ZINN
& *the*
ART
of
MOUNTAIN BIKE
MAINTENANCE

3rd Edition

LENNARD ZINN

Illustrated by Todd Telander

VELO
press®

BOULDER, COLORADO

Printed in the United States of America

Distributed in the United States and Canada by Publishers Group West

International Standard Book Number: 1-884737-99-4

Library of Congress Cataloging-in-Publication Data
Zinn, Lennard.
   Zinn & the art of mountain bike maintenance / Lennard Zinn ; illustrated by Todd Telander. — 3rd ed.
      p. cm.
   Rev. ed of Zinn and the art of mountain bike maintenance. c1997.
   Inlcudes bibliographical references and index.
   ISBN 1-884737-99-4 (paper)
   1. All terrain bicycles—Maintenance and repair. I. Title: Zinn & the art of mountain bike maintenance. II. Zinn, Lennard. Zinn & the art of mountain bike maintenance. III. Title.

TL430.Z56 2001
629.28'772—dc21   2001035054

VeloPress
1830 N. 55th Street
Boulder, Colorado 80301-2700 USA
303/440-0601; Fax 303/444-6788; E-mail velopress@7dogs.com

To purchase additional copies of this book or other VeloPress books, call 800/234-8356 or visit us on the web at velopress.com.

Cover design by Susie Alvarez
Interior design by Erin Johnson
Cover photograph © 2001 Galen Nathanson

To Sonny, my wife, without whose support
this book could not have been written;
or at least a few more decades
would have passed before it got done.

contents

A TIP OF THE HELMET TO...

My heartfelt thanks go out to Todd Telander, whose illustrations made the procedures more intelligible and beautiful; to my editors and in-house support system, Charles Pelkey and Mark Saunders, for separating the wheat from the chaff and adding more wheat when necessary; to Terry Rosen, for bugging me to write this book for so many years; to Mike Sitrin, formerly of VeloPress, for doing the same and promising to publish the first edition when I did; to Felix Magowan and John Wilcockson of Inside Communications for their vision, financial support and encouragement; to John Muir and Robert Pirsig, for writing such great books to encourage this effort. Special thanks to Erin Johnson for making it look beautiful, and to Amy Sorrells, Theresa van Zante, and Rick Rundall for their countless efforts to improve it.

For technical assistance with the details, thanks to Wayne Stetina, Steve Hed, Ken Beach, and to Scott, John, and Rusty at Louisville Cyclery (Louisville, Colorado), as well as to folks at Shimano, RockShox, Manitou, Cane Creek, Hayes, Avid, ITM, 3T, Cinelli, Deda, Easton, Salsa, Mavic, Selle San Marco, Cannondale and Ritchey. Thanks go especially to Portia Masterson of Self Propulsion in Golden, Colorado, for her suggestions for the second edition and to Charlie Hancock, Sander Rigney, Doug Bradbury and Chris DiStefano for assistance with the third edition.

I also want to thank my entire family for all of their support and inspiration: Emily and Sarah, my daughters, for showing me that books can be written, completed, and published at a prolific rate; Dad and Mom, for encouraging me my whole life; Rex and Steve, for their suggestions; Kai, Ron, and Dad, for being authors themselves and an inspiration to me; and Marlies, for taking the kids when I needed it.

Thanks, Sarah, for proving Groucho Marx right.

introduction

Peace of mind isn't at all superficial, really. It's the whole thing. That which produces it is good maintenance; that which disturbs it is poor maintenance. What we call workability of the machine is just an objectification of this peace of mind. The ultimate test's always your own serenity. If you don't have this when you start and maintain it while you're working, you're likely to build your personal problems right into the machine itself.

— ROBERT M. PIRSIG, from Zen and the Art of Motorcycle Maintenance

ABOUT THIS BOOK

This book is intended for those with an interest in maintaining their own mountain bikes. Most importantly, this book has been written for mountain bike owners who do *not* think they're capable of maintaining their own bikes. In *Zen and the Art of Motorcycle Maintenance*, Robert Pirsig explores the dichotomy between the purely classical and purely romantic views of the world, a dichotomy that also applies to mountain biking. Riding a mountain bike is generally a romantic experience of emotion, inspiration and intuition, even when solving the complex physics of how to negotiate a technical section of trail without putting your foot down. Mountain bike mechanics, however, is a purely classical structure of underlying form dominated by reason and physical laws. The two fit eloquently together. Each is designed to function in a particular way, and one without the other would be missing out on half the fun.

The romantic can appreciate how success at bike mechanics requires that the procedures be done with love, without which the care you imagined putting into your mountain bike will be lost. And even the pure romantic can follow the simple step-by-step procedures and "exploded" diagrams in this book and discover a passion for spreading new grease on old parts.

Zinn & the Art of Mountain Bike Maintenance is organized in such a way that you can pick maintenance tasks appropriate for you. The repairs illustrated on these pages require no special skills to

i.1 the basic beast

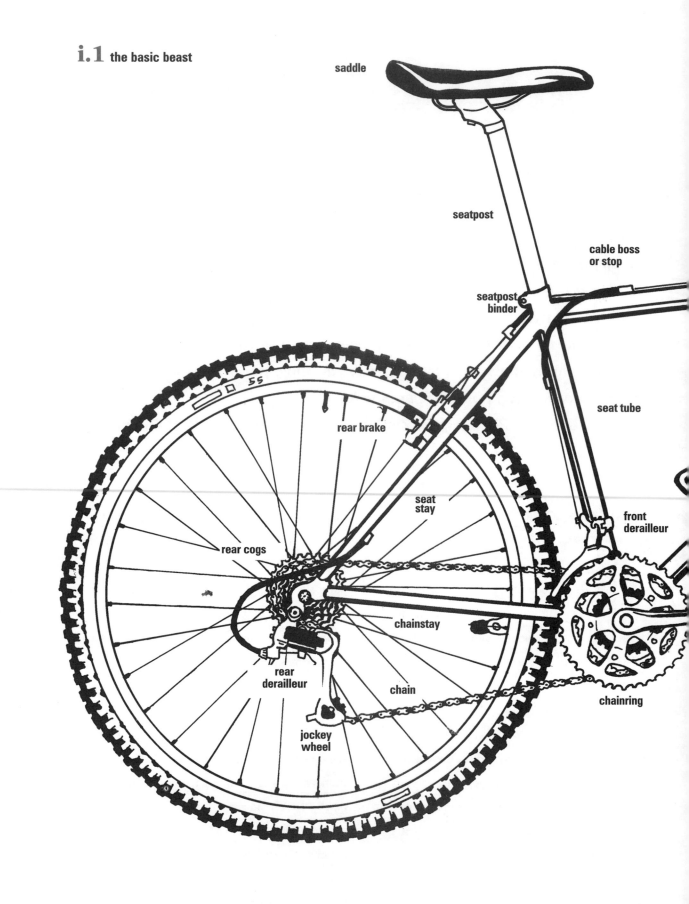

saddle

seatpost

cable boss
or stop

seatpost
binder

seat tube

rear brake

front
derailleur

seat
stay

rear cogs

chainstay

rear
derailleur

chain

jockey
wheel

chainring

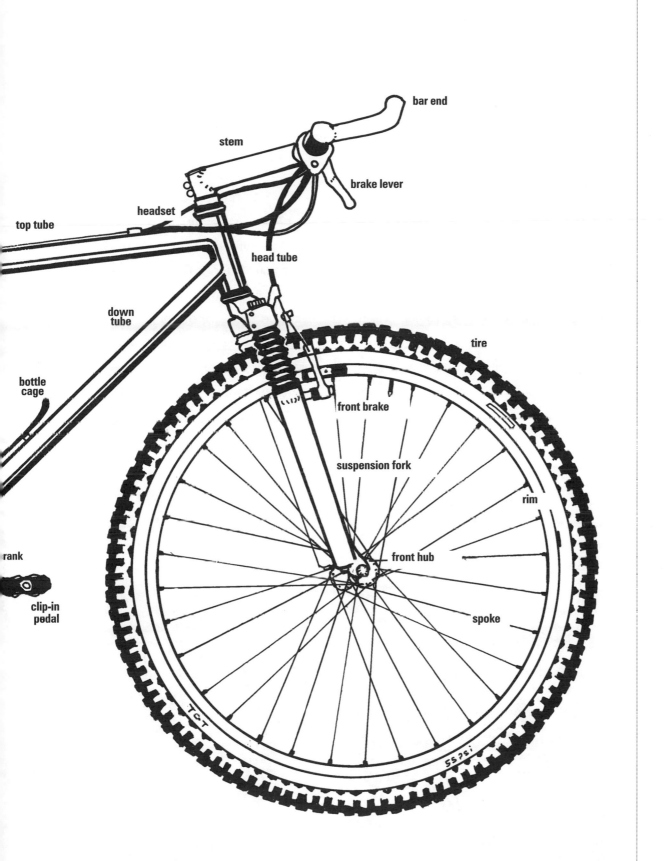

bar end

stem

brake lever

headset

top tube

head tube

down
tube

tire

bottle
cage

front brake

suspension fork

rim

rank

front hub

clip-in
pedal

spoke

perform; anyone can do them. It takes only a willingness to learn.

Mountain bikes are notoriously resilient creatures. You can keep one running an awfully long time just by changing the tires and occasionally lubricating the chain. Chapter 2 is about the most minimal maintenance your bike requires. Even if that is the only part of this book you end up using, you'll have gotten your money's worth by avoiding some unpleasant experiences out on the trail.

This book was originally intended for home enthusiasts, not shop mechanics. For that reason, I have not included the long and precise lists of parts specifications that a shop mechanic might need. Nonetheless, when combined with a speci-fication manual, this book can be a useful, easy-to-follow reference for shop mechanics, too.

WHY DO IT YOURSELF?

There are a number of reasons why you would want to maintain your own mountain bike. Obviously, if done right, it is a lot cheaper to do it yourself than to pay someone else to do it. This is certainly an important factor for those riders who live to ride and have no visible means of support. Self-maintenance is a necessity for that crew.

As your income goes up and the time available to maintain your bike goes down, this becomes less and less true. If you're a well-paid professional

i.2 rigid

with limited free time, it probably does not make as much *economic* sense to maintain your own bike. Yet you may find that you enjoy working on your bike for reasons other than just saving money. Unless you have a mechanic whom you trust and to whom you bring your bike regularly, you are not likely to find anyone else who cares as much about your bicycle's smooth operation and cleanliness as you do. Furthermore, if you love to ride and have limited time to do it, you probably can't afford *not* to be able to fix mechanical breakdowns that occur on the trail.

It is a given: Breakdowns *will* happen, even if you have the world's best mechanic working on your bike. It takes away from my enjoyment of a ride if I have something on my bike that I do not under-stand well enough to know whether it is likely to last the ride, and how to fix it if it does not.

There is an aspect of bicycle mechanics that can be extremely enjoyable in and of itself, almost independent of riding the bike. Bicycles are the epitome of elegant simplicity. Bicycle parts, particu-larly high-end components, are meant to work well and last a long time. With the proper attention, they can shine both in appearance and in perfor-mance for years to come. There is real satisfaction in dismantling a filthy part that is not functioning well, cleaning it up, lubricating it with fresh grease and reassembling it so that it works like new again. Knowing that I made those parts work so smoothly and that I can do it again when they get dirty or worn is rewarding. I am eager to ride hard to see

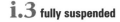

i.3 fully suspended

i.4 the beast exploded

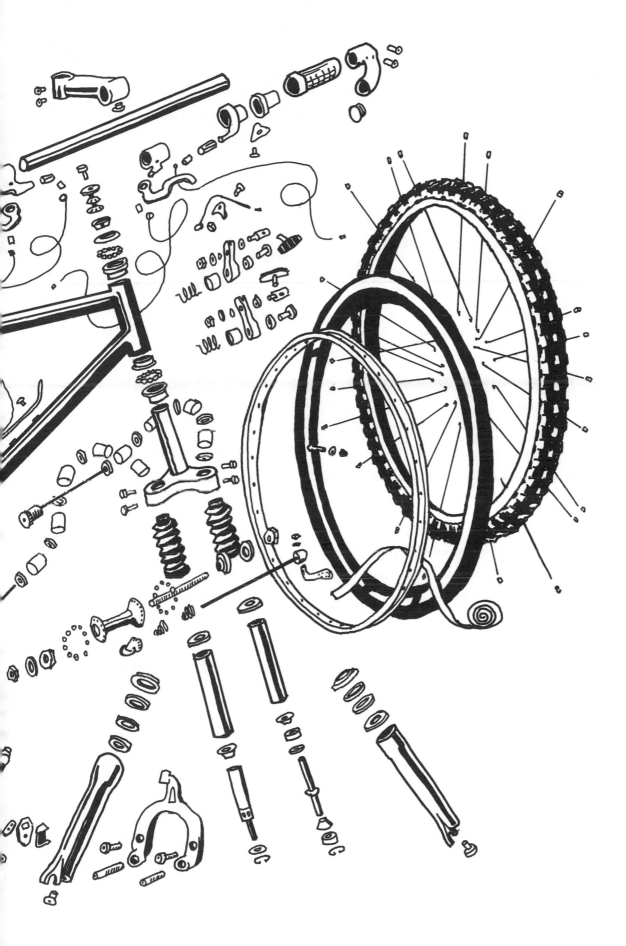

how they hold up, rather than being reluctant to ride for fear of breaking something.

There is also something very liberating about going on a long ride and knowing that you can fix just about anything that might go wrong with your bike out on the trail. Armed with this knowledge and the tools to put it into action, you'll have more confidence to explore new areas and go further than you might otherwise.

In 1995, I took a day to ride the entire 110-mile White Rim Trail loop in Utah's Canyonlands. It is as desolate as you can imagine out there, and I was completely alone with the sky, the sun and the rocks for long stretches. I had a good mileage base in my legs, so that I knew I was physically capable of doing the ride during the limited daylight hours of late October. I had checked, replaced or adjusted practically every part of my bike in the days before the ride. I had also tried out the bike on long rides close to town. Finally, I added to my saddlebag tool kit a few tools that I do not ordinarily carry.

I knew that there was very little chance of anything going wrong with my bike, and, with the tools I had, I could fix almost anything short of a broken frame on the trail. Armed with this knowledge and experience, I *really* enjoyed the ride! I stopped and gawked at almost every breathtaking vista, vertical box canyon or colorful balanced rock or arch. I took scenic detours. I knew that I had a good cushion of safety, so I could totally immerse myself in the pleasure of the ride. I had no nagging fear of something going wrong to dilute the experience.

Confidence in your mechanical ability allows you to be more courageous about what you will try. And armed with this confidence, you'll be more willing to share your love of the sport with other, less-experienced, riders. Bringing new people along on rides is a lot more fun if you know that you can fix their bikes and won't be stranded with an old junker that won't roll.

HOW TO USE THIS BOOK

Skim through the entire book. Skip the detailed steps, but look at the exploded diagrams and get the general flavor of the book and what's inside. When it is time to perform a particular task, you'll know where to find it, and you'll have a general idea of how to approach it.

Illustrator Todd Telander and I have done our best to make these pages as understandable as possible. Exploded diagrams are purposefully used instead of photographs to show more clearly how each part goes together. The first time you go through a procedure, you may find it easier to have a friend read the instructions out loud as you perform the steps.

Obviously, some maintenance tasks are more complicated than others. I am convinced that anyone with an opposable thumb can perform virtually any repair on a bike. Still, it pays to spend some time getting familiar with the really simple tasks, such as fixing a flat, before throwing yourself into complex jobs, such as building a wheel.

Tasks and tools required are divided into three levels indicating their complexity or your proficiency. Level 1 tasks need Level 1 tools and require of you only an eagerness to learn. Level 2 and Level 3 also have corresponding tool sets and are progressively more difficult. All repairs mentioned in this

book are classified as Level 1 unless otherwise indicated. Tools are shown in Chapter 1. At the end of Chapter 2 (Section II-16), the "General Guide to Performing Mechanical Work" is a must-read; it states general policies and approaches that apply to all mechanical work.

Each chapter starts with a list of required tools in the margin. If a section involves a higher level of work, there will be an icon designating the level and tools necessary to perform the tasks in that section. Tasks and illustrations are numbered for easy reference.

At the end of some chapters, there is a troubleshooting section. This is the place to go to identify the source of a certain noise or particular mal-

function in the bike. There is also a comprehensive troubleshooting guide in Appendix A.

There is a wealth of other valuable information in the appendixes. Get used to using the appendixes; many tasks will be simplified.

Appendix B is a complete gear chart and includes instructions on how to calculate your gear with nonstandard size wheels. Appendix C is an extensive section on selecting the proper size bike and positioning it to fit you. The glossary (Appendix D) is a comprehensive dictionary of mountain bike technical terms. Appendix E lists the tightening specifications of almost every bolt on the bike. Appendix F reveals which clip-in pedals work with which cleats, and vice versa; knowing which pedals your cleats work in can save you lots of time switch-

i.5 hybrid

introduction

ing pedals when trading bikes around with friends or trying demo bikes. Appendix G is a listing of the illustrations in the book, if you want to quickly look up what something looks like.

THE MOUNTAIN BIKE

This is the creature to which this book is devoted (Figs. i.1 and i.4). All of its parts are illustrated and labeled here. Take a minute to familiarize yourself with these now, and refer back to these diagrams whenever necessary.

The mountain bike comes in a variety of forms, from models with rigid frames and forks (Figs. i.2 and i.5) to models with high-zoot front and rear suspension systems (Fig. i.3). A mountain bike generally comes with 26-inch knobby tires. Tire sizes and shapes vary widely and include everything from studded snow tires to smooth street tires.

I believe that by clearly spelling out the steps necessary to properly maintain and repair a bicycle, even those who see themselves as having no mechanical skills will be able to tackle problems as they arise. With a little bit of practice and a willingness to learn, your bike will suddenly transform itself from a mysterious black box, too complicated to tamper with, to a simple, very understandable machine that can be a genuine delight to work on. Just allow yourself the opportunity and the dignity to follow along, rather than deciding in advance that you will *never* be able to do this. All you have to do is follow the instructions and trust yourself.

So, set aside your self-image as someone who is "not mechanically oriented" (and any other factors that may stand in the way of you making your mountain bike ride like a dream), and let's start playing with your bike!

tools

Behold, we lay a tool here and on the morrow it is gone.

— The Book of Mormon

You can't do much work on a bike without tools. Still, it's not always clear exactly which tools to buy. This chapter will clarify what tools you should consider owning, based on your level of mechanical experience and interest.

As I mentioned in the introduction, the maintenance and repair procedures in this book are classified by their degree of difficulty. All repairs mentioned are classified as Level 1, unless otherwise indicated. The tools for Levels 1, 2 and 3 are pictured and described on the following pages. Lists of the tools needed in each chapter are shown in the margin at the beginning of each chapter.

For the uninitiated, there is no need to rush out and buy a large number of bike-specific tools. With only a few exceptions, the "Level 1 Tool Kit" (Fig. 1.2) consists of standard metric tools. In a more compact and lightweight form, this is the same collection of tools I recommend carrying with you on rides (Figs. 1.6 and 1.7). The "Level 2 Tool Kit" (Fig. 1.3) contains several bike-specific tools, allowing you to do more complex work on the bike. "Level 3" (Fig. 1.4) tools are extensive (and expensive), and they ensure that your riding buddies will show up not only to ask your sage advice but to borrow your tools as well.

And if you really want to go all out and be set up like a pro (and even have mechanics wanting to borrow your tools), you can splurge on the set shown in Fig. 1.5. If you are one to loan tools, you might consider marking your collection so as to help recover those items that might otherwise take a long time finding their way back to your workshop. It wouldn't hurt writing down the details about what tool you lent to whom and on what date. You would be surprised how easy it is to forget who has your fancy Shimano chain tool, even if it's marked.

I-1: LEVEL 1 TOOL KIT

Level 1 repairs are the simplest and do not require a workshop, although it is nice to have a good space to work. You will need the following tools (Fig. 1.2):

- **Tire pump** with a gauge and a valve head to match your tubes (either Presta or Schrader valves; see Fig. 1.1).

- **Standard screwdrivers:** small, medium and large (one of each).

  - **Phillips-head screwdrivers:** one small and one medium.

  - Set of three plastic **tire levers**.

  - At least two **spare tubes** of the same size and valve type as those on your bike.

  - Container of regular **baby powder**. It works well for coating tubes and the inner casings of tires. Do not inhale this stuff; it's bad for the lungs.

1.1 valve types

- **Patch kit.** Choose one that comes with sandpaper instead of a metal scratcher. At least every 18 months, check that the glue has not dried up, whether open or not.

- **One 6-inch adjustable wrench** (a.k.a. "Crescent wrench").

- **Pliers:** regular and needle-nose.

- Set of **metric Allen wrenches** (a.k.a. "hex keys") that includes 2.5mm, 3mm, 4mm, 5mm, 6mm

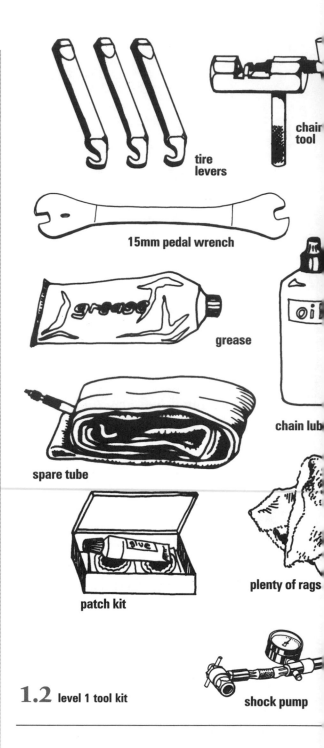

tire levers

chain tool

15mm pedal wrench

grease

oil

chain lub

spare tube

patch kit

plenty of rags

1.2 level 1 tool kit

shock pump

and 8mm sizes. Folding sets are available and work nicely to keep your wrenches organized. I also recommend buying extras of the 4mm, 5mm, 6mm and 8mm sizes.

- Set of **metric open-end wrenches** that includes 7mm, 8mm, 9mm, 10mm, 13mm, 14mm, 15mm and 17mm sizes.

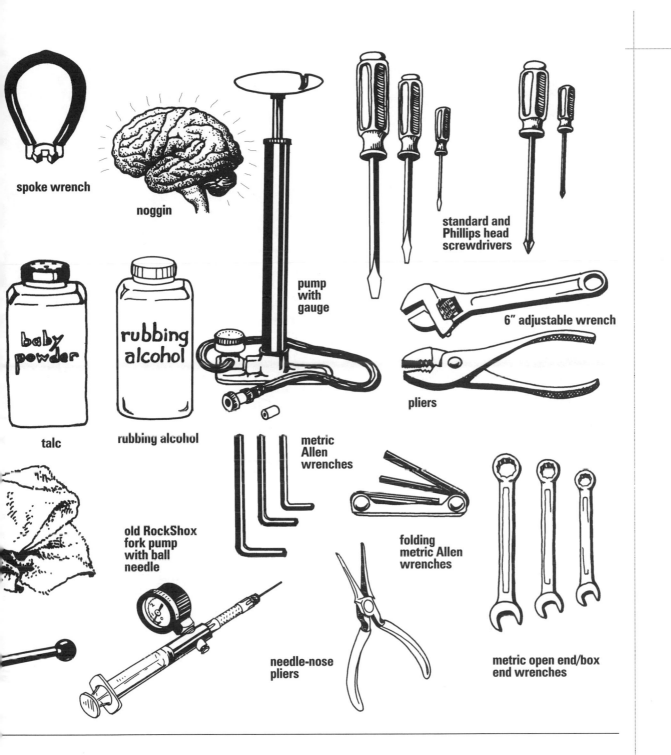

spoke wrench

noggin

pump
with
gauge

standard and
Phillips head
screwdrivers

6" adjustable wrench

talc

rubbing alcohol

pliers

metric
Allen
wrenches

old RockShox
fork pump
with ball
needle

folding
metric Allen
wrenches

needle-nose
pliers

metric open end/box
end wrenches

- **15mm pedal wrench**. This is thinner and longer than a standard 15mm wrench and thicker than a cone wrench.
- **Chain tool** for breaking and reassembling chains.
- **Spoke wrench** to match the size of nipples used on your wheels.
- **Tube or jar of grease**. I recommend using

grease designed specifically for bicycles; however, standard automotive grease is okay, except in suspension forks and twist shifters.

- Drip bottle or can of **chain lubricant**. Please choose a nonaerosol; it is easier to control, uses less packaging and wastes less in overspray.
- **Rubbing alcohol** for removing and installing

handlebar grips and for cleaning disc brake pads, rotors and internal parts.

- A lot of **rags**!

Other

- If you have an air-sprung suspension fork or rear shock, you need a **shock pump**. Get one with a no-leak head if your front or rear shock has standard Schrader valves, and get the adapter you need if you have an earlier RockShox system requiring either a ball needle or a special adapter to insert down inside a deep Schrader valve.
- You'll also want stuff like **tape, zip-ties, safety glasses** and **rubber dish gloves** or a box of cheap **latex gloves**.

I-2: LEVEL 2 TOOL KIT

Level 2 repairs are a bit more complex, and I recommend that you use a well-organized workspace with a shop bench. Keeping your workspace well organized is probably the best way to make maintenance and repair easy and quick. You will need the entire Level 1 Tool Kit (Fig. 1.2) plus the following tools (Fig. 1.3):

- **Portable bike stand.** Be sure that the stand is sturdy enough to remain stable when you're really cranking on the wrenches.
- **Shop apron** (this is to keep your nice duds nice).
- **Hacksaw** with a fine-toothed blade.
- Set of **razor blades** or a sharp **shop knife**.
- **Files:** one round and one flat.
- **Cable cutter** for cutting brake and shifter cables without fraying the ends.
- **Cable-housing cutter** for cutting coaxial-indexed cable housing. If you purchase a Shimano, Park

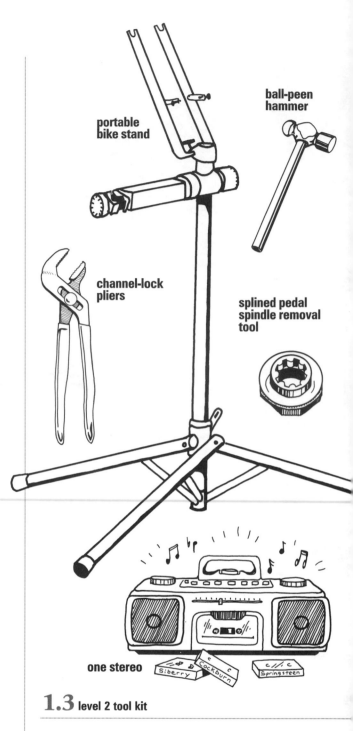

portable bike stand

ball-peen hammer

channel-lock pliers

splined pedal spindle removal tool

one stereo Siberry Cockburn Springsteen

1.3 level 2 tool kit

or Wrench Force housing cutter, you won't need to buy a separate cable cutter, since either of these cleanly cuts both cables and housings.

- Set of **metric socket wrenches** that includes 7mm, 8mm, 9mm, 10mm, 13mm, 14mm and 15mm sizes.
- **Crank puller** for removing crank arms.
- **Chainring-nut tool** for holding the nut while

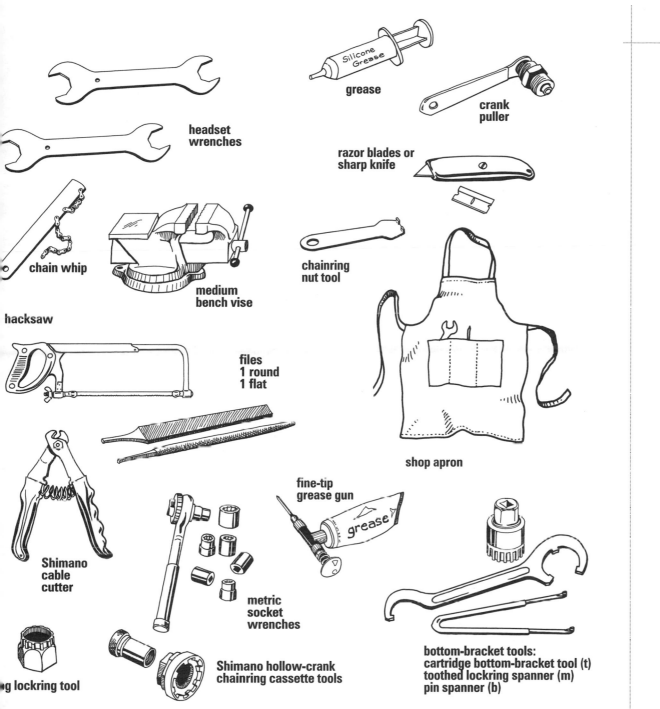

grease

crank
puller

headset
wrenches

razor blades or
sharp knife

chain whip

chainring
nut tool

medium
bench vise

hacksaw

files
1 round
1 flat

shop apron

fine-tip
grease gun

grease

Shimano
cable
cutter

metric
socket
wrenches

bottom-bracket tools:
cartridge bottom-bracket tool (t)
toothed lockring spanner (m)
pin spanner (b)

g lockring tool

Shimano hollow-crank
chainring cassette tools

you tighten or loosen a chainring bolt.

- **Chainring-cassette removal tools** for Shimano
  hollow cranks.

- Medium **ball-peen hammer**.

- **Two headset wrenches.** Be sure to check the size
  of your headset before buying these. This purchase is unnecessary if you have a threadless
  headset and plan only to work on your own

bike. Some suspension forks have fittings requiring headset wrenches.

- **Medium bench vise.**

- **Cog lockring tool** for removing cogs from the
  rear hub.

- **Chain whip** for holding cogs while loosening
  the cassette lockring.

- **Bottom bracket tools.** For Shimano cartridge

bottom brackets and clones of them, you'll
need the splined tool specifically made for this
type of bottom bracket. For cup-and-cone bottom brackets, you'll need a lockring spanner
and a pin spanner to fit your bottom bracket.

- **Channel-lock pliers.**
- **Splined pedal spindle removal tool.**
- **Fine-tipped grease gun.**
- Tube of **silicone-based grease** if you have
  Grip Shift and other nonlithium grease for
  suspension forks.
- One **stereo** with good tunes. This is especially
  important if you plan on spending a lot of
  time working on your bike.

I-3: LEVEL 3 TOOL KIT

If you are an accomplished Level 3 mechanic,
you can even build up brand-new frames. That is
assuming, of course, that these tools (Fig. 1.4) are
neatly organized in your shop.

- **Parts washing tank.** Please use an environmentally safe degreaser. Dispose of used solvent responsibly; check with your local environmental safety office.
- **Fixed bike stand** with a clamp.
- Large **bench-mounted vise** to free stuck parts.
- **Headset press** used to install headset bearing
  cups. The press should fit all cup sizes and may
  require adapters for internal cups or for cups
  with pressed-in bearings.
- **Fork crown race punch** (a.k.a. "slide hammer")
  for installing the fork crown headset race.
- **Headset cup remover.**
- **Star-nut installation tool** for threadless headsets.
- An **extra chain whip for** disassembling free-
  wheels or old-style cassettes.

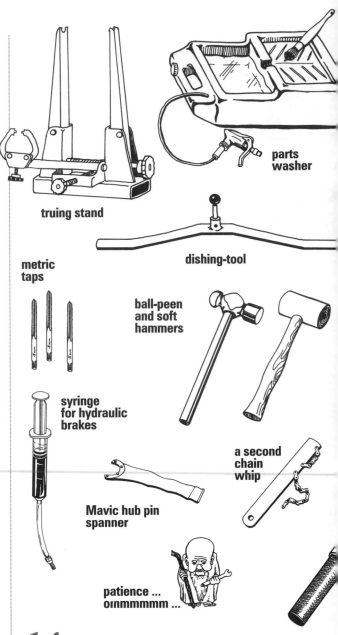

parts
washer

truing stand

metric
taps

dishing-tool

ball-peen
and soft
hammers

syringe
for hydraulic
brakes

a second
chain
whip

Mavic hub pin
spanner

patience ...
ornmmmmm ...

1.4 level 3 tool kit

- **Freewheel removers for** Shimano, Sachs and
  Suntour freewheels.
- **Large ball-peen hammer.**
- **Soft hammer.** Choose a rubber, plastic or wood-
  en mallet to prevent damage to parts.
- **Torque wrench.** Torque wrenches are great for
  checking proper bolt tightness. Following manu-
  facturer-specified torque settings prevents parts from
  stripping as well as from falling off while riding.

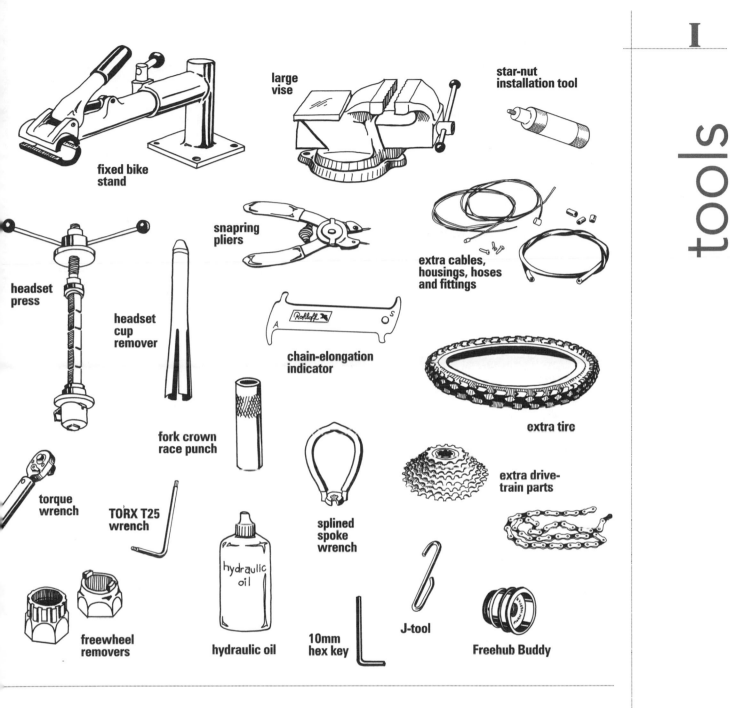

fixed bike
stand

large
vise

star-nut
installation tool

headset
press

snapring
pliers

extra cables,
housings, hoses
and fittings

headset
cup
remover

chain-elongation
indicator

fork crown
race punch

extra tire

torque
wrench

TORX T25
wrench

splined
spoke
wrench

extra drive-
train parts

hydraulic
oil

J-tool

freewheel
removers

hydraulic oil

10mm
hex key

Freehub Buddy

- Set of **metric taps** that includes 5mm by 0.8mm, 6mm by 1mm, and 10mm by 1mm for fixing mangled frame threads.
- Pair of **snapring pliers** for removing snaprings from suspension forks, pedals, derailleurs and other parts.
- **Chain elongation gauge** to determine if a chain needs replacing. An accurate 12-inch ruler will substitute adequately.

- **Truing stand** for truing and building wheels.
- **Dishing tool** for checking that the set of wheels you just finished building is properly centered.
- **Spoke wrenches** of all sizes.
- **Splined spoke wrench** for Mavic.
- **Pin spanner** for adjusting Mavic hubs.
- **Morningstar Freehub Buddy** for flushing and lubricating freehubs.

- **Morningstar J-tool** for removing freehub dust covers.
- **Hydraulic fluids** of different types and viscosities for different hydraulic brakes, suspension forks and rear shocks.
- **Syringe** for hydraulic brakes — the type varies with brake brand.
- **TORX wrenches.** These have star-shaped tips and fit some disc-brake rotor bolts. TORX T25 is the size for disc brakes.
- **10mm hex keys**, for some suspension pivots.
- One healthy dose of **patience** and an equal willingness to work and rework jobs until they have been properly finished.

Other

- **Spare parts** to save you from last-minute runs to the bike shop, like several sizes of ball bearings, spare cables, cable housing and a lifetime supply of those little cable-end caps. Keep on hand spare tires, tubes, chains and cogsets. If you expect to be working on suspension forks and hydraulic brakes, be sure to have spare springs, hoses and fittings.
- **Various fluids.** Special **suspension oils** and **greases, threadlock fluid, titanium anti-seize compound, outboard-motor gear** oil or specialty **freehub lubricants** are required for some jobs.

I-4: NOW, IF YOU *REALLY* WANT A WELL-STOCKED SHOP

The following tools (Fig. 1.5) are not even part of the Level 3 kit and are not often needed for bike repairs. That said, they sure do come in handy when you need them.

- English-threaded **bottom bracket tap set.** This

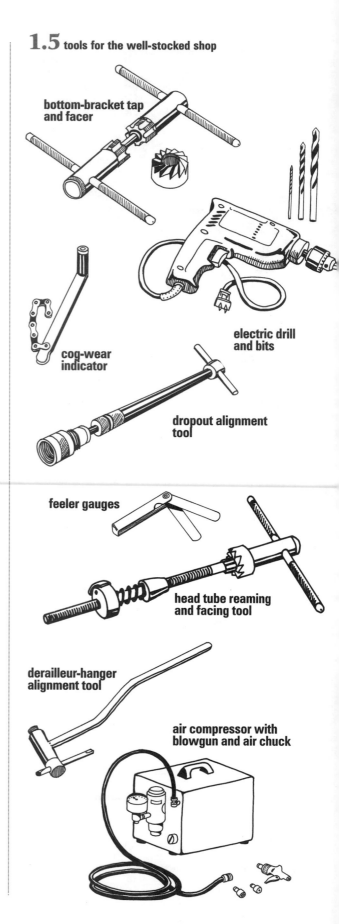

1.5 tools for the well-stocked shop

bottom-bracket tap and facer

electric drill and bits

cog-wear indicator

dropout alignment tool

feeler gauges

head tube reaming and facing tool

derailleur-hanger alignment tool

air compressor with blowgun and air chuck

cuts threads in both ends of the bottom bracket while keeping the threads in proper alignment.

- **Bottom bracket shell facer.** Like a bottom bracket tap, this tool cuts the faces of the bottom bracket shell so they are parallel to each other.
- **Head tube reamer/facer.** This tool keeps both ends of the head tube perfectly parallel and properly sized for the headset cups.
- **Electric drill** with drill bit set.
- **Dropout alignment tools** (a.k.a. "tip adjusters").
- **Derailleur hanger alignment tool** to straighten the hanger after you shift it into the spokes or crash on it.
- **Cog-wear indicator gauge** to determine if cogs are worn out.
- **Feeler gauges** for precise adjustment of some disc brakes.
- **Air compressor** with **blowgun** and **air chuck.** Useful for lots of things, including overhauling disc brakes and seating tubeless tires.

I-5: SETTING UP YOUR HOME SHOP

I recommend keeping this area clean and very well organized. Lame as it sounds, remember that a "clean shop is a happy shop!" Make it comfortable to work in and easy to find the tools you need. Hanging tools on peg-board or slat-board or placing them in bins or trays are all effective ways to maintain an organized work area. Being able to find the tools you need will increase the enjoyment of working on a bike immensely. It is harder to do a job with love if you're frustrated about not being able to find the cable cutter. Placing small parts in one of those bench-top organizers with several rows of little drawers is another good way to keep chaos from taking over.

I-6: TOOLS TO CARRY WITH YOU WHILE RIDING

A. For most riding

Keep all of this stuff (Fig. 1.6) in a bag under your seat or somehow attached to your bike. Some people may prefer to keep it in a hydration (a.k.a. "CamelBak") pack or a fanny pack. The operative words here are "light" and "serviceable." Many of these tools are combined into some of the popular "multi-tools." Make sure you try all tools at home before depending on them on the trail.

- **Spare tube.** This is a no-brainer. Make sure the valve matches the ones on your bike and pump. If rarely needed, keep the tube in a plastic bag to prevent deterioration.
- **Tire pump** and/or **CO_2 cartridge.** Larger pumps are faster than itty-bitty mini-pumps. Make sure the pump or cartridge is set up for your type of valves.
- **Patch kit.** You'll need something after you've used your spare tube. Check it at least every one and a half years to make sure the glue is not dried up.
- At least two plastic **tire levers**, preferably three.
- **Chain tool** that works.
- 8mm and 10mm **open-end wrenches**.
- **Spoke wrench** sized to your spokes.
- Small **screwdriver** for adjusting derailleurs and other parts.
- Compact set of **Allen wrenches** that includes 2.5mm, 3mm, 4mm, 5mm and 6mm sizes. (Some of you might need to bring along an 8mm, too.)
- A good **multi-tool** to replace some or all of the above six items with less weight and bulk.
- **TORX T25 wrench** if you have disc-brake rotors with TORX screws.

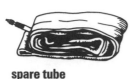

1.6 tools to take on all rides

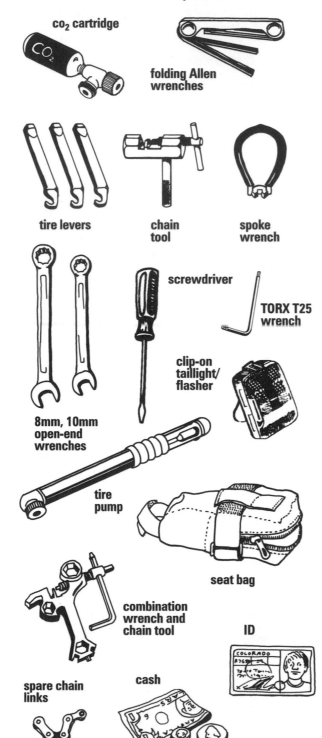

spare tube

patch kit

co₂ cartridge

folding Allen wrenches

tire levers

chain tool

spoke wrench

screwdriver

TORX T25 wrench

8mm, 10mm open-end wrenches

clip-on taillight/ flasher

tire pump

seat bag

combination wrench and chain tool

ID

spare chain links

cash

- **Spare chain links** from your chain. If you're using a Shimano chain, bring at least two "sub-pin" rivets. If you use SRAM or Sachs chains, bring along an extra "magic link." Like the Shimano subpin, you'll never need it ... unless, of course, you forget to bring one.

- **Identification.**

- **Cash** for obvious reasons *and* to boot sidewall cuts in tires.

B. For long or multi-day trips

These items in Fig. 1.7 are, of course, in addition to proper amounts of food, water, and extra clothes.

- **Spare spokes.** Innovations in Cycling sells a really cool folding spoke made from Kevlar. It's worth getting one or two for emergency repairs on a long ride.

- Another **spare tube.**

- Small plastic bottle of **chain lube.**

- Small tube of **grease.**

- Compact 15mm **pedal wrench.** One with a headset wrench on the other end can be particularly handy.

- **Pliers.** Useful for innumerable purposes.

- **Shock pump** for your front and/or rear shock.

- **Wire** and/or a small **bungee cord** can be very handy for all kinds of things.

- **Duct tape.** It's like The Force. It has a light side, a dark side and it holds the universe (and sometimes your bike or your shoes) together.

- **Money,** or its plastic equivalent, which can get you out of lots of scrapes.

- **Matches,** because you never know when you can be stranded overnight.

- A lightweight aluminized folding **emergency blanket.**

1.7 tools for extended backcountry riding

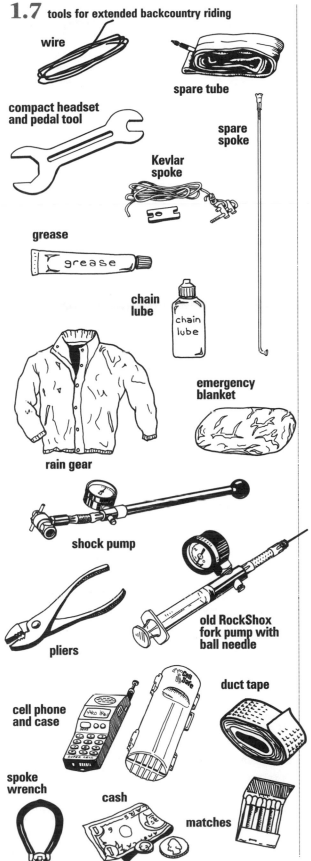

wire

spare tube

compact headset and pedal tool

spare spoke

Kevlar spoke

grease

chain lube

rain gear

emergency blanket

shock pump

pliers

old RockShox fork pump with ball needle

cell phone and case

duct tape

spoke wrench

cash

matches

- **Rain gear.**
- **Cell phone** with protective case.

  Note: Read Chapter 3 on emergency repairs before embarking on a lengthy trip.

  If you are planning a bike-centered vacation, be sure to bring along a Level 1 tool kit in the car, some headset wrenches and incidentals like duct tape and sandpaper.

I

tools

basic stuff

PRE-RIDE INSPECTION, WHEEL REMOVAL AND GENERAL CLEANING

Everything should be made as simple as possible, but not simpler.

— *ALBERT EINSTEIN*

aking sure your bike is safe is essential. It's a good idea to get in the habit of checking your bike *before* heading out on a ride. Performing the pre-ride inspection regularly could help you avoid delays due to parts failure. I won't even mention the injury risks you face by riding a poorly maintained bike.

After that, unless you always have a mechanic with you, you need to know how to take your wheels on and off or you won't be able to effectively deal with minor annoyances like flat tires or jammed chains. And if you do absolutely nothing else to your bike, keeping your chain and a few other parts clean will enhance the enjoyment of the ride. This chapter's three very basic cleaning

and maintenance procedures are fundamental to keeping your bike running smoothly.

All mechanics should read the last section in this chapter, a "General Guide to Performing Mechanical Work."

II-1: PRE-RIDE INSPECTION

1. Check to be sure that the quick-release levers or axle nuts (the ones that secure the hub axle to the dropouts) are tight.

2. Check the brake pads for excessive or uneven wear.

3. Grab and twist the brake pads and brake arms to make sure the bolts are tight.

4. Squeeze the brake levers. This should bring the pads flat against the rims (or slightly toed-in), without hitting the tires. Make certain that you can-

not squeeze the levers all of the way to the handle-bars (see Section VII-3 in Chapter 7 on brake cable-tension adjustment).

5. Spin the wheels. Check for wobbles while sighting on the rims, not the tires. (If a tire wobbles excessively on a straight rim, it may not be fully seated in the rim; check it all of the way around on both sides.) Make sure that the rims do not rub on the brake pads.

6. Check the tire pressure. On most mountain bike tires, the proper pressure is between 30 and 60 pounds per square inch (psi). Look to see that there are no foreign objects sticking in the tire. If there are, you may have to pull the tube out and repair or replace it. For some, it might be worth your time to look at the section on tire sealants (i.e., goop inside the tube that fills any small holes you may get) in Chapter 6, Section VI-9.

7. Check the tires for excessive wear, cracking or gashes.

2.1 releasing the noodle from the link on a V-brake

8. Be certain that the handlebar and stem are tight and that the stem is lined up with the front tire.

9. Check that the gears shift smoothly and the chain does not skip or shift by itself. Make sure that indexed (or "click") shifting moves the chain one cog, starting with the first click.

Make sure that the chain does not overshift the smallest or biggest rear cog or the smallest or biggest front chainring.

10. Check the chain for rust, dirt, stiff links or noticeable signs of wear. It should be clean and lubricated. (Be cautious about overdoing it, though. Overlubricated, gooey chains pick up lots of dirt, particularly in dry climates.) The chain should be replaced on a mountain bike about every 500 to 1000 miles of off-road riding or every 2000 miles of paved riding.

11. Apply the front brake and push the bike forward and back. The headset should be tight and not make clunking noises or allow the fork any fore-aft play.

12. If all this checks out, go ride your bike! If not, check the table of contents, go to the appropriate chapter and fix the problems before you go out and ride.

II-2: REMOVING THE FRONT WHEEL

You can't transport your mountain bike easily if you can't remove the front wheel, since it is required for most roof racks and for jamming a mountain bike inside your car. As outlined in the following sections, wheel removal involves releasing the brake and opening the hub quick-release or bolt-on skewer, or the axle nuts on the low-end models.

If you have a single-leg fork (i.e., Cannondale

2.2 releasing a cantilever brake

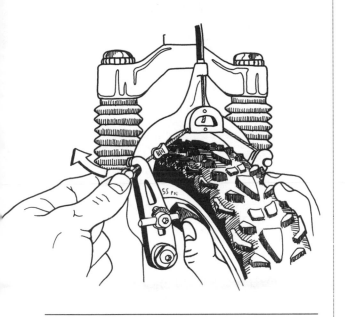

2.3 opening quick-release skewer

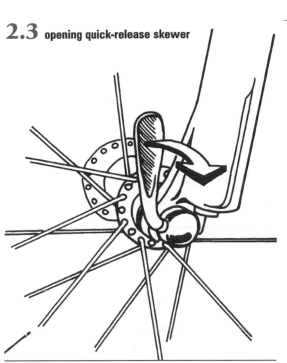

Lefty) wheel removal is different. See the note at the end of Section II-5.

II-3: RELEASING THE BRAKE

Most brakes have a mechanism to release the brake arms so that they spring away from the rim (Figs. 2.1 and 2.2), allowing the tire to pass between the pads. V-brakes (a.k.a. "sidepull cantilevers" — Fig. 2.1) are released by pulling the end of the curved cable guide tube (a.k.a. the "noodle") out of the horizontal link atop one of the brake arms while either holding the link or squeezing the pads against the rim with the other hand (Fig. 2.1). Most cantilevers (Fig. 2.2) and U-brakes (Fig. 7.45) are released by pulling the enlarged head of the straddle cable out of a notch in the top of the brake arm while holding the pads against the rim with the other hand (Fig. 2.2).

Most disc brakes (Figs. 7.18 and 7.19) allow the disc to fall away without releasing the pads. Old (mid-1990s) Dia-Compe cable-actuated hydraulic

disc brakes require opening a latch under the caliper, securing it to the fork. The entire caliper can then be swung up and forward, allowing the wheel to come out.

Roller-cam brakes (Fig. 7.46) are released by pulling the cam down and out from between the two rollers while holding the pads against the rim. Many linkage brakes (Fig. 7.44) are released like V-brakes or cantilevers. Hydraulic rim brakes (Fig. 7.39) usually require detaching the U-shaped brake booster connecting the piston cylinders together, if installed, followed by unscrewing or quick-releasing one wheel cylinder.

II-4: DETACHING A WHEEL WITH A QUICK-RELEASE SKEWER

This is easy, and you don't need a tool.

1. Pull the lever out to open it (Fig. 2.3).

2. After opening the quick-release lever, unscrew the nut on the opposite end of the quick-release skewer's shaft until it clears the fork's wheel-retention tabs.

2.4 bolt-on skewer

3. Pull the wheel off.

Note: *Some bikes have non-quick-release superlight titanium bolt-on skewers (Fig. 2.4). The wheel is removed by unscrewing the skewer with a 5mm Allen wrench.*

II-5: DETACHING A WHEEL WITH AXLE NUTS

1. Unscrew the nuts on the axle ends (usually with a 15mm wrench) until they allow the wheel to fall out (Fig. 2.5).

2. Most mountain bikes have some type of wheel-retention system consisting of nubs or bent tabs on the fork ends (also known as "dropouts"), or an axle washer with a bent tooth hooked into a hole in the fork end. These systems prevent the wheel from falling out if the axle nuts loosen. Loosen the nuts enough to clear the retention tabs on the fork ends.

3. Pull the wheel out.

Note: *For Cannondale Lefty forks, first remove the disc brake with a 5mm hex key then unscrew the axle bolt (usually with a 5mm hex key as well). This pulls the wheel right off without any further encouragement from you. On reinstallation, grease the bearing seats on the axle (the thing sticking out from the fork). Slide the hub back on, line it up, and tighten the bolt. Mount the brake again, assuring that you keep the same spacers between it and the mounting tabs on the fork.*

II-6: INSTALLING THE FRONT WHEEL

Leave the brake open and lower the fork onto the wheel so that the bike's weight pushes the

dropouts down onto the hub axle. This will seat the axle fully into the fork and center the rim between the brake pads. If your fork or wheel is misaligned, you'll need to hold the rim centered between the brake pads when securing the hub.

With a disc brake, drop the slot in the caliper (the part attached to the fork) over the rotor (the big disc attached to the wheel). Make sure that the rotor does not dislodge either pad.

Continue with the appropriate hub-securing step.

II-7: TIGHTENING THE QUICK-RELEASE SKEWER

The quick-release skewer is not a glorified wing nut and should not be treated as such.

1. Hold the quick-release lever in the "open" position.

2. Tighten the opposite end nut until it snugs up against the face of the dropout.

2.5 loosening axle nut

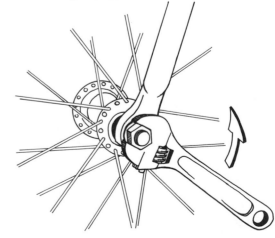

2.6 tightening the quick release

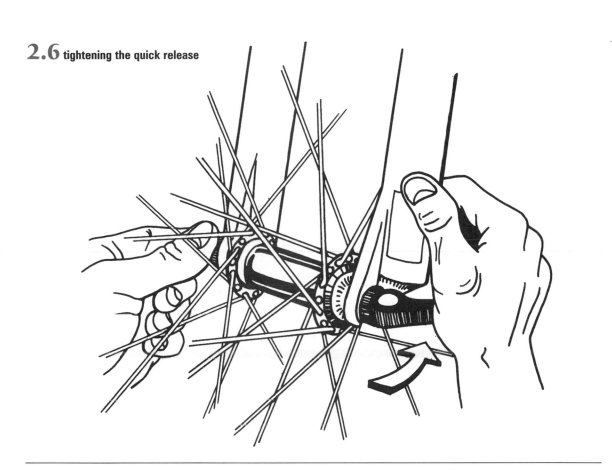

3. Push the lever over (Fig. 2.6) to the "closed" position (it should now be at a 90-degree angle to the axle). If done right, it should have taken a good amount of hand pressure to close the quick-release lever properly; the lever should have left its imprint on your palm for a few seconds.

4. If the quick-release lever does not close tightly enough, open the lever again, tighten the end nut one quarter-turn and close the lever again. Repeat until tight.

5. If, however, the lever cannot be pushed down perpendicular to the axle, then the nut is too tight. Be careful, because forcing an overly tight skewer to close can snap the shaft. Open the quick-release lever, unscrew the end nut one quarter-turn or so, and try closing the lever again. Repeat this procedure until the quick-release lever is fully closed and snug. When you are done, it is important to have

the lever pointing straight up or toward the back of the bike so that it cannot hook on obstacles and be accidentally opened.

6. Check that the axle is tightened into the fork by trying to pull the wheel out.

II-8: TIGHTENING BOLT-ON SKEWERS

Hold the end nut with one hand and tighten the skewer with a 5mm Allen wrench. Control tech recommends 65 inch-pounds (in-lbs) of tightening torque for steel bolt-on skewers and 85 in-lbs for titanium versions. You can come close to the right amount of torque by using a short Allen wrench and tightening as tightly as you can with your fingers. It is easy to overtighten these skewers, so try to avoid that by approximating the pressure a quick-release skewer applies, and do not go higher than that.

2.7 removal and installation of rear wheel

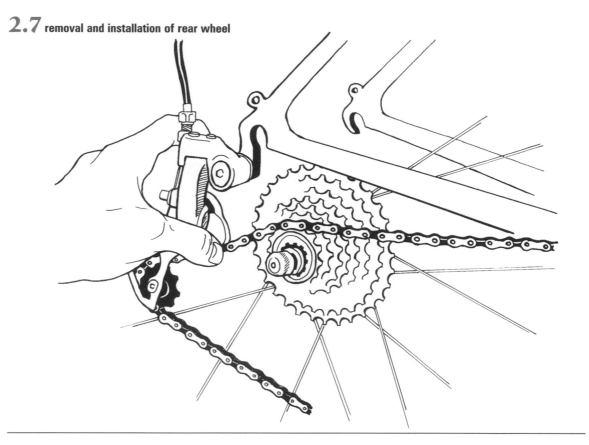

II-9: TIGHTENING AXLE NUTS (MASS-MERCHANT BIKES)

Snug up the nuts clockwise (opposite direction of Fig. 2.5) with a wrench (usually 15mm), a little from each side until they are quite tight.

II-10: CLOSING THE BRAKES

1. The steps required to close the brakes are the reverse of what you did to release them. With a V-brake (sidepull cantilever), hold the link in one hand, pull the noodle back, push the cable coming out of the noodle into the slot in the end of the link, and pop the end of the noodle back into the slotted hole (Fig. 2.1 in reverse). With a cantilever or U-brake, hold the brake pads against the rim with one hand and hook the enlarged end of the straddle cable back into the end of the brake arm with your other hand (Fig. 2.2 in reverse). With

most disc brakes, the brake is ready to apply as soon as the wheel is installed. Do the reverse of Section II-3 to reconnect the more rare types of brakes, or find the brake in Chapter 7 and read up on it.

2. Check that the brake cables are connected securely by squeezing the levers. Lift the front end of the bike and spin the front wheel, gently applying the brakes several times. Check that the pads are not dragging, and recenter the wheel (or adjust the brakes as described in Chapter 7, under your type of brake). If everything is reconnected and centered properly, you're done. Go ride your bike.

II-11: REMOVING THE REAR WHEEL

Removing the rear wheel is just like removing the front (Sections II-2–II-5), with the added complication of the chain and cogs.

1. Shift the chain onto the smallest cog. Do this by lifting the rear wheel off of the ground and shifting while turning the cranks.

2. To release the wheel from the rear dropouts and the brakes, follow the same procedure as with the front wheel. When you push the wheel out, you'll need to move the chain out of the way. This is usually a matter of grabbing the rear derailleur, pulling it back so the jockey wheels (pulley wheels) move out of the way, while pushing forward on the quick release or axle nuts with your thumbs and letting the wheel fall as you hold the bike up (Fig. 2.7). If the bottom half of the chain catches the wheel as it falls, lift the wheel and jiggle it upward to free it.

II-12: INSTALLING THE REAR WHEEL

1. Check to make sure that the rear derailleur is shifted to its outermost position (over the smallest cog [Fig. 5.4]).

2. Slip the wheel up between the seatstays and maneuver the upper section of chain onto the smallest cog (Fig. 2.7).

3. Set the bike down on the rear wheel, and as you let the bike drop down, pull the rear derailleur back with your right hand and pull the axle ends back into the dropouts with your index fingers. Your thumbs push forward on the rear dropouts, which should now slide over the axle ends. (If the axle does not slip into the dropouts, you may need to spread the dropouts apart or squeeze them toward each other to get them to clear the axle ends.) If you have a rear disc brake, guide the rotor in between the brake pads.

4. Check that the axle is fully seated in the dropouts, which should result in the wheel being centered between the brake pads. If it is not, hold the rim in a centered position as you secure the axle.

5. Tighten the quick-release skewer, bolt-on skewer, or axle nuts the same way as explained for the front wheel.

6. Reconnect the rear brake the same way as you did on the front wheel.

You're done. Go ride your bike.

II-13: CLEANING THE BICYCLE

Most cleaning can be done with soap, water and a brush. Soap and water are easier on you and the earth than stronger solvents, which are generally only needed for the drivetrain, if at all. Avoid using the high-pressure sprayers you find at pay car washes to clean your bike. The soaps are corrosive, and the high pressure forces them into bearings, pivots and frame tubes, causing extensive damage over time.

A bike stand is highly recommended when scrubbing the bike. In the absence of a bike stand, the bike can be hung from a garage ceiling with rope, or it can be stood upside down on the saddle and handlebars, or on the front of the fork and the bars with the front wheel removed.

1. The wheels can be cleaned easily while on the bike. Remove the wheels to clean the frame, fork and components.

2. If the bike has a chain hanger (a little nub attached to the inner side of the right seatstay, a few centimeters above the dropout), hook the chain over it. If not, pull the chain back over a dowel stick (Fig. 2.8) or old rear hub secured into the dropouts.

3. Fill a bucket with hot water and dish soap. Using a stiff nylon-bristle scrub brush, scrub the entire bike and wheels. Leave the chain, cogs, chainrings and derailleurs for last.

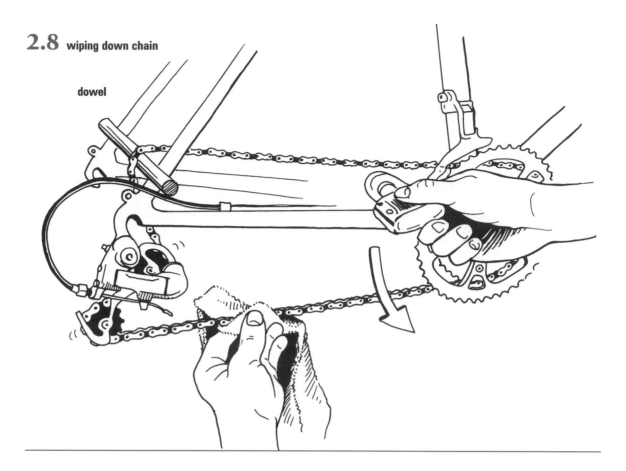

2.8 wiping down chain

dowel

4. Rinse the bike with water (low pressure!), either by hosing it off or by wiping it with a wet rag.

Avoid getting water in the bearings of the bottom bracket, headset, pedals or hubs. Also avoid getting water into the lip seals of suspension forks, as well as any pivots or shock seals on rear-suspension systems. Most frames and rigid forks have vent holes in the tubes to allow expanding hot gases to escape during welding. The holes are often open to the outside on the seatstays, fork legs, chainstays, and seatstay and chainstay bridges. Avoid getting water in these holes. This is especially true when using high-pressure car washes. Taping over the vent holes, even when riding, is a good idea.

II-14: CLEANING DRIVETRAIN

The drivetrain consists of an oil-covered chain running over gears and derailleurs. It is all exposed to the elements, so it picks up lots of dirt. Since the drivetrain is what transfers your energy into the bike's forward motion, it should move freely. Frequent cleaning and lubrication keep it rolling well and extend the life of your bike.

The drivetrain can often be cleaned sufficiently by using a rag and wiping down the chain, derailleur jockey wheels and chainrings.

1. To wipe the chain, turn the cranks while holding a rag in your hand and grabbing the chain (Fig. 2.8).

2. Holding a rag, squeeze the teeth of the jockey wheels in between your index finger and thumb as you turn the cranks (Fig. 2.9). This will remove almost any buildup on the jockey wheels.

3. Slip a rag in between cogs of the freewheel and work it back and forth to clean each cog (Fig. 2.10).

4. Lastly, thoroughly wipe down the derailleurs

2.9 cleaning jockey wheels

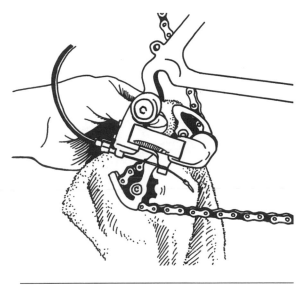

and the front chainrings with the rag.

Your chain will last much longer if you perform this sort of quick cleaning regularly, followed by dripping chain lube on the chain and another light wipe down. You'll also be able to skip those heavy-duty solvent cleanings that are necessary when a chain gets really grungy. You can get it just as clean as with a solvent if you wipe the chain down thoroughly after lubricating it and clean in between all of the outer link plates with cotton swabs (they won't fit in between the inner link plates, but the roller will spin with them).

You can also remove packed-up mud from derailleurs and cogs with the soapy water and scrub brush. The soap will not dissolve the dirty lubricant that is all over the drivetrain; but the brush will smear it all over the bike if you're not careful. Use a different brush than the one you use for cleaning the frame. Follow it with a cloth wipe down.

II-15: SOLVENT CLEANING OF THE CHAIN

If you frequently wipe down and lubricate your chain sparingly by putting lube only on the chain

rollers where it is needed (Fig. 4.1), rather than all over the chain, you can minimize the need for solvent cleaning with its associated disposal and toxicity problems. If you determine that using a solvent is necessary, work in a well-ventilated area, use as little solvent as necessary, and pick an environmentally friendly one. Using one of the many citrus solvents on the market will minimize the danger of breathing the stuff or getting it onto and into your skin, and it will reduce a major disposal problem. If you are using a lot of solvents, organic ones like diesel fuel can be recycled, which may be a preferable solution to using citrus solvents, as long as you protect yourself from the fumes with a respirator.

Because all solvents suck the oils out of your skin, I recommend using rubber gloves, even with "green" solvents. A self-contained chain cleaner with internal brushes and a solvent bath is a quick and convenient way to clean a chain (Fig. 2.11), but it does not clean well deep inside the rollers. A nylon brush or an old toothbrush dipped in a solvent is good for cleaning cogs, pulleys and chainrings, and it can be used for a quick clean of the chain as well.

2.10 cogset cleaning

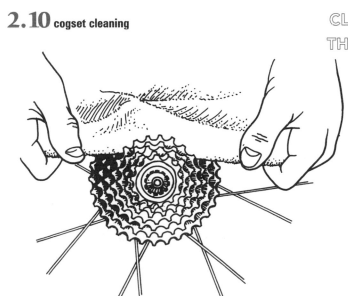

2.11 using a solvent-bath chain cleaner

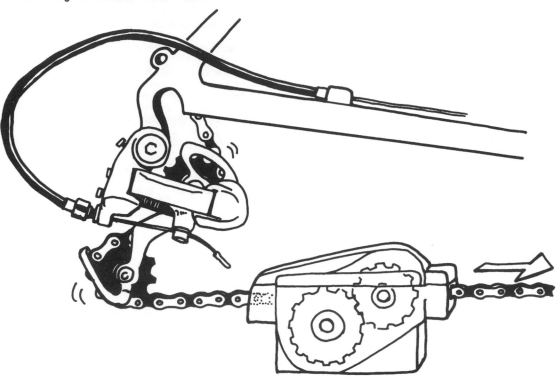

A way to thoroughly clean the chain is to remove it and put it in a solvent bath, but opening the chain often can be hard on the chain and lead to breakage while riding.

1. Follow the directions in Chapter 4, Section IV-7, for removing the chain.

2. Put the chain in an old water bottle that is about one-fourth full of a solvent.

3. Shake the bottle vigorously to clean the chain. Do this close to the ground, in case the water bottle leaks.

4. Hang the chain up to dry completely, especially inside the rollers.

5. Install the chain on the bike, following the directions in Chapter 4, Sections IV-8–IV-11.

6. Drip chain lubricant into each of the chain's links and rollers.

7. Lightly wipe down the chain with a rag.

You can reuse much of the solvent by allowing it to settle in a clear container over a period of days or weeks. Decant and save the clear stuff and dispose of the sludge.

A clean bike invites you to jump on it, and it will feel faster. Corrosion problems are minimized, and you can see problems as they arise. A clean bike is a happy bike.

II-16: GENERAL GUIDE TO PERFORMING MECHANICAL WORK

A. Threaded parts

All threads must be prepped before tightening

Depending on the bolt in question, prep with lubricant, thread-lock compound or an anti-seize compound. Clean off excess thread-prepping compound to minimize dirt attraction.

1. Lubricated threads: Most threads should be

lubricated with grease or oil. If a bolt is already installed, you can back it out and drip a little chain lube on it, and tighten it back down. Lube items like crank bolts, pedal axles, cleat bolts on shoes, derailleur- and brake-cable-anchor bolts and control-lever mounting bolts.

2. Locked threads: Some threads need to be locked to prevent them from vibrating loose; these are bolts that need to stay in place but are not supposed to be tightened down fully for some reason or other, usually to avoid seizing a moving part or stripping threads in a soft material. Examples of bolts of this type are derailleur limit screws, jockey wheel center bolts, brake mounting bolts, and spokes. Use Loctite, Finish Line Threadlock or the equivalent; use Wheelsmith Spoke-Prep or the equivalent on spokes (tight spokes can be greased).

3. Anti-seize threads: Some threads have a tendency to bind up and gall, making full tightening as well as extraction problematic. They need an anti-seize compound on them to prevent galling. Examples of this are any steel or aluminum bolt threaded into a titanium part (this includes any parts mounted to titanium frames, like bottom bracket cups) and any titanium bolt threaded into a steel or aluminum part. Use Finish Line Ti-Prep or the equivalent.

IMPORTANT

Never thread a titanium bolt into a titanium part. Even with an anti-seize compound, these will almost certainly gall and rip apart when you try to remove them.
Wrenches (Fig. 2.12) must be fully engaged before tightening or loosening

1. Allen wrenches (hex keys) and TORX wrenches must be fully inserted into the bolt head or the wrench and/or the bolt hole will round off. A good

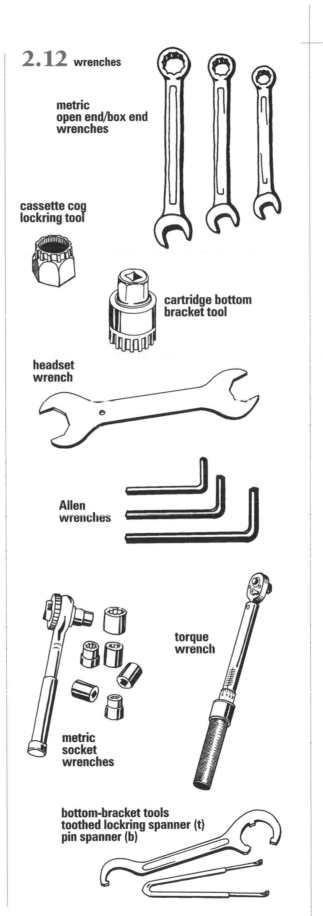

2.12 wrenches

metric open end/box end wrenches

cassette cog lockring tool

cartridge bottom bracket tool

headset wrench

Allen wrenches

torque wrench

metric socket wrenches

bottom-bracket tools toothed lockring spanner (t) pin spanner (b)

GENERAL GUIDE TO MECHANICAL WORK

example is a shoe cleat bolt; clean dirt and rocks out of them and tap the hex key in fully.

2. Open-end, box-end and socket wrenches must be properly seated around a hex bolt, or the bolt head will round off. A good example is an aluminum headset nut.

3. Splined wrenches must be fully engaged or the splines will be damaged or the tool will snap. If you strip the splines in a cassette lockring, you will not be able to get it off.

4. Toothed-lockring spanners need to stay lined up on the lockring; if they slide off, they will not only tear up the lockring, they will also damage the frame paint. Such a lockring can be found on a bottom bracket adjustable cup.

5. Pin spanners need to be fully seated in the holes to prevent slipping out and damaging the holes in the part. You can find pinholes in some bottom bracket adjustable cups, crank-bolt collars and cartridge-bearing hubs.

Tightening torque: A full list of specific tightening torques can be found in Appendix E

Generally, tightness can be classified in three levels:

1. Snug (10–30 in-lbs): small setscrews (like Grip Shift mounting screw), bearing preload bolts (like on threadless headset top caps) and screws going into plastic parts need to be snug.

2. Firmly tightened (30–80 in-lbs): cable anchor bolts, shoe cleat bolts and brake mounting bolts need to be firmly tightened.

3. Tight (70–240 in-lbs): wheel axles and stem and seatpost bolts need to be tight.

4. Really tight (280–600 in-lbs): crank arm bolts, pedal axles, cassette lockring bolts and bottom bracket cups are large parts that need to be really tight.

B. Cleanliness

1. Do not expect parts to work by just squirting or slathering lubricant on them (meanwhile patting yourself on the back for maintaining your bike). The lube will pick up lots of dirt and get very gunky.

2. Do not expect parts to work by washing them and not lubricating them. They will get dry and squeaky.

C. Test Riding

Always test ride the bike after adjusting in the bike stand. Parts behave differently under load.

GENERAL
GUIDE TO
MECHANICAL
WORK

emergency repairs

*Always carry a flagon of whiskey in case of a snakebite,
and furthermore, always carry a small snake.*

— *W. C. FIELDS*

This chapter is included so you do not face disaster if you have a mechanical problem on the trail. If you ride your bike out in the boonies, sooner or later you will encounter a mechanical problem that has the potential to turn into an emergency. The best way to avoid such an emergency is to plan ahead and be prepared before it happens. Proper planning involves steps as simple as bringing along a few tools, spare tubes and a little knowledge.

If you have something break on the trail, there are procedures in this chapter to deal with most "emergencies," whether or not you have all of the tools that you need. You always have the option of walking, but this chapter is designed to get you home pedaling.

Finally, you may find yourself with a perfectly functioning bicycle and still be in dire straits because you're either lost, bonking (i e , your body has run out of fuel) or injured on the trail. Carefully read the final portion of this chapter for pointers on how to avoid getting lost or injured and what to do if the worst does happen.

If this chapter does nothing other than alert you to some of the dangers facing you out in the backcountry, then hopefully you'll prepare for them and this chapter will have accomplished its purpose.

III-1: RECOMMENDED TOOLS

The take-along tool kit for your seat bag is described in Chapter 1, Section I-6 (Fig. 1.6). If you're going to be a long way from civilization, take along the extra tools recommended for longer trips (Fig. 1.7).

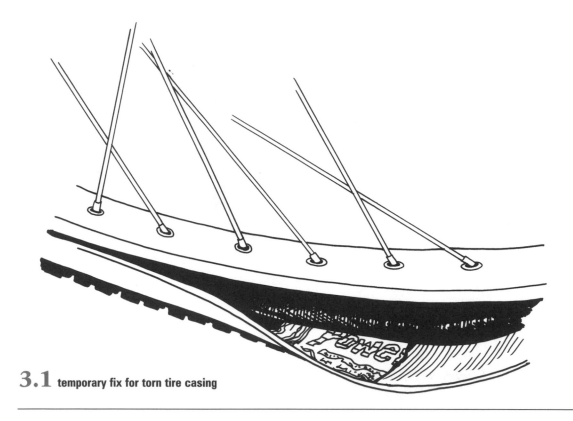

3.1 temporary fix for torn tire casing

III-2: FLAT TIRE PREVENTION

Flat tires can be prevented with the use of some tire sealants. "Slime" is one that works well. The stuff is a viscous liquid with chopped fibers in it that plug holes in the tube as they happen (use of Slime is covered in Chapter 6, Section VI-9); it can be injected into your tube, or you can purchase tubes with sealant already inside.

If you have Slime or another tire sealant in your tube and your tire gets low (this is most likely to happen when you stop riding for a while), put more air in and spin the wheel or ride for a couple of miles to get the sealant to flow out to the hole. A large hole will not be filled, although amazingly big holes can be plugged enough to get you home if you locate where the sealant is squirting out through the tire. Rotate the wheel so that the puncture is at the bottom and wait. The sealant may pool up enough there to plug the hole. Add more air and continue riding.

I recommend against older, plastic tire liners that go between the tire and tube. They are so stiff that they decrease traction and cornering ability, and they can slip sideways and cut into the tube.

There is, however, a new generation of liners made from Kevlar. These liners are considerably lighter than their stiff plastic counterparts. They are fairly expensive, though. A pair of "Spin Skins" for mountain bike tires can run around $33.

Tubeless tires (Section VI-7) can also eliminate many possible flat tires, especially when coupled with Slime (Section VI-9).

III-3: FIXING FLAT TIRES

A. If you have a spare or a patch kit

Simple flat tires are easy to deal with. The first flat you get on a ride is most easily fixed by installing your spare tube (Chapter 6, Section VI-6). Make sure you remove all thorns from the tire and feel around the inside of the tire for any other sharp objects. Check the rim to see that your flat wasn't caused by a protruding spoke or nipple, a metal shard from the rim, or the edge of a spoke hole protruding through a worn rim strip. Many rim strips are totally inadequate, being either too narrow or prone to cracking or tearing. Also, metal hunks left from the drilling of rims during manufacture can work their way out into the tube. Endeavor to eliminate these problems before leaving on a backcountry ride by shaking out any metal fragments and using good rim strips or a couple of layers of fiberglass packing tape (with those lengthwise superstrong fibers inside) as rim strips. If the hole in the tube is on the rim side, tire sealant will not fill the hole because the liquid will be thrown to the outside when the wheel turns.

After you run out of spare tubes, additional flats must be patched (also covered in Chapter 6, Sections VI-3–VI-5).

B. Torn sidewall

Rocks and glass can cut tire sidewalls. The likelihood of sidewall problems is reduced if you do not venture into the backcountry on old tires with rotten and weakened sidewall cords. If your tire's sidewall is torn or cut, the tube will stick out. Just patching or replacing the tube isn't going to solve the problem. Without reinforcement, your tube will blow out again very soon. First, you have to look for something to reinforce the sidewall (Fig. 3.1). Dollar bills work surprisingly well as tire boots. The paper is pretty tough and should hold for the rest of the ride if you are careful. (I told you that cash would get you out of bad situations. Just don't try putting a credit card in there; tire cuts don't take American Express or Visa!) Business cards are a bit small but work better than nothing. You might even

try an energy bar wrapper. A small piece of a tire liner cut into an oval might be a good addition to your patch kit for this purpose. A piece of a plastic soda bottle can also work. You get the idea.

1. Lay the cash or other reinforcement inside the tire over the gash (Fig. 3.1), or wrap it around the tube at that spot. Place several layers between the tire and tube to support the tube and prevent it from bulging out through the hole in the sidewall.

2. Put a little air in the tube to hold the makeshift reinforcement in place.

3. Mount the tire bead on the rim. You may need to let a little air out of the tube to do so.

4. After making sure that the tire is seated and the boot is still in place, inflate the tube to about 40 psi, if you are good at estimating without a gauge. Much less than 40psi will allow the boot to move around and may also lead to a pinch flat if you're riding on rocky terrain. This is not a perfect solution, so you will need to check the boot periodically to make certain that the tube is not bulging out again.

C. No more spare tubes or patches

Now comes the frustrating part: You have run out of spare tubes, and have used up all of your patches (or your CO_2 cartridge is empty and you don't have a pump) and still you have a flat tire. The solution is obvious. You are going to have to walk or ride home without air in your tire. Riding a flat for a long way will trash your tire and will probably damage your rim, yet there are ways to minimize that damage. Try filling the space in the tire with grass, leaves or similar materials. Pack it in tightly and then remount the tire on the rim. This should make the ride a little less dangerous, by minimizing the flat tire's tendency to roll out from under the bike during a turn.

III-4: CHAIN JAMMED BETWEEN THE CHAINRING AND THE CHAINSTAY

If your chain gets jammed between the chainring and the chainstay, it may be hard to get it out if the clearance is tight. You may find that you tug and tug on the chain, and it won't come out. Well, chainrings flex, and if you apply some mechanical advantage, the chain will come free quite easily. Just insert a screwdriver or similar thin lever between the chainring and the chainstay, and pry the space open while pulling the chain out (Fig. 3.2). You will probably be amazed at how easy this is, especially in light of how much hard tugging would not free the chain.

If you still cannot free the chain, disassemble the chain with a chain tool (Chapter 4, Section IV-7), pull it out, and put it back together (Sections IV-9–IV-11).

III-5: BROKEN CHAIN

Chains can break when mountain bike riding, usually while shifting the front derailleur under load. The side force of the derailleur on the chain coupled with the high tension can pop a chain plate off the end of a rivet. As the chain rips apart, it can cause collateral damage to other parts. The open chain plate can snag the front derailleur cage, bending it or tearing it off, or it can jam into the rear dropout.

When a chain breaks, the end link is certainly shot, and some others in the area may be as well.

1. Remove the damaged links with the chain

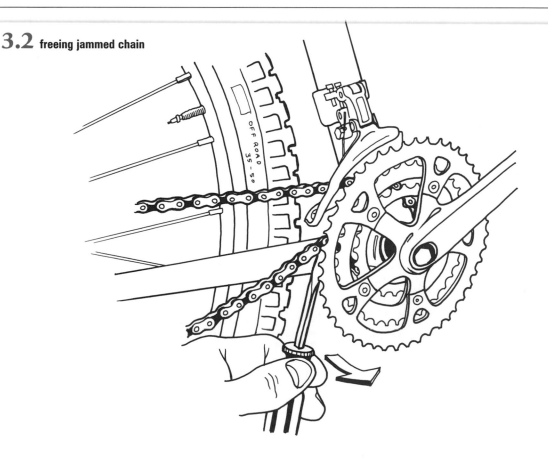

3.2 freeing jammed chain

CHAINS

3.3 fixing broken chain

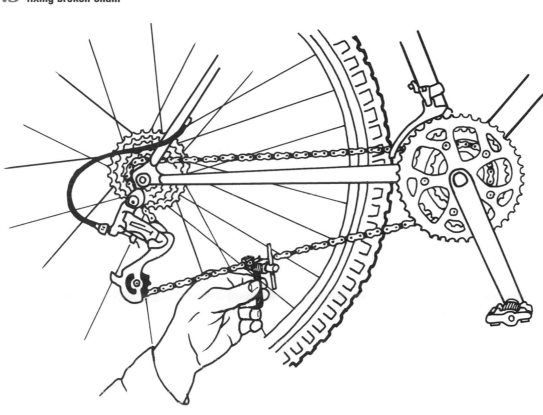

emergency repairs

tool. (You or your riding partner *did* remember to bring a chain tool, right?) Again, the procedures for removing the damaged links and reinstalling the chain are covered in Chapter 4, Sections IV-7–IV-11.

2. If you have brought along extra chain links, replace the same number you remove. If not, you'll need to use the chain in its shortened state — it will still work.

3. Join the ends and connect the chain (Fig. 3.3); procedure is in Chapter 4, Sections IV-9 and IV-10. Some lightweight chain tools and multi-tools are more difficult to use than a shop chain tool. Some flex so badly that it is hard to keep the push rod lined up with the rivet. Others pinch the plates so tightly that the chain link binds up. It's a good idea to find these things out before you perform repairs on the trail. Try the tool out at home or at your

local bike shop. This way you know what you're getting into before you reach the trailhead.

III-6: BENT WHEEL

 If the rim is banging against the brake pads, or worse yet the frame or fork, pedaling becomes very difficult. It can happen due to a loose or broken spoke or to a badly bent or even broken rim.

III-7: LOOSE SPOKES

If you have a loose spoke or two, the rim will wobble all over the place.

1. Find the loose spoke (or spokes) by feeling all of them. The really loose ones, which would cause a wobble of large magnitude, will be obvious. If you find a broken spoke, skip to the next section

3.4 loose spoke

3.5 brake lever adjusting barrel

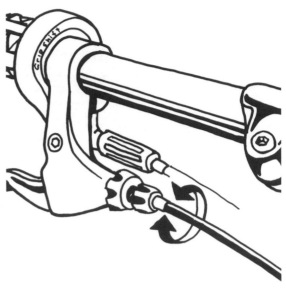

(III-8). If you have no loose or broken spokes, skip ahead to Section III-10.

2. Get out the spoke wrench that you carry for such an eventuality. If you don't have one, skip to Section III-9 below.

3. Mark the loose spokes by tying blades of grass, sandwich bag twist-ties, tape or the like around them.

4. Tighten the loose spokes (Fig. 3.4), and true the wheel, following the procedures in Chapter 6, Section VI-10.

III-8: BROKEN SPOKES

 If you break a spoke, the wheel will wobble wildly.

1. Locate the broken spoke.

2. Remove the remainder of the spoke, both the piece going through the hub and the piece threaded

into the nipple. If the broken spoke is on the freewheel side of the rear wheel, you may not be able to remove it from the hub, because it will be behind the cogs. If so, skip to step 6 after wrapping it around neighboring spokes (Fig. 3.6) to prevent it from slapping around.

3. Get out your spoke wrench. If you have no spoke wrench, skip to Section III-9 below.

4. If you brought a spare spoke of the right length or the Kevlar replacement spoke mentioned in Chapter 1, Section I-6B, you're in business. If not, skip to step 6. Put the new spoke through the hub hole, weave it through the other spokes the same way the old one was, and thread it into the spoke nipple that is still sticking out of the rim. Mark it with a pen or a blade of grass tied around it. With the Kevlar spoke, thread the Kevlar through the hub hole, attach the ends to the enclosed stub

3.6 wrapping broken spoke

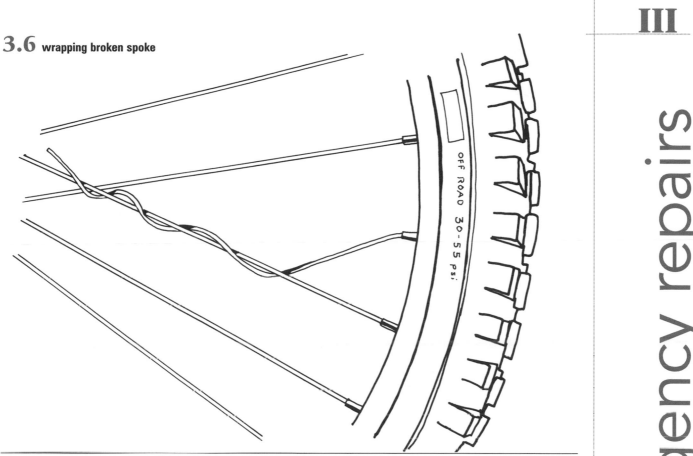

of spoke, adjust the ends to length, tie them off, and tighten the spoke nipple.

5. Tighten the nipple on the new spoke with a spoke wrench (Fig. 3.4), checking the rim clearance with the brake pad as you go. Stop when the rim is straight, and finish your ride.

6. If you can't replace the spoke and you do have a spoke wrench, bring the wheel into rideable trueness by loosening the spoke on either side of the broken one. These two spokes come from the opposite side of the hub and will let the rim move toward the side with the broken spoke as they are loosened. A spoke nipple loosens clockwise when viewed from its top. Ride home, conservatively, as this wheel will rapidly get worse.

7. Once at home, replace the spoke, following the procedure in Chapter 6, Section VI-11, or take it to a bike shop for repair. After you have had a

broken spoke more than once on a wheel, it should be relaced with new spokes, and the rim may need replacement as well.

III-9: NO SPOKE WRENCH

If the rim is banging the brake pads, but the tire is not hitting the chainstays or fork legs, just open the brake so that you can get home.

1. Loosen the brake cable tension by screwing in (clockwise) the barrel adjuster on the brake lever (Fig. 3.5). Remember that braking on that wheel is greatly reduced or nonexistent, so ride slowly and carefully

2. If the rim is still banging the brakes, and you have a wrench to loosen the brake cable (usually a 5mm Allen), do so, and then clamp it back down. You now have no brake on this wheel; ride carefully and walk the bike through difficult sections.

3.7 fixing bent rim

BENT RIM

3. If the bent wheel still will not turn, you can remove both brake arms from the cantilever posts, put them in your pocket, and pedal home slowly. You will usually need a 5mm Allen wrench for this. Do not attempt to ride a bike with brakes still attached to the frame or fork but disconnected from the cable. The brake arms will flap around as you ride and may get caught in the spokes, which could crack your seatstay or fork, not to mention your head, in a heartbeat.

If you want to straighten the wheel without using a spoke wrench, follow the next procedures for dealing with a bent rim, Section III-10. Recognize that if you bend the rim by smacking it on the ground to correct for a loose or broken spoke, you will permanently deform the rim. Try to get home without resorting to this, since you will have to replace the rim.

III-10: BENT RIM

LEVEL 2 If your rim is only mildly out of true, and you brought your spoke wrench, you can fix it. The procedure for truing a wheel is explained in Chapter 6, Section VI-10.

If the wheel is really whacked out, spoke truing won't do much. To get it to clear the brakes so that you can pedal home, follow the steps under III-9: "No Spoke Wrench."

If the wheel is bent to the point that it won't turn, even when the brake is removed, you can beat it straight as long as the rim is not broken.

1. Find the area that is bent outward the most and mark it.

2. Leaving the tire on and inflated, hold the wheel by its sides with the bent part at the top facing away from you.

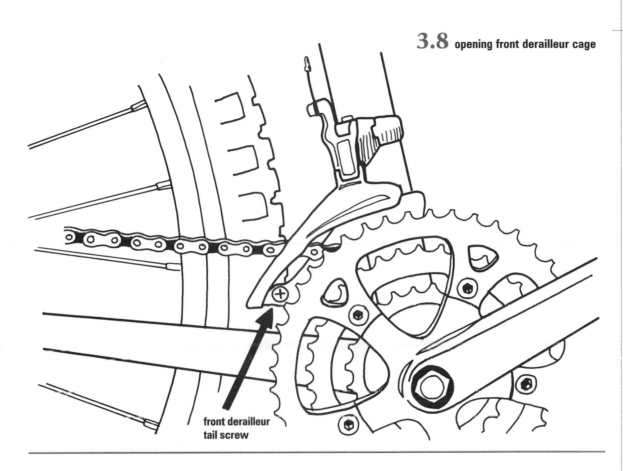

3.8 opening front derailleur cage

front derailleur
tail screw

3. Smack the bent section of the rim against the flat ground (Fig. 3.7).

4. Put the wheel back in the frame or fork, and see if anything has changed.

5. Repeat the process until the wheel is rideable. You may be surprised how straight you can get a wheel this way. Of course, you can also make it a lot worse if you hit it too hard or at the wrong spot.

III-11: DAMAGED FRONT DERAILLEUR

If the front derailleur is mildly bent, straighten it with your hands or leave it until you get home.

If it has simply rotated around the seat tube (the chain, your foot, or a pants leg can catch it and turn it), reposition it so the cage is just above and parallel to the chainrings, then tighten the derailleur in place with a 5mm Allen wrench. If the derailleur is broken or so bent that you can't ride,

you will need to remove it or route the chain around it as described below.

A. With only a screwdriver

1. Get the chain out of the derailleur cage. To do this, open the derailleur cage by removing the screw at its tail (Fig. 3.8).

2. Bypass the derailleur by putting the chain on a chainring that does not interfere with it (either shift the derailleur to the inside and put the chain on the big chainring or vice versa).

B. With Allen wrenches and a screwdriver (or a chain tool)

1. Remove the derailleur from the seat tube, usually with a 5mm Allen wrench.

2. Remove the screw at the tail of the derailleur cage with a screwdriver (Fig. 3.8).

3. Pry open the cage, and separate it from the chain. You could also disassemble the chain, pull it out of the derailleur, and reconnect it (Chapter 4, Sections IV-7–IV-11).

4. Manually put the chain on whichever chainring is most appropriate for the ride home. If in doubt, put it on the middle one.

5. Tie the cable up so it won't catch in your wheel.

6. Stuff the derailleur in your pocket and ride home.

III-12: DAMAGED REAR DERAILLEUR

If the derailleur gets bent just a bit, you can probably straighten it enough to get home. If only a jockey wheel fell out, you may be able to fix that as in Section III-13. Or if the return spring breaks and the chain hangs slack, you can try the fix in Section III-14. But if the rear derailleur gets really

bent or broken, then you will not be able to continue to pedal with the chain routed through it.

If you only need to descend back to your home or car, tie up your chain to the chainstay with tape, wire or string, and coast back down.

To pedal back, you can also route the chain around the derailleur, effectively turning your bike into a single-speed for the duration of your ride (Fig. 3.9). However, the only rear-suspension bikes that can be set up as a single speed are "unified-rear-triangle" bikes, where the dropouts are rigidly attached to the bottom bracket shell. Other rear suspension systems will alternately yank on and slacken the chain as they move. Taking the derailleur out of the equation means that there is nothing to take in or let out the slack. If you have a lockout on the rear shock, you can use that and continue with the fol-

3.9 bypassing damaged rear derailleur

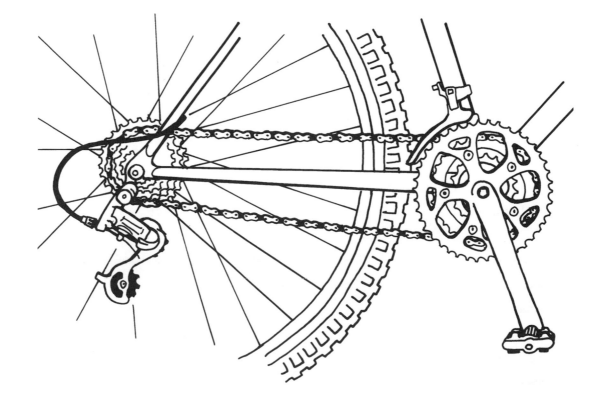

DAMAGED
REAR
DERAILLEUR

lowing instructions. Otherwise, you must try another way to repair the derailleur (like the repair in section III-13), or you will be walking home.

1. Open the chain with a chain tool (Chapter 4, Section IV-7) and pull it out of the derailleur.

2. Pick a gear combination in which you think you can make it home most effectively, and set the front derailleur over the chainring you have picked. Be aware that the chain line must be straight (i.e., the chain must parallel the frame), or the chain will fall off of the cog and chainring and frustrate any attempts to pedal.

3. Wrap the chain over the chainring and the rear cog you have chosen, bypassing the rear derailleur entirely.

4. Remove any overlapping chain, making the chain as short as you can and still be able to connect the ends together. Push the wheel a bit forward in the dropouts to get a bit more slack.

5. Connect the chain with the chain tool as described in Chapter 4, Section IV-9. Pull the wheel back in the dropouts as far as you can to tension the chain.

6. Ride home.

III-13: REAR DERAILLEUR JOCKEY WHEEL FELL OUT

If you can find the jockey wheel and the bolt, just reassemble the parts onto the derailleur (see Section V-29 in Chapter 5).

If you find the wheel and not the bolt, you can reattach it with one of the bolts holding a water bottle cage on (provided you did not try to save weight by using short bottle-boss bolts!). The thread should be the same, although if the bolt is too long, you will need to be careful you don't

shift the derailleur inward far enough to catch it on the spokes as you ride.

If you cannot find the jockey wheel, you can still rig up the derailleur to work, or at least to pedal without shifting. If you lost the upper jockey pulley and your derailleur is a type with the same bolts top and bottom, then put the lower pulley on top first. Now, if you found the bolt for the lost pulley, just tighten it back in where it was, making sure the chain is routed over it in the normal fashion as if the pulley were still on it. If the bolt is also missing, you can still rig it up to work. Collect three threaded collars from the Presta valves on both of your wheels and your spare tube. String them up between the cage plates with a twist tie, wire or zip-tie.

III-14: BROKEN REAR-DERAILLEUR RETURN SPRING

If the spring in the rear derailleur's lower knuckle breaks, it will not pull tension on the chain. If you have a bungee cord, you can hook it to the derailleur's jockey-wheel cage and around the end of the quick-release skewer. Reverse the skewer so that the lever is on the drive side. Hook the other end of the bungee to wherever you can to maintain good tension, like a water-bottle cage or the seat tube.

III-15: BROKEN FRONT DERAILLEUR CABLE

Your chain will be on the inner chainring, and you will still be able to use all of your rear cogs. You have three options, depending on which chainring you want for your return ride:

Option 1. Leave it on the inner ring and ride home.

Option 2. Tighten the inner derailleur stop screw until the derailleur sits over the middle

III

emergency repairs

BROKEN
FRONT
DERAILLEUR
CABLE

3.10 tightening the inner front
derailleur stop screw

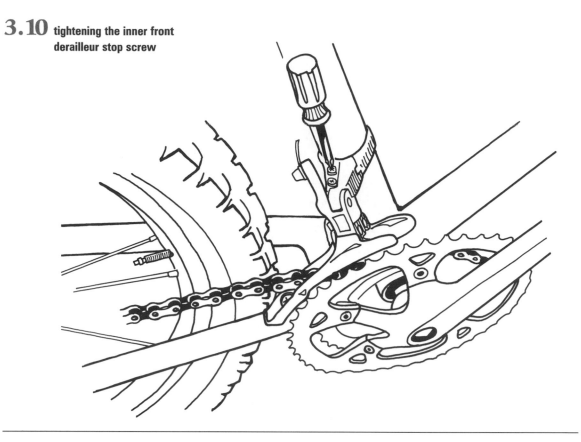

chainring (Fig. 3.10). Leave the chain on the middle ring and ride home.

Option 3. Bypass the front derailleur by removing the chain from the derailleur and putting it on the big chainring. You can do this either by opening the derailleur cage with a screwdriver (Fig. 3.8) or by disconnecting and reconnecting the chain with a chain tool (Chapter 4, Sections IV-7 and IV-9–IV-11).

Note: You have probably noticed by now that a chain tool is one of the handiest items you can take along. Like the ad says: "Don't leave home without it."

III-16: BROKEN REAR DERAILLEUR CABLE

Your chain will be on the smallest rear cog, and you will still be able to use all three front chainrings. You have three options:

Option 1. Leave it on the small cog and ride home.

Option 2. Move the chain to a larger cog, push inward on the derailleur with your hand, and tighten the high-end adjustment screw on the rear derailleur (usually the upper one of the two screws) until it lines up with a larger cog (see Fig. 3.11). Move the chain to that cog and ride home. You may have to fine-tune the adjustment of the derailleur stop screw to get it to run quietly without skipping.

Option 3. If you do not have a screwdriver, you can push inward on the rear derailleur while turning the crank with the rear wheel off of the ground to shift to a larger cog. Jam a stick in between the derailleur cage plates to prevent it from moving back down to the small cog (Fig. 3.12).

III-17: BROKEN BRAKE CABLE

Walk home, or ride slowly and carefully home if the trail is not dangerous.

3.11 broken rear derailleur cable — option 2

III-18: FLAT SUSPENSION FORK

Not much you can do here. If you have a blown or leaking air-spring fork and can't pump it, you will just have to ride back with it bottoming out the whole way. Go slowly and keep your weight back.

III-19: BROKEN SEAT RAILS OR SEATPOST CLAMP

If you can't tape or tie the saddle back on, try wrapping your gloves or some clothing over the top of the seatpost to pad it. Otherwise, remove the seatpost and ride home without it.

III-20: BROKEN SEATPOST

If the elastomer breaks or falls out of a suspension seatpost, you may be able to replace the elastomer with a piece of wood.

If the seatpost shaft breaks, you can splint it internally with a stick, tape it up, and ride very carefully. Failing that, remove the seatpost and ride home standing up.

III-21: BROKEN HANDLEBAR

It's probably best to walk home. You could splint it by jamming a stick inside and wrapping it with duct tape. If the break is right next to the stem clamp, you could also loosen the clamp, move the bar over so the break is inside the clamp, and retighten it. In either case, you must ride very carefully. The stick could easily break or the clamp could let go of the broken bar, leaving you with no way to control the bike. A sudden collision of your face with the ground would follow. From what I've heard, that can be a painful experience. In fact, now that I think of it, you might want to consider just walking your bike home.

3.12 broken rear derailleur cable — option 3

III

emergency repairs

BROKEN SEAT
RAILS
—
BROKEN
SEATPOST
—
BROKEN
HANDLEBAR

47

III-22: BROKEN LINKAGE BOLT ON REAR SUSPENSION SYSTEM

Try sticking a hex key in where the bolt was and tape it in place.

III-23: FROZEN FREEHUB OR FREEWHEEL

If your rear cogs will not freewheel, you cannot coast. The frozen cogs will pull the chain around and rip up the rear derailleur. Try squirting some chain lube into the front and back of the freewheel mechanism. No chain lube and it is above freezing? Try squirting water in to get it to turn. If it is below freezing, believe it or not, you can sometimes free a frozen freehub by peeing on it. Hey, don't laugh. It's warm!

No matter what liquid you lubricate it with, you may need to hit the freehub with a stick to get it to turn.

III-24: TRAIL SAFETY: AVOIDING GETTING LOST OR HURT, AND DEALING WITH IT IF YOU DO

Mountain biking in the backcountry can be dangerous. You need to prepare properly and to take personal responsibility for your own and others' safety when riding in deserted country. Two deaths near Moab, Utah, in the summer of 1995 highlight the risks facing anyone who rides off into the backcountry.

The two who died in Moab were riding the popular Porcupine Rim Trail. The account of these riders pinpoints a number of details that cost them their lives. The pair got lost on the descent off Porcupine Rim, missed the turn into Jackass Canyon and then headed instead into Negro Bill Canyon — which divides the Porcupine Rim Trail

from Moab's most famous ride, the Slickrock Trail. It may come as a surprise that people could die and go undiscovered for 17 days so close to a main highway into town (which was right below them) and to two heavily traveled trails. But apparently, they hadn't told anyone of their plans, so no one in town noticed when they did not return.

Their parents, not hearing from them for a few days, called the sheriff, and a search was mounted.

Once lost, they abandoned their bikes and tried to walk down to the road, instead of riding back the way they had come. That road and the Colorado River are very close as the crow flies and are visible at a number of points ... but, due to the numerous cliffs, are quite difficult to reach. The two climbed, fell or slid down to a ledge from which they apparently were unable to climb either up or down, and there they slowly perished from exposure.

They died on a ledge, in such a way that they were very difficult to spot from the air. They had placed no items to indicate their positions to airborne spotters. Had searchers found their bikes, they could have concentrated the search on a small area. Regrettably, their bikes and helmets were picked up by a pair of passing riders who then did not leave word with the authorities.

Eventually, a helicopter searcher saw the bodies on the ledge, and a Forest Service ranger rappelled 160 feet down to them. He was able to then walk out unaided, indicating that perhaps the riders were so injured, exhausted, delirious or hypothermic that they had been unable to take the same route out.

Cliffs, steep hills and an array of other natural features can also pose a risk. In the fall of 1995, another Moab rider barely managed to jump off his bike before it went hurtling over the edge of a

BROKEN LINKAGE BOLT

—

FROZEN FREEHUB

—

TRAIL SAFETY

cliff and dropped some 400 feet. Anyone who has ridden much in Moab can tell you that there are countless other places exposed enough to present a similar threat.

Even in seemingly safe areas, the risks can be high. Pro rider Paul Willerton came close to meeting his end on a relatively standard, cliffless, but isolated trail near Winter Park, Colorado. Unable to walk after crashing and breaking his leg, Willerton had to drag himself many miles using only his arms.

We all tend to think that nothing like this will ever happen to us. But things like this can happen, far too easily. This shouldn't discourage you from riding in the backcountry. It should encourage you to think and utilize the following 12 basic backcountry survival skills — they could make the difference between life and death.

1. Always take plenty of water. You can survive a long time without food but not without water.

2. Tell someone where you are going and when you expect to return. If you know of someone who is missing, call the police or sheriff.

3. If you find personal effects on the ground, assume it could indicate that someone is lost or in trouble. Report the find and mark the location.

4. If you get lost, backtrack. Even if going back is longer, it is better than getting stranded.

5. Don't go down something you can't get back up.

6. Bring matches, extra clothing and food, and perhaps a flashlight and an aluminized emergency blanket, in case you have to spend the night out or need to signal searchers.

7. If the area is new to you, go with someone who is familiar with it, or take a map and compass, and know how to use them.

8. Wear a helmet. It's hard to ride home with a cracked skull.

9. Bring basic first aid and bike tools, and know how to use them well enough to keep yourself and your bike going.

10. Walk your bike when it's appropriate. Falling off a cliff is a poor alternative to taking a few extra seconds or displaying less bravado. Try riding difficult sections to improve your bike handling, but if the exposure is great or a mistake leaves you injured a long way from help, find another place to practice those moves.

11. Don't ride beyond your limits if you are a long way out. Take a break. Get out of the hot sun. Avoid dehydration and bonk by drinking and eating enough.

12. Teach your friends all these things.

The above 12 rules are in addition to the below International Mountain Bike Association (IMBA) Rules of the Trail, which we would all do well to adhere to.

1. Plan ahead.
2. Always yield trail.
3. Never scare animals
4. Ride on open trails only.
5. Control your bicycle.
6. Leave no trace.

Keep in mind that your decisions affect not only you, but they could also affect your riding partners, your families and countless others. It is important to understand that endangering yourself can also endanger the person trying to rescue you. Search and rescue parties are usually made up of helpful people who will gladly come and save you, but no one appreciates being put in harm's way unnecessarily.

In summary, make appropriate decisions when cycling the backcountry. Learn survival skills, and prepare well. Recognize that even though you have a $4000 bike and are riding on popular trails, you are not immune to danger. When ignorance makes us oblivious to danger, it sadly becomes the danger itself.

chains

A chain is only as strong as its weakest link.
— *ANONYMOUS*

A sausage is only as good as its last link.
— *BLUTO*

bike chain is a simple series of links connected by rivets. Rollers surround each rivet between the link plates and engage the teeth of the cogs and chainrings. It is an extremely efficient method of transmitting mechanical energy from your pedals to your rear wheel. In terms of weight, cost and efficiency, the bicycle chain has no equal ... and believe me, people have tried to improve on it.

To keep your bike running smoothly, you do have to pay at least some attention to your chain. It needs to be kept clean and well lubricated in order to utilize your energy most efficiently, shift smoothly and maximize chain life. Chains need to be replaced frequently to prolong the working life of other, more expensive, drivetrain components.

This is because, as a chain's internal parts wear, it gets longer, thus contacting gear teeth differently than intended.

IV-1: LUBRICATION

When lubricating the chain, use a lubricant intended for bicycle chains. If you want to get fancy about it, you can assess the type of conditions in which you ride and choose a lubricant intended for those conditions. Some lubricants are dry and pick up less dirt in dry conditions; some are sticky and therefore less prone to washing off in wet conditions.

1. Drip a small amount of lubricant across each roller (Fig. 4.1), periodically moving the chain to give easy access to the links you are working on. If you are in a hurry, you can turn the crank slowly while dripping lubricant onto the chain as it goes

4.1 lubing chain

4.2 wiping chain with rag

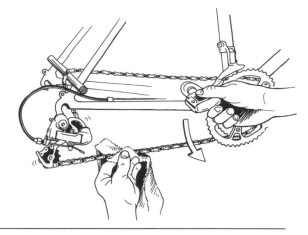

by. This is better than not lubricating the chain, but it will cause you to apply too much lubricant. That, in turn, will cause the chain to pick up dirt faster, and you'll then wear out your chain sooner.

2. Wipe the chain off lightly with a rag. In wet conditions, expect to require more lubricant (after every ride, or even several times during a rainy ride). The lubricant for wet conditions needs to adhere well to the chain and not be easily washed off; this usually means a thick and sticky lubricant — even grease. For dry conditions, less quantity of a dry lubricant that does not pick up dirt is preferable.

IV-2: CLEANING BY FREQUENT WIPING AND LUBRICATION

Cleaning the chain can be accomplished in a number of ways. The simplest method to maintain a chain is to wipe it down frequently and then lubricate it. If this is done before every ride, you will never need to clean your chain with a solvent. The lubricant softens the old sludge buildup, which is driven out of the chain when you ride. The problem is that the lubricant also picks up new dirt and grime. If new dirt and grime is wiped off before it's driven deep into the chain, and the

chain is relubricated frequently, it will stay clean and supple. Chain cleaning can be performed with the bike standing on the ground or in a bike stand.

1. With a rag in your hand, grasp the lower length of the chain (between the bottom of the chainring and the rear derailleur lower jockey wheel).

2. Turn the crank backward a number of revolutions, pulling the chain through the rag (Fig. 4.2). Periodically rotate the rag to present a cleaner section of it to the chain.

3. Lubricate each chain roller as above.

IV-3: CHAIN-CLEANING UNITS

Several companies make chain-cleaning units that scrub the chain with a solvent while it is still on the bike. These types of chain cleaners are generally made of clear plastic and have two or three rotating brushes that scrub the chain as it moves through the solvent bath (Fig. 4.3). These units offer the advantage of letting you clean your chain without removing it from the bike. Regularly removing your chain is a pain and it shortens chain life. Most chain cleaners come with a non-toxic, citrus-based solvent. For your safety and other environmental reasons, I strongly recom-

4.3 using solvent-bath chain cleaner

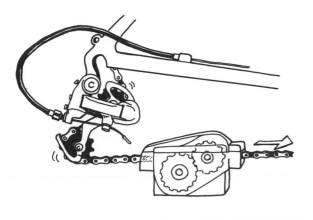

mend that you purchase nontoxic citrus solvents for your chain cleaner, even if the unit already comes with a petroleum-based solvent. If you recycle used petroleum solvents, then go ahead and use them. In either case, wear gloves when using any sort of solvent, citrus or petroleum based.

Citrus chain solvents often contain some lubricants, so they won't dry the chain out. The effective combination of lubricant and solvent is why diesel fuel used to have such a following as a chain cleaner. A really strong solvent without lubricant (acetone, for example) will displace the oil from inside the rollers. It will later evaporate, leaving a dry, squeaking chain that is hard to rehabilitate. The same can happen with a citrus-based solvent without a lubricant included, especially if the chain is not allowed to dry long enough.

Procedure

1. Remove the top and pour in the solvent up to the fill line.

2. Place the chain-cleaning unit up against the bottom of the chain, and reinstall the top so that the chain runs through it.

3. Turn the bike's crank backward (Fig. 4.3).

4. Lubricate as above (Section IV-1).

IV-4: REMOVAL AND CLEANING

You can also clean the chain by removing it from the bicycle and cleaning it in a solvent. I recommend against it, because repeated disassembly weakens the chain, except in the case of a chain with a master link.

On a road bike, chain breakage is not much of an issue, but mountain bike chains are prone to breakage because of the conditions in which they are used. A chain that breaks while riding generally does it during shifting of the front derailleur while pedaling hard. This can pry a link plate open so that the head of a rivet pops out of it, tearing the chain apart. Chain disassembly and reassembly expands the size of the rivet hole where you put it together, allowing the rivet to pop out more easily. Shimano supplies special "subpins" for reassembly of its chains that are meant to prevent this. A hand-opened "master link" can avoid the chain weakening of pushing pins out. Master links are standard on Taya chains and on SRAM and Sachs chains of 1998 and later. Lickton Cycle's aftermarket Super Link can also be installed into any chain.

If you do disassemble the chain (see Section IV-7 for instructions), you can clean it well, even without a solvent tank. Just drop your chain into an old jar or water bottle half filled with solvent. Using an old water bottle or jar allows you to clean the chain without touching or breathing the solvent — something to be avoided even when you are using citrus solvents.

Procedure

1. Remove the chain from the bike (Section IV-7 below).

2. Drop it in a water bottle or jar.

3. Pour in enough solvent to cover the chain.

4.4 checking chain wear ... If the curved tooth with the *S* (indicating steel cogs) falls completely into the chain, replace it. (The *A* side is for aluminum cogs.)

4. Shake the bottle vigorously (low to the ground, in case the top pops off).

5. Hang the chain to air dry.

6. Reassemble it on the bike (see Sections IV-8–IV-11 below).

7. Lubricate it as above (Section IV-1).

Allow the solvent in the bottle to settle for a few days so you can decant the clear stuff and use it again. I'll say it throughout the book — it is important to use a citrus-based solvent. It is not only safer for the environment, it is gentler on your skin and less harmful to breathe. Wear rubber gloves when working with any solvent, and use a respirator meant for volatile organic compounds if you are not using a citrus-based solvent. There is no sense in fixing your bike so it goes faster if you end up becoming a slower, sickly bike rider.

IV-5: CHAIN REPLACEMENT

As the rollers, pins and plates wear out, the chain lengthens. That, in turn, hastens the wear and tear on other drivetrain parts. An elongated chain concentrates the load on each individual gear tooth, rather than distributing it over all of the teeth that the chain contacts. This results in the gear teeth becoming hook-shaped and the tooth valleys becoming wider. If such wear has already occurred, a new chain will not solve the problem. A new

chain will not mesh with deformed teeth, and it is likely to skip whenever you pedal hard. So before all of that extra wear and tear takes place, get in the habit of replacing your chain on a regular basis.

How long it takes for the chain to stretch will vary, depending on chain type, maintenance, riding conditions and strength and weight of the rider. Figure on replacing your chain every 500 to 1000 miles, especially if ridden in dirty conditions by a large rider. Lighter riders riding mostly on paved roads can extend replacement time to 2000 miles.

IV-6: CHECKING FOR CHAIN ELONGATION

The simplest method is to employ a chain-elongation indicator; one example is the model made by Rohloff (Fig. 4.4). The indicator falls completely into the chain if the chain is worn out. If the chain is still in good shape, the indicator's tooth will not go all of the way in. Another way is to measure it with an accurate ruler. Chains are measured on an inch standard, and there should be exactly an integral number of links in one foot.

1. Set one end of the ruler on a rivet edge, and measure to the rivet edge at the other end of the ruler.

2. The distance between these rivets should be 12 inches exactly. If it is 12-1/8 inches or greater, replace the chain; if it is 12-1/16 inches or more, it

is a good idea to replace it (and a necessity to do so if you have any titanium or alloy cogs or an 11-tooth small cog). Chain manufacturer Sachs (now SRAM) recommends replacement if elongation is 1 percent, or 1/2 inch in 100 links (50 inches). If the chain is off of the bike, you can hang it next to a new chain for comparison; if it is more than a half-inch longer for the same number of links, replace it.

IV-7: CHAIN REMOVAL

The following procedure applies to all standard derailleur chains except those with a "master link." Master-link equipped chains include all Taya chains, chains with Lickton's Super Link, and Power Link-equipped SRAM or Sachs chains; all of these chains snap open by hand at the master link (see Section IV-11), although they can also be opened at any other link with a chain tool as described below.

1. Place any link over the back teeth on a chain tool (Fig. 4.5).

2. Tighten the chain-tool handle clockwise to push the link rivet out. Unless you have a Shimano chain and a new subpin for it, be careful to leave a millimeter or so of rivet protruding inward from the chain plate to hook the chain back together when reassembling.

IV-8: CHAIN INSTALLATION

1. Determine the chain length: If you are putting on a new chain, determine how many links you'll need in one of two ways.

Method 1. Assuming your old chain was the correct length, compare the two and use the same number of links.

Method 2. If you have a standard long-cage mountain bike rear derailleur on your bike, wrap the chain around the big chain ring and the biggest cog without going through either derailleur. Bring the two ends together until the ends overlap; one full link (Fig. 4.6) should be the amount of overlap (Fig. 4.7). Remove the remaining links and save them in your spare tire bag so you have spares in case of chain breakage on the trail.

2. Route the chain properly: Shift the derailleurs so that the chain will rest on the smallest cog in the rear and on the smallest chainring up front.

Starting with the rear derailleur pulley that is farthest from the derailleur body (this will be the bottom pulley once the chain is taut), guide the chain up through the rear derailleur, going around the two jockey pulleys. Make sure the chain passes inside of the prongs on the rear derailleur cage.

Guide the chain over the smallest rear cog.

4.5 removing rivet

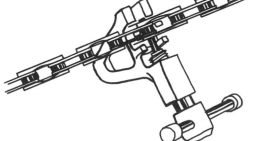

4.6 one complete chain link

4.7 determining chain length

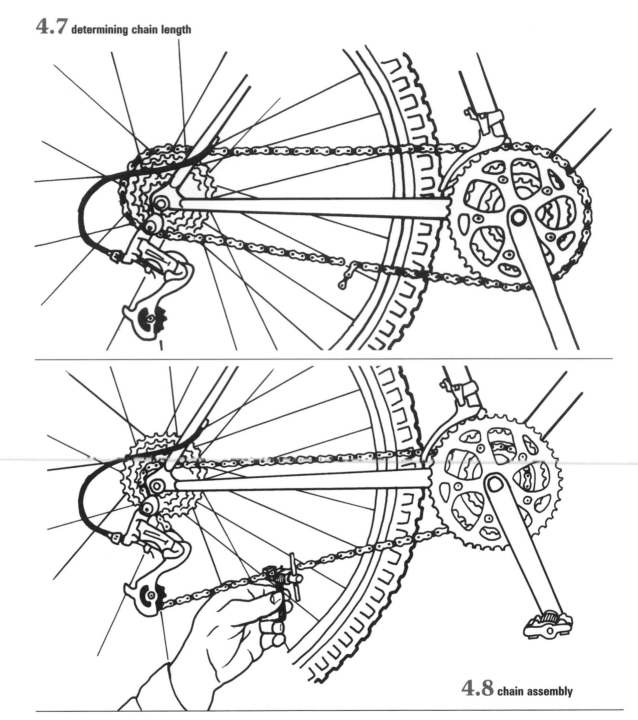

4.8 chain assembly

Guide the chain through the front derailleur cage. Wrap the chain around the smallest front chainring. Bring the chain ends together so they meet.

3. Connect the chain: Connecting a chain is much easier if the link rivet that was partially removed when the chain was taken apart is facing toward you. Positioning the link rivet this way

allows you to use the chain tool (Fig. 4.8) in a much more comfortable manner (driving the rivet toward the bike, instead of back at you).

IV-9: CONNECTING A STANDARD CHAIN

1. Push the ends together, snapping the end link over the little stub of pin you left sticking out to

4.9 replacing rivet

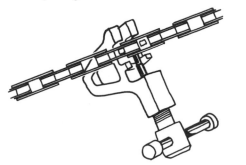

4.10 loosening a stiff link

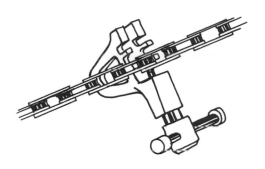

4.11 snapping end off Shimano subpin

the inside between the opposite end plates. You will need to flex the link open as you push the link in to get the pin to snap into the hole.

2. Push the rivet through with the chain tool (Fig. 4.9) until the same amount protrudes on either end.

3. Free the stiff link (Fig. 4.15), either by flexing it back and forth with your fingers (Fig. 4.16) or, better, by using the chain tool's second set of teeth as below.

4. Put the link over the set of teeth on the tool closest to the screw handle (Fig. 4.10).

5. Push the pin a fraction of a turn to spread the plates apart.

IV-10: CONNECTING A SHIMANO CHAIN

1. Make sure you have a Shimano subpin, which looks like a black rivet with a point on one end. It is twice as long as a standard rivet and has a breakage groove at the middle of its length. It comes with a new Shimano chain. If you are reinstalling an old Shimano chain, get a new subpin at a bike shop. If you don't have a subpin and are going to connect it anyway, follow the procedure above in Section IV-9, but be aware that the chain is now more likely to break than if it had been assembled with the proper subpin.

2. Remove any extra links, pushing the appropriate rivet completely out.

3. Line up the chain ends.

4. Push the subpin in with your fingers, pointed end first. It will go in about halfway.

5. With the chain tool, push the subpin through (Fig. 4.9) until there is only as much left protruding at the tail end as the other rivets in the chain.

6. Break off the leading half of the subpin with a pair of pliers (Fig. 4.11).

7. The chain should move freely. If not, flex it back and forth with your thumbs at this rivet (Fig. 4.16).

IV-11: CONNECTING AND DISCONNECTING A MASTER LINK

A. Lickton's Super Link and SRAM (Sachs) Power Link (Fig. 4.12)

These links are the same; SRAM (Sachs) licenses Lickton's design. The master link is made up of two symmetrical links, each of which has a single pin

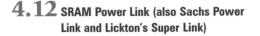

4.12 SRAM Power Link (also Sachs Power Link and Lickton's Super Link)

4.13 Taya chain master link

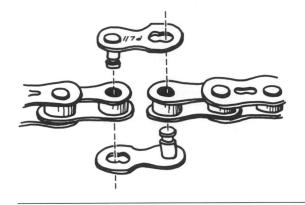

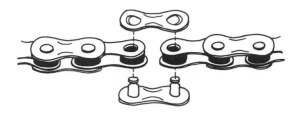

sticking out of it. There is a round hole in the center of each plate that tapers into a slot on the end opposite the pin.

Connecting

1. Put the pin of each half of the link through the hole in each end of the chain; one pin will go down and one up (Fig. 4.12).

2. Pull the links close together so that the each pin goes through the keyhole in the opposite plate.

3. Pull the chain ends apart so that the groove at the top of each pin slides to the end of the slot in each plate.

Disconnecting

1. While squeezing the master link plates together to free the pins, push the chain ends toward each other so that the pins come to the center hole in each plate.

2. Pull the two halves of the master link apart.

Note: In practice, this is often almost impossible to do with an old chain. You may have to just open the chain somewhere else, reassembling it as in Section IV-9, or using another master link.

B. Taya Master Link (Fig. 4.13)

1. Connect the two ends of the chain together

with the master link that has two rivets sticking out of it (Fig. 4.13).

2. Snap the outer master link plate over the rivets and into their grooves. To facilitate hooking each keyhole-shaped hole over its corresponding rivet, flex the plate with the protruding rivets so that the ends of the rivets are closer together.

Disconnecting

1. Flex the master link so that the pins come closer together.

2. Pull the plate with the oval holes off of the rivets.

TROUBLESHOOTING CHAIN

IV-12: CHAIN SUCK

Chain suck occurs when the chain does not release from the bottom of the chainring and pulls up rather than running straight to the lower rear derailleur jockey wheel. It will come around and get "sucked" up by the inner or middle chainring until it hits the chainstay (Fig. 4.14). Sometimes, the chain becomes wedged between the chainstay and the chainring.

A number of things can cause chain suck. To eliminate it, try the simplest methods first.

Reducing chain suck

1. Clean and lube the chain and see if it improves; a rusty chain will take longer to slide off of the chainring than will a clean, well-lubed chain.

2. Check for tight links by watching the chain move through the derailleur jockey wheels as you slowly turn the crank backwards. Loosen tight links by flexing them side to side with your thumbs.

3. If chain suck persists, check that there are no bent or torn teeth on the chainring. Try straightening any broken or torn teeth you find with pliers.

4. If your chain still sucks, try another chain with wider spacing between link plates (if it is too narrow, it can pinch the chain ring). You can use a caliper to compare link spacing of various chains.

5. Another approach is to replace the inner (and perhaps middle) chainring with a thin stainless steel (or shiny chromed) chainring. The thin,

slick rings will release the chain more easily.

6. If the problem still persists, a new chainring or an anti–chain suck device that attaches under the chainstays may help. Ask at your bike shop about what is available.

IV-13: SQUEAKING CHAIN

Squeaking is caused by dry or rusted surfaces inside the chain rubbing on each other.

1. Wipe down and lubricate the chain (Sections IV-1 and IV-2).

2. If the squeak does not go away after a single ride with fresh lubricant, replace the chain. (If the initial remedy does not work, the chain is too dry inside and probably rusted as well. Chains seldom heal from this condition. Life is too short and bike riding is too joyful to put up with the sound of a squeaking chain.)

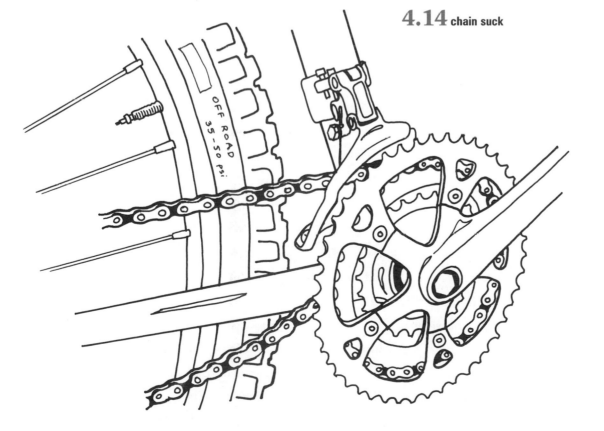

4.14 chain suck

OFF ROAD
35 - 50 psi.

IV-14: SKIPPING CHAIN

There can be a number of causes for a chain to skip and jump as you pedal.

A. Stiff links

1. Turn the crank backward slowly to see if a stiff chain link (Fig. 4.15) exists; a stiff link will be visible because it will be unable to bend properly as it goes through the rear derailleur jockey wheels. It will deflect the jockey wheels when passing through.

2. Loosen stiff links by flexing them side to side between the index finger and thumb of both hands (Fig. 4.16) or by using the second set of teeth on a chain tool (Fig. 4.10). Set the stiff link over the teeth closest the screw handle, and push the pin a fraction of a turn to spread the link.

3. Wipe down and lubricate the chain.

B. Rusted chain

A rusted chain will squeak. If you watch it move through the rear derailleur, it will look like many links are tight; they will not bend easily and will cause the jockey wheels to jump back and forth.

1. Lubricate the chain.

2. If this does not fix the problem after a few miles of riding, replace the chain.

C. Worn-out chain

If the chain is worn out, it will be elongated and will skip because it does not mesh well with the cogs. A new chain will fix the problem, if it has not gone on long enough to ruin some cogs.

1. Check for chain elongation as described above in Section IV-6.

2. If the chain is stretched, replace it.

4.15 stiff link

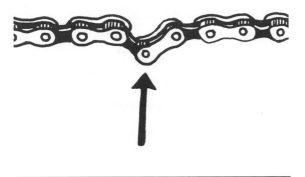

3. If replacing the chain does not help or makes matters worse, see the next section.

D. Worn cogs

If you just replaced the chain, and it is now skipping, at least one of the cogs is worn out. If this is the case, the chain will probably skip on the cogs you use most frequently and not on others.

1. Check each cog visually for wear. If its teeth are hook-shaped, the cog is shot and should be replaced. Rohloff makes a simple tool that checks for cog wear by putting tension on a length of chain wrapped around the cog (see Fig. 1.5 in Chapter 1). If chain links on the tool can be lifted off of the cog while under tension, the cog is worn out.

2. Replace the offending cogs or the entire cassette or freewheel. See cog change in Chapter 6, Section VI-18.

3. Replace the chain as well, if you have not just done so. An old chain will wear out your new cogs rapidly.

E. Misadjusted rear derailleur

If the rear derailleur is poorly adjusted or bent, it can cause the chain to skip by lining up the chain between gears.

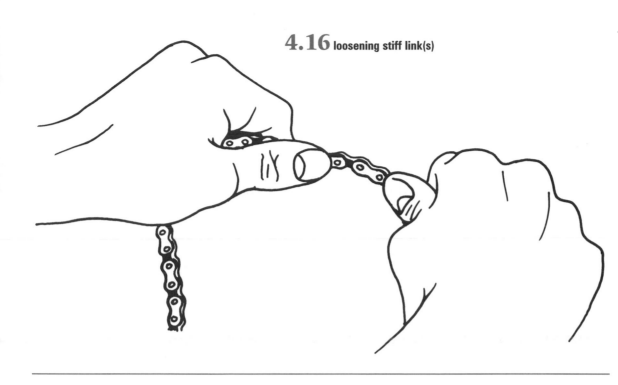

4.16 loosening stiff link(s)

1. Check that the rear derailleur shifts equally well in both directions and that the chain can be pedaled backward without catching.

2. Adjust the rear derailleur by following the procedure described in Section V-2 in Chapter 5.

F. Sticky shift cable

If the shift cable does not move freely enough to let the derailleur's spring return the chain to be lined up under the cog, it will jump off under load. Frayed, rough, rusted or worn cables or housings will cause the problem, as will overly thick cables or kinked or sharply bent housings.

Replacing the shift cables and housings (Sections V-6–V7 in Chapter 5) should eliminate the problem.

G. Loose rear derailleur jockey wheel(s)

A loose jockey wheel on the rear derailleur can cause the chain to skip by letting it move too far laterally.

1. Check that the bolts holding the jockey wheel

to the cage are tight, using an appropriately sized (usually 3mm) Allen wrench.

2. Tighten the jockey-wheel bolts if necessary. Hold the Allen wrench close to its bend so that you don't have enough leverage to overtighten the bolts. If the jockey wheel bolts loosen regularly, put Loctite on them.

H. Bent rear derailleur or rear-derailleur hanger

If the derailleur or derailleur hanger is bent, adjustments won't work. You will probably know when it happened, either when you shifted your derailleur into your spokes, when you crashed onto the derailleur, or when you pedaled a stick or a tumbleweed through the derailleur.

1. Unless you have a derailleur hanger alignment tool and know how to use it (Chapter 14, Fig. 14.3), take the bike to a shop and have it checked and the dropout hanger alignment corrected. Some bikes, especially those made out of aluminum, have a replaceable (bolt on) right rear

dropout and derailleur hanger, which you can purchase and bolt on yourself.

2. If a straight derailleur hanger does not correct the misalignment, your rear derailleur is bent. This is generally cause for replacement of the entire derailleur. (See Chapter 5, Section V-1.) With some derailleurs, you can just replace the jockey wheel cage, which is usually what is bent. If you know what you are doing and are careful, you can sometimes bend a bent derailleur cage back with your hands. It seldom works well, but it's worth a try if your only other alternative is to replace the entire rear derailleur. Just make sure you don't bend the derailleur hanger in the process.

I. Worn derailleur pivots

If the derailleur pivots are worn, the derailleur will be loose and will move around under the cogs, causing the chain to skip. Replacing the derailleur is the solution.

J. Bent rear derailleur mounting bolt

If the mounting bolt is bent, the derailleur will not line up straight. To fix the derailleur, get a new bolt and install it following the instructions in Chapter 5, Section V-33, "Upper Pivot Overhaul." Be sure to observe how the spring-loaded assembly goes together during disassembly to ease reassembly.

TROUBLE-
SHOOTING
SKIPPING
CHAIN

the transmission

DERAILLEURS, SHIFTERS AND CABLES

Most Americans want to be somewhere else, but when they get there, they want to go home.

— *HENRY FORD*

tools

3mm, 4mm, 5mm and 6mm Allen wrenches

flat-blade and Phillips screwdrivers (small and medium)

cable cutter

Indexed housing cutter

pliers

grease

chain lubricant

rubbing alcohol

There is nothing like having your derailleurs working smoothly, predictably and quietly under all conditions. Knowing that you can shift whenever you need to inspires confidence when riding on difficult single-track sections. It really is a lot more pleasant to ride through beautiful terrain without the grinding and clunking noises of an out-of-whack derailleur.

Improperly adjusted rear derailleurs are a pretty common problem, which is surprising because derailleur adjustments are easy, provided the equipment is clean and in good working order. A few simple adjustments to the limit screws and the cable tension and you're on your way. Once you see how easy it is, you will probably keep yours in adjustment all of the time.

V.A: THE REAR DERAILLEUR

The rear derailleur is one of the more complex parts on a bike (Fig. 5.1). It moves the chain from one rear cog to another, and it also takes up chain slack when the bike bounces or the front derailleur is shifted.

The rear derailleur bolts to a hanger on the rear dropout (Fig. 5.2). Two jockey wheels (pulley wheels) hold the chain tight and help guide the chain as the derailleur shifts. Depending on the model, a rear derailleur has one or two springs that pull the jockey wheels tightly against the chain, creating a desirable amount of chain tension.

Except on Shimano's reverse-action "Rapid-Rise" derailleurs, increasing the tension on the rear derailleur cable moves the derailleur inward toward the larger cogs. When the cable tension is released,

5.1 rear derailleur exploded

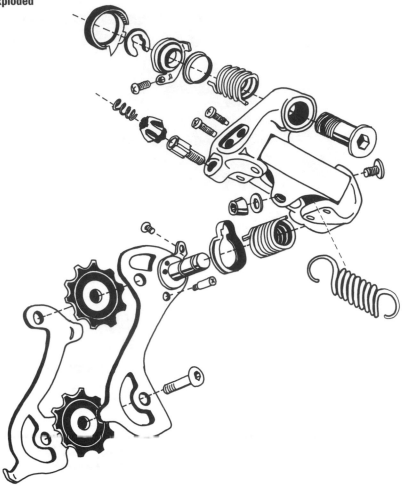

a spring between the derailleur's two parallelogram plates pulls the chain back toward the smallest cogs. The Rapid-Rise derailleurs work in exactly the opposite fashion.

The chain length and the balance between the springs in the upper and lower pivots determine how well the derailleur tracks the cogs and retains the chain. The two limit screws on the rear derailleur (Fig. 5.3) prevent the derailleur from moving the chain too far to the inside (into the spokes) or to the outside (into the dropout). In addition to limit screws, most rear derailleurs have a cable-tensioning barrel adjuster located at the back of the derailleur, where the cable enters it (Fig. 5.3). This can be used

to fine-tune the shifting adjustment to land the chain precisely on each cog with each click of the shifter. Rear derailleurs also often have a "b" tension screw at the back of the derailleur rotating it around its mounting point to control the space between the bottom of the cogs and the upper jockey wheel.

V-1: REAR DERAILLEUR INSTALLATION

1. Apply a small amount of grease to the derailleur's mounting bolt and then thread the bolt into the large hole on the right rear dropout.

2. Pull the derailleur back so that the "b" adjusting screw or tab on the derailleur ends up behind the tab on the dropout (Fig. 5.2).

5.2 right rear dropout

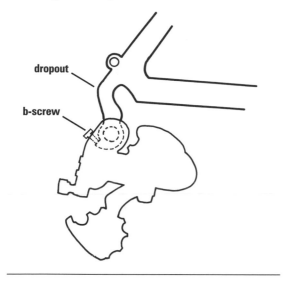

5.3 rear derailleur adjustments

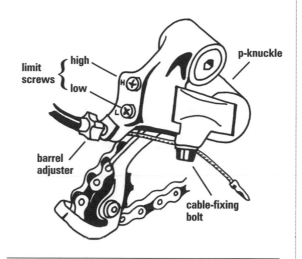

3. Tighten the mounting bolt until the derailleur fits snugly against the hanger.

4. Route the chain through the jockey wheels and connect it, making sure it is the correct length (see Chapter 4, Sections IV-8–IV-11).

5. Install the cables and housings (see Sections V-6–V-13 below).

6. Pull the cable tight with a pair of pliers, and tighten the cable-fixing bolt.

7. Follow the adjustment procedure described below.

V-2: ADJUSTMENT OF REAR DERAILLEUR AND RIGHT-HAND SHIFTER

Perform all of the following derailleur adjustments with the bike held in a stand or hung from the ceiling. That way, you can turn the crank and shift gears while you put the derailleur through its paces. After adjusting it off of the ground, test the shifting while riding. Derailleurs often perform differently under load than in a bike stand.

Before starting, lubricate or replace the chain (see Chapter 4) so that the whole drivetrain runs smoothly.

A. Limit-screw adjustments

The first, and most important rear derailleur adjustment is the limit screws. Properly set, these screws (Fig. 5.3) should make certain that you will not ruin your frame, wheel or derailleur by shifting into the spokes or by jamming the chain between the dropout and the smallest cog. It is never pleasant to see your expensive equipment turned into shredded metal. All it takes is a small screwdriver to turn these limit screws. Remember, it's "lefty loosey, righty tighty" for these screws.

B. High-gear limit-screw adjustment

This screw limits the outward movement of the rear derailleur. You tighten or loosen this screw until the derailleur shifts the chain to the smallest cog quickly but does not overshift.

How do you determine which limit screw works on the high gear? Often, it will be labeled with an "H," and it is usually the upper of the two screws (Fig. 5.3). If you are not certain, just try both screws. Whichever screw, when tightened, moves the derailleur when the chain is on the

5.4 high gear

5.5 low gear

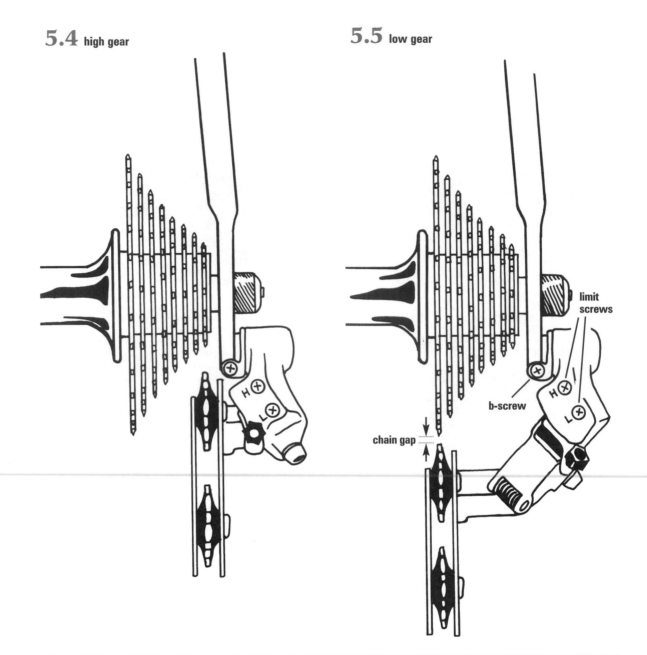

smallest cog is the one you are looking for. On most derailleurs, you can also see which screw to adjust by looking in between the derailleur's parallelogram side plates. You will see one tab on the back end of each plate. Each tab is designed to hit a limit screw at one end of the movement. Shift into your highest gear, and notice which screw is touching one of the tabs; that is the high-gear-limit screw.

Procedure

1. Shift the chain to the large front chainring.

2. While slowly turning the crank, shift the rear derailleur to the smallest rear cog (highest gear) (Fig. 5.4).

3. If there is hesitation in the chain's shifting movement, loosen the cable a little to see if it is stopping the derailleur from moving out far enough. Do this by turning the barrel adjuster on

the derailleur or shift lever clockwise, or by loosening the cable-fixing bolt.

4. If the chain still won't drop smoothly and without hesitation to the smallest cog, loosen the high-gear-limit screw one quarter-turn at a time, continuously repeating the shift, until the chain repeatedly drops quickly and easily.

5. If the derailleur throws the chain into the dropout, or it tries to go past the smallest cog, tighten the high-gear-limit screw one quarter-turn and redo the shift. Repeat until the derailleur shifts the chain quickly and easily into the highest gear without throwing the chain into the dropout.

C. Low-gear limit-screw adjustment

This screw stops the inward movement of the rear derailleur, preventing it from going into the spokes. This screw is usually labeled "L," and it is usually the bottom screw (Fig. 5.3). You can check which one it is by shifting to the largest cog, maintaining pressure on the shifter, and turning the screw to see if it changes the position of the derailleur.

1. Shift the chain to the inner chainring on the front. Shift the rear derailleur to the lowest gear (largest cog) (Fig. 5.5). Do it gently, in case the limit screw does not stop the derailleur from going into the spokes.

2. If the derailleur touches the spokes or shoves the chain over the largest cog, tighten the low-gear-limit screw until it does not.

3. If the derailleur cannot bring the chain onto the largest cog, loosen the screw one quarter-turn. Repeat this step until the chain shifts easily up to the cog but does not tap the spokes.

D. Cable-tension adjustment: indexed rear shifters

With an indexed shifting system (one that "clicks" into each gear), it is the cable tension that determines whether the derailleur moves to the proper gear with each click.

1. With the chain on the large chainring in the front, shift the rear derailleur to the smallest cog. Keep clicking the shifter until you are sure it will not let any more cable out (or keep pushing the thumb lever with Rapid-Rise).

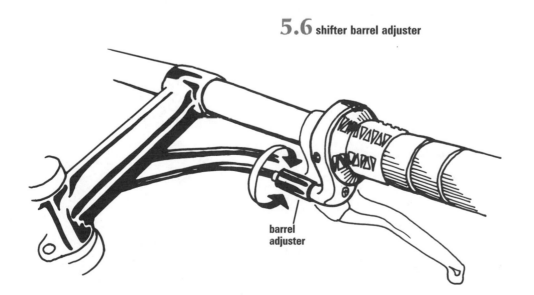

5.6 shifter barrel adjuster

barrel
adjuster

V

the transmission

LOW-GEAR
LIMIT-SCREW
ADJUSTMENT

—

CABLE-
TENSION
ADJUSTMENT

2. Shift back one click; this should move the chain smoothly to the second cog.

3. If the chain does not climb to the second cog, or if it does so slowly, increase the tension in the cable by turning either the derailleur cable barrel adjuster (Fig. 5.3) or the shifter barrel adjuster (Fig. 5.6) counterclockwise. Do the opposite with a Rapid-Rise derailleur. If you run out of barrel adjustment range, retighten both adjusters, loosen the cable-fixing bolt and pull some of the slack out of the cable. Tighten the fixing bolt and repeat the adjustment. Note that Shimano Rapid-Rise, SRAM and Sachs DiRT derailleurs have no barrel adjuster — use the barrel adjuster on the shifter alone.

4. If the chain overshifts the second cog or comes close to overshifting, decrease the cable tension by turning one of the barrel adjusters clockwise (or increase the tension with a Rapid-Rise derailleur).

5. Keep adjusting the cable tension in small increments while shifting back and forth between the two smallest cogs until the chain moves easily in both directions.

6. Shift to the middle chainring in the front and onto one of the middle rear cogs. Shift the rear derailleur back and forth a few cogs, again checking for precise and quick movement of the chain from cog to cog. Fine-tune the shifting by making small adjustments to the cable-tensioning barrel adjuster.

7. Shift to the inner ring in the front and to the largest cog in the rear. Shift up and down one click in the rear, again checking for symmetry and precision of chain movement in either direction between the two largest cogs. Fine-tune the barrel adjuster until you get it just right.

8. Go back through the gears. With the chain in the middle chainring in front, the rear derailleur should shift smoothly back and forth between any pair of cogs. With the chain on the big chainring, the rear derailleur should shift easily on all but perhaps the largest one or two cogs in the rear. With the chain on the inner chainring, the rear derailleur should shift easily on all but perhaps the two smallest cogs.

Note: If the shifter barrel adjuster does not hold its adjustment, your derailleur will get steadily worse as you ride. This has been a problem with some XTR shifters, which have no springs or notches to hold the adjuster in place, as most barrel adjusters have. If you have this problem, there are a couple of things you can do, besides getting a new shifter. One is to put Finish Line "Ti-Prep" on the threads to create a bit more friction; I have found this to be a temporary fix only. Loctite or crosswise scoring the threads may also help, although I have not tried either. One foolproof solution, though a bit of a hassle, is to keep the shifter barrel adjuster turned all of the way in and make all cable tension adjustments with the barrel adjuster on the rear derailleur. This fix will not work with adjuster-free Rapid-Rise rear derailleurs, though.

5.7 chain gap adjustment of early SRAM derailleur

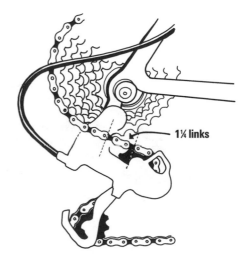

1¼ links

E. Cable-tension adjustment: Nonindexed rear shifters

If you do not have indexed shifting, adjustment is complete after you remove the slack in the cable. With proper cable tension, when the chain is on the smallest cog, the derailleur should move as soon as the shift lever does. If there is free play in the lever, tighten the cable by turning the cable barrel adjuster on the derailleur or shifter counterclockwise. If your rear derailleur and shifter don't have barrel adjusters, loosen the cable clamp bolt, pull some slack out of the cable with pliers, and retighten the clamp bolt.

Fine details of rear derailleur adjustment

In most cases, you can stop after adjusting the cable tension, but there is more you can do if you are a stickler for optimum performance. If you are still having shifting trouble, you would be well advised to proceed to at least step F, maybe step G and its following note as well. And if you have a problem with your chain bouncing off, attend to step G.

F. Chain gap: The "b-screw" adjustment

You can get a bit more precision by adjusting the small screw (b-screw) that changes the derailleur's position against the derailleur hanger tab on the right rear dropout. Viewing from behind with the chain on the inner chainring and largest cog (Fig. 5.5), adjust the screw so that the upper jockey wheel is close to the cog, but not pinching the chain against the cog. Repeat on the smallest cog (Fig. 5.4). You'll know that you've moved it in too closely when it starts making noise.

SRAM (a.k.a. "Grip Shift") suggests setting the b-screw on its early ESP derailleurs with the chain on the middle chainring and largest cog. Viewing from

5.8 removing the p-knuckle screw with a 2mm hex key

the drive side, turn the screw so that the length of chain across the "chain gap" (from where the chain leaves the bottom of the cog to its first contact at the top of the upper jockey wheel) is one to one-and-a-quarter links (Fig. 5.7), where one link is a complete male-female link pair (Fig. 4.6). SRAM derailleurs from 2000 and later specify a 6mm vertical distance from the tip of the jockey wheel to the bottom of the large cog (the chain gap depicted in Fig. 5.5), when in the small-chainring/large-cog combination.

G. Lower knuckle pivot spring ("p-spring") tension adjustment

 The lower pivot spring twists the derailleur forward and puts pressure on the chain through the jockey wheels. You can bring the upper jockey wheel closer to the cogs and increase chain retention over rough terrain by increasing the lower knuckle pivot spring tension. It puts more drag on the chain, so I wouldn't do it on a cross-country bike unless I had to. But increasing the p-spring tension can be worth doing for downhill.

This is definitely a complex adjustment requiring

V

the transmission

B-SCREW
ADJUSTMENT
—
P-SPRING
TENSION
ADJUSTMENT

5.9 increasing the p-spring tension by putting the spring end in another hole

5.10 removing the stopper screw that prevents the jockey cage from twisting all of the way around

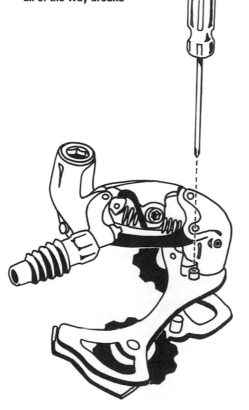

P-SPRING TENSION ADJUSTMENT

disassembly of the derailleur pivot, so be sure it is justified. Also, if you were thinking about replacing your steel pivot bolt with a lightweight aluminum one, now is the time to do it.

On post-1997 Shimano XT, LX and STX rear derailleurs, there is a setscrew on the side of the lower pivot that makes it possible to disassemble the pivot without disconnecting the derailleur from the cable and the chain, but I recommend removing the derailleur first. You would have to unscrew the mounting bolt anyway, and the derailleur will get so twisted around that it will be hard to tell which way is up with the cable and chain connected. You could end up turning the jockey cage the wrong direction and deforming the spring so it would not fit back in the knuckle.

The setscrew on the lower pivot engages a groove in the pivot shaft to keep it from pulling apart. Remove the screw with a 2mm hex key (Fig. 5.8), and pull the jockey cage away from the spring. Put the spring in the next spring hole to increase its tension (Fig. 5.9), push the pivot assembly back together, and replace the setscrew. Shimano derailleurs come with the p-spring in the low-tension hole.

Increasing p-spring tension on XTR and older model Shimano derailleurs is more complicated because there is no setscrew on the lower knuckle housing. After removing the derailleur from the bike, remove the tall stopper screw that prevents the jockey cage from twisting all of the way around (Fig. 5.10). Remove the upper jockey wheel and unscrew the pivot bolt from the back with a 5mm hex key (Fig. 5.11). Pull the derailleur cage off the end of the spring and move the end of the spring into the other spring hole. Wind the jockey wheel

5.11 unscrewing the pivot bolt with a 5mm hex key to pull the derailleur cage off of the p-spring

5.12 front derailleur

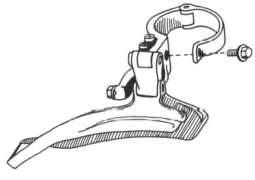

5.13 XTR bottom-bracket-mount front derailleur and band-clamp adapter (below)

cage back around, screw it all back together with the pivot bolt, and replace the stopper screw.

Note: If you cannot get the rear derailleur to shift well, or it makes noise in even mild cross gears no matter what you do, or it throws the chain off despite your best efforts, refer to the chain-line discussion under the troubleshooting section at the end of this chapter.

V.B: THE FRONT DERAILLEUR

The front derailleur moves the chain between the chainrings. The working parts consist of a steel cage, a linkage and an arm attached to the shifter cable. The front derailleur is attached to the frame, usually by a clamp surrounding the seat tube (Fig. 5.12). Some Shimano models attach to the face of the bottom bracket. Shimano's top-of-the-line XTR front derailleur mounts both to the face of the bottom bracket and to a braze-on boss (or band clamp) on the seat tube (Fig. 5.13); Shimano also offers an XTR front derailleur with a standard seat-tube band clamp.

V-3: FRONT DERAILLEUR INSTALLATION: BAND TYPE

1. Clamp the front derailleur around the seat tube.

2. Adjust the height and rotation as described in Section V-5A on the following page.

3. Tighten the clamp bolt (Fig. 5.12).

V-4: FRONT DERAILLEUR INSTALLATION: BOTTOM-BRACKET-MOUNTING TYPE

1. Remove the bottom bracket (see Chapter 8, Sections VIII-10 and VIII-11).

2. Slip the derailleur bracket over the right-hand bottom bracket cup, and start the cup into the bottom bracket shell a few threads.

V

the transmission

FRONT DERAILLEUR

5.14–5.15 proper cage alignment

5.16 proper clearance

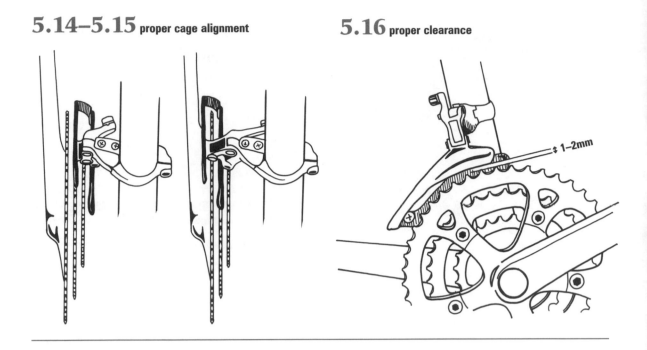

1–2mm

3. With less expensive models, place the C-shaped stabilizer around the seat tube to fix the rotational adjustment. With the XTR bottom-bracket-mounted derailleur (Fig. 5.13), loosely screw the mounting bolt into the special braze-on designed for it. (If the frame does not have the braze-on, a separate XTR seat-tube band clamp with a threaded hole in the side is used [see Fig. 5.13]. The band will need to be bent to fit an ovalized seat tube.)

4. Tighten the right-hand bottom bracket cup against the bottom bracket face.

5. With the XTR bottom-bracket-mounted derailleur, tighten the mounting bolt into the braze-on (or band clamp hole).

6. Complete the bottom bracket installation (see Chapter 8, Sections VIII-7–VIII-9).

Note: There are no (or limited) height and rotational adjustments on these derailleurs, and they must be used with the chainring size for which they were intended. They can be turned only slightly to line up better with the chain.

The XTR front derailleur has two mounting-bolt

holes for either a 46- or 48-tooth chainring. The derailleur's rotational adjustment can be fine-tuned without the braze-on; the band clamp can be twisted around the seat tube a few degrees.

V-5: FRONT DERAILLEUR AND LEFT-HAND SHIFTER ADJUSTMENT

A. Position adjustments

With a seat-tube-clamp front derailleur, the position is adjusted with a 5mm Allen (or 8mm box) wrench on the band clamp bolt. Bottom-bracket face-mounted front derailleurs have no vertical or rotational (twist about the seat tube) adjustments.

1. Position the height of the front derailleur so that the outer cage passes about 1–2mm (1/16–1/8 inches) above the highest point of the outer chainring (Fig. 5.16).

2. Position the outer plate of the derailleur cage parallel to the chainrings (or to the chain in the lowest and highest gears) when viewed from above. Check this by shifting to the big chainring and smallest cog and sighting from the top (Fig. 5.15).

5.17 limit screws

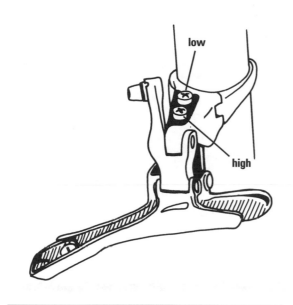

Many derailleurs (Sachs, most Shimano, SunTour) need the outer face of the cage exactly parallel to the chainring; check this by measuring the space between the cage and the inner side of the crankarm as it passes by. The cage of some derailleurs flares wider at the tail (Shimano XTR is one example). The outer tail of the derailleur cage on these models needs to be out a bit from parallel to the plane of the frame in order to parallel the chain. Similarly, when on the inner chainring and largest cog, the inner cage plate should parallel the chain, making the tail a bit in from parallel with the plane of the frame (Fig. 5.14).

Note: *Height and rotational adjustments of the seat-tube-clamp version of Shimano's differential-plate XTR front derailleur are set in the same manner as standard front derailleurs.*

B. Limit-screw adjustments

The front derailleur has two limit screws that stop the derailleur from throwing the chain to the inside or outside of the chainrings. These are usually labeled "L" for low gear (small chainring) and "H" for high gear (large chainring) (Fig. 5.17). On most derailleurs, the low-gear screw is closer to the frame; however, Shimano XTR differential-plate derailleurs have the limit-screw positions reversed, but their adjustment is the same.

If in doubt, you can determine which limit screw controls which function by the same trial-and-error method outlined above for the rear derailleur. Shift the chain to the inner ring, then tighten one of the limit screws. If turning that screw moves the front derailleur outward, then it is the low-gear-limit screw. If turning that screw does not move the front derailleur, then the other screw is the low-gear-limit screw.

C. Low-gear limit-screw adjustment

1. Shift back and forth between the middle and inner chainrings.

2. If the chain drops off of the little ring to the inside, tighten the low-gear limit screw (clockwise) one quarter-turn and try shifting again.

3. If the chain does not drop easily onto the inner chainring when shifted, loosen the low-gear limit screw one quarter-turn and repeat the shift.

D. High-gear limit-screw adjustment

1. Shift the chain back and forth between the middle and outer chainring.

2. If the chain jumps over the big chainring, tighten the high-gear limit screw one quarter-turn and repeat the shift.

3. If the chain is sluggish going up to the big chainring or does not go up at all, loosen the high-gear limit screw one quarter turn and try the shift again.

LOW-GEAR
AND
HIGH-GEAR
LIMIT-SCREW
ADJUSTMENT

E. Cable-tension adjustment

1. With the chain on the inner chainring, remove any excess cable slack by turning the barrel adjuster on the shifter (as in Fig. 5.6, except on left shifter) counterclockwise (or loosen the cable-fixing bolt, pull the cable tight with pliers, and tighten the bolt).

2. Check that the cable is loose enough to allow the chain to shift smoothly and repeatedly from the middle to the inner chainring.

3. Check that the cable is tight enough so that the derailleur starts to move as soon as you move the shifter.

Note: This tension adjustment should work for indexed as well as friction shifters. With indexed front shifting, you may want to fine-tune the barrel adjuster to avoid noise from the chain dragging on the derailleur in some cross gears, or to get more precise shifting.

Another note: Some front derailleurs have a cam screw at the end of the spring to adjust spring tension. For quicker shifting to the smaller rings, increase the spring tension by turning the screw clockwise.

Note on shifting trouble: If you cannot get the front derailleur to shift well, or it rubs in cross gears no matter what you do, or it throws the chain off despite your best efforts, refer to the chain-line discussion under the troubleshooting section at the end of this chapter.

V.C: THE SHIFT CABLES AND HOUSINGS

In order for your derailleurs to function properly, you need to have clean, smooth-running cables (also called "inner wires"). Because of all the muck and guck that you encounter on a mountain bike, you need to regularly replace those cables. As with replacing a chain, replacing cables is a maintenance operation, not a repair operation. Do not wait until

5.18 cable-housing types and end caps

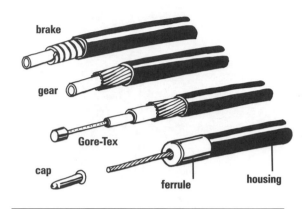

cables break to replace them. Replace any cables that have broken strands, kinks or fraying between the shifter and the derailleur. You should also replace housings (also called "outer wires") if they are bent, mashed, just plain gritty or the color clashes with your bike (this is really important).

CABLE INSTALLATION/ REPLACEMENT

V-6: PROCEDURE FOR BUYING CABLES

1. Buy new cables and housing with at least as much length as the ones you are replacing.

2. Make sure that the cables and housing are for indexed systems. These cables will stretch minimally, and the housings will not compress in length. Under its external plastic sheath, indexed housing is not made of steel coil like brake housings; it is made of parallel (coaxial) steel strands of thin wire. If you look at the end, you will see numerous wire ends sticking out surrounding a central Teflon tube (make sure it has this Teflon liner, too) (Fig. 5.18).

3. Buy two cable crimp caps (Fig. 5.18) to prevent fraying, and a tubular cable housing end (ferrule) for each end of every housing section. These ferrules will prevent kinking at the cable entry

points, cable stops, shifters and derailleurs.

While you're at it, buying rubber cable donuts (Fig. 5.30) or sheathing for bare-cable runs is worthwhile to protect your frame.

4. It is a good idea to buy a bunch of cables, cable caps and ferrules (Fig. 5.18) to keep on hand in your work area. They're cheap, and you should be changing cables regularly, without having to have to make a special trip to the bike shop every time you need a little cable-end cap.

V-7: CUTTING THE HOUSING TO LENGTH

1. Use a special cable-housing cutter like those from Park, Shimano or Wrench Force (see Section I-2 in Chapter 1). Standard wire cutters will not cut index-shift housing.

2. Cut the housing to the same lengths as your old ones. If you have no old housings to compare

5.19–5.20 housing length

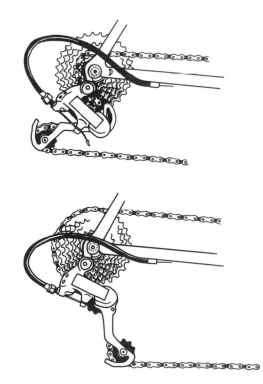

with, cut them so that the housing sections curve smoothly from cable stop to cable stop, and turning the handlebars does not pull or kink them. Allow for enough length at the rear derailleur so that the derailleur can freely swing forward (Fig. 5.20) and backward (Fig. 5.19 for chainstay cable, Fig. 5.27 for seatstay cable). Current SRAM and Sachs DiRT rear derailleurs use a short housing section without a cable loop (the bare cable runs over a pulley), and they are particularly sensitive to housing length. The housing should curve gently into its receptacle without being so short that it limits derailleur movement or long enough to have a sharp bend; the latter is particularly important to watch for with a seatstay cable as the derailleur swings backward.

3. With a nail or toothpick, open each Teflon sleeve-end that has been smashed shut by the cutter.

4. Place a ferrule (Fig. 5.18) over each housing end.

V-8: REPLACING CABLE IN THUMB SHIFTERS, SHIMANO RAPIDFIRE LEVERS OR SRAM TRIGGER LEVERS

1. Disconnect the cable at the derailleur and clip off the end cap.

2. Shift the lever (on Rapidfire or SRAM, the upper, chain-dump lever) to the gear setting that lets the most cable out. This will be the highest gear position for the rear shift lever (small cog), and the lowest for the front (small chainring).

3. If installed, unscrew the large plastic plug that covers the cable-access hole on many Shimano Rapidfire levers. On SRAM trigger levers, open the rubber cable-change flap. Push out the old cable and recycle it.

4. The recessed hole into which the cable head seats should be visible right up against the barrel

5.21 thumb shifter   **5.22** Rapidfire shifter

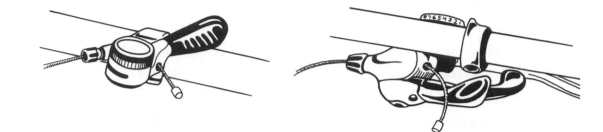

adjuster. Thread the cable through the hole and out through the barrel adjuster (Figs. 5.21 and 5.22).

5. Guide the cable through each housing segment and cable stop. Slotted cable stops allow you to slip the cable and housing in and out from the side. Replace the plastic plug or rubber flap over the cable-access hole in the shifter.

V-9: XTR RAPIDFIRE CABLE-REPLACEMENT INSTRUCTIONS

The 1996–2000 Shimano XTR shifters have a plastic cover over the wire-end hook (Fig. 5.23) and also have a slotted barrel adjuster and shifter body.

1. Shift the smaller (upper and forward) finger-operated lever until the shifter lets all of the cable out; i.e., the rear shifter is in high-gear (small-cog) position — "H" on the indicator; the front shifter is in the low-gear (small-chainring) position — "L" on the indicator.

2. Turn the shifter barrel-adjuster so the cable slit is lined up with the slot in the shifter body (Fig. 5.23); the slot is on the opposite side from the gear indicator. Post-1999 XTR barrel adjusters are in a plastic housing that pulls out of the lever body. Pull it out to simplify cable replacement.

3. Unscrew the Phillips-head screw on the plastic cover; it will not come completely out (where you could lose it), being retained in the cover by a plastic ring. Open the cover.

4. Pull the old cable down out of the slot, and

5.23 replacing cable in 1996–2000 XTR shifter

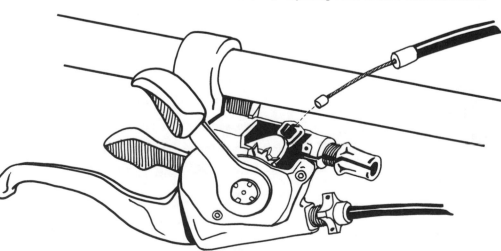

5.24 **SRAM Half Pipe shifter cable change**

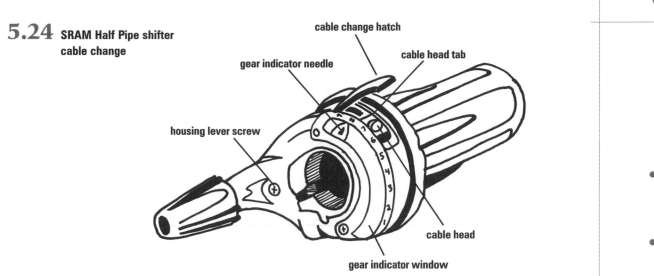

cable change hatch

gear indicator needle

cable head tab

housing lever screw

cable head

gear indicator window

the transmission

then pull the cable head out of the hook.

5. Slip the new cable head into the cable hook (Fig. 5.23), and pull the cable into the slot. Turn the barrel adjuster so the slots no longer line up.

6. Close the cover and tighten the screw (gently!).

7. Guide the cable through each housing segment and cable stop. Slotted cable stops allow you to slip the cable and housing in and out from the side.

Note: Replacing the thin cables connected to the XTR "Rapidfire Remote" bar-end-mounted shifters requires buying the thin double-headed cables and housings from Shimano. The small heads simply slip through the holes in both sets of shift levers (on the bar and on the bar end) from the back side. You install the little plastic cable head caps onto the metal cable heads to keep them from pulling back through. That's it.

V-10: REPLACING CABLE IN SRAM (GRIP SHIFT) AND SACHS TWIST SHIFTERS FROM 1998 AND LATER

Changing cables is easy on current Grip Shift and Half Pipe shifters via the cable-hole cover. High-end shifters got this feature in 1998, and by 2000, all SRAM shifters had the quick-cable-change system.

1. Disconnect the cable at the derailleur and cut off the end cap.

2. Twist the shifter to let out the maximum amount of cable (shift to "9" with the rear shifter and "1" with the front).

3. Getting at the end of the cable differs with each model. Some, such as Half Pipe shifters, for instance, have a rectangular rubber hatch that you pull open (Fig. 5.24). While pushing back on the cable, you then pry up the plastic tab that obscures half of the cable head. Use a small screwdriver. The cable should pop out from under the hook on the tab.

Other high-end SRAM shifters have a plastic hatch that you slide off to the side. Once the hatch is off, you will see the cable head on the front shifter, and on the rear shifter, you will see a small setscrew that you remove with a 2.5mm hex key to reveal the cable head.

On current low-end shifters, you peel back the corner of the rubber grip cover, and you will see the cable head.

4. Push out the old cable.

5. Slide in the new cable and pull it snug. Replace the setscrew, if present, and carefully screw it in until

5.25 pre-1998 Grip Shift right shifter

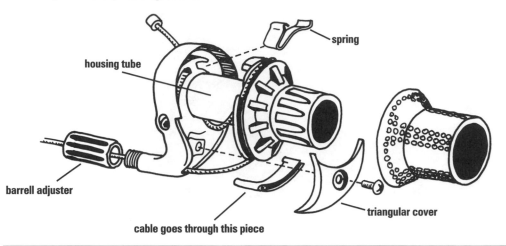

spring

housing tube

barrell adjuster

cable goes through this piece

triangular cover

5.26 pre-1998 Grip Shift left shifter

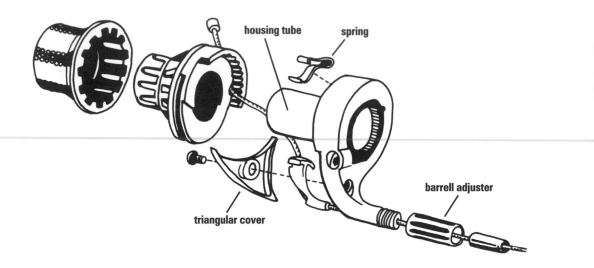

housing tube   spring

triangular cover

barrell adjuster

it contacts the cable head. If it feels like it has stripped the threads, it hasn't — it just has gone in beyond the threads and is turning freely. No worries.

6. Push the cover that conceals the cable head back into place.

V-11: REPLACING CABLE IN (AND OVER-HAULING) PRE-1998 GRIP SHIFT

Prior to 1998, all Grip Shifts had to be disassembled to replace the cable; 1998-2000 low-end shifters still require disassembly for cable changing.

1. Disconnect the derailleur cable.

2. Move the brake lever inboard to make room for pulling the grip apart. If a bend in the handle-bar or other obstruction prevents this, you must roll or slide the handlebar grip away from the Grip Shift to allow room for the shifter to slide apart.

3. With a Phillips screwdriver, remove the triangular plastic cover holding the two main sections together (Figs. 5.25 and 5.26).

4. Pull the outer shifter section away from the main body to separate it from the inner housing.

Watch for the spring to ensure that it does not fall out. It can be nudged back into place if it does (Figs. 5.25 and 5.26).

5. Pull the old cable out and recycle it.

6. Clean and dry the two parts if they are dirty; a rag and a cotton swab are usually sufficient. Finish Line offers a cleaning and grease kit specifically designed for Grip Shift shifters. A really gummed-up shifter may require a solvent and compressed air to clean and dry it.

7. Using a nonlithium grease, lubricate the inner housing tube and spring cavity, all cable grooves and the indexing notches in the twister. Use SRAM Jonnisnot or Finish Line's silicone-based Teflon grease.

8. Thread the cable through the hole, seating the cable end in its little pocket.

9. For the rear shifter, loop the cable once around the housing tube, and exit it through the barrel adjuster (Fig. 5.25). For the front shifter, the cable routes directly into its guide (Fig. 5.26).

10. Make sure the spring is in its cavity in the housing; hold the spring in with a small amount of grease if need be.

11. Slide the outer (twister) body over the inner tube. Be sure that the shifter is in the position that lets the most cable out (on models with numbers, line up the highest number with the indicator mark on rear shifters, lowest number on front shifters).

12. Lift the cable loop into the groove in the twister (Fig. 5.25), and push straight inward on it as you pull tension on the cable exiting the shifter. The twister should slide in until flush under the housing edge; you may have to jiggle it back and forth slightly while pushing in to get it properly seated.

13. Replace the cover and screw.

14. Check that the shifter clicks properly.

15. Slide the grip back into place.

16. Guide the cable through each housing segment and cable stop. Slotted cable stops on your frame allow you to slip the cable and housing in and out from the side — use them that way to save yourself some effort.

V-12: ATTACH CABLE TO REAR DERAILLEUR

1. Put the chain on the smallest cog so the rear derailleur moves to the outside.

2. Run the cable through the barrel adjuster, and route it through each of the housing segments until you reach the cable-fixing bolt on the derailleur. Make sure that the rear shifter is on the highest gear setting; this ensures that the maximum amount of cable is available to the derailleur.

3. Pull the cable taut and into its groove under the cable-fixing bolt (Fig. 5.27).

4. Tighten the bolt. On most derailleurs this takes a 5mm Allen wrench.

5.27 **attaching rear derailleur cable**

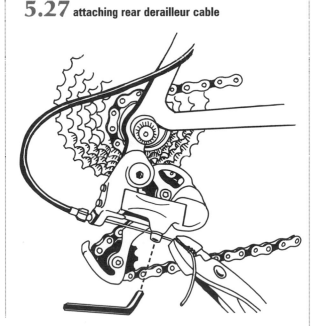

5.28 pull cable tight before tightening with Allen wrench

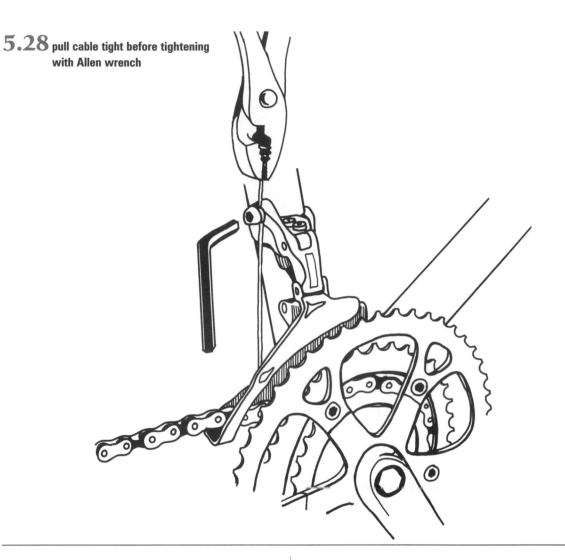

V-13: ATTACH CABLE TO FRONT DERAILLEUR

1. Operate the shifter to allow the most cable out (granny gear setting). Shift the chain to the inner ring so that the derailleur moves farthest to the inside. This ensures that the maximum amount of cable is available to the derailleur.

2. Place the cable into its groove under the fixing bolt on the derailleur arm while pulling the cable taut with pliers (Fig. 5.28), and tighten the bolt. Make sure you do not hook up a top-pull front derailleur from the bottom, or vice versa. Also note that some older derailleur models require housing to run the full length of cable.

V-14: FINAL CABLE TOUCHES

A high-quality cable assembly includes the cable-housing-end ferrules throughout, and crimped cable caps (Fig. 5.29); cables are clipped about 1cm or 2cm past the cable clamp-bolts. Also, little rubber cable donuts (Fig. 5.30) or pieces of thin cable sheathing are installed to keep the bare cables from scratching the frame's finish.

V-15: GORE-TEX CABLES

If you are using Gore-Tex cables, follow the instructions on the package, as these require very special treatment in order to work properly. The Gore Tex needs to be removed from the cable at

5.29 crimp cable ends

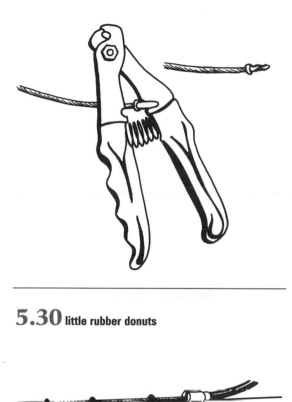

5.30 little rubber donuts

the last inch or so before the cable fixing bolt, as well as from all of the cable that is inside the shift lever or Grip Shift. A plastic tube covers the cable (Fig. 5.18) over its entire length from shifter to derailleur. A little rubber accordion seal (called a "Grub") at the fixing bolt covers the end of the cable-cover tube and keeps dirt and water out of it.

V-16: CABLE LUBRICATION

New cables and housings with Teflon liners do not need to be lubricated. Old cables can be lubricated with chain lubricant. Grease sometimes slows cable movement, but various manufacturers recommend (and some even supply) their own molybdenum disulfide grease for cables.

1. Pull the housing segments out of their slotted cable stops; there is no reason to disconnect the cable.

2. Coat with lubricant the areas of the cable that will be inside of the cable housing segments.

Note: *If you do not have slotted cable stops, you might as well replace the cables and housings because an old cable will have a frayed end and will be hard to put back through the housing after lubrication. That's another reason to keep cables, housing ferrules and cable ends in stock.*

V-17: EASY STEPS TO REDUCE CABLE FRICTION

Besides replacing your cables and housings with good-quality cables and lined housings, there are other steps you can take to improve shifting efficiency.

1. The most important friction-reducing step is to route the cable so that it makes smooth bends, and so that turning the handlebars does not increase the tension on the shift cables.

2. Choose cables that offer particularly low friction. "Die-drawn" cables, which have been mechanically pulled through a small hole in a piece of hard steel called a die, move with lower friction than standard cables. Die-drawing flattens all of the outer strands and smoothes the cable surface. Thinner cables and lined housings with a large inside diameter also reduce friction. Gore-Tex cables are cables coated with Gore-Tex. They are lower friction and are further sealed end-to-end with a plastic sheath (Fig. 5.18).

3. Shifting to smaller cogs can be quickened by increasing the size of the derailleur-return spring. You can buy an after-market stiffer spring designed specifically for your derailleur.

CABLE
LUBRICATION
—
REDUCING
CABLE
FRICTION

5.31 Grip Shift

5.32 Rapidfire

5.33 thumb

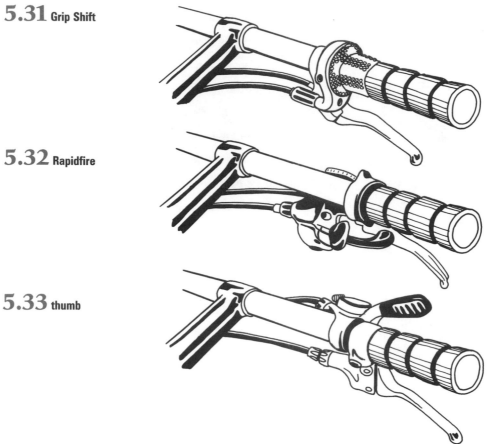

V.D: THE SHIFTERS

Twist shifters, thumb shifters and Rapidfire levers (Figs. 5.31through 5.33) all move the derailleurs, but they go about it in very different ways.

V-18: BAR END AND GRIP
REPLACEMENT/INSTALLATION

Replacing shifters requires removing at least grips and bar ends, and often brake levers as well. Shifters are generally labeled right and left, but if you're in doubt, you can tell which is which because the right one has a lot more clicks. Obviously, this is not true with friction shifters.

1. Remove bar ends, usually with a 5mm Allen wrench.

2. Remove grips by peeling them back at either end, squirting water or rubbing alcohol underneath and twisting back and forth while sliding them off. If you are planning on replacing them, you can cut the grips off.

3. Squirt rubbing alcohol inside when replacing grips.

V-19: REPLACING SHIFTER AND INTE-
GRATED BRAKE LEVER (FIG. 5.32)

If you are replacing the entire brake lever/shift lever unit:

1. Remove the old brake lever and shifter.

2. Slide the new brake lever/shifter onto the bar, making sure that you put the right shifter on the right side and vice versa.

3. Slide the grip back into position.

4. Mount the bar end, if you have one.

5. Rotate the brake lever to the position you like.

6. Tighten the brake-lever fixing bolt.

V-20: REPLACING THE SHIFTER UNIT ON INTEGRAL BRAKE/SHIFT LEVER (I.E., RAPIDFIRE — FIGS. 5.23 AND 5.32)

1. After shifting to the high-gear position to release the maximum amount of cable, unbolt the old shift lever from the brake lever body.

2. Position the new shifter exactly like the old one was.

3. Replace the bolt and tighten it.

4. Reinstall/replace the cable and tighten it.

Note: *Rapidfire Remote installation: Mount the remote lever to the end of the bar end with a 2mm hex key. Hook up the cables as described in Section V-9.*

V-21: REPLACING GRIP SHIFT (FIG. 5.31), HALF PIPES (FIG. 5.34) AND OTHER TWIST SHIFTERS

1. Remove the old shifter. Replace the brake lever if you had to remove it to get the old shifter off.

2. Loosen and slide the brake lever inward to allow room for the shifter.

3. Slide the appropriate (right or left) new shifter on with the cable-exit barrel pointing inward.

4. Slide on the plastic washer over the bar that separates the grip from the Grip Shift. This step is not necessary with Half Pipes or 2001 and later Shorties, as the plastic washer is integrated within the shifter.

5. Replace the grip (and bar end).

6. Butt the Grip Shift up against the plastic washer. Rotate the shifter until the cable-exit barrel is oriented so it will not interfere with the brake lever.

7. Tighten the mounting bolt to the handlebars with a 2.5mm or 3mm Allen wrench.

8. Slide and rotate the brake lever to the position you like, and tighten it down.

9. Reinstall/replace the cable and tighten it.

V-22: TOP-MOUNTED THUMB SHIFTERS (FIG. 5.33)

1. Remove the bar end, grip, brake lever and old shifter.

2. Slide on the replacement shifter.

3. Slide on the brake lever, grip and bar end.

4. Tighten the bar end and brake lever in the position you want.

5. Tighten the shifter in the position that is comfortable for you that allows easy access to the cable-barrel adjuster and free cable travel.

6. Reinstall/replace cable and tighten it.

V.E: SHIFTER MAINTENANCE

V-23: GRIP SHIFT

Grip Shift (Figs. 5.24 and 5.31) requires periodic cleaning and lubrication, as described below. Clean only with soap and water and lubricate only with nonlithium (preferably silicone-based Teflon) grease, like Grip Shift Jonnisnot (they pay people to come up with these names, too!).

If shifting has gotten poor on Half Pipes and other Grip Shifts with the quick cable-change feature, try replacing the cable and housing first before disassembling the shifter for cleaning.

Short Grip Shifts

The exploded diagrams in Figs. 5.25 and 5.26 and the text in Section V-11 detail how to take apart, clean and grease a short-length Grip Shift (except for

5.34 squeezing the two tabs together to release the Half Pipe retaining washer

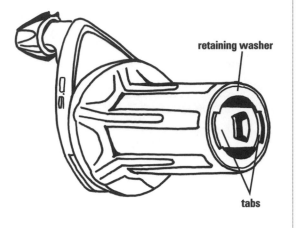

the 2001 and later Shortie, which follows the same disassembly as Half Pipes described below). With older models and some current low-end models, as long as you have the shifter disassembled, you might as well replace the cable (Section V-11), since shifter disassembly is required for the task.

Long (Half Pipe) twist shifters

This section also applies to SRAM's Shortie shifters from 2001 and later. First, remove the cable (Section V-10) and the fixed grip (Section XI-3). Note that, unlike with older Grip Shift models, you do not remove the triangular housing cover to get the twist grip off.

1. Twist the shifter away from you to let out all of the cable (turn it to "1" on the front shifter and "9" on the rear).

2. Remove the shifter from the bar using a 3mm hex key on the setscrew.

3. Squeeze the tabs (Fig. 5.35) on the end of the housing tube together (you may have to pry inward on them with a screwdriver on each), and remove the plastic retainer (Fig. 5.34).

4. Slowly slide the grip outward as you twist the shifter gently away from you in the cable-release direction. If you pull too fast, the long coil spring inside (Fig. 5.35) may pop out. Pull out the long coil spring.

5. Remove the two Phillips screws and pop off the clear plastic window covering the gear-indicator needle (Fig. 5.24).

6. Pull straight out on the gear-indicator needle (Fig. 5.24) and remove it.

7. After carefully noting the position of the small leaf spring — it looks like a flat bent piece of steel (Fig. 5.35), pull the spring up and out using needle-nosed pliers or tweezers.

8. With a Phillips screwdriver (or, in some cases, a 2.5mm hex key), remove the housing-cover screw (Fig. 5.24).

9. Slide the outer parts (the housing cover and cable spool) away from the housing (Fig. 5.36), being careful not to break the tab on the housing cover. To get the housing cover to come up, you may need to push up on it with the end of a paper

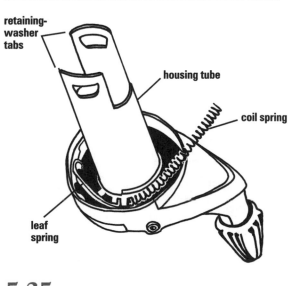

5.35 Half Pipe springs

5.36 Half Pipe disassembled

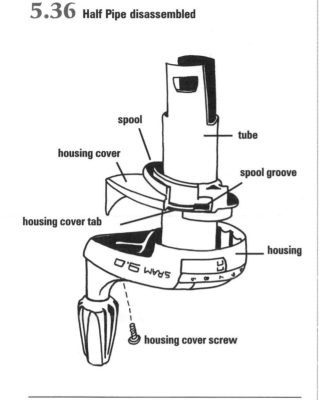

- spool
- tube
- housing cover
- spool groove
- housing cover tab
- housing
- SRAM 9.0
- housing cover screw

5.37 indexed thumb shifter exploded

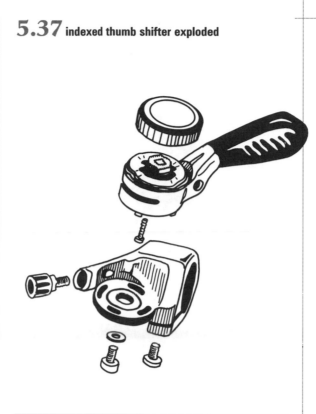

clip through the housing-cover-screw hole.

10. Clean all of the parts with soap, water and clean rags. Use no solvents.

11. With nonlithium (preferably silicone-based Teflon) grease, lubricate the large tube extending from the housing, the cable track and all detents for the springs.

12. Slide the housing cover and spool back down onto the housing tube, after having first slipped the cover's tab into the spool's groove (Fig. 5.36). Replace the housing-cover screw.

13. Set the leaf spring in place into the spool in the same position that you remember it was before (Fig. 5.35). Carefully press down on one end of the spring as you work to seat the other end in place.

14. Install one end of the coil spring onto its tab (Fig. 5.35). Slide the outer grip onto the tube, angle the other end of the spring up toward the

grip, and pop the other end of the spring onto the tab inside the grip.

15. Rotating the grip slightly away from you to compress the coil spring, slide the grip inward until it engages in the housing.

16. Replace the plastic retaining washer over the tabs on the housing tube (Fig. 5.34).

17. Rotate the shifter away from you to the position that would let out the most cable.

18. Peer into the curved slot the gear-indicator needle slides in. If you followed step 17, you should see the receptacle for the needle at one end of the slot. Slip the gear-indicator needle (Fig. 5.24) back into its receptacle, replace the plastic window, and install the two screws that hold it on.

19. Install the shifter onto the bar with a 3mm hex key. Check that it works.

20. Install a new cable (Section V-10), connect it to the derailleur, and go ride your bike.

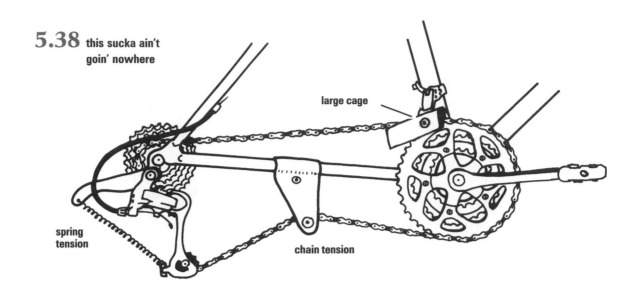

5.38 this sucka ain't goin' nowhere

large cage

spring tension

chain tension

V-24: RAPIDFIRE SL AND RAPIDFIRE PLUS

Shimano Rapidfire SL (Fig. 5.23) and Rapidfire Plus shifters (Fig. 5.32) are not designed to be disassembled by the consumer. Squirting a little chain lube inside every now and then is a good idea, though. If a Rapidfire lever stops working, it requires purchasing a new shifter unit. On an integrated unit, the brake lever does not need to be replaced; just bolt the new shifter to it (Section V-20).

Sometimes the gear indicator unit stops working, and it can even jam the lever and stop it from reaching all of the gears. This was most common in the 1993 and 1994 models. The indicators can be removed from the shifter with a small screwdriver. The indicator's little link arm needs to be stuck back into the hole from whence it came. Once the indicator jams, you can expect it to happen again; eventually, you will want to replace the lever or dispense with the indicator.

V-25: ORIGINAL RAPIDFIRE

Shimano's first attempt at a two-lever mountain shifter did not work very well. If you are having trouble with yours, I recommend throwing it out and getting a new system. You know you have original Rapidfire if the thumb operates both the down- and up-shift levers. Newer Rapidfire SL and Plus levers (Figs. 5.23 and 5.32) require the thumb only for downshifting; the forefinger reaches back to perform the upshifts.

V-26: THUMB SHIFTERS

Indexed (click) thumb shifters (Fig. 5.33) are not to be disassembled further than removing them from their clamp. Periodic (semi-annual or so) lubrication with chain lube is recommended and is best accomplished from the back side once the shifter assembly is removed from its clamp (Fig. 5.37).

Frictional (nonclicking) thumb shifters can be disassembled, cleaned, greased and reassembled. Put the parts back the way you found them. You can avoid the hassle of disassembly by squirting chain lube in instead.

V-27: SPECIAL DOWNHILL-SPECIFIC DRIVETRAIN ADAPTATIONS

Tension arms, rollers, giant front derailleur cages (Fig. 5.38) and other chain-retention systems have become a part of downhill racing, due to the extraordinary demands the sport places on the drive system. Downhill-specific products are outside of the scope of this book, but, at least once assembled on the bike, many of these drivetrain items are fairly obvious in their function and maintenance.

V.F: DERAILLEUR MAINTENANCE

V-28: JOCKEY WHEEL MAINTENANCE

The jockey wheels (a.k.a. "guide pulleys" — Fig. 5.39) on a derailleur will wear out over time. For best performance, standard jockey wheels should be overhauled every 200–500 miles. That should take care of the gunk that the chain and the trail regularly deliver to them. The mounting bolts on jockey wheels also need to be checked regularly. If a loose jockey-wheel bolt falls off while you are riding, you'll need to follow the procedure for a broken rear derailleur on the trail in Chapter 3.

Some expensive guide pulleys have cartridge bearings (Fig. 5.39), whereas standard ones have a center bushing sleeve made of either steel or ceramic (SRAM upper jockey wheels have an oversized steel center bushing). A washer with a curved rim facing inward is usually installed on both sides of a standard jockey wheel. Some guide pulleys also have rubber seals around the edges of these washers.

V-29: PROCEDURE FOR OVERHAULING STANDARD JOCKEY WHEELS

1. Remove the jockey wheels by undoing the bolts that hold them to the derailleur (Fig. 5.39). This usually takes a 2.5mm or 3mm Allen wrench.

2. Wipe all parts clean with a rag. A solvent is usually not necessary but can be used.

3. If the teeth on the jockey wheels are broken or worn off, replace the wheels.

4. Smear grease over each bolt and sleeve and inside each jockey wheel.

5. Reassemble the jockey wheels on the derailleur. Be sure to orient the cage plate properly (the larger part of the cage plate should be at the bottom jockey wheel).

V-30: CARTRIDGE-BEARING JOCKEY WHEEL OVERHAUL

If the cartridge bearings (bottom, Fig. 5.39) in high-end jockey wheels do not turn freely, they can usually be overhauled.

1. With a single-edge razor blade, pry the plastic cover off one or, preferably, both sides of the bearing (Fig. 6.26).

2. With a toothbrush and solvent, clean the bearings. Use a citrus-based solvent, and wear gloves and glasses to protect skin and eyes.

3. Blow the solvent out with compressed air or your tire pump and allow the parts to dry.

4. Squeeze new grease into the bearings and replace the covers.

5.39 jockey wheel exploded

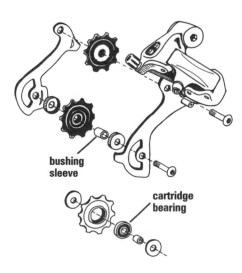

bushing sleeve

cartridge bearing

V-31: REAR DERAILLEUR OVERHAUL

Except for the jockey wheels and pivots, most rear derailleurs are not designed to be disassembled. If the pivot springs seem to be operating effectively, all you need to do is overhaul the jockey wheels (see above), and clean and lubricate the parallelogram and spring as follows.

V-32: MINOR WIPE AND LUBE

1. Clean the derailleur as well as you can with a rag, including between the parallelogram plates.

2. Drip chain lube on both ends of every pivot pin

3. If you have the clothespin-type spring in the parallelogram (as opposed to the full coil spring running diagonally from one corner of the parallelogram to the other), put a dab of grease where the spring end slides along the underside of the outer parallelogram plate.

V-33: UPPER PIVOT OVERHAUL

1. Remove the rear derailleur; it usually takes a 5mm Allen wrench to unscrew it from the frame and to disconnect the cable.

2. With a screwdriver, pry the circlip (Fig. 5.40) off of the threaded end of the mounting bolt. Don't lose it; it will tend to fly when it comes off.

3. Pull the bolt and spring out of the derailleur.

4. Clean and dry the parts with or without the use of a solvent.

5. Grease liberally, and replace the parts.

6. Each end of the spring has a hole that it needs to go into. If there are several holes, and you don't know which one it was in before, try the middle one. (If the derailleur does not keep tension on the chain well enough, you can later try

5.40 rear derailleur pivots

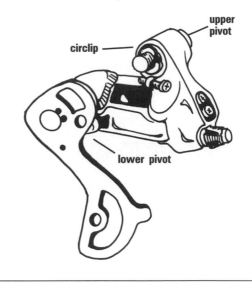

another hole that increases the spring tension.)

7. Push it all together, and replace the circlip with pliers.

V-34: LOWER PIVOT OVERHAUL

1. Remove the derailleur from the bike.

2. Shimano derailleurs can be divided into two types: ones that have a setscrew on the side of the lower pivot, and ones that do not. If yours has a setscrew (Fig. 5.8), remove it with a 2mm hex key and pull the jockey cage away from the derailleur.

If your derailleur has no setscrew, find and unscrew the tall cage-stop screw on the derailleur cage (Fig. 5.10); it is located near the upper jockey wheel. It is designed to maintain tension on the lower pivot spring and prevent the cage from springing all of the way around. Once the screw is removed, slowly guide the cage around until the spring tension is relieved. Remove the upper jockey wheel and unscrew the pivot bolt from the back with a 5mm (sometimes 6mm) hex key (Fig. 5.11).

REAR
DERAILLEUR
OVERHAUL
—
UPPER &
LOWER PIVOT
OVERHAUL

Be sure to hold the jockey wheel cage to keep it from twisting.

3. Determine in which hole the spring end has been placed, then remove the spring.

4. Clean and dry the bolt and the spring with a rag. A solvent may be used if necessary.

5. Grease all parts liberally.

6. Replace the spring ends in their holes in the derailleur body and jockey-wheel cage (Fig. 5.9). Put the spring in the adjacent hole if you want to increase its tension (see Section V-2G).

7. If your derailleur has a setscrew, push the assembly together, wind the spring, and replace the setscrew. If your derailleur does not take a setscrew, wind the jockey wheel cage back around, screw it all back together with the pivot bolt, and replace the stopper screw.

V-35: PARALLELOGRAM OVERHAUL

Very few derailleurs can be completely disassembled. Those that can (Mavic, first generation SRAM and 2002 high-end SRAM) have removable pins holding them together. The pins have circlips on the ends that can be popped off with a screwdriver, after which you can pull out the pins. Disassemble the derailleur carefully in a box so the circlips do not fly away and make note of where each part belongs so that you can get it back together again. Clean all parts, grease them, and reassemble.

V-36: REPLACING STOCK BOLTS WITH LIGHTWEIGHT VERSIONS

Lightweight aluminum and titanium derailleur bolts are available as replacement items for many derailleurs. Removing and replacing jockey wheel bolts is simple, as long as you keep all of the jockey wheel parts together and put the inner cage plate back on the way it was. Upper and lower pivot bolts are replaced following the instructions in Sections V-33 and V-34.

V.G: TROUBLESHOOTING REAR DERAILLEUR AND RIGHT-HAND SHIFTER PROBLEMS

Once you have made the adjustments outlined above, your drivetrain should be quiet and should stay in gear, even if you turn the crank backwards. If you cannot fine-tune the adjustment so that each click with the right shifter results in a clean, quick shift, you need to check some of the following possibilities. For skipping- and jumping-chain problems, see also the troubleshooting section at the end of Chapter 4.

V-37: SHIFTER COMPATIBILITY

Check to see if your shifter is compatible with your derailleur and your cogs. This is especially important if any of these parts were not original equipment on your bike. It should be obvious that a 7-speed shifter will not work on an 8- or 9-speed cassette, but components of different brands for the same number of speeds often will not work together either. Be certain, if the shifter is a different brand than your derailleur, that they are nonetheless designed to work together. The most common example of this is SRAM's Grip Shift, some models of which are specifically designed to work with a Shimano rear derailleur. SRAM ESP derailleurs work only with a longer-pull ESP twist shifter designed for it and incompatible with other derailleurs.

If your shifter and derailleur are incompatible,

TROUBLE-
SHOOTING
DERAILLEUR
AND
HAND SHIFTER
PROBLEMS

you will need to change one of them. Quality being equal, I suggest replacing the less costly item (generally the shifter).

V-38: STICKY CABLES

Check your derailleur cables to confirm that they run smoothly through the housing. Sticky cable movement will cause sluggish shifting. Lubricate the cable by smearing it with chain lube or a specific lubricant that came with your shifters (Section V-16).

If lubricating the cable does not help, replace the cable and housing (see Sections V-6–V-15).

V-39: BENT REAR DERAILLEUR HANGER

A bent hanger will hold the derailleur crooked and bedevil shifting. Instructions for straightening the hanger are in Chapter 14, Section XIV-5.

V-40: BENT REAR DERAILLEUR CAGE

A bent derailleur cage will line the jockey wheels up at an angle. Mild bending can be straightened by hand, eyeballing the crank for reference.

V-41: LOOSE PIVOTS (WORN-OUT REAR DERAILLEUR)

A loose and floppy rear derailleur will not shift well. Replace it.

V.H: TROUBLESHOOTING FRONT DERAILLEUR AND LEFT HAND SHIFTER PROBLEMS

V-42: CHAIN SUCK

For chain suck problems (Fig. 4.14), you should refer to the troubleshooting section at the end of Chapter 4.

5.41 measuring chain line

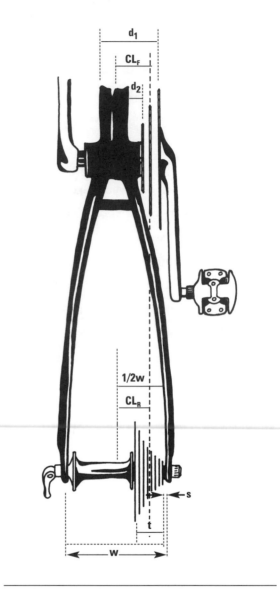

V-43: CHAIN LINE

You have chain line problems if: (1) your chain falls off to the inside no matter how much you adjust the low-gear-limit screw, cable tension and derailleur position; (2) you have chain rub, noise or auto-shift problems in mild cross-gears that are not corrected with derailleur adjustments; or (3) your front derailleur cannot move your chain onto the large chainring.

Chain line is the relative alignment of the front

chainrings with the rear cogs; it is the imaginary line connecting the center of the middle chainring with the middle of the cogset (Fig. 5.41). This line should in theory be straight and parallel with the vertical plane of the bicycle. Even owners of new bikes may find they have poor chain lines, due to mismatched cranks and bottom brackets.

Chain line is adjusted by moving or replacing the bottom bracket to move the cranks left or right. You can roughly check the chain line by placing a long straight edge against the middle chainring and back to the rear cogs; it should come out in the center of the rear cogs. Continue on for a more precise method, if you want to get your shifting as good as possible.

V-44: PRECISE CHAIN LINE MEASUREMENT

LEVEL 2 You will need a measuring caliper. The position of the middle chainring, as measured from the center of the seat tube to the center of the middle chainring, is often called the chain line, although this is only the front end point of the line.

1. Finding the middle chainring position, or front end point of the chain line (CL_F in Fig. 5.41):

a. Measure from the left side of the *down tube* to the outside of the large chainring (d_1 in Fig. 5.41). (*Do not* measure from the seat tube, as it may be oval where it meets the bottom bracket shell. The frame tubes are labeled in Fig. 14.1.)

b. Measure the distance from the right side of the *down tube* to the inside of the inner chainring (d_2 in Fig. 5.41).

c. Add these two measurements and divide the sum by two.

$$CL_F = (d_1 + d_2)/2$$

2. Finding the rear end point of the chain line (CL_R in Fig. 5.41), which is the distance from the center of the plane of the bicycle to the center of the cogset:

a. Measure the thickness of the cog stack, end to end (t in Fig. 5.41).

b. Measure the space between the face of the smallest cog and the inside face of the dropout (s in Fig. 5.41).

c. Measure the length of the axle from dropout to dropout (w in Fig. 5.41); this dimension is also called "axle overlock dimension," referring to the distance from locknut face to locknut face on either end. Generally, on any mountain bike since 1989 or so, this will be 135mm.

d. Subtract one-half of the thickness of the cog stack and the distance from the inside face of the right rear dropout from one-half of the rear axle length.

$$CL_R - w/2 - t/2 - s$$

3. If $CL_F = CL_R$, your chain line is perfect. This, however, almost never occurs on a mountain bike, due to considerations about chainstay clearance, prevention of chain rub on large chainrings in cross gears, and inward movement range of the front derailleur. Shimano specifies a "chain line" (meaning CL_F, the front end point of the chain line) as 47.5mm for bikes with a 68mm-width bottom bracket shell, and 50mm for 73mm-width shells (both of these specified dimensions are plus or minus 1mm). CL_F, the rear end point of the chain line, on the other hand, usually comes out around 44.5mm. Shimano's specifications, then, are primarily intended to avoid chainring rub on chainstays, not on ideal shifting.

Your bike will shift best and run quietest if you

the transmission

TROUBLE-
SHOOTING
DERAILLEUR
AND
HAND SHIFTER
PROBLEMS

get the chain line at around 45mm, but you may have some problems there, such as: (a) your inner and middle chainrings might rub the chainstay, (b) your front derailleur may bottom out on the seat tube before moving inward enough to shift to the inner chainring (this is particularly a problem with bikes with oversized seat tubes), and (c) when crossing to the smallest cog from the inner and even middle chainring, the chain may rub on the next larger ring (this is not a problem if you simply avoid those cross gears).

I recommend having the chainrings in toward the frame as far as you can, without rubbing the frame or losing front derailleur shifting performance due to bottoming out on the seat tube.

4. To improve the chain line, move the chainrings, since there is little or nothing you can do with the rear cog position. The chainrings are moved by using a different bottom bracket, by exchanging bottom bracket spindles with a longer one, or by moving the bottom bracket right or left (bottom bracket installation and overhauling is covered in Chapter 8).

Note: *Some brand-new bikes have terrible chain lines that can only be corrected by buying a new bottom bracket. This usually has to do with a conceptually impaired bean-counting product manager selecting the parts for a given bike model. Product managers know that customers often pay attention to the quality and brand of the cranks on the bike and pay little heed to*

5.42 Third Eye Chain Watcher

the quality of the bottom bracket — the unseen part of the mix. With a cheap bottom bracket, the cranks may sit way too far out, and the chain line will stink. You will end up having to replace the longer bottom bracket with a shorter one if you want the bike to shift decently. In such a case, good shops will replace the bottom bracket before selling the bike to you.

Another note: *The chain line can also be off if the frame is out of alignment (Chapter 14, Section XIV-6). If that's the case, it is probably not something you can fix yourself.*

5. If improving the chain line does not fix your problem, or if you don't want to mess with the chain line, buy and install a Third Eye Chain Watcher (Fig. 5.42) or a Deda Elementi Dog Fang. Both are inexpensive plastic gizmos that clamp around the seat tube next to the inner chainring. Clamp one on and adjust the position so that the prong (or "fang") nudges the chain back on when it tries to fall off to the inside.

TROUBLE-
SHOOTING
DERAILLEUR
AND
HAND SHIFTER
PROBLEMS

the wheels

TIRES, RIMS, HUBS AND COGS

tools

spoke wrench

13mm, 14mm, 15mm, 16mm cone wrenches

17mm open-end wrench (or an adjustable wrench)

screwdriver

5mm, 6mm and 10mm Allen wrenches

grease

oil

chain whip

cassette lockring remover

large adjustable wrench

freewheel remover, if your bike does not have a cassette

pump

tire levers

tube patch kit

optional

truing stand

wheel-dishing tool

linseed oil

tweezers

cog-wear indicator

I'm just sitting here watching the wheels go round and round.
I really love to watch them roll.

— *JOHN LENNON*

Early bicycles may have existed without pedals and steering systems, but they *always* had wheels. After all, without wheels, it ain't a bike!

With the exception of recent molded composite versions, wheels on mountain bikes are strung together with spokes. The hub is at the center, and its bearings allow the wheel to turn freely around an axle. The rim is supported and aligned by the tension on the spokes. On most bikes, the rim serves as both support for the tire and as a braking surface.

On the rear wheel, a cassette freehub or freewheel allows the wheel to spin while coasting and engages when force is applied to the pedals (Fig. 6.1).

The tires provide grip and traction for propulsion and steering. The air pressure in the tire is your first line of suspension. On virtually all mountain bikes, inner tubes keep the air inside the tires.

This chapter addresses how to fix a flat or replace a tire or tube, true a wheel, fix a broken spoke or bent rim, overhaul hubs, change rear cogs and lubricate cassettes and freewheels. Have at it.

VI.A TIRES: REPLACING OR REPAIRING TIRES AND INNER TUBES

VI-1: REMOVING A STANDARD TIRE AND TUBE

Note: If you have tubeless tires, skip to Section VI-2.

1. Remove the wheel (See Chapter 2, Sections II-2 and II-11). If the wheel is on a Cannondale "Lefty" one-legged fork, you can skip this step, since you can change the tire with the wheel on the bike!

6.1 **the whole thing**

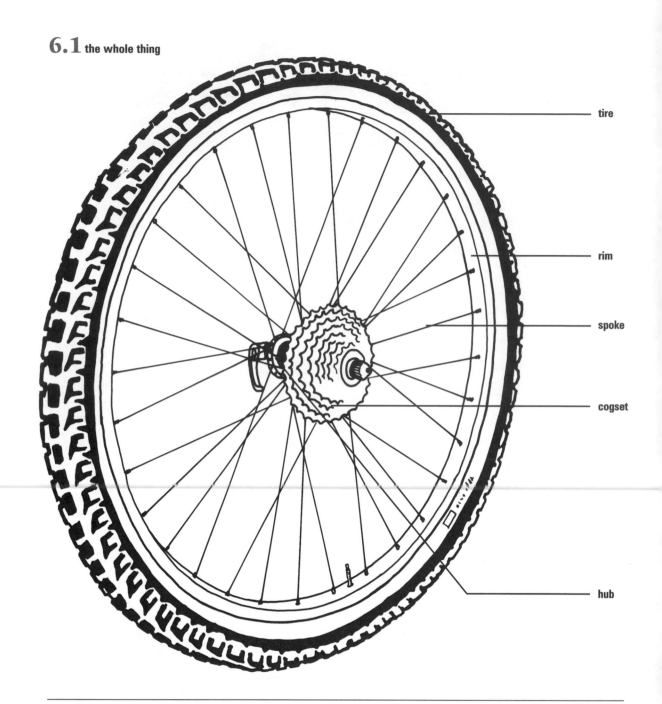

tire

rim

spoke

cogset

hub

TIRES

2. If your tire is not already flat, deflate it.

To deflate a Schrader valve (the kind of valve you would find on your car's tire), push down on the valve pin with something thin enough to fit in that won't break off, like a pen cap or a paper clip (Fig. 6.3).

Presta, or "French," valves are thinner and have a small threaded rod with a tiny nut on the end. To let air out, unscrew the little nut a few turns, and push down on the thin rod (Fig. 6.2). To seal, tighten the little nut down again (with your fingers only!); leave it tightened down for riding.

Note: If you have deep-section rims (i.e., Spinergy, Zipp or Hed), you will probably have "valve extenders" — thin threaded tubes that screw onto the valve stems. To deflate most of them, you need to insert a

6.2 presta valve

6.3 schrader valve

35-50 psi

35-50 psi

fzhsssss.......

psssssSszht......

letting air out

6.4–6.5 removing tires with levers

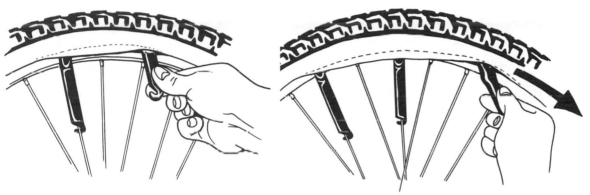

thin rod (a spoke is perfect) inside to release the air. To install valve extenders so they seal properly and allow easy inflation, you need to unscrew the little nut on the Presta valve against the mashed threads at the top of the valve shaft (they are mashed to keep the nut from unscrewing completely off). Back the nut firmly into these mashed threads with a pair of pliers so it stays unscrewed and does not tighten back down against the valve stem and prevent air from going in when you pump it. Spinergy extenders do not require this and actually allow you to tighten and loosen the valve nut with the extender in place.

You also should wrap a turn or two of Teflon pipe thread tape around the top threads on the valve stem before screwing on the valve extender to seal it; if you do not, air will leak out when pumping, and your pressure gauge on your pump will not give an accurate reading of the pressure in the tire. Tighten the valve extender onto the valve stem with a pair of pliers.

3. If you can push the tire bead off of the rim with your thumbs without using tire levers, by all means do it, for there is less chance of damaging either the tube or the tire. It is easiest to start just one side or the other of the valve stem.

PRO TIP

TIRE REMOVAL

Removal of the tire is most easily accomplished by starting near the valve stem. That way, the beads of the deflated tire can have fallen into the dropped center of the rim on the opposite side of the wheel, mak-

ing it effectively a smaller-circumference rim off of which you are pushing the tire bead. If you try to push the tire bead off of (or onto) the rim on the side opposite the valve stem, the circumference on which the bead is resting is larger, because the valve stem is forcing the beads to stay up on their seating ledges opposite where you are working.

4. If you can't get the tire off with your hands alone, insert a tire lever, scoop side up, between the rim sidewall and the tire until you catch the edge of the tire bead. Again, this is most easily done adjacent the valve stem.

5. Pry down on the lever until the tire bead is pulled out over the rim (Figs. 6.4 and 6.5). If the lever has a hook on the other end, hook it onto the nearest spoke. Otherwise, keep holding it down.

6. Place the next lever a few inches away, and do the same thing with it (Fig. 6.4).

7. If needed, place a third lever a few inches farther on, pry it out, and continue sliding this lever around the tire, pulling the bead out as you go (Fig. 6.5). Some people slide their fingers around under the bead, but beware of cutting your fingers on sharp tire beads.

6.6 removing the inner tube

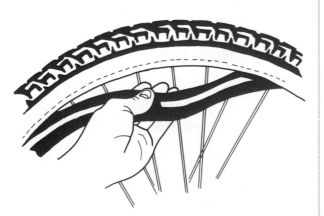

6.7 UST tubeless tire and rim cross-section

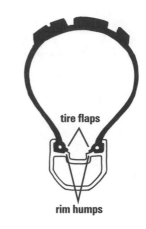

tire flaps

rim humps

Note: *There are various "quick" tire levers on the market that only require the one lever. But if the tire is really stubborn, the tried-and-true three-lever method outlined above may be the only way you can get the tire off.*

8. Once the bead is off on one side, pull the tube out (Fig. 6.6). If you are patching or replacing the tube, you do not need to remove the other side of the tire from the rim. If you are replacing the tire, the other bead should come off easily with your fingers. If it does not, use the tire levers as outlined above.

VI-2: REMOVING A TUBELESS TIRE

If you have tubeless tires, you must do all removal and installation with your hands only, as tire levers can damage the sealing flap extending beyond the tire bead (Fig. 6.7), and then your tire will not seal. If you are planning on patching the tire, you must find the leak before removing it from the rim (Section VI-3).

Because the "UST" tubeless system — originated by Mavic, Michelin and Hutchinson and since adopted by others — is the only one in wide use, this section specifically addresses that system.

1. Remove the wheel (See Chapter 2, Sections II-2 and II-11). If the wheel is on a Cannondale "Lefty" one-legged fork, you need not remove the wheel!

2. If your tire is not already flat, deflate it at the valve.

Tubeless tire valves just screw into the rim with rubber seals around them. They can be either Schrader valves (the kind of valve you would find on your car's tire), Presta, or "French," valves (Fig. 1.1), or both. UST valves are both. Unscrew and remove the outer, Schrader-size externally threaded tube to make it a Presta valve. To use it as a Schrader valve, screw on the Schrader tube after unscrewing the little nut on the end of the inner Presta valve.

To deflate a Schrader valve, push down on the valve pin with something thin enough to fit in that won't break off, like a pen cap or a paper clip (Fig. 6.3).

To let air out of a Presta valve, unscrew the little nut a few turns, and push down on the thin rod (Fig. 6.2). To seal, tighten the little nut down again (with your fingers only!). Leave it tightened down for riding.

3. Push inward on the tire beads all of the way around with your thumbs to get them to pop off of the "hump" (Fig. 6.7) and fall into the dropped center of the rim.

4. Starting adjacent the valve stem, push the tire off of the rim with your thumbs.

VI-3: FINDING LEAKS

1. If the leak location is not obvious, put some air in the tube to inflate it until it is two to three times larger than its deflated size. Be careful. You can explode it if you put too much air in, especially with latex or urethane tubes.

6.8 checking for puncture

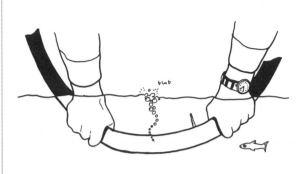

Note: For tubeless tires, leave the tire on the rim and inflate it to 25–50 psi, then continue with steps 2 and 3.

2. Listen/feel for air coming out, and mark the leak(s).

3. If you cannot find the leak by listening, submerge the tube (or tubeless tire mounted on the rim) under water. Look for air bubbling out (Fig. 6.8), and mark the spot(s).

Keep in mind that you can only patch small holes. If the hole is bigger than the eraser end of a pencil, a round patch is not likely to work. A slit of up to an inch or so can be repaired with a long oval patch.

Note on patching tubeless tires: The following instructions apply to patching a tube, but the procedure is same for patching a tubeless tire, except that you patch the inside of the tire vs. the outside of a tube. Also, you can always stick a tube inside a tubeless tire if you don't want to deal with patching the tire. And for using a tubeless tire where there are a lot of cacti or thorns, it is arduous and next to impossible to find and patch all of the holes. Rather than throw the (expensive) tire out, fill it with Slime (Section VI-9).

6.9 smearing patch glue

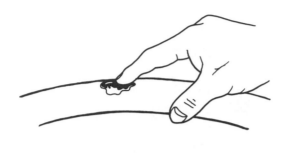

6.10 removing cellophane

6.11–6.12 installing tire by hand

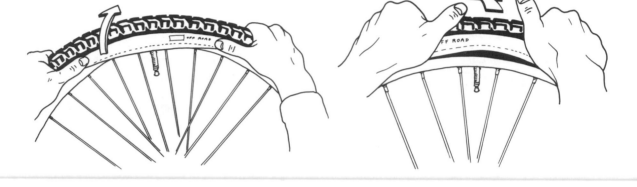

PATCHES

VI-4: USING STANDARD PATCHES

1. Dry the tube thoroughly near the hole.

2. Rough up and clean the surface about a 1-inch radius around the hole with a small piece of sandpaper (usually supplied with the patch kit). Do not touch the sanded area, and don't rough up the tube with one of those little metal "cheese graters" that come with some patch kits. They tend to do to your tube what they do to cheese.

3. Use a patch kit designed for bicycle tires that have the thin, usually orange, gummy edges surrounding the black patches. Rema and Delta are common brands.

4. Apply patch cement in a thin, smooth layer all over an area centered on the hole (Fig. 6.9). Cover an area that is bigger than the size of the patch.

5. Let the glue dry until there are no more shiny, wet spots (5–10 minutes).

6. Remove the foil backing from the patch (but not the cellophane top cover).

7. Stick the patch over the hole, and push it down in place, making sure that all of the gummy edges are stuck down.

8. Although there is no need to do so, the standard procedure is to remove the cellophane top covering. Be careful not to peel off the edges of the patch (Fig. 6.10). Oftentimes, the cellophane atop the patch is scored. If you fold the patch, then this cellophane will split at the scored cuts, allowing you to peel outward and avoid pulling the newly adhered patch away from the tube.

VI-5: USING GLUELESS PATCHES

There are a number of adhesive-backed patches on the market that do not require cement to stick them on. Most often, you simply need to clean the area around the hole with the little alcohol pad supplied with the patch. Let the alcohol dry, peel the backing, and stick on the patch. The advantage of glueless patches is that they are very fast to use, take little room in a seat bag and you never open your patch kit to discover that your glue tube is dried up. On the downside, I have not found any that stick nearly as well as the standard type. With a standard patch installed, you can inflate the tube without having it in the tire to look for more leaks. If you do that with a glueless patch, it usually lifts the patch enough to start it leaking. You must install it in the tire and on the rim before putting air in it after patching. And don't expect a permanent fix, as you can with a Rema-style patch.

VI-6: INSTALLING TUBE AND TIRE

Feel around the inside of the tire to see if there is anything sticking through that can puncture the tube. This is best done by sliding a rag all the way around the inside of the tire. The rag will catch on anything sharp and saves your fingers from being cut by whatever is stuck in the tire.

1. Replace any tire that has worn-out areas (inside or out) where the tread-casing fibers appear to be cut or frayed.

2. Examine the rim to be certain that the rim tape is in place and that there are no spokes or anything else sticking up that can puncture the tube. Replace the rim tape if necessary. With an asymmetrically drilled rim, make sure the adhesive and/or the fit of the rim tape is very good. The rim tape only needs

to slide over a little bit to expose the edge of one of the offset holes and puncture your tube.

By hand, push one side bead of the tire onto the rim. Ideally, you first want to check the tire-rotation direction and orient the tire label so it is next to the valve stem for ease of finding both.

PRO TIP

TIRE DIRECTION

Tire direction makes a difference for technical riding. On the front, you want the scooping edges of the tread blocks forward for braking, while on the rear, you want them pointed back for propulsion traction. Some tires have an arrow indicating rotation direction for use either on the front or the rear. If not, hold the tire up above your head and look at the tread as the ground sees it. Consider which way the wheel is rotating and what happens during braking and driving. The best way to orient the tread will then be apparent.

4. Optional: Smear baby powder around the inside of the tire and on the outside of the tube, so the two do not adhere to each other. Don't inhale the stuff.

5. Put just enough air in the tube to give it shape. Close the valve, if a Presta.

6. Push the valve through the valve hole in the rim.

7. Push the tube up inside the tire all of the way around.

8. Starting at the side opposite the valve stem, push the tire bead onto the rim with your thumbs. Be sure that the tube doesn't get pinched between the tire bead and the rim.

9. Work around the rim in both directions with your thumbs, pushing the tire onto the rim (Fig. 6.11). Finish from both sides at the valve (Fig. 6.12). You can usually install a mountain bike tire without tools. If you cannot, first try deflating the tube when

6.13 seating the tube by pushing up on the valve

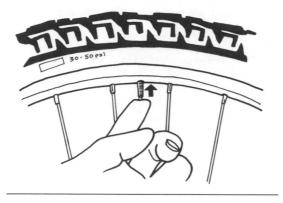

you have gotten as far around as you can with your hands. You should now be able to push the tire on the last bit, as deflating the tube will allow the beads on the far side, opposite the valve stem, to drop into the lower center of the rim. If this does not allow you to complete the mounting by hand, use tire levers to pry the tire bead on, but make sure you don't catch any of the tube under the edge of the bead. Finish the same way, at the valve.

10. Reseat the valve stem and suck up any folds of the tube stuck under the tire bead by pushing up on the valve after you have pushed the last bit of bead onto the rim (Fig. 6.13). You may have to manipulate the tire so that all the tube is tucked under the tire bead.

11. Go around the rim and inspect for any part of the tube that might be protruding out from under the edge of the tire bead. If you have a fold of the tube under the edge of the bead, it can blow the tire off the rim either when you inflate it or while you are riding. It will sound like a gun went off next to you and will leave you with an unpatchable tube.

12. Pump the tire up. Generally, 35-45 psi is a good amount. Much more, and the ride gets harsh.

Much less, and you run the risk of a pinch flat, or "snake bite."

PRO TIP

LOW TIRE PRESSURE

If you have an anti-pinch-flat tube, like Hutchinson's thick green tube, you can get a smoother ride, better traction on side hills and lower rolling resistance on rough terrain by running lower tire pressure (under 30 psi).

VI-7: INSTALLING TUBELESS TIRE

Again, these instructions apply to the UST tubeless system. Tire levers are not to be used to prevent damage to the seal.

1. Examine the rim to be sure the tire will seal to it. First of all, it must be a UST rim (and tire) — only a rim without spoke holes on the inside and with the "hump" along the edge of each bead ledge will seal with the tire (Fig. 6.7). Furthermore, the rim edges and the hump must not be dented or gouged, or air will escape there.

2. Wet the edges of the tire to facilitate sealing it on initial inflation.

3. Determine rotation direction (see "Pro Tip" under Section VI-6), and locate the label at the valve stem. Starting opposite the valve, push the tire onto the rim with your thumbs and fingers only, finishing at the valve.

4. Push the other bead onto the rim by hand, again starting on the side of the rim opposite the valve stem and finishing at the valve stem. If you start at the valve stem, you will have to work harder, because the valve holds the tire bead up on the ledge and forces the rim to stretch around a larger circle.

5. Pump the tire up with a floor pump, getting air in as fast as possible initially until you hear the

INSTALLING
TUBE AND
TIRE
—
INSTALLING
TUBELESS
TIRE

100

tire seat. Just like with a tubeless car tire, seating the bead is a lot more effective with an air compressor (Fig. 1.5), but it can be done with a manual pump. Sometimes, a UST tire can even be seated with a head pump, but be aware that you have to get a lot of air into the tire in a hurry to force the beads to pop up over the humps and then onto the ledges.

6. Pump up (or deflate) to your desired riding pressure.

PRO TIP
LOW TIRE PRESSURE

You can get a smoother ride, better traction on side hills and lower rolling resistance on rough terrain by running lower tire pressure (under 30 psi). You can't pinch-flat a tubeless tire (there is no tube to pinch!), although you can dent your rim. Begin by experimenting with tire pressures, and don't be afraid to even try less than 20 psi with tubeless tires — you might discover that you like it!

VI-8: PATCHING TIRE CASING (SIDEWALL)

Unless it is an emergency, don't do it! If your casing is cut, it's best to get a new tire because patching the tire casing is dangerous. No matter what you use as a patch, the tube will find a way to bulge out of the patched hole, and when it does, your tire will go flat immediately. Imagine coming down a steep descent and suddenly your front tire goes completely flat — you get the picture. In emergency situations, you can put layers of non-stretchable material, such as a dollar bill, an empty energy bar wrapper (or two), even a short section of the exploded tube (double thickness is better) between the tube and tire (see Chapter 3, Section III-3B and Fig. 3.1).

VI-9: TIRE SEALANTS

Slime is primordial green goo with chopped fibers in it; when it sloshes around in an inner tube (or inside a tubeless tire), it flows to punctures and seals them. There are other brands of tire sealants besides Slime; these instructions generally apply to them as well. Although they are messy and add weight to your wheels, tire sealants can virtually eliminate flat tires due to simple punctures.

Only use Slime in a tube without cuts in it and with a Schrader valve (Fig. 6.3) in good condition. You can put Slime in a tube with a slow leak; simply inject it as below, pump it up, and spin the wheel for about five minutes. Be forewarned that after about a year, the stuff dries up and doesn't work well anymore.

A. Putting tire sealant in a tubeless tire

Simply pop the tire off of one side of the rim (Section VI-2), shake the bottle, and squirt 2–4oz. or so of sealant into the tire. Push the tire bead back onto the rim (Section VI-7) and inflate.

B. Slime installation into a tube that's already installed in a tire

Note: The tube must be of proper size. If it is too small (for instance, a 26-by-1.325–1.5-inch tube inside a 26-by-2.0-inch tire) and stretches when inflated in the tire, any holes will stretch open and won't seal.

1. Shake Slime bottle.

2. Remove Schrader valve core using valve cap/core-remover packaged with the Slime.

3. Rotate the wheel so the valve stem is at the 4 o'clock position.

4. Cut off the bottle spout, and connect the bottle spout and valve stem with the supplied surgical tubing.

5. Squeeze the bottle slowly to inject the Slime.

6. Stop squeezing after injecting 4oz.; wait several minutes to clear the stem.

7. Remove the surgical tube.

8. Screw the valve core firmly back into the valve stem in a clockwise direction.

9. Inflate the tube.

If the tube has a leak, spin the wheel for five minutes to spread the Slime around in the tube.

Note: *If you have Presta valves (Figs. 1.1 and 6.2) and you want to use tire sealant, you can purchase tubes with it already installed.*

C. Maintaining tire-sealant-filled tubes

Pumping: Always have the stem at 4 o'clock and wait a minute for Slime to drain away; if you don't, Slime will leak out, eventually clogging the valve.

Sealing punctures:

1. If you find your tire flat, pump it up and ride it a bit to see if it seals.

2. If you get numerous punctures, you may need to pump repeatedly and ride before the tube seals up.

3. Pinch flats, caused by pinching the tube between the tire and rim, are hard to seal because the two "snake-bite" holes are on the side. Try laying the bike on the same side as the holes.

4. Imbedded nails and other foreign objects can be removed; spin the wheel to seal the hole.

5. Punctures on the rim side of the tube will not seal because the Slime is thrown to the outside.

6. Sidewall gashes need to be patched, and the tire needs to be replaced.

7. Replace the tube after a year or so. The sealant will have become too viscous to work properly anymore.

VI-10: TRUING A WHEEL

For more information on truing wheels, see Chapter 12 on wheel building, Section XII-4.

If your wheel has a wobble in it, you can fix it by adjusting the tension on the spokes. An extreme bend in the rim cannot be fixed by spoke truing alone, since the spoke tension on the two sides of the wheel will be so uneven that the wheel will rapidly fall apart.

Get a spoke wrench of the right size for your spoke nipples — they come in different sizes (as well as square or splined shapes), and you will wreck your nipples if you use a spoke wrench that is too large.

1. Check that there are no broken spokes in the wheel, or any spokes that are so loose that they flop around. If there is a broken spoke, follow the replacement procedure in the following section, VI-11. If there is a single loose spoke, check to see that the rim is not dented or cracked in that area. I recommend replacing the rim if it is. If the rim looks okay, mark the loose spoke with a piece of tape, and tighten it up with the spoke wrench until it feels the same tension as adjacent spokes on the same side of the wheel (pluck the spoke and listen to the tone). Then follow the truing procedure below.

2. Grab the rim while the wheel is on the bike, and flex it side to side to check the hub bearing adjustment. If the bearings are loose, the wheel will clunk side to side. The hub will need to be tightened before you true the wheel, or the wheel will behave erratically. Follow the hub adjustment procedure, Section VI-14D, steps 28-31.

3. Put the wheel in a truing stand, if you have

6.14 tightening and loosening spokes

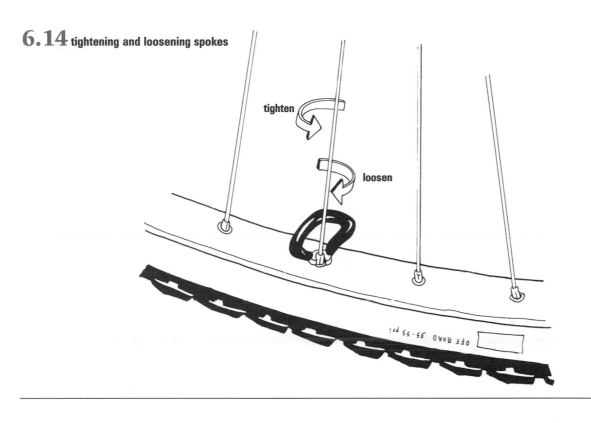

one. Otherwise, leave it on the bike. Suspend the bike in a bike stand or from the ceiling, or turn it upside down on the handlebars and saddle.

4. Adjust the truing stand feeler, or hold one of your brake pads so that it scrapes the rim at the biggest wobble.

5. Where the rim scrapes, tighten the spoke (or spokes) that come(s) to the rim from the opposite side of the hub, and loosen the spoke(s) that

come(s) from the same side of the hub as the rim scrapes (Figs. 6.15–6.16). This will pull the rim away from the feeler or brake pad.

When correcting a wheel that is laterally out of true (wobbles side to side), always adjust spokes in pairs: one spoke coming from one side of the wheel, the other from the opposite side. Tightening spokes is like opening a jar upside down. With the jar right-side up, turning the lid to the left opens

6.15–6.16 lateral truing

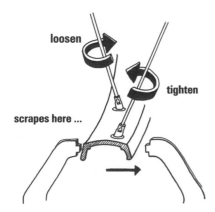

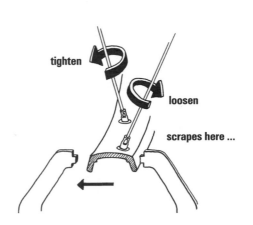

the jar, but this reverses when you turn the jar upside down (try it and see). Spoke nipples are just like the lid on that upside-down jar. In other words, when the nipples are at the bottom of the rim, counter-clockwise tightens, and clockwise loosens (Fig. 6.14). The opposite is true when the nipples you are turning are at the top of the wheel. It may take you a few attempts before you catch on, but you will eventually get it. If you temporarily make the wheel worse, simply reverse what you have done and start over.

It is best to tighten and loosen by small amounts (about a quarter-turn at a time), decreasing the amount you turn the spoke nipples as you move away from the spot where the rim scrapes the hardest. If the wobble gets worse, then you are turning the spokes the wrong direction.

Note: Some wheels (Shimano's complete wheels, for instance) have the spoke nipples at the hub and not at the rim. You need a special spoke wrench (it should come with the wheels) to get in there at them. You must be particularly careful about the rotation direction (note the discussion above about jar lids) to make sure you are tightening or loosening as you intend.

6. As the rim moves more toward center, readjust the truing-stand feeler or the brake pad so that it again finds the most out-of-true spot on the wheel.

7. Check the wobble first on one side of the wheel and then the other, adjusting spokes accordingly, so that you don't end up pulling the whole wheel off-center by chasing wobbles only on one side. As the wheel gets closer to true, you will need to decrease the amount you turn the spokes to avoid overcorrecting.

8. Accept a certain amount of wobble, especially if truing in a bike, for the in-the-bike method of wheel

truing is not very accurate and is not at all suited for making a wheel absolutely true. If you have access to a wheel-dishing tool, check to make sure that the wheel is centered (Chapter 12, Section XII-5).

VI-11: REPLACING A BROKEN SPOKE

LEVEL 2

Go to the bike store and get a new spoke of the same length. Remember: The spokes on the front wheel are usually not the same length as the spokes on the rear. Also, the spokes on the drive side of the rear wheel are almost always shorter than those on the other side. Same goes for a disc-brake front wheel.

1. Make sure you are using the proper thickness and length spoke.

2. Thread the spoke through the spoke hole in the hub flange. If the broken spoke is on the drive side of the rear wheel, you will need to remove the

6.17 weaving in a new spoke

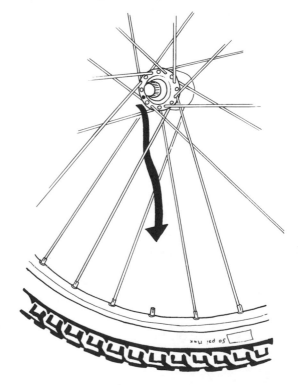

6.18 front hub with cartridge bearing

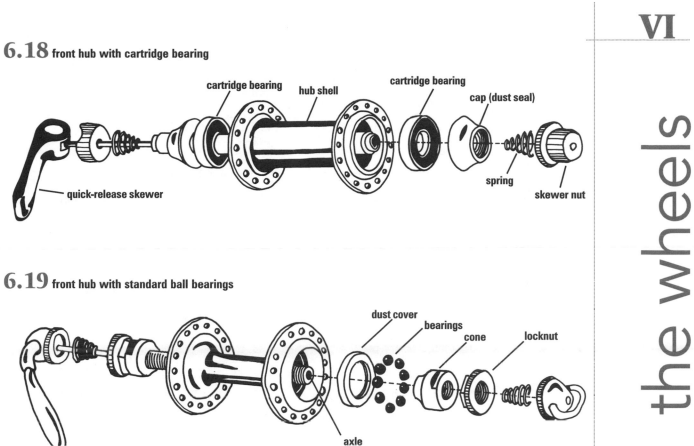

cartridge bearing · hub shell · cartridge bearing · cap (dust seal)

quick-release skewer · spring · skewer nut

6.19 front hub with standard ball bearings

dust cover · bearings · cone · locknut

axle

cassette cogs or the freewheel to get at the hub flange (Sections VI-18 and VI-19). If the spoke is adjacent to the disc-brake rotor, remove the rotor (Section VII-14A).

3. Weave the new spoke in with the other spokes just as it was before (Fig. 6.17). It may take some bending to get it in place.

4. Thread it into the same nipple, if the nipple is in good shape. Otherwise, use a new nipple; you'll need to remove the tire, tube, and rim strip to install it.

5. Mark the new spoke with a piece of tape, and tighten it up about as snugly as the neighboring spokes on that side of the wheel.

6. Follow the steps for truing a wheel as outlined above, Section VI-10.

VI.C HUBS

VI-12: OVERHAULING HUBS

Hubs should turn smoothly and noiselessly. If they are regularly maintained, you can expect them to still be running smoothly when you are ready to give up on the rest of your bike.

There are two general types of hubs: the standard "cup and cone" type and the "sealed bearing" (or "cartridge bearing") type. All hubs have a "hub shell" that contains the axle and bearings and is connected to the rim with spokes.

Standard cup-and-cone hubs have loose ball bearings that roll along very smooth bearing surfaces called the "bearing races," or "cups," with an axle going through the center of the hub. These hubs also have conical-shaped nuts threaded onto the axle called "cones" (Fig. 6.19). These cones press the bearings gently inside the cups and guide the bearings as they travel along the bearing races. The cone surface that comes in contact with the bearings has been machined in high-quality hubs to minimize friction. The operation of the hub depends on the smoothness and lubrication of the cones, ball bearings and bearing races. Outside of the cones are one or more spacers (or washers) followed by threaded locknuts that tighten down against the cones and spacers to keep the hub in proper adjustment. The rear hub will have more spacers on both sides, especially on the drive side (Fig. 6.28).

The term "sealed-bearing" hub is a bit of a misnomer, since many cup and cone hubs offer better protection against dirt and water than some sealed-bearing hubs. The phrase "cartridge-bearing hub" is more accurate, since the distinguishing feature of these hubs is that the bearings, races and cones are all assembled as a complete unit at the bearing factory, and then plugged into a hub shell machined to accept the cartridge. Cartridge-bearing front hubs have two bearings, one on either end of the hub shell (Fig. 6.18). Rear hubs (Fig. 6.27) have at least that, and come with additional bearing cartridges to stabilize the rear cassette (the part onto which the rear cogs are attached).

Cartridge-bearing hubs can have any number of axle assembly types. Some have a threaded axle with locknuts quite similar to a cup-and-cone hub. Much more common on mountain bikes are aluminum axles, often very large in diameter with correspondingly large bearings. Their end caps usually snap on, screw on or are held on with setscrews or circlips. The large diameter axles and bearings are meant to

prevent independent movement of the legs of suspension forks or rear suspension assemblies.

VI-13: ALL HUBS

1. Remove the wheel from the bike (Chapter 2, Sections II-2–II-5 and II-11).

2. Remove the quick-release skewer or the nuts and washers holding the wheel onto the bike.

VI-14: OVERHAUL STANDARD CUP-AND-CONE HUB, FRONT OR REAR

Take some time to evaluate the hub's condition before disassembling it. That will help you to isolate problems. Spin the hub while holding the axle, and turn the axle while holding the hub. Does it turn roughly? Is the axle bent or broken? Wobble the axle side to side. Is the bearing adjustment loose?

Note: Some hubs with large rubber seals covering the axle nuts (Shimano STX comes to mind) can squeal hideously, even though the inside workings of the hub are in good shape. The squeal can be caused by dust in the seal, or mis-seating of it against the hub face. The seal can be pulled off by squeezing and yanking it. Brush it off, put it back into its mating grooves on the hub, and it will probably be silent.

A. Disassembly

1. Set the wheel flat on a table or workbench. Slip a cone wrench of the appropriate size (usually 13mm, 14mm or 15mm) onto the wrench flats on one of the cones. On a rear wheel, work on the noncog side.

2. Put an appropriately sized wrench or adjustable wrench on the locknut on the same side.

3. While holding the cone with the cone wrench, loosen the locknut (Fig. 6.20). This may

6.20 loosening and tightening locknut

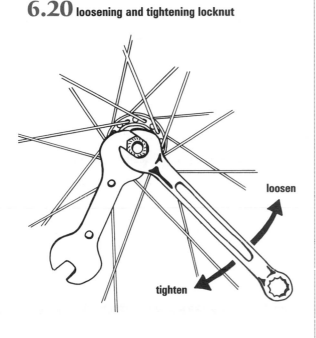

loosen

tighten

6.21 removing dustcap

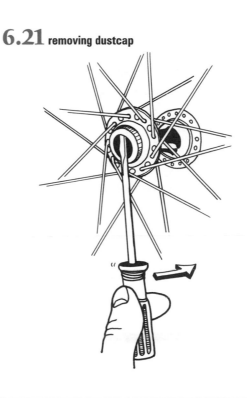

the wheels

OVERHAULING
CUP-AND-
CONE HUBS

take considerable force, as these are often fastened together very tightly to maintain the hub's adjustment. Make sure that you are unscrewing the locknut counterclockwise ("lefty loosey, righty tighty").

4. As soon as the locknut loosens, move the cone wrench from the cone on top to the cone on the opposite end of the axle, in order to hold the axle in place as you unscrew the locknut. It will generally unscrew with your fingers; use a wrench on it if necessary to get past any damaged threads.

5. Slide any spacers off. If they will not slide off, the cone will push them off when you unscrew it. Please note that some spacers have a small tooth or "key" that corresponds to a groove along the axle.

6. Unscrew the cone off of the axle. Again, you may need to hold the opposite cone with a wrench and use a wrench on this cone. An easy way to keep track of the various nuts, spacers and cones is to lay them down on your workbench in the order they were removed (Fig. 6.19), or you can slide a

twist-tie through all the parts in the correct order and orientation. Either method serves as an easy guide when reassembling the hub.

7. Put your hand over the end of the hub from which you removed the nuts and spacers (to catch any bearings that might fall out), and flip the wheel over. Have a rag underneath the wheel to catch stray bearings.

8. Pull the axle up and out, being careful not to lose any bearings that might fall out of the hub or that might be stuck to the axle. Leave the cone, spacers and locknut all tightened together on the opposite end of the axle from the one you disassembled. If you are replacing a bent or broken axle, measure the amount of axle sticking out beyond the locknut. Put the cone, spacers and locknut on the new axle identically.

9. Remove all of the ball bearings from both sides of the hub. They may stick to a screwdriver with a coating of grease on the tip, or you can push

them down through the center of the hub and out the other side with the screwdriver. Tweezers or a small magnet might also be useful for removing bearings. Put the bearings in a cup, a jar lid or the like. Count the bearings, and make sure you have the same number from each side.

10. With a screwdriver, gently pop off the seals that are pressed into either end of the hub shell (Fig. 6.21). Be careful not to deform them; leave them in if you can't pop them out without damage. If they are not removed, it is tedious, but not impossible, to clean the dirty grease out of their concave inside with a rag and a thin screwdriver.

B. Cleaning

11. Wipe the hub shell out with a rag. Remove all dirt and grease from the bearing surfaces. Using a screwdriver, push a rag through the axle hole through the hub and spin it to clean out any grease or dirt. Wipe off the outer faces of the shell. Finish with a very clean rag on the bearing surfaces. They should shine and be completely free of dirt or grease. If you let your hub go too long between overhauls, the grease may have solidified and glazed over so completely that you will need a solvent to remove it.

If you are working on a rear cassette hub, take this opportunity to lubricate the cassette. (See "Lubricating Freehub Mechanisms," Section VI-20.)

12. Wipe down the axle, nuts and cones with a rag. Clean the cones really well with a clean rag. Again, a solvent may be required if the grease has solidified. Get any dirt out of the threads on the disassembled axle end, as the cone will then push the dirt into the hub upon reassembly.

13. Wipe the grease and dirt off of the seals. A rag over the end of a screwdriver is sometimes useful to get inside. Again, glaze-hard grease may have to be removed with a solvent. Keep the solvent out of the freehub body.

14. Wipe the bearings off by rubbing all of them together between two rags. This may be sufficient to clean them completely, but small specks of dirt can still adhere to them, so I prefer to take the next step as well.

15. If you are overhauling low-quality hubs, skip to step 16.

Super clean and polish the bearings. I prefer to wash them in a plugged sink with an abrasive soap like Lava, rubbing them between my hands as if I were washing my palms. This really gets them shining, unless they are caked with glaze-hard grease. Make sure you have plugged the sink drain! This method has the added advantage of getting my hands super clean for the assembly step. It is silly to contaminate your super clean parts with dirty hands. If there is hardened glaze on the bearings, soak them in a solvent. If that does not remove it, go buy new bearings at the bike shop. Take a few of the old bearings along so you are sure to buy the right size.

16. Dry all bearings and any other wet parts. Inspect the bearings and bearing surfaces carefully. If any of the bearings have pits or gouges in them, replace all of them. The same goes for the cones. A lack of sheen or a patina on either balls or cones indicates wear and is cause for replacement. Most bike shops stock replacement cones. If the bearing races (or cups) in the hub shell are pitted, the only thing you can do is buy new hubs. Regular maintenance and proper adjustment can prevent pitted hub bearing races.

Note: *Using new ball bearings when overhauling*

CLEANING
CUP-AND-
CONE HUBS

6.22 push inward on the axle and flip the wheel over

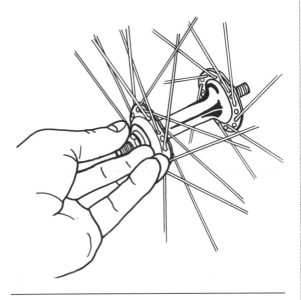

standard cup-and-cone hubs assures round, smooth bearings; however, do not avoid performing an overhaul just because you don't have any new ball bearings. Inspect the ball bearings carefully. If there is even the slightest hint of uneven wear or pitting on the balls, cups or cones, throw the bearings out and complete the overhaul with new bearings. Err on the side of caution.

C. Assembly and lubrication

17. Press the seals or dust covers in on both ends of the hub shell.

18. Smear grease with your clean finger into the bearing race on one end of the hub shell. I like using light-colored or clear grease so that I can see if it gets dirty, but any bike grease will do. Grease not only lubricates the bearings, it also forms a barrier to dirt and water. Use enough grease to cover the balls halfway. Too much grease will slow the hub by packing around the axle.

19. Stick half of the ball bearings into the grease, making sure you put in the same number of bear-

ings that came out. Distribute them uniformly around in the bearing race.

20. Smear grease on the cone that is still attached to the axle, and slide the axle into the hub shell. Lift the wheel up a bit (30-degree angle), so you can push the axle in until the cone slides into position, and keeps all the bearings in place. It is important to replace the axle and cone assembly into the same side of the hub from which it was removed on rear hubs due to spacing for cogs.

21. Holding the axle pushed inward with one hand to secure the bearings, turn the wheel over (Fig. 6.22).

22. Smear grease into the bearing race that is now facing up. Lift the wheel and allow the axle to slide down just enough so that it is not sticking up past the bearing race. Make sure no bearings fall out of the bottom. If the race and bearings are properly greased and the axle remains in the hub shell, they are not likely to fall out.

23. While the top end of the axle is still below the bearing race, place the remaining bearings uniformly around in the grease. Make sure you have inserted the correct number of bearings.

6.23 setting the axle on the floor to keep the cone in contact with the bearings

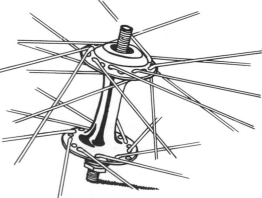

6.24 tightening and loosening locknut

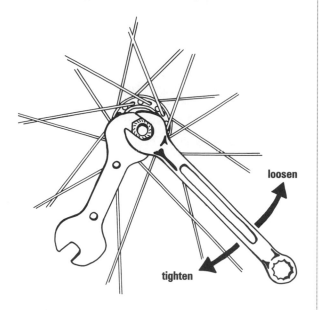

loosen

tighten

24. Slide the axle back up into place by setting the wheel down on the table, so that the wheel rests on the lower axle end, seating the cone up into the bearings (Fig. 6.23).

25. Using your fingers, screw the top cone down into place, seating it snugly onto the bearings. Covering the top cone with a film of grease is also a good idea.

26. In correct order, slide on the washer and any spacers. Watch for those washers with the little tooth or "key" that fits into the lengthwise groove in the axle.

27. Use your finger to screw on the locknut. Note that the two sides of the locknut are not the same. If you are unsure about which way the locknut goes back on, check the orientation of the locknut that is on the opposite end of the axle (this locknut was not removed during this overhaul and is assumed to be in the correct orientation). As a general rule, the rough surface of the locknut faces out so that it can get a better bite into the dropout.

D. Hub adjustment

28. Thread the cone onto the axle until it lightly contacts the bearings. The axle should turn smoothly without any roughness or grinding, and there should be a small amount of lateral play. Thread the locknut down until it is snug against the cone. The slight looseness will be taken out when the quick-release skewer is tightened down with the wheel in the frame. If the hub is a bolt-on type without a quick-release skewer, you don't want any play in it.

29. Place the cone wrench into the flats of the hub cone. Tighten the locknut with another wrench (Fig. 6.24). Tighten it about as tightly as you can against the cone and spacers, in order to hold the adjustment. Be aware that you can ruin the hub if you accidentally tighten the cone down against the bearings instead of against the locknut.

30. If the adjustment is off, loosen the locknut while holding the cone with the cone wrench. If the hub is too tight, unscrew the cone a bit. If the hub is too loose, screw the cone in a bit.

31. Repeat steps 28–30 until the hub adjustment feels right. It should have a slight amount of end play so that the pressure of the quick release skewer will compress it to a perfect adjustment. Tighten the locknut firmly against the cone to hold the adjustment.

Note: You may find that tightening the locknut against the cone suddenly turns your "Mona Lisa" perfect hub adjustment into something slightly less beautiful. If it is too tight, back off both cones (with a cone wrench on either side of the hub, each on one cone) a fraction of a turn. If too loose, tighten both locknuts a bit. If still off, you might have to loosen one side and go back to step 29. It's rare that I get a

HUB
ADJUSTMENT

hub adjustment perfectly "dialed-in" on the first try, so expect that you might have to tinker with the adjustment a bit before it's right.

32. Put the skewer back into the hub. Make sure that the conical springs have their narrow ends to the inside (see Fig. 6.19).

33. Install the wheel in the bike, tightening the skewer. Check that the wheel spins well without any side play at the rim. If it needs readjustment, go back to step 31.

34. Congratulate yourself on a job well done! Hub overhaul is a delicate job, and it makes a difference in the longevity and performance of your bike.

VI-15: OVERHAUL CARTRIDGE-BEARING HUB

Cartridge-bearing hubs (Figs. 6.18 and 6.27) generally do not need much maintenance; however, if you ride through water above your hubs, you can expect water and dirt to get through any kind of seal. If the ball bearings inside the cartridges get

wet, they should be overhauled or replaced.

There are many types of cartridge-bearing hubs, and it is outside the scope of this book to explain how to disassemble every one of them. Some have a threaded axle with locknuts similar to loose-ball hubs. Others have an end cap (Fig. 6.18) that can be removed by just pulling it off, by loosening a set screw on the cap or by unscrewing the axle from either end with two 5mm Allen wrenches; the ends of the axle on this latter type will have a 5mm hex cut inside either end. Older Mavic hubs have cup-shaped end flanges held on with snaprings. Current Mavic hubs have one end cap with a 5mm hex hole, while the other end cap pulls off. To get the axle out, you have to unscrew and remove either the end cap with the hex hole, or the threaded collar on the other end. You can hold the collar with a pin tool that comes with the hubs while fixing the other end of the axle with a 5mm hex key. Alternatively, if you have a 10mm hex key, you can insert it into the collar end of the axle after you

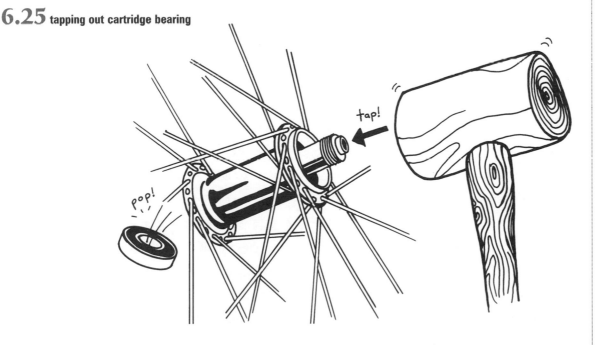

6.25 tapping out cartridge bearing

pull off the end cap on that end. Hold the axle with the 10mm hex key while you unscrew the 5mm end cap from the other end.

If your hub has dust covers concealing the bearings, pry them off after the axle end caps have been removed.

Once the end cap and dust covers have been removed, you can usually smack the end of the axle with a soft hammer or on a table, and it will either pop the axle out, or it will push the opposite bearing out (Fig. 6.25). The axle may have a shoulder on either side, internal to the bearings, which can be used to force the bearings out, or you will push the axle end into the center of the hub, behind the bearing, and use the end of the axle (or a large drift punch) to push the bearing out. A tap with a soft hammer, and the axle shoulder, the axle end or the drift punch should force the bearing out of the hub. Pop the other bearing out the same way.

If the bearings don't want to come out without undue force, you can leave them in the hub shell and pop off the outer bearing seal on each with the tip of a knife blade (Fig. 6.26). If the grease inside is pretty clean, you can just wipe it out and pack new grease in from the outside. That may be all that is necessary.

Cartridge bearings are vulnerable to lateral stress; if you have to use a lot of force to pound them out, they will need to be replaced.

Once the cartridge bearings are out, you can sometimes overhaul them (otherwise you'll need to buy new ones):

1. Gently pop the bearing covers off with a single-edge razor blade (Fig. 6.26).

2. Squirt a citrus-based solvent into the bearing under pressure (wear rubber gloves and protective

OVERHAULING CARTRIDGE-BEARING HUB

6.26 removing bearing seal

glasses) to wash out the grease, water and dirt. Scrub with a clean toothbrush. Brush your teeth later with a different toothbrush.

3. Blow out the bearing with compressed air to dry it out.

4. Pack it with grease and snap the bearing covers back on.

5. Reassemble the hub the opposite way it came apart.

Note: Reinstalling the bearings in most new cartridge-bearing hubs is relatively easy: Simply press the bearings in with your hand, or use the shoulder on the axle as a punch to press the bearings into place. In most cases, even a soft hammer is not necessary; however, with older cartridge-bearing hubs (SunTour, Sanshin, Specialized and others), it isn't so easy. The tolerance between the hub cups and the outer surface of the bearing is so tight that these bearings must be pressed in or pounded in with a hammer. A direct blow from a hammer would ruin the bearing, so with these types of hubs, it is best to use either an old cartridge bearing or a similar-sized piece of metal to tap the bearings into the hub.

6. Adjustment: Sometimes the bearings will be slightly out of alignment after installation, making the hub noticeably hard to turn. A light tap on either end of the axle with a soft hammer will often free them. With Mavic hubs, once the wheel

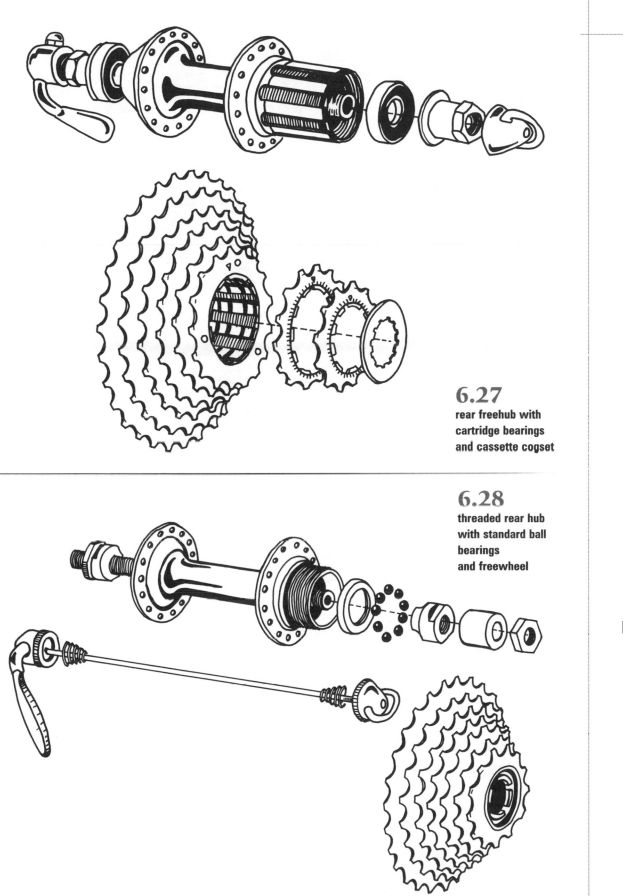

VI

the wheels

6.27
rear freehub with
cartridge bearings
and cassette cogset

6.28
threaded rear hub
with standard ball
bearings
and freewheel

REAR HUBS

is mounted in the frame or fork with the skewer tightened, turn the threaded ring on one face of the hub (the side opposite the cogs on the rear) with the Mavic pin tool. Screw it in to remove side play, unscrew it to eliminate hub binding.

VI-16: GREASE GUARD HUBS

Wilderness Trail Bikes, SunTour and others have made high-end hubs, some labeled Grease Guard, that have small grease ports on them that accept a small-tipped grease gun. The tip in this type of grease gun is about the size of the tip of a pencil. Injecting grease into these grease ports forces grease through the bearings from the inside out, squeezing the old grease out of the outer end. Grease injection systems do not eliminate the need for overhauling your hubs. Grease injection merely extends the amount of time between overhauls; furthermore, these systems are only as good as you are about using them.

VI.D: FREEHUBS, FREEWHEELS AND COGS

Both freehubs and freewheels are freewheeling mechanisms, meaning that they allow the rear wheel to turn freely while the pedals are not turning.

A freehub is an integral part of the rear hub. The cogs slide onto the freehub body, engaging longitudinal grooves, or "splines" (Fig. 6.27). A freehub can also be called a "cassette hub," the group of cogs being called the "cassette."

A freewheel is a separate unit with the cogs attached to it. The entire freewheel threads onto the drive side of the rear hub (Fig. 6.28). Thread-on freewheels have fallen out of fashion relative to freehubs; interchanging cogs on a freewheel is

6.29 cleaning cogs

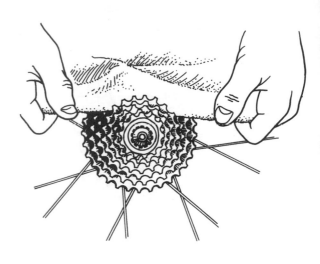

more difficult, and a freewheel does not support the drive side of the hub axle. Freewheels can be removed with a freewheel tool made to fit the specific freewheel. Entire freewheels with different gear combinations can be changed in this way.

Freehubs and freewheels usually rely on a series of spring-loaded pawls that engage internal teeth when pressure is applied to the pedals but allow the bike to freewheel when the rider is coasting. The pawls riding over the teeth as they rotate past makes the familiar clicking noise when coasting.

Most freehubs can be lubricated without removing them from the hub. Changing gear combinations is accomplished by removing the cogs from the freehub body and putting on different ones.

VI-17: CLEANING REAR COGS

The quickest, though perfunctory, way to clean the rear cogs is to slide a rag back and forth between each pair of cogs (Fig. 6.29). The other way is to remove them (see Section VI-18 below) and wipe them off with a rag or immerse them in solvent.

CLEANING COGS

VI

VI-18: CHANGING CASSETTE COGS

1. Get out a chain whip, a cassette lockring remover, a wrench (adjustable or open) to fit the remover and the cog(s) you want to install. (Some very old cassettes have a threaded smallest cog instead of a lockring. These require two chain whips and no lockring remover.)

2. Remove the skewer.

3. Wrap the chain whip around a cog at least two up from the smallest cog, wrapped in the drive direction to hold the cassette in place.

4. Insert the splined lockring remover into the lockring — the metallic ring with a splined hole holding the smallest cog in place. Unscrew the lockring in a counterclockwise direction while holding the chain whip to keep the cassette from turning (Fig. 6.30). If the lockring is so tight that the tool pops out and damages it, put the skewer without its

springs through the hub and tool and tighten it. Loosen the lockring a fraction of a turn, remove the skewer, and unscrew the lockring the rest of the way.

5. Pull the cogs straight off. Some cassette cogsets are all single cogs separated by loose spacers, some cogsets are bolted together, and some cogsets are a combination of both.

6. Clean the cogs with a rag or a toothbrush — use a solvent if necessary, and don't put the toothbrush back by the bathroom sink!

7. Inspect the cogs for wear. If the teeth are hook-shaped, they may be ripe for replacement. Rohloff also makes a cog wear indicator tool (Fig. 1.5). If you have access to one, use it according to its supplied instructions.

8. a. If you are replacing the entire cogset, just slide the new one on. Usually, one spline is wider than the others to assure proper alignment (Fig. 6.31).

6.30 removing a freewheel lockring

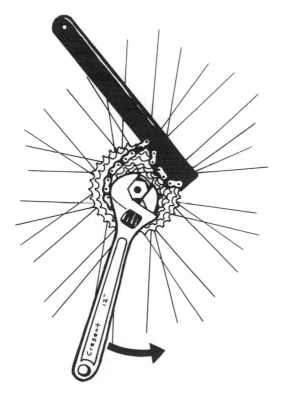

6.31 spline vs. spleen

large spline

large spleen (not to scale)

b. If you are installing a 9-speed cassette, see the notes under step 9.

c. If you are replacing some individual cogs within your cogset, be certain that they are of the same type and model. For example, not all 16-tooth Shimano cogs are alike. Most cogs have shifting ramps, differentially shaped teeth and other asymmetries. They differ with model as well as with sizes of the adjacent cogs, so you need to buy one for the exact location and model. Install them in decreasing numerical sequence with the numbers facing out.

Some bolt-together cogsets are held together by three long bolts (Fig. 6.27) and can be disassembled for cleaning and then reinstalled onto the freehub as separate cogs to facilitate future cog changes and cleaning. But high-end cogsets usually have lightweight splined aluminum carriers onto which the cogs are mounted. These cannot be disassembled, and you replace the entire carrier with cogs assembled onto it.

9. When all the cogs are on, tighten the lockring with the lockring remover and wrench. (If you have the old freehub type with the thread-on first cog, tighten that on with a chain whip instead.) Make sure that all of the cogs are seated and can't wobble side to side, which would indicate that the first or second cog is sitting against the ends of the splines. If the cogs are loose after tightening the lockring, loosen the lockring, line up the first and second cog until they fall in place and tighten the lockring again.

Note on compatibility: The above instructions for removing and replacing cogs apply for 9- 8-, 7-, and 6-speed cogsets. But the freehub bodies vary, so make sure you only use, for example, an 8-speed cogset on a freehub body designed for eight cogs.

Note on 11-speed cogs: Some 8/9-speed freehub bodies will not accept 11-tooth cogs (for example, 1992–1994 XTR freehub bodies will not accept 11–28 or 11–30 cogsets). To accept the small 11-tooth cog, the splines of current freehub bodies stop about 2mm before the outer end of the freehub body. If you are motivated to do so, you can grind the last 2mm of splines off of an old-style 8-speed freehub so it will accept an 11-tooth cog. But be aware that the steel is very hard, and you may need a grindstone to do the job!

Note on 9-speed cassettes: Ritchey's 2-by-9 system (front double, rear nine) features a 9-speed cassette that fits on an 8-speed freehub. The ninth cog is large (33 teeth or more) and bowl-shaped. It takes advantage of some unused space on the inboard end of the freehub body and spaces the teeth the same distance from the next cog as the spacing throughout the cassette.

Installing a Ritchey 9-speed cassette: Many freehubs from Shimano as well as other companies have a steel ring against the inboard end of the cassette body. You should remove this ring (it pulls straight off), and then put on the Ritchey ninth cog in its place. Some XT and XTR freehubs have a thicker aluminum ring inboard; replace this thick ring with the thinner steel ring supplied with the Ritchey cog, and put on the ninth cog. Slide on the 8-speed cassette and tighten it down with the lockring as in step 9.

Caution on Ritchey 9-speed: To avoid the derailleur hitting the spokes when on the bowl-shaped Ritchey cog, you must use an "OCR" ("Off-Center Rear") rim; Ritchey, Bontrager and others supply them. The spoke holes on these rims are offset to the nondrive side and angle the drive-side spokes further away from the cogs.

CHANGING
CASSETTE
COGS

VI-19: CHANGING FREEWHEELS

If you have a freewheel (Fig. 6.28) and want to switch it with another one, follow this procedure. Replacing individual cogs on an existing freewheel is beyond the scope of this book and is rarely done these days due to unavailability of spare parts.

1. Get out the appropriate freewheel remover for your freewheel, a big adjustable wrench to fit it, and the freewheel you are replacing it with.

2. Remove the quick-release skewer, and take the springs off of it.

3. Slide the skewer back in from the nondrive side, place the freewheel remover into the end of the freewheel so that the notches or splines engage, and thread the skewer nut back on, tightening it against the freewheel remover to keep it from popping out of its notches.

4. Put the big adjustable wrench onto the flats of the freewheel remover, and loosen it (counterclockwise). It may take considerable force to free it, and you may even need to put a large pipe on the end of the wrench for more leverage. Have the tire on the ground for traction as you do it. Once the freewheel pops loose, be careful to not keep unscrewing it without loosening the skewer nut, as this could snap the skewer in two.

5. Loosen the skewer nut a bit, unscrew the freewheel a bit more, etc., until it spins off freely and there is no longer any danger of having the freewheel remover pop out of the notches it engages.

6. Remove the skewer and spin off the freewheel.

7. Grease the threads on the hub and on the new freewheel.

8. Thread on the new freewheel by hand.

Tighten it either with a chain whip, the freewheel remover and a wrench, or by putting it on the bike and pedaling.

9. Replace the skewer with the narrow ends of its conical springs facing inward.

VI-20: LUBRICATING FREEHUB MECHANISMS

Most people ignore their freehubs, even though they may maintain the rest of their bicycle very well. This could explain why replacement freehubs are one of the most oft-purchased replacement parts in bike shops. But a little simple lubrication on a regular basis can prevent their demise.

Many freehubs can be cleaned and lubricated reasonably well simply by dripping chain lube into them, once the axle assembly is out (step A explains how). But you can only flow in a thin lubricant this way, which will not protect or hold up as long as a thicker formulation. See step B for how to inject cleaning solvents as well as thicker, more protective lubricants into a Shimano freehub.

Some high-end freehubs have grease-injection holes on the freehub body that accept a fine-tip grease gun; you remove the cogs to get at the hole. Rather than using bearing grease, inject a thinner lube in them, like Manitou fork Microlube to avoid grease thickening up inside and sticking the pawls in the cold, preventing engagement of the freehub.

If the freehub has teeth on the faces of the hub shell and freehub (DT-Hügi or old Mavic freehubs have these radial teeth), you can just drip oil into the crease between the freehub and the hub shell as you turn the freehub counterclockwise. Recent DT-Hügi hubs pull apart easily for lubrication; follow the instructions in part C.

A. Oiling a standard freehub

1. Disassemble the hub axle assembly (see Sections VI-12–VI-15).

2. Wipe clean the inside of the drive-side bearing surface.

3. With the wheel lying flat and the freehub pointed up toward you, flow chain lube between the bearing surface and the freehub body as you spin the freehub counterclockwise. You will hear the clicking noise of the freehub pawls smooth out as lubricant reaches them. Keep it flowing until old black oil flows out of the other end of the freehub.

4. Wipe off the excess lube, and continue with the hub overhaul.

B. Thorough Shimano freehub lubrication

By far the best way to lubricate a Shimano freehub is to inject lubricant under pressure into it with a Morningstar "Freehub Buddy" tool (Fig. 6.34). Once the hub is apart, most of the work is done. This tool is easy to use, but you may want to first order a dust cap from Morningstar (see the note after step 4).

1. To use this tool, you must first disassemble the hub axle assembly as in Section VI-14.

2. Pry out the freehub dust cover — ideally with the Morningstar J-tool, Fig. 6.32 — to expose the hub bearing race. On newer, deeper freehubs for 9 speeds, you can only start moving the dust cap by prying against the freehub fixing bolt. Then you drop a 6mm bolt down into the fixing bolt and use it as a fulcrum for the J-tool to pry against the rest of the way.

3. Once the dust cover is off, push the Freehub Buddy into the bearing race (Fig. 6.33).

4. Inject diesel fuel (as a cleaning solvent) followed by a lubricant into the threaded hole (or the smaller tapered section below the threads) in the center of the Freehub Buddy; it will exit through the lube galley hole in the side of the tool between the two rubber O-rings (Fig. 6.34). The smaller O-ring at the closed end of the Freehub Buddy seals off the center of the hub to prevent lubricant from going in there, and the larger O-ring prevents lube from squirting back out the front of the freehub.

I recommend force-threading the tip of a turkey baster filled with diesel fuel into the threaded hole

6.32 prying out a Shimano freehub dust cover with a J-tool

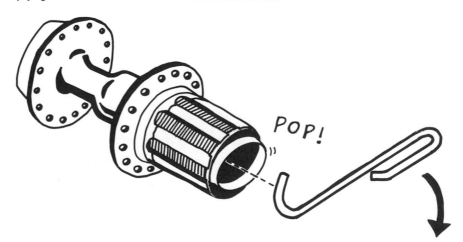

POP!

6.33 Freehub Buddy tool installed in the end of a Shimano freehub body

6.34 Morningstar Freehub Buddy

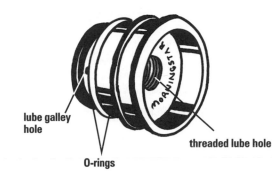

lube galley hole

O-rings

threaded lube hole

in the center of the Freehub Buddy and squirting it in as you slowly turn the freehub. Tilt the wheel with a bucket below to catch the dirty fuel oil. Then force-thread the tip of a tube of outboard motor gear oil into the Freehub Buddy's threaded hole (Fig. 6.34) and squeeze the gear oil in. Outboard gear oil works great — it's the perfect weight for a freehub, and it comes in a huge tube whose end fits nicely into the center hole of the tool. You can also force-thread a tube of grease, or, better, the tip of a glue syringe or turkey baster filled with oil or your own custom mixture of compatible (i.e., synthetic with synthetic or petroleum with petroleum) oil and grease into the Freehub Buddy. Aerosol chain lube can also be squirted into the Freehub Buddy via an included plastic adapter that fits inside the threaded hole and accepts the long, thin tube that comes with the spray lube.

Whatever lubricant you use, squeeze it into the Freehub Buddy until all the old dirty lubricant squeezes through the freehub and out the back end of it. Keep going until clean lube oozes out.

The Freehub Buddy is the only way you can get a lubricant thicker than thin chain lube into your freehub, and a thicker lubricant protects better. Be

certain that it's not *too* thick, however. Filling a freehub with thick grease in cold weather may cause the pawls to stick and not spring back into the freehub teeth to lock it up when you want to pedal forward. You could end up freewheeling in both directions! Always spin it by hand and check it first, and, if it does not engage well, purge it again with lighter oil that is compatible with the grease you put inside.

Note: *Many freehub dust caps will be ruined upon removal; they are usually made of stamped sheet metal. Shimano does not sell them separately, complicating freehub service considerably. Morningstar sells machined removable dustcaps with an O-ring seal as well as freehub tools and lubricants. Contact Morningstar Tooling at P.O. Box 213, Bodfish, CA 93205-0213; e-mail: fhb@qnet.com.*

5. Once the freehub is done, overhaul the hub and replace the axle assembly.

Note: *You can also disassemble a Shimano freehub by unscrewing (clockwise — it's left-hand threaded) the hub bearing race. Morningstar sells a tool that fits into its two notches. I won't go into the details here, but I do illustrate it in the* Mountain Bike Performance Handbook *published by MBI.*

C. DT-Hügi freehub lubrication

1. Recent DT-Hügi high-end free-hubs pull apart easily for cleaning and lubrication.

2. Remove the skewer.

3. Lay the wheel on its side, cogs up, grasp the cogset, and pull up. The freehub body will come off, bringing the axle end-cap with it.

4. Clean and grease the spring, both star-shaped ratchets, and the teeth that engage on the freehub body and hub shell.

5. Push the freehub and end-cap back on, and replace the skewer. That's it!

VI-21: LUBRICATING FREEWHEELS

1. Wipe dirt off of the face of the fixed part of the freewheel surrounding the axle.

2. With the wheel lying flat, and the cogs facing up toward you, drip lubricant into the crease between the fixed and moving parts of the freewheel as you spin the cogs in a counterclockwise direction. You will hear the clicking noise inside get smoother as you get lubricant in there. Be sure to keep the flow of lubricant going until the old, dirty oil flows out the back side around the hub flange.

3. Wipe off the excess oil.

FREEHUB AND
FREEWHEEL
LUBRICATION

brakes

Well, I predict that if you think about it long enough you will find yourself going round and round and round and round until you finally reach only one possible, rational, intelligent conclusion. The law of gravity and gravity itself did not exist before Isaac Newton. No other conclusion makes sense.

— *ROBERT M. PIRSIG, from* Zen and the Art of Motorcycle Maintenance

Oh, well. We came after Newton, so we'd better have a good set of brakes.

tools

2.5mm, 3mm, 4mm, 5mm, 6mm Allen wrenches

9mm and 10mm open end wrenches

small adjustable wrench

pliers

grease

screwdrivers, flat and Phillips

TORX T25 wrench

cable-housing cutter

sharp knife

TYPES OF BRAKES

Not that long ago (1996 — when we published the first edition of this book), by far the most common brake for mountain bikes was the cable actuated center pull cantilever (Figs. 7.23–7.38). But "sidepull cantilevers," otherwise known as "V-brakes" (Fig. 7.12), completely eliminated standard cantilevers (except on bikes using road levers, like for cyclo-cross and some tandems) in a single season after Shimano introduced them. And now, disc brakes similar to those found on a car or motorcycle (Figs. 7.18 and 7.19) appear on large numbers of bikes as well.

There is good reason that the use of both brakes has become so widespread. V-brakes offer more flexibility than cantilevers; since they do not require a cable hanger, V-brakes can be used on rear suspension frames without added complexity, and parallel-push V-brake designs allow use of different rims without pad readjustment. V-brakes are also more powerful than cantilevers because their arms are longer, and the direct cable pull from one arm to the other is more efficient than yanking up on straddle cable tying the two arms together, as cantilevers do. Adjusting V-brakes is also much quicker and simpler than adjusting cantilevers.

Disc brakes, which squeeze the pads against a hub-mounted disc (or "rotor"), stay much cleaner than rim brakes, as mud is thrown away from them by the tires, rather than into them. Additionally, the rim does not heat up on braking, which can burst the tire, so disc brakes can offer consistent performance over a wide range of conditions. Like car brakes, they can also have very high stopping power as well as good modulation of that power. Even more so than a V-brake, a disc brake does not get in the way of movement of a suspension frame. Disc brakes have become an attractive option with the advent of lighter and simpler brake designs at a lower price, combined with built-in mounts for them on frames and suspension forks.

Still, there are a lot of old-style center-pull cantilever brakes out there; hence, working on them is thoroughly covered in this chapter. They're light and simple, they offer good mud clearance, and, above all, they stop your bike. Like V-brakes, cantilevers pivot on bosses attached to the frame and fork.

There are several other options when it comes to mountain bike brakes as well. For rear-suspension frames, linkage brakes that mount on the cantilever bosses offer the same advantage of operating without a cable stop as V-brakes and disc brakes. They rely an on articulated linkage that pulls both brake arms toward one another. The introduction of the V-brake has pretty much dried up the market for other linkage designs.

Some hydraulic rim brakes (Fig. 7.39) mount on the cantilever bosses and are also useful on rear-suspension bikes. On these brakes, the pads are driven straight toward the rim by hydraulic pressure.

Roller-cam brakes (Fig. 7.46) and U-brakes (Fig. 7.45) also mount on bosses attached to the frame and fork. You should know that the brazed-on bosses for these brakes are positioned higher than those used for standard cantilevers and V-brakes. Roller-cams and U-brakes peaked in popularity in the late 1980s, but there are still a few around.

VII-1: RELEASING BRAKES TO REMOVE A WHEEL

V-brakes (Fig. 7.12): Hold the brake-arm link while pulling back and up on the cable "noodle" until it comes out of the slotted hole in the link (see Chapter 2, Fig. 2.1). You can also hold the pads against the rim and pull the cable noodle back and up to release it from the link, but this requires more force.

Disc brakes (Figs. 7.18 and 7.19): Just drop the wheel right out. The disc falls straight out of the caliper (other than in a couple of old designs for frames and forks without built-in disc-brake mounts).

Cantilevers (Fig. 7.29) and **U-brakes** (Fig. 7.45): hold the pads against the rim and pull the head of the straddle cable out of the hook at the end of one brake arm (see Chapter 2, Fig. 2.2).

Magura hydraulic rim brakes (Fig. 7.39): If the brake has a stiffening arch over the wheel (Fig. 7.39), pull its left end off of the bolt head it slips over. If the brake has a quick-release lever on one side, open it and pull the brake bracket off of the brake boss (Fig. 7.40). If there is no quick release, you will have to unscrew the mounting bolt on one side to pull the brake bracket off.

Other types: See the section on the particular brake.

VII.A: CABLES & HOUSINGS

Given that cables transfer braking force from the levers to most brakes, their proper installation and maintenance are critical to good brake performance. If there is excess friction in the cable system, the brakes will not work properly, no matter how well the brakes, calipers and levers are adjusted. Each cable should move freely and be replaced if there are any broken strands.

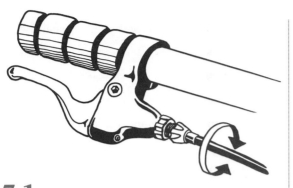

7.1 changing cable tension

VII-2: CABLE TENSIONING

As brake pads wear and cables stretch, the cable needs to be shortened. The barrel adjuster on the brake lever (Fig. 7.1) offers adjustment to mitigate these kinds of changes. The cable should be tight enough that the lever cannot be pulled to the grip, yet loose enough that the brakes (assuming they are centered and the wheels are true) are not dragging on the rims.

VII-3: INCREASING CABLE TENSION

1. Back out the barrel adjuster (exploded in Fig. 7.2) by turning it counterclockwise (Fig. 7.1) after loosening the locknut. Some barrel adjusters have no locknut (Fig. 7.11); just turn them, and they hold their adjustment by friction.

2. Adjust the cable tension so that the brake lever does not hit the grip when the brake is applied. Lock in the tension by tightening the locknut down against the lever body while holding the barrel adjuster. Again, some levers, like Shimano XTR (Fig. 7.11), do not have a locknut on the barrel adjuster and stay in place without it.

3. You may find that you need to tighten the cable more than by simply fiddling with the barrel adjuster. If you need to take up more slack than the barrel adjuster allows you to, tighten the cable at the brake. First, screw the barrel adjuster most of the way in. This leaves some adjustment in the system for brake setup and cable stretch over time. Loosen the bolt clamping the cable at the brake. Check the cable for wear. If there are any frayed strands, replace it. (See "Cable Installation," Section VII-6.) Otherwise, pull the cable tight, and retighten the clamping bolt. Tension the cable as needed with the barrel adjuster.

VII-4: REDUCING CABLE TENSION

1. Back out the locknut on the barrel adjuster (Fig. 7.2) a few turns (counterclockwise), unless yours is the type without a locknut.

7.2 cable installation at brake lever

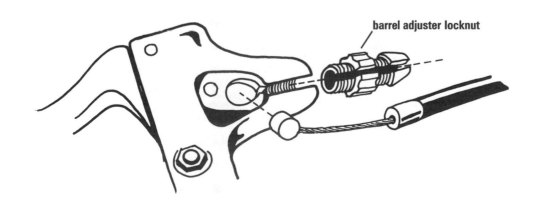

barrel adjuster locknut

2. Turn the barrel adjuster clockwise (Fig. 7.1) until your brake pads are properly spaced from the rim.

3. If your lever has a locknut, tighten it clockwise against the lever body to lock in the adjustment.

4. Double-check that the cable is tight enough so that the lever cannot be squeezed all the way to the grip.

VII-5: CABLE MAINTENANCE

1. If the cable is frayed or kinked or has any broken strands, replace it. (See "Cable Installation," Section VII-6.)

2. If the cable is not sliding well, lubricate it. If you have it, use molybdenum disulfide grease; otherwise, try a chain lubricant. Standard lithium-based greases can eventually gum up cables and restrict movement.

3. To lubricate, open the brake (via the cable quick release as when you remove a wheel; see Section VII-1).

4. Pull each section of cable housing out of each slotted cable stop. If your bike does not have slotted cable stops, you will have to pull out the entire cable.

5. Slide the housing up the cable, rub lubricant with your fingers on the cable section that was inside the housing, and slide the housing back into place.

6. If the cable still sticks, replace it.

VII-6: CABLE INSTALLATION

1. Remove the old cable, making sure not to lose any parts of the cable clamps or straddle-cable holders.

Note: When installing a new cable, it is a good idea to replace the housings as well, even if you don't think they need to be. Daily riding in particularly dirty conditions means that cables and housings may have to be replaced every couple of months. As with chains and derailleur cables, brake cable replacement is a maintenance operation, not a repair operation; don't wait until a cable breaks or seizes up to replace it.

2. Purchase good-quality cables and lined housings.

Cables: Try using die-drawn cables; they have been pulled through a constricting die and will pull with less friction, because the exterior strands have been flattened.

Note: Some cables even come coated in Teflon or Gore-Tex. Gore-Tex RideOn cables and housings, when properly installed, can reduce friction significantly and stay that way, by virtue of being completely sealed. The Gore-Tex must be peeled off of the cable the last couple of inches on either end — where it enters the brake lever and clamps to the brake; if this is not done, the Gore-Tex coating can get completely wadded up and prevent cable movement. A thin plastic tube sheaths the cable, end-to-end against crud, including through the housing sections. A rubber accordion-like seal (called the "Grub") covers the end of the plastic tube at each brake and prevents the access of dirt at its one possible entry point.

Housing: Most brake-cable housing is spiral-wrapped to prevent splitting under braking pressure (see Chapter 5, Fig. 5.18). Teflon-lined housing reduces friction and is a must on a mountain bike.

3. Cut the housing sections long enough to reach the brakes, and route them so that they do not make any sharp bends. If you are replacing existing housing, look at the bends before removing it. If the bends are smooth and do not bind when the wheel is turned, cut the new housings to the same lengths. If not, cut each new segment longer than you think necessary and keep trimming it back until it gives the smoothest path pos-

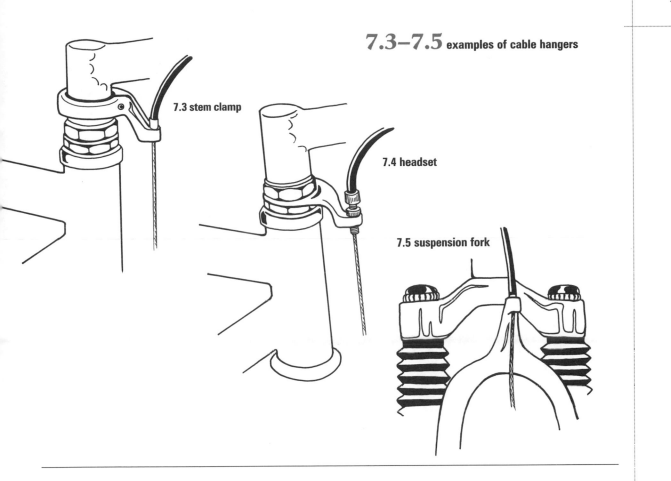

7.3–7.5 examples of cable hangers

7.3 stem clamp

7.4 headset

7.5 suspension fork

sible for the cable, without the cable tension being affected by turning the handlebars. Use a cutter specifically designed for cutting housings, or a sharp side-cutter.

4. After cutting, make sure the end faces are flat. If not, flatten them with a file or a clipper.

5. If the end of the Teflon liner is mashed shut after cutting, open it up with a sharp object like a nail or a toothpick.

6. Slip a ferrule over each housing end for support (see Chapter 5, Fig. 5.18).

7. Decide which hand you want to control which brake (the standard is the right hand controlling the rear brake).

8. Tighten the adjusting barrel to within one turn of being screwed all of the way in. Rotate the barrel adjuster and locknut so that their slots line up with those on the lever and lever body (Fig. 7.2).

9. Insert the round head of the cable into the lever's cable hook (Figs. 7.2, 7.9 and 7.11).

10. Pull the cable down into the lined-up slots on the barrel and nut. Once the cable is in place, turn the barrel so that the slots are offset to prevent the cable from slipping back out. If you have an old lever that is not slotted, you will have to feed the entire length of the cable from the cable hook out through the hole in the lever body.

11. For the front brake, skip to step 12.

Hopefully, you have slotted cable stops on your frame. They make cable installation a lot easier. Assuming that you do, slide the rear brake cable through the housing sections and then route the cable and housing from the brake lever to the brake, snapping the housing and cable into the slot

7.6 tightening cantilever brake cable

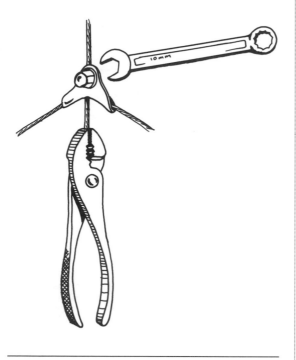

in each stop. If you don't have slotted stops, you will have to feed the cable through the hole in each cable stop.

Note: With new cables and lined housing, it is usually best not to use a lubricant on the cable. It can gum up inside the housing and attract dirt. Some manufacturers, however, supply lubricants specifically for this purpose with their cables and housings.

For the rear brake, skip to step 13.

12. With a V-brake, terminate the housing in the top of the "noodle" guide tube (Fig. 7.12). On a cable-actuated disc brake (Fig. 7.19), the housing usually terminates at a stop on the brake caliper. With a cantilever brake and a suspension fork, terminate the front brake housing at the stop on the brake arch (Fig. 7.5). For cantilevers without suspension, you may have a cable stop that is integral to the stem or one attached to the headset (Fig. 7.4). If your brake cable passes through an integral

cable stop on the stem or a stem through-hole, I recommend bypassing it, as these require readjustment of the front brake with any change in stem height. Instead, use a collar that slips around the stem above the headset (Fig. 7.3) or one that slips into the headset stack between locknuts (Fig. 7.4).

13. Attach the cable to the brake. (See section on your type of brake.) Pull it taut and tighten the cable-clamping bolt (Fig. 7.6 for cantilevers, 7.12 for V-brakes). Pull the lever as hard as you can and squeeze it repeatedly for about a minute to stretch the new cable.

14. Adjust cable tension with the lever barrel adjuster (as in Sections VII-2–VII-4).

15. Cut off cable ends about 2-1/2 inches past the cable-fixing bolts. Crimp end caps on all exposed cable ends to prevent fraying (Fig. 5.29 in Chapter 5), and bend the extra to the side. Follow adjustment procedure for your brake, if need be.

Note: Once the cable has been properly installed, the lever should snap back quickly when released. If it does not, recheck the cables and housings for free movement and sharp bends. Release the cable at the brake, and check the levers for free movement. With the cable still loose, check that the brake pads do not drag on the tire as they return to the neutral position; make sure the brake arms rotate freely on their pivot bosses, and check that the brake arm return springs pull the pads away from the rims.

VII.B: BRAKE LEVERS

The levers must operate smoothly and be set up so that you can easily reach them while riding.

VII-7: LEVER LUBRICATION/SERVICE

1. Lubricate all pivot points in the lever with grease or oil.

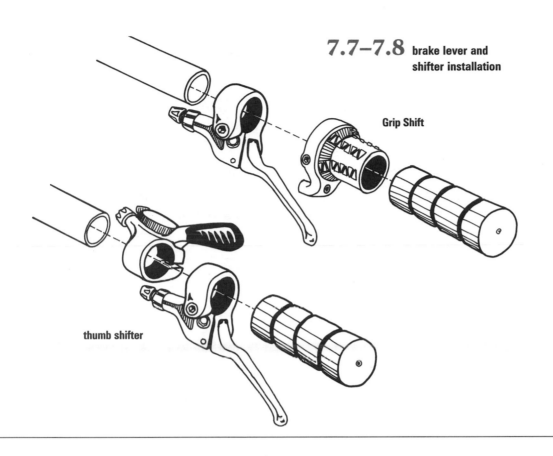

7.7–7.8 brake lever and
shifter installation

Grip Shift

thumb shifter

2. Check return-spring function for levers that have them.

3. Make sure that the lever or lever body is not bent in a way that hinders movement.

4. Check for stress cracks, and, if you find any, replace the lever.

VII-8: LEVER REMOVAL, INSTALLATION AND POSITIONING

Brake levers mount on the bar inboard of the grip and bar end. They are also mounted inboard of twist shifters and outboard of thumb shifters (Figs. 7.7 and 7.8). Some integrated systems include both brake lever and shifter in a single unit (Fig. 7.11).

Most levers have a wrap-around clamp with a single bolt, and grips, bar ends and twist shifters cannot be on the bars when removing and installing them, as described below. But some high-end levers mount with two bolts and a separate

semicircular band; these can come off and on the bar with the bar ends, grips and shifters already on.

1. If installed, remove the bar end by loosening the mounting bolt and sliding it off.

2. Remove the handlebar grip by lifting the edges on both ends, squirting rubbing alcohol or water underneath, and twisting it until it becomes free and slides off.

3. If installed, remove the twist shifter by loosening the mounting bolt and sliding it off.

4. Loosen the brake lever's mounting bolt with an Allen wrench and slide the lever off.

5. Slide the new lever on, and replace the other parts in the order in which they were installed. Slide the grips on using rubbing alcohol (it dries quickly) as a lubricant; water works, too, but the grips will twist for a few rides.

6. Make certain the levers do not extend beyond the ends of the bars. Rotate them and slide them

inward to your preference. See the Pro Tip in the next section for positioning for high performance.

7. Tighten all mounting bolts on levers, shifters and bar ends.

VII-9: REACH AND LEVERAGE ADJUSTMENTS

Some levers have a reach adjustment set screw; usually it's on the lever body just under the barrel adjuster (Figs. 7.9 and 7.10). If you have small hands, you may want to tighten the reach set screws so you can reach the levers more easily.

Some brakes also have a leverage adjustment (Figs. 7.9 and 7.11), which moves the cable end in or out relative to the lever pivot. The closer the cable passes by the pivot, the higher the leverage but the less cable the lever pulls, and vice versa. To start with, set it at the position that offers the weakest leverage, where the cable head or cable path is farthest from the pivot. Only increase the leverage if you become very confident in using the brakes.

On Shimano XTR, Avid and recent SRAM brake levers, a long screw performs the leverage adjustment (Fig. 7.11). On Shimano XT and older SRAM, as well as current low-end SRAM levers, leverage is adjusted by installing, relocating or removing a series of inserts. On Shimano DX and M600, leverage is adjusted by loosening a small bolt on the upper face of the lever arm with a 3mm Allen key, sliding the leverage adjuster up and down, and retightening the bolt (Fig. 7.9). These (DX and M600) and SRAM levers have a hook to hold the cable end far out along the lever (Fig. 7.9); the cable passes over a trough whose position away from the pivot determines the leverage. On yet some other levers, a rotating notched eccentric disc

BRAKE LEVERS

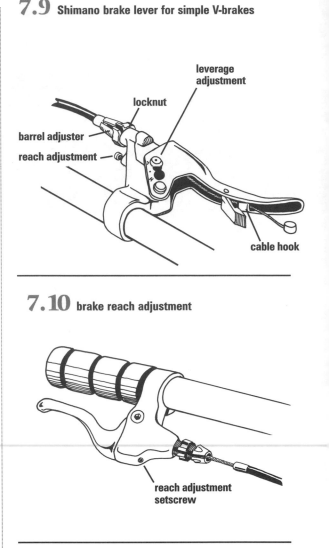

7.9 Shimano brake lever for simple V-brakes

leverage adjustment

locknut

barrel adjuster

reach adjustment

cable hook

7.10 brake reach adjustment

reach adjustment setscrew

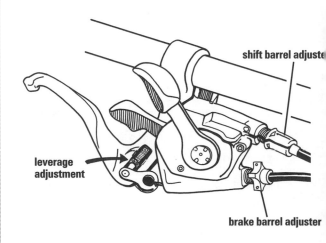

7.11 Rapidfire integrated shift/brake levers

shift barrel adjuster

leverage adjustment

brake barrel adjuster

adjusts the cable-head position relative to the pivot. Again, remember that leverage is increased (and amount of cable pulled is reduced) if the cable head or cable path is closer to the lever pivot, and vice versa.

Safety note: The levers for V-brakes are initially set up with intentionally low leverage (and correspondingly high cable pull), due to the high leverage of the long brake arms. If you use a lever from a cantilever brake with a V-brake, you have more leverage and can end up on your nose. Always start with V-brake levers adjusted to lowest leverage (cable passing farthest from the lever pivot), and increase from there if you wish.

PRO TIP

To get maximum performance out of your V-brakes (sidepull cantilevers) and minimize your effort, you should increase the leverage, but you must also place the lever so that you can only reach it with your forefinger; otherwise you can grab too much brake and do an endo.

Even though a lot of people want a hard feel to the brakes, the harder the brakes feel, the less power you have. The hard feel indicates that you have less mechanical advantage; it feels hard because you are doing all of the work! A softer feel indicates that you have more leverage. You will do less work and stop the bike more easily.

Set your brake levers up for high leverage, even though you may lose some pad travel. You will be trying to move the cable hook (or the cable path) closer to the lever pivot, usually by turning in a screw or by removing some inserts in the lever (Figs. 7.9 and 7.11).

Move your levers inboard so that the tip of the lever is under your index finger. The lever will bypass your second finger and let you pull it to the grip, rather than losing some range by hitting your finger(s). Hold the bar with three fingers and pull the lever with one. *Make sure you pull on the end of the lever, since that is where the leverage is. You will find that you can grip the bars better, and your arms will stay more relaxed when braking. In addition, it will be comfortable to simply rest your forefingers on the levers so that you will be ready to brake at any time. I suggest placing the levers of powerful disc brakes in this position, too.*

Note that it is easy to move the brake lever inboard far enough with twist shifters and with Rapidfire integral brake/shift levers, but it may not be with Rapidfire levers on a separate band clamp. The band clamp goes inboard of the brake lever, and it may prevent the lever from moving inward enough for a rider with large hands (and bar ends taking up some handlebar real estate) to get unimpeded one-finger braking. The shifter band clamp can hit the bulge or curve of the handlebar and stop before it has moved inward enough that the brake lever clears the second finger.

VII.C: BRAKE CALIPERS
VII.C1: V-Brakes

V-brakes (a.k.a. "sidepull cantilevers") have tall, cantilever-like arms, a horizontal cable-hook link on top of one arm, and a cable clamp on the top of the other. A curved aluminum guide pipe, (noodle) hooks into the horizontal link and takes the cable from the end of the housing and out through the link and directs it toward the cable clamp on the opposite arm (Figs. 7.12 and 7.13). V-brakes usually, although not always, have long, thin brake pads with threaded posts. Some V-brakes, like Shimano XT and XTR (Fig. 7.12) and Avid Arch Supreme, have "parallel-push" linkages, which move the brake pads horizontally rather than in an arc around the brake boss like a cantilever. Simple

7.12 Shimano parallel-push V-brake

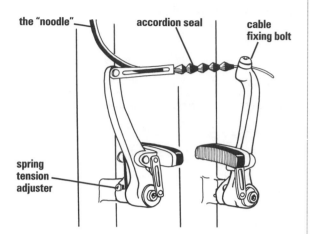

the "noodle"   accordion seal   cable fixing bolt

spring tension adjuster

7.13 simple V-brake (a.k.a. sidepull cantilever brake)

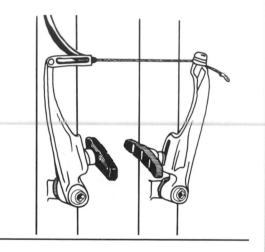

7.14 finalizing pad to rim adjustment

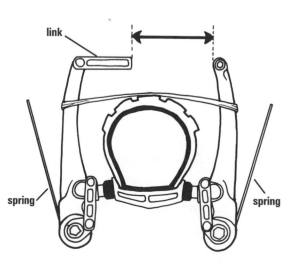

link

spring   spring

V-brake designs mount the pad directly to the arm so that it moves in a cantilever-like arc (Fig. 7.13).

V-brakes are extremely powerful and can be very grabby if used with a cantilever brake lever; it is important that you use the levers that were designed for use with the brake (see Section VII-9 regarding leverage).

VII-10: V-BRAKE INSTALLATION AND ADJUSTMENT

A. V-Brake mounting

1. Grease the brake bosses on your frame or fork.

2. With Shimano, Dia-Compe, and most other V-brakes, slide each brake arm on, inserting the spring pin into the center hole of the boss. Tighten the brake bolt with washer into the boss.

With Avid Arch Supreme brakes, slide two supplied washers onto each brake boss to prevent binding of the brake pivot cartridge bearings. Slide the brake on and tighten the bolt. Bolt each end of the pivot arch, using the supplied bolts and washers, to the hole in the arm adjacent each brake pad.

B. V-Brake pad adjustment

These instructions apply to threaded pad posts. For V-brakes with unthreaded pad posts (Dia-Compe 747), it is best to follow the pad adjustment procedure for cantilever brakes, Section VII-20, coupled with the pad offset in step 4 below. Dia-Compe 747s do not hold the adjustment of their pads well, no matter how much you tighten the eye-bolt nut on the unthreaded pad posts. You may be able to increase the friction between the eye-bolt washers and the curved brake arm by sanding the contacting surfaces on the arms and washers. The brakes will not look as nice, but they may at least work.

3. Roughly adjust each pad by loosening the pad nut, pushing the arm toward the rim, and tightening the pad nut with the pad flat against the rim.

4. Determine the proper amount of pad offset from the brake arms: While holding the pads against the rim, measure the space between the end of the link to the inside edge of the opposite brake arm (Fig. 7.14); this length should be at least 39mm. If it is less than 39mm, the end of the noodle can hit the opposite arm when the brake is applied, particularly as the pads wear. Obviously, this would prevent the brakes from grabbing the rims, which is not what you have in mind when you apply the brakes; this becomes more of an issue the narrower the rim is.

Threaded-post pads are offset from the brake arms by concave washers of various thicknesses nesting over convex washers on either side of the mounting tab (Fig. 7.16). The pad offset, which is adjusted by the spacer stack, should be set so that the top of each brake arm is a little outside of vertical relative to the brake mounting bolt when the brake is applied (i.e., the arms are approximately parallel). On Shimano V-brakes, as they come out of the box, the concave washer on the pad side is 6mm thick, and 3mm thick on the nut side. Avid offers more options, using a 1mm flat washer and 3mm and 5mm concave washers, which can be stacked in combinations. Interchange the washers from side to side to set the offset.

5. Finalize the pad-to-rim adjustment: On brakes with vertical return springs, like Shimano and Avid, flip the springs off of their retention pins and connect the tops of the arms together with a rubber band to lightly hold the pads against the rim (Fig. 7.14). Otherwise, hold the pad against

the rim or put a rubber band around the brake lever after you have connected the cable.

6. Loosen the pad-fixing nut, and then tighten the pad-fixing nut with the pad held flat against the rim. Toe-in (Fig. 7.28) is not necessary in many cases, but it is recommended if you have any brake squeal. To get just a bit of toe-in, slip a paper clip between the tail of the brake pad and the rim, then hold the pad against the rim and tighten it down. The pad's top edge should be about 1mm below the edge of the rim.

7. Rehook the return springs behind the retention pins.

Note: Many high-end V-brakes are "parallel-push," i.e., the linkage attached to the pad mounting bracket keeps the pad moving horizontally as it contacts and leaves the rim surface (Figs. 7.12 and 7.14–7.16). When interchanging wheels with these brakes, as long as the rims have parallel braking surfaces, there is no need to adjust the pads; the only necessary adjustment is to the cable length, if the rim width varies.

C. Threading the cable to the brake through the curved alloy guide pipe (the "noodle")

For the rear brake, pick the one of the two supplied noodles whose curvature and length best fits your frame for a smooth cable path. Bend the noodle if need be. Hook the head of the noodle into the notch in the horizontal link.

7. Slip the rubber accordion dust boot onto the cable, big end first, and over the tip of the noodle (Fig. 7.12). A tight-fitting O-ring ("cable donut" — see Fig. 5.30) on the cable butted up against the narrow end of the boot is a good idea to prevent the boot from falling off of the noodle. If you are using Gore-Tex RideOn cables, you can dispense with the

boot and use Gore's little "Grub" seal instead. The Grub seals the end of the Gore plastic sheath, which should be cut to terminate halfway between the guide pipe tip and the cable-fixing bolt.

8. Connect the cable to the fixing bolt on the opposite arm.

9. Set the cable length so that there is 1–1.5mm of space between each pad and the rim. Tighten the cable-fixing bolt with the lever barrel adjuster screwed out one turn. Make sure the wheel is centered in the frame or fork.

D. V-Brake centering/spring tension adjustment

10. a. Some V-brakes (Shimano) use a vertical return spring (Fig. 7.14) adjusted by a screw at the mounting pivot on each arm (Fig. 7.12); turn the screw clockwise to move the arm farther from the rim, and vice versa. A quick way to increase spring tension or center the brakes on the trail is to bend the vertical springs outward after pulling them off the retention pins on the back of the arms (Fig. 7.14) without fooling with the screws.

b. Dia-Compe 747s use a spring adjuster cam rotated by a 5mm Allen key; turn it toward the imprinted "H" or "L" for more or less spring tension.

c. Avid Arch Supremes have an innovative (and very quick) way to set the spring balance. While lightly squeezing the lever so the pads touch the rim, loosen and retighten the plastic knob at the top of the arch. The W-shaped spring passes through the knob and hooks on the arms; it automatically finds its balance point when the knob is loosened.

d. If your V-brake springs do not adjust with any of the above three methods, look at spring tension adjustment for cantilever brakes, Section VII-22, since any of the spring configurations used in

cantilevers could be built into a V-brake.

Note: If a brake arm does not turn freely on the boss, the boss may be damaged. Bulged or mushroomed bosses can be filed and sanded smaller; bent or broken ones must be replaced (hopefully they are the bolt-on type; otherwise new ones must be welded on).

Another note: Parallel-push V-brakes, like high-end Shimano and Avid, often do not hold their pad centering adjustment, especially when new. You may frequently find that one pad is very close to or rubbing the rim after a ride in which they started centered. This is because, especially as the pivots break in, any bit of grit in any of the numerous pivots will change the return friction on one side relative to the other side. Brake adjustment is an exercise in symmetry; it can be easily thrown off.

11. Squeeze the brake lever hard a number of times to stretch the cable and make sure it does not slip at the anchor bolt.

VII-11: V-BRAKE PAD REPLACEMENT INTO PAD HOLDERS

It is only on high-end brakes that you will find removable pads that slide in and out of permanent pad holders.

1. With a pair of pliers, remove the cotter pin from the top of the pad holder (Fig. 7.15).

2. Slide the old pad out of its groove in the pad holder (Fig. 7.15).

3. Slide in the new pad, paying attention to the "R" and "L" markings for right and left and the "Forward" direction arrow, if present. Right and left must be heeded, as the back of these pads only have a slot for the cotter pin on one end. Avid pads have two cotter pin slots and can be oriented either way.

4. Replace the cotter pin, and check that the pad is secure in the holder.

7.15 pad replacement on V-brakes

7.16 V-brake pad holder assembly

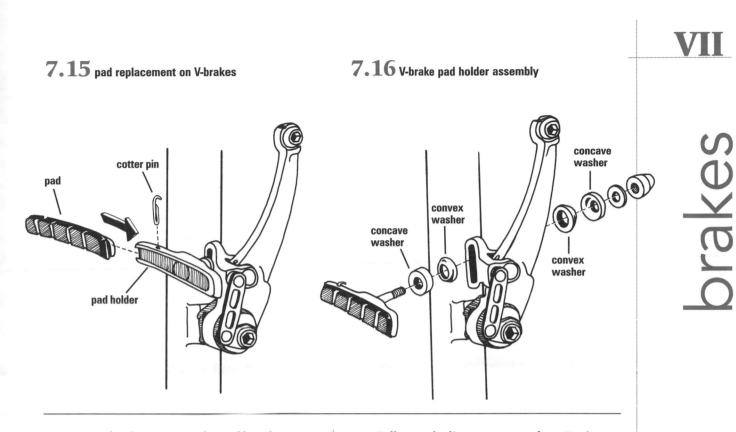

Note: Avid pads are not interchangeable with most other pad holders, which have a curved groove. Avid pad holders have a straight groove, even though the pad itself is curved. The pads are flexible enough that they can be jammed into each other's holders in a pinch, but the outer curvature of the pad will not match that of the rim.

VII-12: PAD REPLACEMENT ON V-BRAKES WITH ONE-PIECE PAD AND THREADED POST

1. Note how the washers are stacked on the pad post (Fig. 7.16).

2. Unscrew the shoe-fixing nut and remove the old pad and post from the arm.

3. Replacing the concave and convex washers as they were, bolt the new pad to the arm. The convex washers are placed on either side of the brake arm with flat sides facing in (Fig. 7.16). The concave washers are placed adjacent to the convex washers so that the concave and convex surfaces meet and allow angular adjustability of the pad.

4. Follow pad adjustment procedure, Section VII-10B.

VII-13: PAD REPLACEMENT ON V-BRAKES WITH UNTHREADED PAD POSTS

Follow pad replacement and adjustment procedures for cantilever brakes, Sections VII-19 and VII-20.

VII-C2: Disc Brakes

Disc brakes can offer a high "gee-whiz" factor as well as great stopping and modulation. But installing them correctly is a must. Once properly installed, discs require less maintenance than do rim brakes, because the tire is not dragging mud into them. But disc brakes do require more care and cleanliness. There is no need to be intimidated, though. While being precise, disc brakes are really quite simple.

VII-14: DISC BRAKE INSTALLATION AND ADJUSTMENT

Once you are used to it, you will find that you

can install and adjust many disc brakes quicker than V-brakes or cantilevers! Simply stated, you just bolt the rotor to the hub, tighten the lever onto the bar, bolt the caliper to the mounts on the frame or fork and tie down the hose or cable. But the space between the pads and rotor is small, and speed of accurate mounting depends on you, the brake and the type of mount the brake accepts.

The two types of mounts built into frames and forks are "International Standard" (IS) mounts (Fig. 7.18) and "post mounts" (Fig. 7.19). IS mounts are drilled transversely and not threaded, whereas post mounts are threaded directly toward the frame or fork. IS mounts, front or rear, are 51.5mm apart. Currently the post-mount standard for forks is 74mm, while original Hayes front post mounts were 2.75 inches (68.8mm) apart. For a brief time, 70mm front post-mount spacing was briefly used as well. (Confused yet?) Rear chainstay post mounts are 21.5mm apart; some seatstay post mounts are also 21.5mm apart, while others are spaced at 74mm.

After installing, don't expect to get full brake performance until you have made a number of hard stops (maybe 10) to wear in the pads and rotor.

Avoid touching the rotor's braking surface and getting grease on it. If brake performance ever drops off, try cleaning the rotor and pads with alcohol.

Never squeeze the lever without a disc or another spacer between the pads, as you can push a piston all of the way out.

A. Rotor mounting and removal
Installation

Rotor bolt patterns vary, too, although Hayes's six-bolt pattern is now widely used as the standard,

7.17 bolting rotor onto hub (Shimano shown)

including by Hayes's competitors, Shimano and Avid.

1. Loosely bolt the rotor to the hub flange (Fig. 7.17). The logo on the rotor should face out so that the rotor turns in the proper direction.

2. Gradually snug the bolts, alternately tightening opposing bolts, rather than adjacent bolts. A hex key or a Torx wrench (like a hex key, but with a star-shaped end [see Fig. 1.4]) is required for this; brakes with Torx bolts usually supply the wrench. Torque for rotor bolts ranges from 18 in-lbs for some manufacturers to 55 in-lbs for others. (Shimano asks you to make one additional step and bend over the corners of small spring-steel plates that should be installed under each pair of bolts [Fig. 7.17]. The heads of the bolts are triangular, and bending the plates over them is designed to ensure that they cannot unscrew.)

3. Install the wheel in the frame or fork.
Removal

When removing a disc rotor, you must loosen all of the screws a portion of a turn before unscrewing any of them. On braking, the rotor may rotate a bit and lean against one side of each

7.18 mounting a hydraulic Shimano International-Standard brake on International-Standard fork mounts

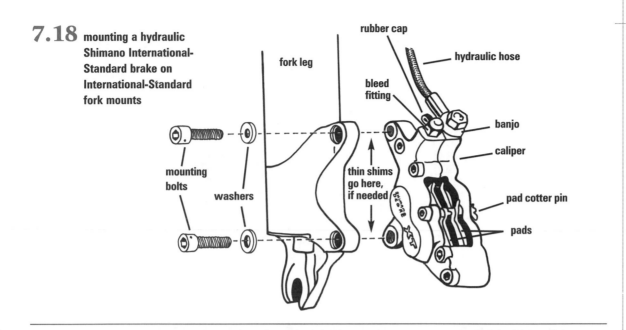

rubber cap

hydraulic hose

fork leg

bleed fitting

banjo

caliper

mounting bolts

washers

thin shims go here, if needed

pad cotter pin

pads

screw. If you remove one screw while the others are still tight, the rotor holes will still be pressed against the side of the screw, and the threads on the screw will be damaged. Then you will wreck the threads in your hub when you put the damaged screw back in.

Note on hubs with adapters: Some disc-brake hubs do not accept a rotor without an adapter. The adapter is attached to the hub, and then the rotor is bolted to the adapter. Some Mavic disc-brake hubs use bolt-on adapters available in several bolt patterns to match various brake brands.

To attach a rotor to a SRAM disc-brake hub, you use a splined disc adapter that slides on and is held in place with three set screws and a thread-on collar tightened with a standard Shimano splined cassette lockring tool.

B. Installing disc-brake caliper onto International Standard mounts

IS mounts (Fig. 7.18) are found on most forks and disc-brake frames.

Note: If you are using a caliper adapter to mount an Avid, Hayes or other post-mount brake to an IS fork or

frame, first bolt the adapter to the frame or fork mounts, then follow the next set of directions (in section C) for installing a caliper onto post mounts.

1. First install the wheel on the bike. Slip the caliper over the rotor and up against the frame or fork mounts.

2. Install and tighten the mounting bolts (torque varies from 53–110 in-lbs, depending on brand). Tightening torque is important, since your stopping ability hangs in the balance. Torque specifications for various disc-brake brands are listed in Appendix E.

3. Spin the wheel and check for rub of the rotor on the pads or caliper slot. If there is some rub, peer through the gap between the rotor and the pads, using a white background for contrast, noting which pad (or worse, which side of the caliper slot) is rubbing. It should be the inboard pad that is rubbing, if at all. (If the outboard pad is rubbing, there is little you can do, unless the rotor is bent (see "Another note" below), although you could shim the rotor away from the hub.)

4. Remove the caliper from the frame or fork

7.19 mounting a cable-activated Avid post-mount brake on Manitou fork post mounts

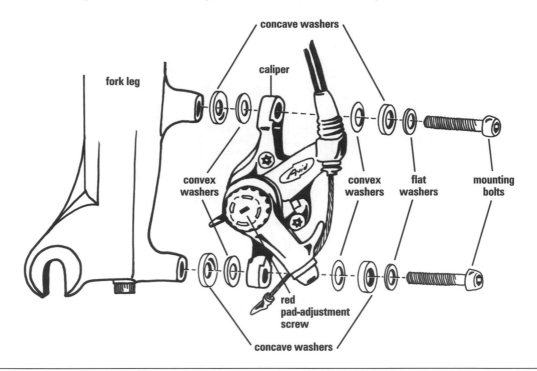

and slip a supplied thin shim washer between the caliper and each mount tab (Fig. 7.18). Repeat steps 2–4 until the brake rub has been eliminated.

Note: Some IS brakes have only one moving pad and instead flex the rotor toward the stationary pad. Magura Louise hydraulic and most mechanical disc brakes are examples. The stationary inboard pad is adjusted independently so that it just clears the rotor without rubbing. Adjust the inboard pad on a Louise with a 5mm hex key and on most mechanical disk brakes with a thumbscrew.

Another note: A bent rotor will rub or at least reduce pad adjustment range. Notice where it rubs on which pad, mark it with a felt pen, and carefully bend it into alignment with your fingers, while it remains mounted to the hub.

"Free-running drag": Some IS brakes use a "floating caliper" in which the entire caliper moves as the pad(s) on the outboard side push against the rotor and pull the stationary pad(s) over to the rotor. Magura Gustav M, Amp, and RockShox brakes have this feature. It is almost impossible to eliminate brake rub with these, as the rotor is the only thing that pushes the brake back over. Another floating feature is the "floating rotor" of the Pro Stop brake. The caliper is fixed, but the rotor slides laterally on plastic bushings. These also tend to rub.

C. Installing disc-brake caliper onto post mounts

Manitou forks have post mounts, as do Trek and many other frames. But mounting post-mount brakes onto an adapter bracket for International Standard mounts — front or rear — follows the same procedure, once the bracket is bolted to the IS mounts. Hayes pioneered the post mount (Fig. 7.19), and Avid and some Magura brakes also bolt directly to them. Mounting any International Standard brake to post mounts is possible with an adapter.

The beauty of post mounts is that the brake can be moved laterally without needing to slip shims (thin washers) between the caliper and the mounts — as you need to with IS mounts. This advantage applies even if you are mounting an IS brake via an adapter to a post-mount frame or fork, or vice versa.

1. If you are using an IS brake with an adapter on a post-mount frame or fork, tighten the adapter to the caliper first.

2. Loosely bolt the post-mount caliper to the post mounts on the frame, fork (Fig. 7.19) or adapter (or, if you have an IS brake, loosely bolt its attached post-mount adapter onto the frame or fork post mounts). The caliper slot will be over the rotor, and the caliper will have some lateral freedom of movement.

3. Slip feeler gauge blades (Fig. 1.5) in between the rotor and the pad on either side. Start with around .015 inches in thickness. Business cards sometimes work instead.

4. Squeeze and hold the brake lever while tightening the mounting bolts.

5. Spin the wheel to check for brake rub. If you hear rub, peer through the gap between the rotor and the pads, using a white background for contrast, noting which pad (or worse, which side of the caliper slot) is rubbing. Loosen the bolts again, and slip a thicker feeler gauge between the rubbing pad and the rotor, and use a thinner one on the other side.

6. Repeat steps 4 and 5 until the rotor spins without rub. If desperate, just loosen the bolts, eyeball the gap, and tighten while holding the caliper; expect some frustration.

Note: Some mechanical disc brakes that work by flexing the rotor toward a fixed pad are adjusted by first turning screws on the pads until they pinch the rotor. On Avid, turn the large red screw on the wheel side until the fixed pad centers the rotor in the caliper slot. Then turn the red screw on the cable side (Fig. 7.19) until the rotor is pinched between the pads and centered in the slot. Tighten the mounting bolts and back off the fixed-pad (wheel-side) screw until the rotor spins freely. Now tighten the cable (see Chapter 2, Section II-14D), and back off on the red screws on either side a few clicks each to get the desired pad-to-rotor spacing. Note that Avids have convex and concave washers (Fig. 7.19) like on a V-brake pad to allow the brake to swing to compensate for misaligned mounts — make sure you retain the original order of these washers.

Similarly, the inboard (stationary) pad on hydraulic Magura Louise and mechanical Hayes, SRAM, Grimeca, and Formula brakes can be adjusted independently to get ideal pad-rotor spacing. On Hayes mechanical, squeeze the brake lever with the caliper loosely mounted over the rotor, shake the caliper into its favored position, and tighten the mounting bolts. Then turn the fixed pad adjuster counterclockwise one-eighth turn with a 4mm hex key to attain a pad-rotor spacing of 0.15 inches. The Magura Louise inboard pad is adjusted with a 5mm hex key until it just clears the rotor without rub. The entire caliper on SRAM, Grimeca, and Formula mechanical brakes can be moved laterally with a thumbscrew.

***Another note:** A bent rotor will rub or at least reduce pad adjustment range. Notice where it rubs on which pad, mark it with a felt pen, and carefully bend it into alignment with your fingers while it is still mounted on the hub.*

D. Hooking up cable-actuated disc brakes

Route the cable housing to the brake, following the procedures in Section VII-6 on cable installation. Zip-tie it down where there are no cable stops. Push the cable through the housing stop on the caliper, and tighten it under the cable anchor bolt.

Note: The above applies to cable-actuated mechanical disc brakes. There are still a few cable-actuated hydraulic disc brakes around, with which the cable is routed similarly but connected differently. RockShox, Amp and Hayes all had systems, but these are now so rare that I did not devote space to them here. Problems like overheating of the small volume of brake fluid inside were the demise of these systems.

E. Cutting hydraulic disc-brake hoses to length

 When you route the hose to the brake, make it curve smoothly without kinks, but also without large loops that can catch on things or with it so short that it is tight across spans where it is vulnerable. If your frame has snap-in disc brake hose guides, use those. Otherwise, tie it down to the frame or fork with zip-ties, tape, little guides that hold the hose and clip or screw into cable guides, or with adhesive-backed hose guides.

Don't expect aftermarket brake hoses to be the right length for your bike; you will likely need to cut them. Generally, there will be a brass ring around the end of the hose crushed by a threaded collar nut to seal against leaks (similar to Magura hydraulic rim brakes — see Fig. 7.43). This brass ring will need to be replaced after you cut the hose. Shimano does not allow cutting its hoses. You must order them to length.

1. Remove the wheel, so you don't accidentally get brake fluid on your disc.

2. At either the caliper or the lever, unscrew the collar nut holding the hose on. It is often covered by a plastic or rubber hose support, which you slide up the hose first.

3. Try gently pulling the hose straight off, but be very careful, because you can break the extension running up into the tube. Many brake fittings have a thin barbed tube extending up inside the hose and the brass ring. Since the ring is crushed on, it may be too tight to come off of the barbs. And if you bend at all while you pull the hose, you can break off the barbed fitting. Do this on a Hayes lever fitting, and you will be replacing the lever guts.

4. If the hose did not pull off easily, carefully cut the brass ring open with a hacksaw and peel it away from the hose.

5. Now pull the hose off and slide the hose support and nut up the hose beyond where you plan to cut.

6. Cut the hose to length with a sharp knife, making a clean, perpendicular cut. If you are careful to keep a "dome" of fluid on the end of the hose and keep it tipped up during the cutting process, it may be possible to avoid the entry of air and allow you to skip the bleeding step.

7. Install the new brass ring, and tighten the hose nut (maximum torque: 40 in-lbs). Slide the hose support back into place over the nut.

8. Install the wheel again, with the rotor between the pads.

9. Squeeze the lever. If the lever does not feel firm and the brake does not stop well, or the lever comes all of the way to the bar, there is air in the line, and you must bleed it (see Section VII-15).

F. Lever pull and pad spacing

Lever-pull and pad spacing are closely related, as the closer the pads are to the rotor, the less pull it

brakes

takes to stop. But they will rub if too close. Adjustments exist on some brakes and not on others.

Lever pull with cable-actuated brakes can be adjusted with the reach adjustment screw on the lever and the cable barrel adjuster, also on the lever (see Sections VIIA and VIIB for details).

Pad spacing, and hence lever pull, on mechanical disc brakes can be adjusted by knobs at the caliper. Pad spacing on Magura Louise hydraulic brakes can also be adjusted with a screw on the caliper.

Some hydraulic brakes have a lever-reach adjustment on the lever. Others have a screw on the lever that pushes the master-cylinder piston in further and reduces the amount of lever travel required. Still others have an adjustment on the master cylinder reservoir to adjust pad position (Hope has a knob on top of the reservoir that you can turn while riding). Coda hydraulic brakes have a knob on the lever resembling a barrel adjuster that adjusts pad spacing.

Sometimes the pads in Hayes hydraulic disc brakes can get pushed out too far, especially when dirty, since the only thing pulling the pistons back in is the reversal of a twist the pistons apply to square-cross-section seals surrounding them. You can pull out the pads, carefully push the pistons back in with the box end of a 10mm wrench and replace the pads.

VII-15: HYDRAULIC DISC BRAKE BLEEDING (OR FILLING)

The procedure for filling an empty system is the same as for bleeding.

IMPORTANT

With all brakes, remove the wheel, and remove the brake pads from the caliper (Section VII-16) to avoid ruining the pads by getting fluid on them.

IMPORTANT

Use the recommended brake fluid for your brake. Some systems use mineral oil, and some use brake fluid. If you put the wrong type of fluid in a brake, you will ruin the seals inside.

A. Brakes with a screw-on reservoir cover at the lever

When bleeding car brakes, you add extra fluid to the master cylinder (at the foot pedal) and squeeze it out through the wheel slave cylinders. Many bicycle disc brakes (Shimano and Magura, for instance) work the same way.

1. Turn the handlebar and the lever so the reservoir is level.

2. Remove the screws securing the lever reservoir cover, and pull off the cover and diaphragm.

3. Add fluid at the lever reservoir.

IMPORTANT

Shimano and Magura brake fluid is mineral oil — make sure you add no automotive brake fluid! And use mineral oil for brakes, not from a pharmacy!

4. Put a hose on the caliper bleed fitting (Fig. 7.18) leading into a bottle and unscrew the bleed fitting one-eighth turn.

5. Squeeze the lever to push the air out, and tighten the fitting before releasing the lever.

6. Repeat steps 3–5 until clean, bubble-free fluid is coming out of the hose into the catch bottle.

7. Install the pads (Section VII-16) and wheel, and squeeze the lever. It should feel firm and not come back to the grip. Repeat bleed if it feels spongy.

8. Refill the reservoir.

9. Put fluid on the diaphragm, flip it and the cover over and into place. Replace the cover screws.

7.20 catching fluid bled from a Hayes brake

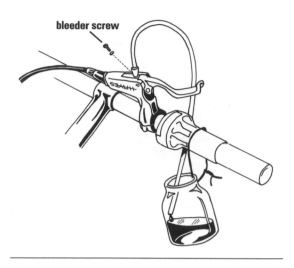

bleeder screw

B. Bleeding Hayes hydraulic disc brakes

Hayes brakes have an expandable reservoir inside the lever, like the plastic sack in a baby bottle. Consequently, they are bled differently than brakes with a fixed-size reservoir, namely, from the bottom.

1. Mount the bike in a stand, turn the handlebar, and rotate the lever on the bar such that the lever is the highest point in the system. Turn the lever until the face of the little bleed screw on the lever points straight up (Fig. 7.20).

2. Stick a clear tube onto the tip of a squeeze bottle of brake fluid, and slip the other end over the bleed fitting (Fig. 7.22) on the caliper.

IMPORTANT

Hayes uses DOT 4 or DOT 3 automotive brake fluid. Make sure you add no mineral oil! And watch out, because automotive brake fluid is corrosive and will remove paint.

3. The brake should have come with a second short clear tube with a plastic fitting on it. Stick the fitting into the bleed hole on the lever after removing the small screw covering it. Hang an old plastic bottle from the bar with wire or a twist-tie, and direct the other end of the tube into it (Fig. 7.20).

4. Before opening the bleed fitting at the caliper, squeeze the fluid bottle repeatedly until any air bubbles in the tube come back into the bottle. The bottle should be pointed straight down.

5. Loosen the fitting on the caliper, and squeeze new fluid in for a count of five. Let off for three counts to draw air out of the caliper and up into the tube and the squeeze bottle. Squeeze for five, let off for three, etc., until no more bubbles come out of the caliper.

6. Squeeze firmly on the bottle until clean fluid without bubbles comes out of the tube at the lever. While still squeezing, close the caliper bleed valve.

7. Remove the tubes from the caliper and the lever and replace the lever bleed screw.

8. Install the pads (Section VII-16) and wheel, and squeeze the lever. It should feel firm and not come back to the grip. Repeat bleed if it feels spongy.

9. With rubbing alcohol, clean the rotor and any paint on the frame that may have contacted brake fluid.

7.21 changing Hayes brake pads (the caliper is shown apart only for the purpose of this illustration — the pads clip in and out without dismantling the caliper)

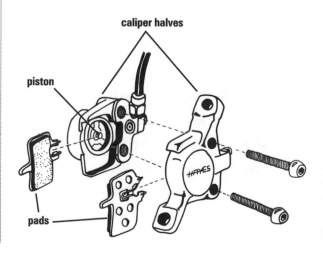

caliper halves

piston

pads

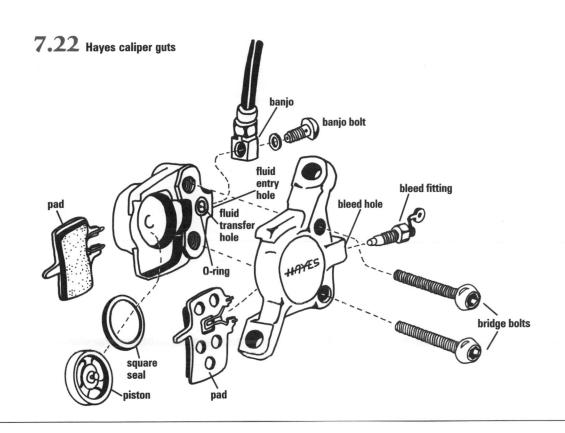

7.22 Hayes caliper guts

banjo

banjo bolt

bleed fitting

fluid
entry
hole

bleed hole

pad

fluid
transfer
hole

O-ring

HAYES

bridge bolts

square
seal

piston

pad

VII-16: DISC BRAKE PAD REPLACEMENT

Most disc brakes have pads that pop in and out easily. The wheel must be off. Usually you grab a tab on the pad with your fingers or needle-nose pliers and pull it toward the center of the caliper slot and out (Fig. 7.21). The pads are constrained by the caliper body, and they may snap into the caliper or onto a nub on the piston with prongs, a wire catch (as on Hayes, Fig. 7.21) and/or magnetically. Some pads (hydraulic Shimano, SRAM, some Grimeca) require that you remove a cotter pin or bolt before the pads will come out (Fig. 7.18).

Check for pad wear, scoring or glazing — anything that could damage the rotor or endanger braking effectiveness.

Replace the pads the way they came out, noting that the left and right pads may differ; it should be obvious if you try to put it in the wrong side. If you reverse the pads, they will not engage because the

piston is usually offset from the center of the cutaway for the pad.

The pads on Shimano, Grimeca and SRAM four-piston hydraulic disc brakes are more complicated to remove and install. All three of these brakes are almost identical and look like Fig. 7.18. You have to remove the pin or bolt on top that holds the pads in; it unscrews on Shimano, while on Grimeca and SRAM you need to pry the circlip off the end and pull it out. There is then a little spring-steel piece that pushes the pads apart that you must pull out with the pads and replace between the new pads.

VII-17: OVERHAULING DISC BRAKES

Eventually, the caliper will need to be overhauled. Obviously, it is different with a mechanical brake and a hydraulic one. (And again, for reasons mentioned under VII-14D, cable-actuated hydraulic disc brakes are not included.)

On many brakes, this is relatively simple, but it normally does require an air compressor.

A. Overhauling hydraulic disc brakes

Regular bleeding cleans dirt out of the system and lengthens the time periods between overhauls. Buy a new set of seals for whichever part of your brake you are overhauling before you start. A speck of dirt or hair in a hydraulic disc brake can cause a leak, so work in a clean area with clean methods.

Caliper (a.k.a. slave cylinder)

1. Remove the caliper from the bike.

2. Disconnect the hose. If there is nothing wrong with the hose or its fittings, you want to save yourself the effort of replacing the brass ring seal on the hose (see Section VII-14E). Some brakes have a fitting screwed into the caliper with a hollow bolt to which the hose nut is attached. This is called a "banjo" (Figs. 7.18 and 7.22) because the head of it looks like a . . . you guessed it. If yours has a banjo, unscrew it, but don't disconnect the hose from the banjo.

3. Remove the bridge bolts holding the caliper clamshell halves together and pull the brake apart.

4. Remove the piston(s). This often requires blowing compressed air into the fluid-transfer hole while plugging the bleed hole, or fluid-entry hole (Fig. 7.22), with your finger. Be careful to not get hit with fluid or parts. Wear safety glasses and cover the piston with your hand so that no springs or other parts fly away.

5. You will often find that there are few parts inside — usually just a couple of pistons and a few seals (Fig. 7.22) and sometimes some return springs. Use a fingernail or a plastic or wooden implement to dig out the piston seals to avoid scratching the cylinder.

6. Clean all parts carefully with isopropyl alcohol, and wipe off the residue.

7. With compressed air, blow out the caliper seal grooves, the bleeder hole and the hole that transfers fluid from one side of the caliper to the other. Wear safety glasses. Check that the seal grooves are completely clean.

8. Lubricate the new seals with the brake fluid recommended for the brake, and put all of the parts back together the way you found them.

9. Bolt the caliper together to the recommended torque. Check Appendix E.

10. Reinstall the hose.

11. Install and center the caliper (Section VII-14B or 14C).

12. Bleed the system (Section VII-15).

Lever (a.k.a. "master cylinder")

Levers rarely need to be overhauled if you bleed your brakes regularly and don't break any fittings on the lever in the process. They are high above the dirt and grime, so any dirt getting into the piston has to travel up from the caliper, which ain't easy.

Generally, you need to remove the lever from the handlebar, disconnect the hose, and remove the lever from the housing. Just keep unscrewing things until it comes apart, noting their order. On some brakes (Hayes, for instance), the cylinder is separate from the lever body, rather than being machined into it. You remove the cylinder assembly, and it is a cartridge that you replace as a unit; you do not take out the little piston and seals.

Clean up and inspect all of the parts, replace any worn ones, and put it back together. Install the lever, mount onto the handlebar, connect the hose, and bleed the system (Section VII-15).

B. Overhauling mechanical disc brakes

Mechanical disc brakes (Fig. 7.19) usually rely on a number of ball bearings rolling in a nautilus-shaped track. Methods to disassemble them vary, and the how-to is usually not in their accompanying instruction manual. But as long as you are careful and you keep the parts in order and don't lose any, it is not particularly complicated to take one apart and put it back together.

Remove the pads, after which the pistons will usually come out one at a time through the rotor slot. If you can do it this way, you can avoid taking the entire brake apart, which is fine, as the pistons are probably all you need to clean anyway. For example, on Avid, to get out either piston, you turn its red plastic screw (Fig. 7.19) clockwise until it pops out. The wheel-side piston is simple threaded on the outside and has a flat rectangular bar sticking out from its back to engage the plastic knurled disc. Once this piston is out, you can snap out the red knob — it just pops in and out with little prongs to hold it. After cleaning the inboard piston and its threaded receptacle, you grease the threads and put it and the red knob back (don't grease the knob). The outboard piston has a rod sticking straight out from its back. A ring of spring steel around it holds it into a hole in the drive mechanism. Don't grease any part of this piston; it doesn't need it, and it will only attract dirt. The pistons are magnetic, so expect a bit of a hassle getting them lined up and back in, since one piston will be attracted by the other one. You can drive in the outboard piston with the inboard piston (turn the red knob). Installing the pads and a spacer in between may help.

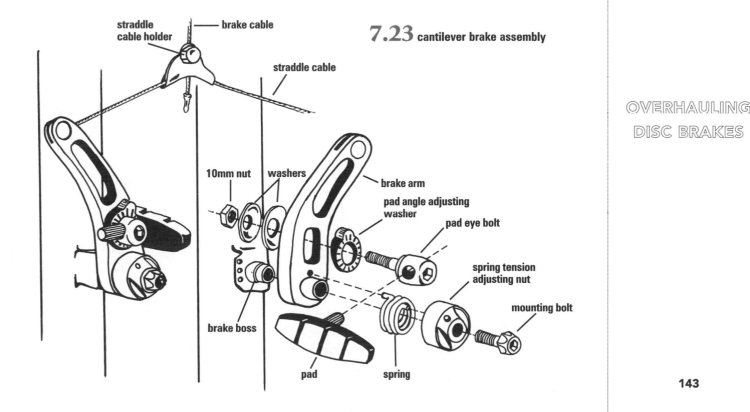

7.23 cantilever brake assembly

straddle cable holder — brake cable

straddle cable

10mm nut   washers

brake arm

pad angle adjusting washer

pad eye bolt

spring tension adjusting nut

mounting bolt

brake boss

pad   spring

If you want to get at the ball-bearing mechanism, you start by unbolting the arm. Simply clean and grease everything and put it back in the way you found it. Be careful, but don't be intimidated.

VII.C3: Cantilever Brakes

VII-18: INSTALLATION

1. Grease the brake bosses (Fig. 7.23). Avoid getting grease inside the brake boss or on the bolt threads; they are treated with thread-lock goop to prevent them from vibrating loose.

2. If you have the installation directions that came with your brakes, follow them. If not, follow the general installation instructions below.

3. Make sure you install the brakes with all of the parts in the order in which they were packaged together. In particular, the springs will often be of different colors not interchangeable from left to right.

4. If the brake has a separate inner sleeve bushing to fit over the cantilever boss, install that first. Slip the brake and return spring over it.

5. Determine what sort of return system your brakes use. If the brake arms have no spring-tension adjustment, or a setscrew on the side of one of the arms for adjusting spring tension, go to step 6. Such brakes use the hole in the cantilever boss to anchor the bottom end of the spring. If the brake arms have a large nut surrounding the mounting bolt for adjusting spring tension behind the brake arm or in front of it (Fig. 7.23), skip to step 8. These brakes do not use the hole in the cantilever boss as a spring anchor.

6. Slip the brake onto the boss, inserting the lower end of the spring into the hole in the cantilever boss (if the boss has three holes, try the center hole first; use a higher hole to make the brake

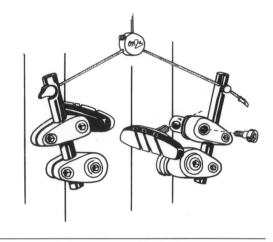

7.24 cylindrical clamp cantilever brake (OnZa)

7.25 threaded post cantilever brake

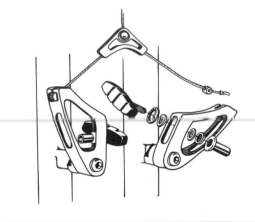

snappier, a necessity with lower-quality or old brakes). You also want to make sure that the top end of the spring is inserted into its hole in the brake arm as well.

7. Install and tighten the mounting bolt into the cantilever boss. Skip the next three steps.

8. Slip the brake (with any included bushings) onto the cantilever boss.

9. Install the spring so that one end inserts into the hole in the brake arm and the other inserts into the hole in the adjusting nut.

10. Install and tighten the mounting bolt while holding the adjusting nut with the appropriate

7.26 distance of pad to fixing bolt (a) and angle against rim (c)

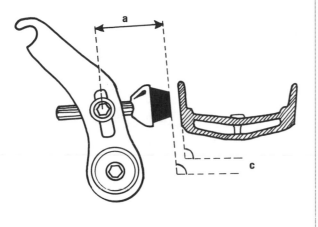

7.27 up and down (b) and twist (d)

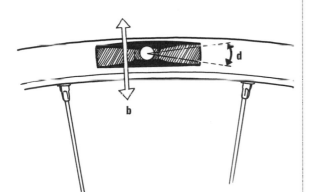

7.28 brake pad toe-in (e)

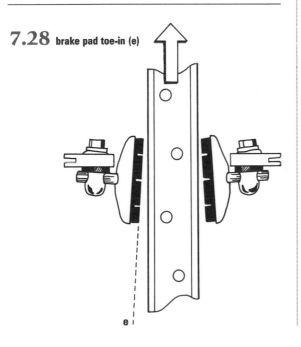

open-end wrench (usually 15mm) so that the pad is touching the rim. This facilitates pad adjustment later.

VII-19: PAD REPLACEMENT AND INSTALLATION

1. Remove the old pad, if applicable.

2. Install the new pad. Most cantilevers rely on an eye bolt with an enlarged head and a hole through it to accept the pad post (Fig. 7.23). Some cantilevers (Avid and OnZa, for example), have a slotted clamp with a hole for the pad post (Fig. 7.24). A few cantis use a threaded pad post that passes through a slot in the brake arm (Fig. 7.25).

3. If your brake spring can be adjusted so that it holds the pad against the rim, set it up that way now. It will make the pad adjustments much easier. If not, you will have to push each arm toward the rim as you adjust the pad.

VII-20: PAD ADJUSTMENT

There are five separate adjustments (a through e in Figs. 7.26–7.28) that must be made for each pad. These adjustments are quite easy with some brakes and a real pain in the rear with others:

a. offset distance of the pad from the brake arm (extension of the pad post) (Fig. 7.26a);

b. vertical pad height (Fig. 7.27b);

c. pad swing in the vertical plane for mating with the rim's sidewall angle (Fig. 7.26c);

d. pad twist to align the length of the pad with the rim's curvature (Fig. 7.27d); and

e. pad swing in the horizontal plane to set toe-in (Fig. 7.28e).

Cantilevers that feature a cylindrical brake arm are by far the easiest to adjust (Fig. 7.24). Pad

VII

brakes

PAD
REPLACEMENT
AND
INSTALLATION
—
PAD
ADJUSTMENT

adjustment is simple because the pad is held to the cylinder with a clamp that offers almost full range of motion. Avid, OnZa, Gravity Research Pipe Dreams, and Dia-Compe VC900 all rely on this type of system. Other cantilevers employ a single pad eye bolt to hold all five adjustments (the eye bolt and washers are exploded in Fig 7.23 and are seen from above in Fig. 7.28). It requires a bit of manual dexterity to hold all five adjustments simultaneously while tightening the bolt.

With all types of cantilevers:

1. Loosen the pad-clamping bolt, lubricate the pad-fixing threads, and set the pad offset, (a, Fig. 7.26), by sliding the post in or out of the clamping hole. The farther the pad is extended away from the brake arm, the greater the angle of the brake arm will be from the plane of the wheel. A benefit of this is that leverage is increased (see straddle cable angle in Figs. 7.31 and 7.32). Drawbacks are: The brake feels less firm, since less lever pull force is required; and clearance between the rider's heel and the rear brake arms is reduced, particularly for small frames. A good initial position is with the post clamped in the center of its length.

7.29 curved-face cantilever brake (Ritchey)

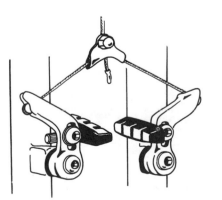

7.30 ball joint cantilever brake (Campagnolo)

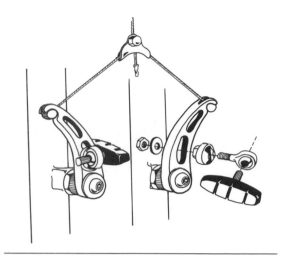

Note: With threaded-post pads (Fig. 7.25), placing spacers between the brake arm and the pad sets pad offset. Lube the pad threads.

2. Roughly adjust the vertical pad height (b, Fig. 7.27), by sliding the pad clamping mechanism up and down in the brake arm slot. With cylindrical-clamp brakes, loosen the bolt clamping the pad holder to the brake arm, and snug the bolt back up, once the rough adjustment is reached. With all other types, leave the pad bolt just loose enough so that you can move the pad easily, and continue.

3. Adjust pad swing in the vertical plane (c, Fig. 7.26), so that the face of the pad meets the rim flat with its top edge 1–2mm below the top of the rim. Fine-tune this adjustment by simultaneously sliding the pad up or down.

4. Adjust the pad twist (d, Fig. 7.27), so that the top edge of the pad is parallel to the top of the rim. Modern pads are quite long and require precision with this adjustment. With cylindrical-clamp brakes, the pad-securing bolt may now be tightened.

5. Finally, adjust the pad toe-in (e, Fig. 7.28). The pad should either be adjusted flat to the rim, or toed-in so that, when the forward end of the

pad touches the rim, the rear end of it is 1mm to 2mm away from the rim.

If the pad is toed-out, the heel of it will catch and tend to chatter, making an obnoxious squealing noise. If the brake arms are not stiff, or they fit loosely on the cantilever boss, the same thing will happen when flat; toe-in is a must and will have to be adjusted frequently as the pads wear to keep them quiet.

On cylindrical-arm brakes with two fixing bolts (Fig. 7.24), the toe-in is adjusted by again loosening the bolt that holds the vertical height adjustment of the pad. Because you have already tightened the other bolt that holds the pad in place, you simply loosen this second bolt and swing the pad horizontally until you arrive at your preferred toe-in or flatness setting. Tighten the bolt again, and you are done with pad adjustment.

With any brake using a single bolt to hold the pad as well as control its rotation, you now have a tricky task of holding all of the adjustments you have made and simultaneously tightening the nut. Most eye-bolt systems are tightened with a 10mm wrench on the nut on the back of the brake while the front is held with a 5mm Allen wrench. Help from someone else to either hold or tighten is useful here. Probably the trickiest brake to adjust has a big toothed or notched washer between the head of the eye bolt and a flat brake arm (Fig. 7.23). The adjusting washer is thinner on one edge than the other, so rotating it (by means of the tooth or notch) toes the pad in or out. With this type, you must hold all of the pad adjustments as you turn this washer, and then keep it and the pad in place as you tighten the nut. It's not an easy job, and the adjustment changes as you tighten the bolt.

The other common type has a convex or concave

shape to the slotted brake arm, and cupped washers separate the eye-bolt head and nut from the brake arm (Shimano, most Dia-Compe, Ritchey [Fig. 7.29], Paul, etc.). The concave/convex surfaces allow the pad to swivel, and tightening the bolt secures everything. Again, you may not get it on the first try. Threaded posts also employ such washers.

Note: Some of these curved-face brakes do not hold their toe-in adjustment well; you may need to sand the brake arm faces and washers to create more friction between them.

Brakes with a cylindrical arm and a clamp secured only by the pad eye bolt (WTB, SRP, etc.) are adjusted functionally the same as the curved-face ones with cupped washers.

A rare, but simple-to-adjust type has a ball joint at each pad eye bolt (Campagnolo, Fig. 7.30).

VII-21: STRADDLE CABLE ADJUSTMENT

The straddle cable should be set so that it pulls on the brake arms in such a way as to provide optimal braking. This is not always the adjustment that produces the highest leverage, for sometimes brake feel (i.e., modulation of braking) is improved when leverage is reduced. In general, I recommend setting it for high leverage and reducing it from there to improve modulation

With any lever arm, the mechanical advantage is highest when the force is applied at right angles to the lever arm. For general purposes, set the straddle cable so that it pulls as close to 90 degrees to the brake arm as you can (Fig. 7.31). An esoteric and more precise argument is that, once the pad hits the rim, the actual lever arm is the line from the face of the pad to the cable attachment point on top of the arm (since the pad, not the brake boss,

7.31 cable angle when open

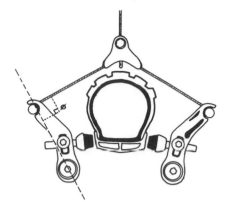

7.32 cable angle when closed

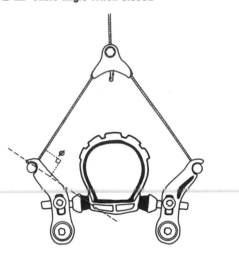

now becomes the fulcrum). If you set the straddle cable at 90 degrees from *this* line, the leverage is maximized (Fig. 7.32).

With low-profile brake arms, a 90-degree straddle cable angle results in a short straddle cable set very low and close to the tire. Make sure that you allow at least an inch of clearance over the tire to prevent mud or a bulge in the tire from engaging the brake.

The straddle cable usually has a metal blob on one end, and the other end is clamped to one brake arm by an anchor bolt (Figs. 7.33–7.35). The blob fits into the slotted brake arm and acts as a quick release for the brake.

With Shimano cantilevers built since 1988, the

brake cable connects directly to the cable clamp on one brake arm, and a link wire hooks to the other arm. On post-1993 Shimano cantilevers, the cable passes through a link-wire holder holding not only a link wire but also a fixed length of cable housing (Fig. 7.35). The brake cable passes directly through the link-wire holder and housing segment to the cable clamp on the brake arm. The mechanic has no choice of straddle cable settings; it is predetermined.

Between 1988 and 1993, Shimano brakes did not have the housing segment on the link wire holder; the holder was instead clamped to the brake cable, and its position was set by a plastic gauge. If you have this type and no gauge, simply set the cable length from link wire holder to brake arm the same on both sides.

Some brakes do not have a cable clamp on either brake arm; both arms are slotted to accept the blob on the end of a straddle cable or link wire. In this case, a small cylindrical clamp forms a second blob on the end of the straddle cable (Fig. 7.34), or a link wire holder that holds two separate link wires is used.

With any straddle cable, after setting its length, the straddle cable holder position is set by loosening the bolt or setscrews that hold it onto the end of the brake cable and sliding it up on the brake cable. Tighten it in place (Fig. 7.6). It is set properly when the brake engages quickly, and the lever cannot be pulled closer than a finger's width from the bar. Some cable slack can be taken up with the barrel adjuster on the brake lever.

The lateral position of the straddle cable holder can be changed with setscrews as well. The holder should generally be centered on the straddle cable, but, sometimes, the brake cable pulls asymmetrically as it comes around the seat tube. In these

7.33–7.35 straddle cables

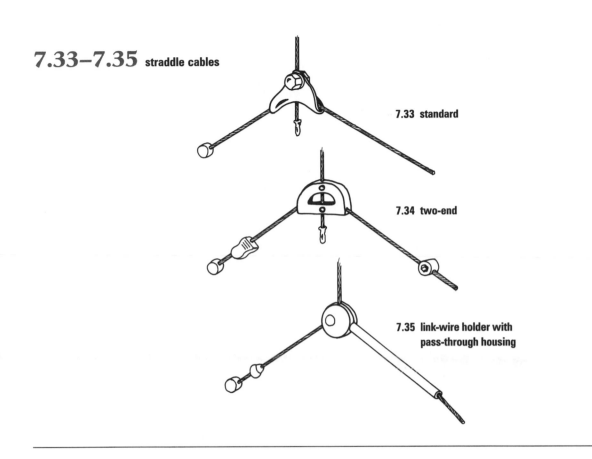

7.33 standard

7.34 two-end

7.35 link-wire holder with pass-through housing

brakes

cases, the straddle cable holder may need to be off-set for the brakes to work (Fig. 7.36).

7.36 an offset straddle cable stop requires an offset straddle hanger

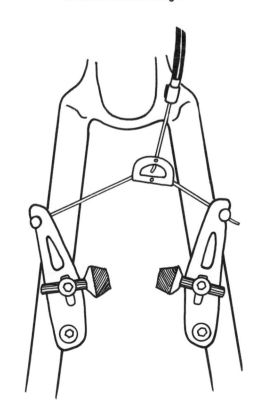

VII-22: SPRING TENSION ADJUSTMENT

The spring tension adjustment centers the brake pads about the rim and also determines the return spring force. There is only one adjustment to make on brakes with a single set screw on the side of one brake arm. Turn the screw until the brakes are centered and the pads hit the rim simultaneously when applied (Fig. 7.37). Higher spring tensions can be achieved by moving the spring to a higher hole in the brake boss.

Some brakes rely on large tensioning nuts surrounding the mounting bolt and do not use the holes in the brake bosses as anchors (Fig. 7.23). On these, the tensioning nuts may be turned on both arms to get the combination of return force and centering you prefer. You must loosen the

7.37 adjusting return spring tension with a setscrew

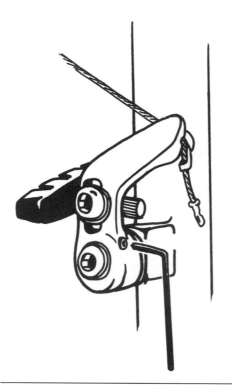

7.38 adjusting return spring tension with tensioning nut

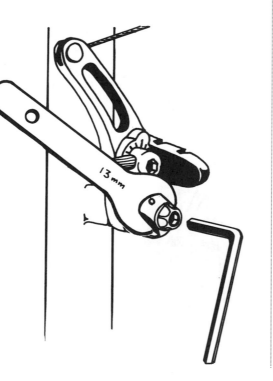

mounting bolt while holding the tensioning nut with a wrench. Turn the nut to the desired tension, and, while holding it in place with the wrench, tighten the mounting bolt again (Fig. 7.38).

On really old brakes without a tension adjustment, centering is accomplished by removing the brake arm and moving the spring to another hole on the boss. It is a rough adjustment at best, and some bosses do not have more than a single hole. When this adjustment fails, you can twist the arm on the boss to tighten or loosen the spring a bit. That, of course, is an even rougher adjustment.

Note: If the brake arms do not rotate easily on the brake post, there is too much friction. Remove the brake and check that the post is not bent or split, in which case a new one needs to be screwed in or welded on. If not bent, the post is probably too fat to slide freely inside the brake arm, either due to paint on it or bulging or mushrooming of the post due to overtightening of the brake mounting bolt. In this case, if it's the replaceable type, screw a new post into the frame or fork. Otherwise, file and sand the circumference of the post to reduce its diameter. File and sand uniformly, only a little at a time; avoid making it too thin.

VII-23: CANTILEVER LUBRICATION/SERVICE

The only lubrication necessary on cantilever brakes is on the cables, levers and brake arms. This should be performed whenever braking feels sticky. Lever and cable lubrication is covered in Section VII-5. Cantilevers can be lubricated by removing them, cleaning and greasing the pivots and replacing them.

VII.C4: Hydraulic Rim Brakes

This refers to brakes that are fully hydraulic and are mounted on the cantilever bosses. The most

7.39 Magura hydraulic brake

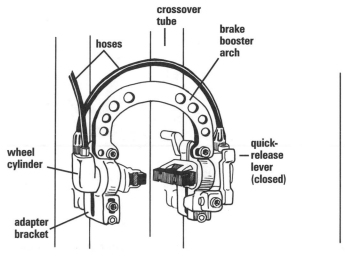

crossover tube

hoses

brake booster arch

wheel cylinder

quick-release lever (closed)

adapter bracket

7.40 Magura brake pad installation and quick-release operation

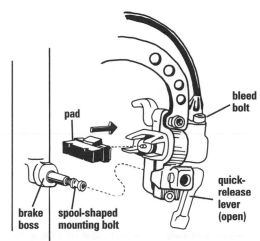

bleed bolt

pad

quick-release lever (open)

brake boss

spool-shaped mounting bolt

brakes

common type is Magura (Fig. 7.39), and these instructions, while possibly applicable to others, focus on Maguras. I cover it in detail, because the Magura owner's manual is an inscrutable translation from German.

The advantages to the Magura brake, in addition to its great stopping power, are that it is practically maintenance free and simple to adjust. The system is completely sealed from dirt, and there are no cables and housings to wear. Pads are replaced simply by pulling them out by hand and pushing new ones in. A screw on the lever adjusts pad-to-rim spacing as easily as turning a barrel adjuster on a cable-actuating lever.

A hydraulic brake works like a car brake in that pressure on brake fluid inside hydraulic tubes transmits the braking force from the lever to the wheel.

Note: The "master cylinder" is the hydraulic cylinder inside the lever, and each "slave cylinder" (or "wheel cylinder") is the cylinder driving each brake pad (one cylinder for each pad).

VII-24: MOUNTING MAGURA BRAKE LEVERS

Hydraulic levers are installed onto the bars with a 4mm or 5mm Allen wrench, as with cable-actuating levers.

VII-25: INSTALLATION AND ADJUSTMENT OF MAGURA BRAKE CALIPERS ONTO CANTILEVER BRAKE BOSSES

1. Snap a C-shaped plastic ring around each slave (wheel) cylinder.

2. Assemble the adapter brackets around the plastic ring on each wheel cylinder with the supplied 4mm bolts, installing the L-shaped elbow behind the top bracket hole (Fig. 7.41). Right and left wheel cylinders are normally determined by orienting the crossover tube connecting the cylinders toward the bike (Fig. 7.39), i.e., the tube from the lever, as well as the bleed hole to the outside.

Note: The adapter brackets (Fig. 7.39) are asymmetrical and can be reversed from left to right to move the slave cylinder closer to the rim or vice versa. Normal mounting is with the bracket imprinted with "Magura" on the right when facing the brake.

3. Slide the included D-shaped washer onto the boss with the flat side of the washer up. A thick washer with a setscrew must be used with some suspension forks to clear the fork brace.

4. Bolt the adapter bracket to the cantilever boss with a bolt and washer. If mounting a bracket with the quick-release feature, first screw the mounting bolt with the spool-shaped head a few turns into the brake boss. Slide the quick-release unit over the mounting slot on the adapter bracket (Fig. 7.40). Push the bracket onto the brake boss so the spool-shaped mounting bolt head comes through the hole in the quick-release unit. Flip the quick-release lever up to its closed position. Tighten the mounting bolt with a 5mm Allen key. You can now remove this side of the brake by merely flipping the quick-release lever down and pulling the bracket straight off (Fig. 7.40). To install, push the bracket onto the boss so the bolt head sticks out through the hole in the quick-release unit, and flip the lever up.

5. Set the pad position: Sliding the adapter bracket up and down adjusts the height of the wheel cylinder. Loosening the mounting bolt and the two bolts holding the bracket together allows the cylinder to be slid in or out and rotated. Using these adjustments in tandem, set the pad-to-rim contact so that the pad hits the rim flat, about 2mm below its upper edge. See to it that the pad holders do not drag on the tire. When retracted, the pads should sit 2–3mm away from the rim.

6. Once the brake is set to the proper position, the elbows need to be positioned (Fig. 7.41) to support the brake and simplify repositioning after

7.41 installing and/or adjusting elbow

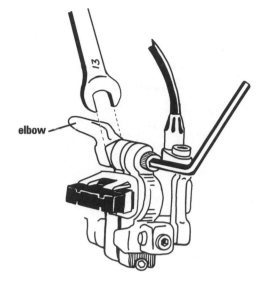

elbow

removal. Loosen the bolt above the wheel cylinder. With a 13mm open-end wrench, rotate the elbow until it contacts the inner side of the seatstay or fork leg, and tighten the bolt (Fig. 7.41). After-market elbows are available to fit certain suspension forks better.

7. If you have the "Brake Booster" arch (Fig. 7.39), loosely bolt it onto the right bracket adapter through its oval mounting hole on the right side. Swing the arch over the wheel and slide it laterally until the booster's bottom left hole lines up with and slips over the bolt head on the left bracket. Tighten the top bolt on the right bracket to fix the booster in place. When releasing the brake, pull the left side of the booster off of the bolt head, and leave it attached to the right cylinder when pulling it off.

8. To fine-tune pad-to-rim spacing, especially as the pads wear, tighten the adjustment screw on the lever. Some systems take a 2mm Allen key; the screw is under the lever. Newer systems have a finger-operated knob on the front of the lever.

VII-26: MAGURA HOSE ROUTING

The hoses cannot go through cable stops, so you secure them to the frame by means of plastic draw ties or with little plastic or aluminum clips that snap over the tube and press or bolt into the frame's cable guides. Make sure there are no kinks in the hoses and that they do not stick out from the bike enough to hit your legs or hook on obstacles. Damaging hoses is to be avoided, as braking goes away if they are punctured.

Unless your frame is very small or very large, you may be able to get away with simply attaching the brakes to the frame as they come out of the box, already filled and bled, saving yourself the time and effort of bleeding the brakes. Skip to Section VII-29 if you are adjusting the hose length.

VII-27: MAGURA PAD REPLACEMENT

Pad replacement is very simple.

1. Once the wheel is off, grab the pad and pull it straight out (Fig. 7.40).

2. Push the new pad in, paying attention to the rotation-indicator arrow on it. That's it!

VII-28: BLEEDING MAGURAS

Sponginess of brakes indicates the need for bleeding air from the lines. Bleeding is a maintenance operation that also clears out dirt that has crept in and should be done every 500 miles or so. If the oil inside comes out clean, you will know you can wait longer next time. There is rarely a need to bleed due to air bubbles, because air does not get in unless the system is opened or gets damaged.

The air bubbles will rise toward the highest point in the system, so they should be up in the

7.42 bleeding and/or filling Magura brake lines

lever after any ride, meaning that it will not take much new fluid to drive them out.

1. Back up the 2mm micro-adjustment screw under the lever and the 2mm reach-adjustment screw on top of the lever, or, on newer models, back up the single knob on the front of the lever.

2. Keeping the bleed bolt at the lever closed, remove the bleed bolt (Fig. 7.40) on the right brake slave cylinder.

IMPORTANT

Never squeeze the lever while the system is open; fluid will squirt out.

3. The Magura syringe has a tube with a barbed fitting on the end (Fig. 7.42). Fill the syringe with Magura brake fluid or low-viscosity mineral oil (never with automotive brake fluid), invert it, and push any air up and out with the plunger. Screw the fitting into the bleed hole on the wheel cylinder (Fig. 7.42). (In a pinch, a squirt bottle of fluid can be used instead of the syringe, but it is easy to allow air in this way. You will need another person to hold the bottle tip tightly into the bleed hole and squeeze the bottle while you open and close the lever bleed bolt.)

VII

brakes

MAGURA
HYDRAULIC
BRAKES

153

7.43 installing hydraulic brake hose

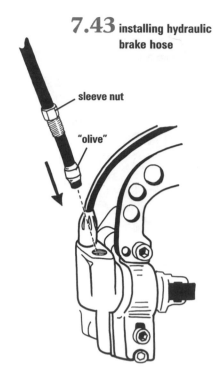

sleeve nut

"olive"

4. Tip the bike or rotate the lever on the bar so the lever bleed bolt is at its highest point, and remove the bolt from the lever.

5. Push fluid into the brake wheel cylinder with the syringe (Fig. 7.42). Let it push fluid out of the lever.

Note: A cleaner way to do this is to screw in a piece of tubing with a barbed fitting into the lever bleed hole. Have the tube drain into a bottle of fluid hanging from the bar (Fig.7.20).

6. While the fluid is still flowing, reinstall the bleed bolt at the lever and tighten it. Make sure the bolt and washer are free of grit.

7. Remove the syringe or bottle from the wheel cylinder, leaving a dome of fluid bulging from the hole. Put the bolt back in, and tighten it; again, the bolt and washer must be free of grit.

If the bubbles have all been driven out, the brake will no longer feel spongy. Repeat until it is right. You may need to bleed it again after riding;

the bubbles will have collected at the lever.

8. Adjust the pad spacing and lever reach as you wish with the two 2mm bolts or the single knob on the lever.

VII-29: CUTTING MAGURA HYDRAULIC BRAKE TUBES

1. Pull the plastic cover off of the crossover tube sleeve nut and slide it up the tube to get it out of the way. Unscrew the main tube sleeve nut with an 8mm wrench and pull the tube out (Fig. 7.43).

IMPORTANT

Again, never squeeze the brake lever while the system is open.

2. Cut the hose to length with a sharp blade, making sure it is a perpendicular cut. For every end you cut, you must have a brass "olive" fitting from Magura (Fig. 7.43); get them in advance.

3. Slide the 8mm sleeve nut up the tube.

4. Slide the brass olive on, with the step-cut end toward the sleeve nut.

5. Stick the hose into the brake cylinder hole (Fig. 7.43), and screw in the sleeve nut by hand. Tighten

7.44 linkage brake

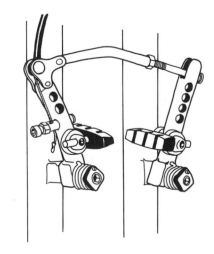

7.45 U-brake (under chainstays)

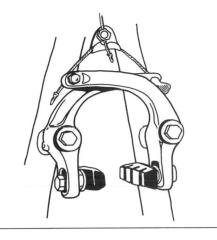

the nut with an 8mm wrench. Push the plastic cover back onto the crossover tube sleeve nut.

6. If shortening the tubing, bleeding may not be necessary unless the brakes feel spongy. (If you cut the tube while holding it pointed up and drip a dome of oil into the tube hole, you can reduce the chances of air getting in.)

If installing new tubing, make the connection at the brake lever the same way. Fill and bleed the line following the bleeding instructions in Section VII-28.

VII.C5: Linkage Brakes

There are so many vastly different linkage brakes (Fig. 7.44) besides V-brakes floating around on older bikes that it would not be possible to include them all in detail here. Linkage brakes are often quite similar to cantilevers or V-brakes and are adjusted, centered and mounted in much the same way.

If in doubt, refer to specific instructions from the manufacturer.

VII.C6: U-Brakes

VII-30: U-BRAKE INSTALLATION

U-brakes (Fig. 7.45) mount on the same bosses that roller-cams do. They *cannot* be mounted on

cantilever bosses, which would be too low.

1. Grease the pivots.

2. Slide the arms onto the pivots.

3. Screw in the mounting bolts.

4. Attach the straddle cable yoke to the brake cable.

5. Attach the straddle cable to the cable clamp on one arm.

6. An easy way to set the position of the straddle cable yoke on a chainstay-mounted U-brake is to squeeze the lever to the grip after slipping the yoke up against the bottom bracket cable guide. Then tighten it in place. This is the highest it could be set on the cable and allows the longest possible straddle cable.

VII-31: U-BRAKE ADJUSTMENT

1. Set the rear straddle cable yoke position on the brake cable as outlined above. On a front brake, set it about 2 inches above the brake.

2. Tighten the straddle cable while pulling it tight with a pair of pliers and squeezing the pads against the rim with your hand. Make sure you have tightened the anchor bolts enough that the cables do not slip.

3. Check that you cannot pull the lever closer than a finger's width from the grip. Tension the cable as needed with the straddle cable yoke or the lever barrel adjuster.

4. Set the spring tension by releasing the straddle cable, loosening the mounting bolt and swinging the pad away from the rim; then tighten the mounting bolt. Center the brake by setting the spring tension on one arm first, followed by the other arm in the same fashion. If your brake has a small Allen set screw on the side of one arm, use it to make fine spring tension adjustments.

VII-32: U-BRAKE PAD REPLACEMENT
AND POSITIONING

U-brakes rely on brake pads with threaded posts. Install them with the original spacers in their original orientation. The pads should hit the center of the braking surface and should have a small amount of toe-in. There is no adjustment for spacing from the brake arm. Hold the pad in place with your hand while tightening the nut with a wrench. As the pads wear, they tend to slide up on the rim and hit the tire, so check this adjustment frequently. You should also regularly clear hardened mud from inside of the brake arms; it can build up here on U-brakes and abrade the tire sidewalls.

VII.C7: Roller-Cam Brakes

VII-33: ROLLER-CAM REMOVAL AND
INSTALLATION

Roller-cam brakes (Fig. 7.46) mount on U-brake bosses attached to the fork and either the chainstays or the seatstays. These are mounted further from the hub than cantilever bosses, and, like U-brakes, they will not work on standard cantilever bosses.

7.46 roller-cam brake

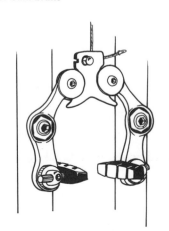

Roller-cams are removed by first pulling the cam plate out from between the rollers on the ends of the arms. Remove the mounting bolt and pull the arms off of the bosses.

Installation is performed in reverse. Grease the bosses and the inside of the pivots as well as the edges of the cam plate and the mounting bolts.

VII-34: ROLLER-CAM ADJUSTMENT

1. Check that the pulleys spin freely, and loosen them with a 5mm Allen wrench on the front and an open-end wrench on the back. The pulleys should rest on the narrow portion of the cam, which gives the greatest mechanical advantage when the brakes are applied. You change pad spacing by changing the location of the cam on the cable.

2. Use a 17mm wrench on the nut surrounding the mounting bolt to center the brake or to adjust spring tension. Loosen the mounting bolt, make small adjustments to the 17mm nut, and tighten the mounting bolt down again.

3. Once the adjustments are set, tighten the cam onto the cable so it will not slip.

VII-35: ROLLER-CAM PAD POSITIONING
AND REPLACEMENT

The pad eye bolt is held on the front with a 5mm Allen wrench. The bolt in the back is adjusted using a 10mm open wrench. The pads should be toed in slightly. As the pads wear, they tend to slide up the rim and rub the tire, so check this adjustment periodically.

BRAKE TROUBLESHOOTING

The first thing to check with any brake is that it stops the bike!

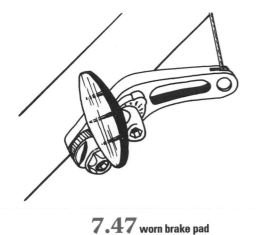

7.47 worn brake pad

7.48 cleaning dirt from brake pad

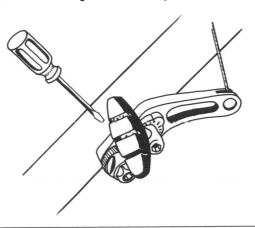

1. While the bike is stationary, pull each lever and see that it firmly engages the brake while the lever still is at least a finger's width away from the handlebar grip. If not, skip to Sections VII-2–VII-4 on cable tensioning (or to Sections VII-14–VII-15 for adjusting and bleeding hydraulic disc brakes or adjusting mechanical disc brakes, or Sections VII-25–VII-28 for adjusting and bleeding hydraulic rim brakes, if that is what you have).

2. Move at 10 mph or so, and apply each brake one at a time. By itself, the rear brake should be able to lock up the rear wheel and skid the tire, and the front brake alone should come on hard enough that it will cause the bike to pitch forward. Careful. Don't overdo it.

If you can't stop the bike quickly, you must make some adjustments and, perhaps, do a little cleaning. A brake works by forcing the brake pads into contact with the rim (or disc) to create friction. Anything that reduces the ability of these surfaces to generate friction against each other compromises braking. With this in mind, it should be obvious that these surfaces need to be clean and dry, that they should line up well with each other, and that the mechanism to pull them into contact

should move freely and pull at an angle that offers high mechanical advantage.

That said, you can probably generate the following brake inspection list to perform frequently:

1. Cable length: Check that the cable is short enough to pull the pads against the rims without the levers contacting the grips, and long enough to allow the wheels to turn without dragging on the pads when centered between them. See cable tensioning sections, VII-2–VII-4, to adjust.

2. Clean rims (or discs): Check for and remove any grease or glaze buildup on rims and pads. Grease can be removed with rags or a solvent, and lightly buffing nonceramic rim surfaces with sandpaper will remove glaze. Solvent residues on pads and rims cause brake squeal. You can remove such residues with soap and water. Disc-brake rotors and pads are cleaned with alcohol. You can also clean disc-brake pads with a file or by rubbing them together.

3. Pad wear: Check that the pads are not excessively worn (Fig. 7.47); if they have grooves, make sure these are not worn off. Make sure the pads contact the rims effectively (Figs. 7.14 and 7.26–7.28). Dig out any rocks or pieces of alu-

minum that are embedded in the pads to prevent rim damage (Fig. 7.48). Beware of lip formation on the top edge of the pad over the rim edge as the lower part of the pad wears away; this lip can prevent the pad from releasing from the rim. Replace or adjust pads as needed, and adjust the brake (refer to the section that applies to your brake) to get the desired response.

4. Cable wear: Check the cables for fraying, wear and free movement, and check that the angle the cable meets each cantilever brake arm is close to 90 degrees (pulling at right angles generates the most leverage [Figs. 7.31–7.32]). If replacing, see "Cable Installation," Section VII-6. Recognize that cables, housings and pads are maintenance items; replace them frequently with good quality ones. Even new, poor-quality pads can require more than twice as much distance to stop as good ones!

5. Centered brakes: Check that the brakes are centered (the pads are spaced equally from either side of the rim) and that they apply and return easily. Readjust as needed (see adjustment section for your brake).

6. Toe-in: If the brakes squeal, and the rims and pads are clean (steps 2 and 3, above), toe the pads in so that the forward corner of each pad touches the rim while the trailing corner is a millimeter or so away from it (Fig. 7.28.). See pad adjustment under your brake type. The flimsier the brake arms, or the looser they are on the brake bosses, the more toe-in that is required.

7. Brake boss flex: If the seatstays or the fork legs are too flexible, applying the brakes will bow them outward and decrease braking pressure. This can be counteracted by attaching a horseshoe-shaped "brake booster" connecting the brake mounting bolts and bridging over the tire. These boosters are available for V-brakes, cantilevers, hydraulic rim brakes (see Fig. 7.39), U-brakes, roller-cams, and other linkage brakes.

TROUBLE-
SHOOTING
BRAKES

cranks and bottom brackets

If you don't have time to do it right the first time, you must have time to do it over again.

—ANONYMOUS

The crank and bottom bracket is the power center for you and your bike. It is through this system that your energy is converted into forward movement of the bike. The crankset consists of the crankarms, bottom bracket, chainrings, chainring bolts and crank bolt (Fig. 8.1).

Any problem in the crankset can result in a large drop in available propulsion. The forces applied here are so large that expensive damage can easily be done if parts are not set up correctly. All parts need to be secured very tightly to oppose these large forces and prevent ruining expensive parts by using them when loose.

VIII.A: CRANKARMS AND CHAINRINGS

VIII-1: CRANK REMOVAL AND INSTALLATION

Depending on the type of crankset you are using, you will either need a socket wrench or a large Allen wrench in order to remove the crank bolt and a crank puller (Figs. 1.2 and 1.3) to take off the crankarms.

Most current crank bolts take either an 8mm Allen wrench or a 14mm socket wrench. Older systems may take a 15mm socket or a 7mm Allen, and you may still run across a few of those old French TA cranks with 16mm bolts.

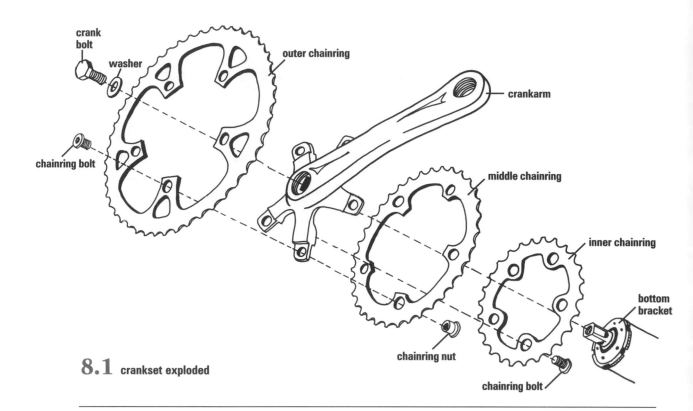

8.1 crankset exploded

A. Removal

1. Older cranksets have a dust cap covering the crank bolt. If it's there, remove it with either a 5mm Allen wrench, a two-pin dust cap tool, or a screwdriver.

2. Remove the crank bolt, using the appropriate wrench (Fig. 8.2). Make sure you bring the washer out with the bolt (Fig. 8.1), if there is one (if you leave it in, you will not be able to pull the crank off).

Note: Some cranks, like Shimano's XTR (Fig. 8.8),

are self-pulling and don't require a crank puller. The crank bolt has a lip held down by a ring threaded into the crank; as the bolt is unscrewed, its lip pushes on the ring and pushes the crank off. Sometimes it doesn't work and the ring unscrews. In this case, you need to hold the ring with an adjustable pin tool while you unscrew the bolt with an 8mm Allen key.

3. Holding the crank puller (Fig. 1.3) in your hand, unscrew its center push bolt so that the

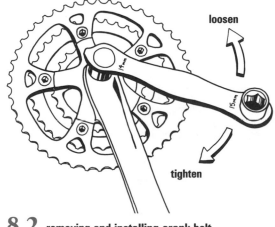

8.2 removing and installing crank bolt

8.3 using crank puller

inner and outer threaded ends of the tool are flush.

4. Thread the crank puller into the hole in the crankarm. Be sure that you thread it in (by hand) as far as it can go; otherwise, you will not engage sufficient crank threads when you tighten the push bolt, and you will damage the threads. Future crank removal depends on those threads being in good condition.

5. Tighten the push bolt clockwise (Fig. 8.3), either with the socket wrench or the included handle, until the crankarm pulls off of the spindle. Unscrew the puller from the crankarm.

B. Installation

1. Slide the crankarm onto the bottom bracket spindle. Clean off all grease from both parts. Grease allows the soft aluminum crank to slide too far onto the steel spindle and could deform the square hole in the crank. Grease has no effect on the new splined spindles, so don't worry if there is a little bit on the crankarm.

2. Install the crank bolt. Apply grease to the threads, and tighten (Fig. 8.2). Here is where a torque wrench comes in handy; tighten it to about 300–435 foot-pounds. If you're not using a torque wrench, make sure the bolt is really tight, but don't muscle it until your veins pop.

3. Replace the dust cover, if your crank has one.

4. Removing and reinstalling the right crank arm could affect shifting, so check the front derailleur adjustment. (See Chapter 5, Section V-5.)

5. You're done. Go ride your bike.

VIII-2: CHAINRINGS

You should get into the habit of checking your chainrings regularly. They do wear out and need to

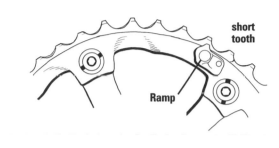

8.4 chainring shifting ramps

short tooth

Ramp

be replaced. It's hard to say how often, so include chainrings as part of your regular maintenance checklist. Check your chainrings for wear when you replace your chain.

The chainring teeth should be checked periodically for wear; the chainring bolts should be checked periodically for tightness; the chainrings themselves should be checked for trueness by watching them as they spin past the front derailleur.

1. Wipe the chainring down and inspect each tooth. The teeth should be straight and uniform in size and shape. Caution: Don't be deceived by the seemingly erratic tooth shapes designed to facilitate shifting; check if they repeat regularly. Shifting ramps on the inner side (Fig. 8.4) meant to speed chain movement between the rings often look like cracks.

If the teeth are hook-shaped, the chainring needs to be replaced. The chain should be replaced as well (see Chapter 4, Section IV-5), because this tooth shape effectively changes the spacing between teeth and accelerates wear on the chain.

Note: Another wear evaluation method is to lift the chain from the top of the chainring; the greater the wear of either part, the further the chain separates. If it lifts more than one tooth, at least the chain, and perhaps the chainring, needs to be replaced.

VIII

cranks and bottom brackets

CHAINRINGS

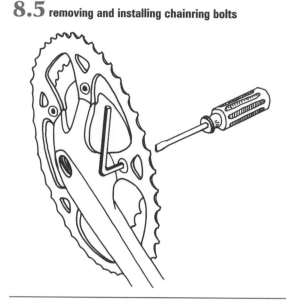

8.5 removing and installing chainring bolts

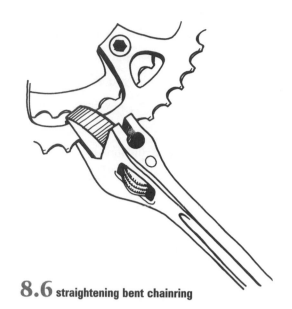

8.6 straightening bent chainring

2. Remove minor gouges in the chainrings with a file.

3. If an individual tooth is bent, try carefully bending it back with a pair of pliers or a crescent wrench. It will likely break off; take the message and buy a new chainring.

4. While turning the crank slowly, watch where the chain exits the bottom of the chainring. See if any of the teeth are reluctant to let go of the chain. That can cause chain suck. Locate any offending teeth and see if you can correct the problem. If the teeth are really chewed up or cannot be improved with pliers and a file, the chainring should be replaced.

VIII-3: CHAINRING BOLTS

Check that the bolts are tight by turning them clockwise with a 5mm Allen wrench (Fig. 8.5). If, as you try to tighten the bolt, the nut on the backside turns, hold it with a two-pronged chainring-nut tool designed especially for this purpose (Fig. 1.3). If you don't have this tool, use a screwdriver — but do so with caution; it is difficult to grip the nut with a screwdriver (Fig. 8.5).

VIII-4: WARPED CHAINRINGS

Looking down from above, turn the crank slowly and see whether the chainrings wobble back and forth relative to the plane of the front derailleur.

If they do, make sure there is no play in the bottom bracket. If there is play, adjust your bottom bracket (Section VIII-8, step 15). It is normal to have a small amount of chainring wobble and flex when you pedal hard, but excessive wobbling will compromise shifting. Small, localized bends can be straightened with a Crescent wrench (Fig. 8.6). If it's really bent, replace it.

8.7 outer and middle chainrings

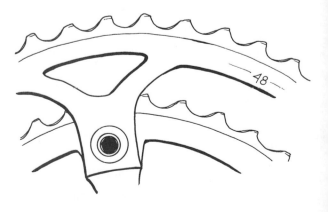

CHAINRING
BOLTS
—
WARPED
CHAINRINGS

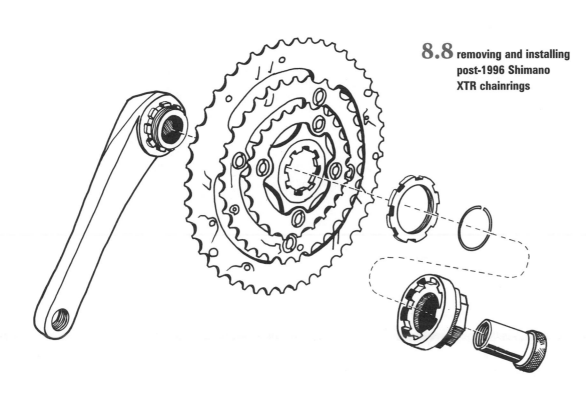

8.8 removing and installing post-1996 Shimano XTR chainrings

VIII-5: BENT CRANKARM SPIDERS

If you installed a new chainring and are still seeing serious back-and-forth wobble, chances are good that the spider arms on your crank are bent. If the crank is new, this is a warranty item, so take it to your bike shop.

VIII-6: CHAINRING REPLACEMENT

A. Replacing either of the two largest chainrings (Fig. 8.7) is easy

1. Simply unscrew the five 5mm Allen bolts holding them on the chainring (Fig. 8.5). You may need to hold the nut on the backside with either a pronged chainring-nut tool or a thin screwdriver.

2. Install the new rings, lubricate the bolts, and tighten them (Fig. 8.5).

Note: Any time you change the outer chainring size, you must reposition the front derailleur for proper chainring clearance, as described in Chapter 5, Section V-5.

B. To replace the inner chainring

1. Pull off the crankarm (Section VIII-1, Figs. 8.2 and 8.3).

2. Remove the 5mm Allen bolts holding the chainring on. They are threaded directly into the crankarm (Fig. 8.1).

3. Install the new ring, and lube and tighten the bolts.

Note: Some chainrings do not accept separate chainrings.

At the high end, 1996 and later Shimano XTR cranks rely on a thread-on cassette system that allows you to spin off all three chainrings from the crankarm as a single unit (Fig. 8.8). After removing a circlip (by prying it off with a screwdriver), a special lockring tool loosens the chainring-cassette-securing lockring; a female-threaded tool that goes on the crank bolt holds the lockring tool in place (Fig. 8.8). Once the cassette is off, you can interchange chainrings within the set or simply pop on a whole new set.

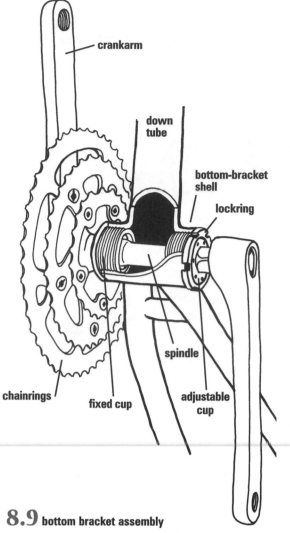

8.9 bottom bracket assembly

Economical cranks often have chainrings riveted to the crank or riveted to each other and bolted to the crank as a unit. In either case, if you want to replace a chainring, you must either replace the entire crank or the chainring set.

4. Replace the crankarm (Section VIII-1, Fig. 8.2). Now ride your bike.

VIII.B: BOTTOM BRACKETS

Most bottom brackets thread into the frame's bottom bracket shell (Fig. 8.9). Simple enough, but it's important to remember that not all of these threads are the same.

Almost all mountain bikes use English standard threads. That translates into a 1.370-inch diameter and a thread pitch of 24 threads per inch. These numbers are usually engraved on the bottom bracket cups. If you are replacing a bottom bracket, make sure that the new cups have the same threads. It is important to remember that the threads on the drive side of an English standard bottom bracket are left-hand threads. In other words, you tighten the right-hand cup by turning it counterclockwise (Fig. 8.16). Meanwhile, the threads on the left cup are right-hand threads and are, therefore, tightened clockwise.

English-threaded mountain bike bottom brackets come in two bearing spacing widths for two different bottom bracket shell widths. One bottom bracket shell width is 68mm, and most bottom brackets will have stamped or printed on them something like "68–114," which means that the shell is 68mm wide, and the spindle is 114mm long. The other bottom bracket shell width is 73mm, and the bottom bracket would have a demarcation like "73–118."

Other threads you may run across are Italian (with a 36mm diameter), French and Swiss (both of these come in 35mm diameter but use different thread directions). These thread patterns are very rare on mountain bikes.

The most common type of bottom bracket currently is the Shimano-style cartridge bottom bracket with splined cups (Fig. 8.10). The most common bottom bracket in the 1980s and before was the "cup and cone" style with loose ball bearings (Fig. 8.11). Another older type has cartridge bearings secured by an adjustable cup and lockring at either end (Fig. 8.12). Shimano's latest high-end

8.10–8.14 types of bottom brackets

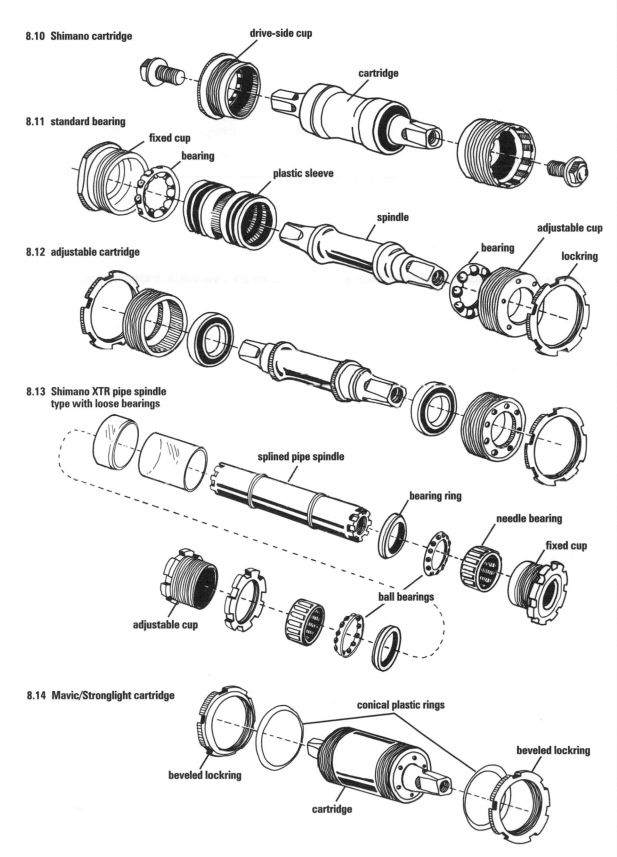

8.10 Shimano cartridge

drive-side cup

cartridge

8.11 standard bearing

fixed cup

bearing

plastic sleeve

spindle

adjustable cup

bearing

lockring

8.12 adjustable cartridge

8.13 Shimano XTR pipe spindle
type with loose bearings

splined pipe spindle

bearing ring

needle bearing

fixed cup

adjustable cup

ball bearings

8.14 Mavic/Stronglight cartridge

conical plastic rings

beveled lockring

beveled lockring

cartridge

bottom brackets have a large spindle with splined ends, rather than square-taper ends (Fig. 8.13). Most of these are still the cartridge type shown in Fig. 8.10 but with a large splined axle. The first generation of splined pipe-spindle Shimano bottom brackets had four sets of loose, adjustable and overhaulable bearings: two sets of tiny balls and two sets of needle bearings (Fig. 8.13).

Some bottom brackets do not thread into the bottom bracket shell. One type utilizes cartridge bearings held into an unthreaded bottom bracket shell by snaprings in machined grooves. Another type is the Mavic (now Stronglight) cartridge threaded on each end (Fig. 8.14); it slips into the bottom bracket shell and is held in place by lockrings threaded onto the cartridge. The latter type is great for frames with damaged threads, as the bottom bracket secures on itself by compressing against the sides of the bottom bracket shell and not on the frame's threads.

VIII.B1: BOTTOM BRACKET INSTALLATION

LEVEL 2 The most important item in bottom bracket installation is to put the right bottom bracket in. If a bike has the wrong length bottom bracket spindle, the chainrings will not line up well with the rear cogs (i.e., the center ring should be in line with the center of the cogset; this is called chain line [see Fig. 5.41]). Some bikes come from the factory with the wrong length bottom bracket. No amount of fiddling with the derailleurs will get such a bike to shift properly. Get a bottom bracket specifically recommended for your crankset and with the proper thread and bottom bracket shell width for your

frame. Before installing a new bottom bracket of a different brand and model than your crank, see Fig. 5.41, and read the chain line section (V-44) at the end of Chapter 5.

VIII-7: INSTALLATION OF SHIMANO CARTRIDGE-SEALED BOTTOM BRACKETS (AND CLONES)

As of this writing, most mountain bike bottom brackets are Shimano-style sealed cartridge units (Fig. 8.10) that are installed with a splined tool (Fig. 1.3). A Shimano cartridge bottom bracket can have either a square tapered axle (Fig. 8.10) or a large tubular axle with splined ends like the spindle in Fig. 8.13.

1. Slide the cartridge into the bottom bracket shell, paying particular attention to the right and left markings on the cartridge. The cup with the raised lip and left-hand thread is the drive-side cup (the left-hand cup in Fig. 8.10).

8.15 tightening and loosening Shimano-style cartridge bottom bracket with socket wrench and splined bottom-bracket tool

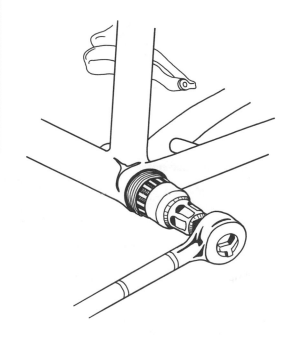

2. Using the splined cup tool with either an open-end wrench or a 3/8-inch drive socket wrench on it, tighten the right (drive-side) cup until the lip seats against the face of the bottom bracket shell (as in Fig. 8.15, except on the drive side). Recommended torque is in Appendix E.

Note: Since almost all mountain bikes have English threads, this cup should tighten counterclockwise.

3. Insert the nondrive side cup, and, with the same tool, turn it clockwise until it fits tightly against the cartridge (Fig. 8.15). (See Appendix E for recommended torque.) There is no adjustment of the bearings to be done; you can put on the crank now.

VIII-8: INSTALLATION OF CUP-AND-CONE BOTTOM BRACKETS

Cup-and-cone (or "loose-ball") bottom brackets (Fig. 8.11) use ball bearings that ride between cone-shaped bearing surfaces on the spindle and cup-shaped races in the threaded cups. One cup, called the fixed cup (the left-hand cup in Fig. 8.11), has a lip on it and fits on the drive side of the bike. The other, called the adjustable cup, has a lockring that threads onto the cup and against the face of the bottom bracket shell. The individual ball bearings are usually held together by a retaining cage, which varies in shape depending on bottom bracket. Some folks prefer to do without the retainer; it works fine either way.

For loose-ball bottom brackets to turn smoothly, the bearing surfaces of the cups must be parallel. Because the cups thread into the bottom bracket shell, the threads on both sides of the shell must be lined up with each other, and the end faces of the shell must be parallel. If you have any doubts

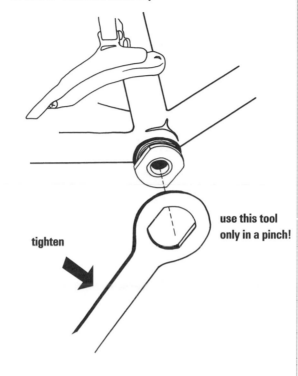

8.16 driveside fixed cup

tighten

use this tool only in a pinch!

about your frame and are installing an expensive bottom bracket, it is a good idea to have the bottom bracket shell tapped (threaded) and faced (ends cut parallel) by a qualified shop possessing the proper tools.

1. Unless you have a shop fixed-cup tool, have a shop install the fixed cup for you. The shop tool assures that the cup goes in straight and very tightly. The tool pictured in Fig. 8.16 can be used in a pinch, but it can let the cup go in crooked and will slip off before you get it really tight. The fixed cup must be very tight (see Appendix E for torque) so it does not vibrate loose. Remember that English-threaded fixed cups are tightened counterclockwise.

2. Wipe the inside surface of both cups with a clean rag, and put a thin layer of clean grease on the bearing surfaces. Put enough that the balls will be half-covered; any more is wasted and attracts dirt.

3. Wipe the axle with a clean rag.

8.17 placing axle in shell

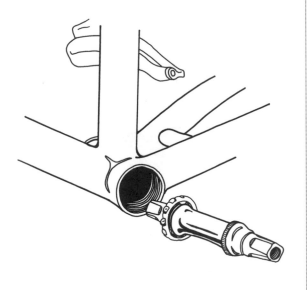

4. Figure out which end of your bottom bracket spindle (axle) is toward the drive side. The drive side may be marked with an "R," or you can simply choose the longer end (when measured from the bearing surface). If there is writing on the spindle, it will usually read right side up for a rider on the bike. If there is no marking and no length difference, the spindle orientation is irrelevant.

5. Slide one set of bearings onto the drive-side end of the axle (Fig. 8.17). If you're using a retainer cage, make sure you orient it correctly. The balls, rather than the retainer cage, should rest against the axle-bearing surfaces. Since there are two types of retainers with opposite designs, you need to be careful to avoid binding, as well as smashing of the retainers. If you're still confused, there is one easy test: If it's right it will turn smoothly; if it's wrong it won't.

If you have loose ball bearings with no retainer cage, stick them into the greased cup. Most rely on nine balls; you can confirm that you are using the correct number by inserting and removing the axle and checking to make sure that they are evenly dis-

tributed in the grease with no extra gap for more balls.

6. Slide the axle into the bottom bracket so it pushes the bearings into the fixed cup (Fig. 8.17). You can use your pinkie from the fixed-cup end to stabilize the end of the axle as you slide it in.

7. Insert the protective plastic sleeve (shown in Fig. 8.11) into the shell against the inside edge of the fixed cup. The sleeve keeps dirt and rust from falling from the frame tubes into the bearings, so if you don't have one, get one.

8. Now turn your attention to the other cup. Place the bearing set into the greased adjustable cup. If you are using a bearing retainer, make sure it is properly oriented.

9. Without the lockring, thread the adjustable cup (clockwise) by hand into the shell over the axle, assuring that it is going in straight. Screw the cup in as far as you can by hand, ideally all the way until the bearings seat between the axle and cup.

10. Locate the appropriate tool for tightening the adjustable cup. Most cups have two holes that accept the pins of an adjustable cup wrench called a "pin spanner" (Fig. 8.18) or a splined end like a cartridge bottom bracket that fits a tool as in Fig. 8.15. The other common type of adjustable cup has two flats for a wrench; on this type, you may use an adjustable wrench.

11. Carefully tighten the adjustable cup against the bearings, taking great care not to overtighten. Turn the axle periodically with your fingers to ensure that it moves freely. If it binds up, you have gone too far; back it off a bit. The danger of overtightening is that the bearings can force dents into the bearing surfaces of the cups, and the bottom bracket axle will never turn smoothly again.

12. Screw the lockring onto the adjustable cup,

CUP-AND-
CONE
BOTTOM-
BRACKET
INSTALLATION

168

8.18 tightening lockring

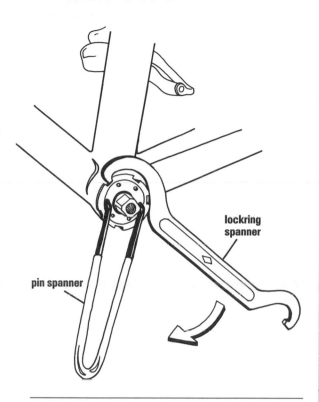

lockring
spanner

pin spanner

and select the proper tool for your lockring. Lockrings come in different shapes, and so do lockring spanners — make sure yours mate properly with each other.

13. Tighten the lockring against the face of the bottom bracket shell with the lockring spanner, while holding the adjustable cup in place (Fig. 8.18). If you turn the bicycle upside down, you can pull down harder on the wrenches.

14. As you snug the lockring up against the bottom bracket shell, check the bottom bracket spindle periodically, for the lockring pulls the cup out of the shell minutely and loosens the adjustment. The spindle should turn smoothly without free play in the bearings. I recommend installing and tightening the drive-side crankarm onto the drive end of the spindle (Fig. 8.2) at this time so you can push the crank from side to side to check for free play.

15. Adjust the cup so that the axle play is just barely eliminated. While holding the cup in place, tighten the lockring as tightly as you can (Fig. 8.18) so the bottom bracket does not come out of adjustment while riding (recommended torque is in Appendix E; tightening it as tightly as you can is about right). You may have to repeat this step a time or two until you get the adjustment just right.

VIII-9: INSTALLATION OF OTHER TYPES OF BOTTOM BRACKETS

The two bottom bracket types mentioned earlier in this chapter probably represent more than 95 percent of the mountain bikes in circulation. There are, however, a few variations worth mentioning.

A. Cartridge-bearing bottom brackets with adjustable cups (Fig. 8.12) are reasonably easy to install. These come with a pair of adjustable cups for both ends. With this type, you simply install the drive-side cup and lockring, slide the cartridge bearing in (if it is not already pressed into the cup), slip the spindle in, and then install the other bearing, cup and lockring. Tighten each lockring while holding the adjustable cup in place with a pin spanner (Fig. 8.18) or splined cup tool (Fig. 8.15). Adjust for free play as in Section VIII-8, steps 11–15.

The advantage of having two adjustable cups is that you can center the cartridge by moving it side to side in the bottom bracket shell. If the chainrings end up too close or too far away from the frame (see Fig. 5.41 and the "chain line" discussion in the troubleshooting section at the end of Chapter 5, Section V-44), you can move one cup in and one out to shift the position of the entire cartridge.

Sometimes cartridge-bearing bottom brackets

VIII

cranks and
bottom brackets

OTHER
BOTTOM-
BRACKET
INSTALLATION

bind up a bit during adjustment and installation. A light tap on each end of the axle usually frees them.

B. An unthreaded bottom bracket shell with snapring grooves uses just a spindle and cartridge bearings without cups (not pictured); snaprings retain the bearings. This type was popular at the beginning of the 1980s and has virtually disappeared on new bikes. With a cupless bottom bracket, seat the cartridge bearings against the stops on either end of the spindle. Install one snapring with snapring pliers into the groove in one end of the shell. Push the entire assembly of axle and two bearings in from the other side of the bottom bracket shell. Install the other snapring, and you're done.

C. Mavic or Stronglight cartridge bottom brackets (Fig. 8.14) require either end of the bottom bracket shell to be chamfered at an angle to seat the angled lockrings. You need to go to a shop equipped with the Mavic tool for this. Once this is done, you simply slip the cartridge into the shell, slide on one of the angled plastic rings from either end (pictured in Fig. 8.14), and screw on a lockring, angled side inward, from either side. Holding the cartridge with a pin spanner, tighten the lockring on either side (Fig. 8.18). The beauty of Mavic bottom brackets is that they work independently of the bottom bracket shell threads, so they can be installed in shells with ruined threads or nonstandard threads. Mavic stopped producing them in 1995, so they are hard to find.

D. Non-cartridge XTR pipe-spindle bottom brackets (Fig. 8.13) are installed like cup-and-cone bottom brackets (Section VIII-8), with the exception that the ball bearings ride on bearing rings inboard of needle bearings within the cups. Two notched lockring spanners are required to adjust them.

VIII.C: OVERHAULING THE BOTTOM BRACKET

LEVEL 2

A bottom bracket overhaul consists of cleaning or replacing the bearings, cleaning the axle and bearing surfaces, and regreasing them. With any type, both crankarms must be removed.

VIII-10: OVERHAULING SHIMANO CARTRIDGE BOTTOM BRACKETS

Standard Shimano-style cartridge bottom brackets (Fig. 8.10) are sealed units and cannot be overhauled. They must be replaced when they stop performing properly. Remove them by unscrewing the cups with the splined cup tool (Fig. 8.15) after first removing the cranks as in Section VIII-1. Install a new bottom bracket as directed in Section VIII-7.

VIII-11: OVERHAULING CUP-AND-CONE BOTTOM BRACKETS

Cup-and-cone bottom brackets (Figs. 8.11 and 8.13) can be overhauled entirely from the nondrive side, after you have removed the crankarms as described in Section VIII-1.

1. Remove the lockring with the lockring spanner (as in Fig. 8.18, with the lockring spanner and the rotation direction reversed).

2. Remove the adjustable cup with the tool that fits yours (usually a pin spanner [Fig. 1.3], installed into the cup as in Fig. 8.18).

3. Leave the fixed cup in place, and check that it is tightened hard into the frame by putting a fixed cup wrench on it and turning it counterclockwise (Fig. 8.16).

4. Clean the cups and spindle with a rag. Use a solvent only if the parts are really glazed.

5. Clean the bearings, without removing them from their retainer cages, with a citrus-based solvent. A simple way to do it is to shake the bearings about in a plastic bottle with solvent in it. A toothbrush may be required, and a solvent tank is certainly handy if you have access to one. If your bearings are not shiny and in perfect shape, go ahead and replace them. Balls with dull luster and/or rough spots or rust on them should be replaced.

6. Wash the bearings in soap and water to remove the solvent and any remaining grit. Towel them off thoroughly, and then let them dry completely. An air compressor is handy here.

7. Follow the installation procedure described in Section VIII-8.

8. Install the crankarms as in Section VIII-1, Fig. 8.2.

VIII-12: OVERHAULING OTHER TYPES OF BOTTOM BRACKETS

If any cartridge-bearing bottom bracket becomes difficult to turn, the bearings must be replaced. If they are pressed into cups, then you may also have to buy new cups. Be doubly sure to get the correct size.

1. Reverse the installation procedure outlined above in Section VIII-9 to remove your bottom bracket.

2. Replace the bearings.

3. Reinstall your bottom bracket (Section VIII-9) and crankarms (Section VIII-1).

4. You're done. Go ride your bike.

TROUBLESHOOTING CRANK AND BOTTOM BRACKET NOISE

VIII-13: CREAKING NOISES

Those mysterious creaking noises can be enough to drive you nuts. Just as you think you have your bike tuned to perfection, a little noise comes along to ruin your ride, and these annoying little creaks, pops and groans can be a bear to locate. Pedaling-induced noises can originate from almost anything connected to your crankset, like movement of the cleats on your shoes or of the crankarms on the bottom bracket spindle, loose chainrings, or poorly adjusted bearings. Of course, they could also originate from seemingly unrelated components like your seat, seatpost, frame, wheels, or handlebars.

Before spending hours overhauling your drivetrain, spend some time trying to isolate the source of the noise. Try different pedals and shoes and wheels. Pedal out of the saddle, and pedal without flexing the handlebars. If the source of the creak turns out to be the saddle, seatpost, wheels or handlebars, turn to the appropriate chapter for directions on how to correct the problem.

If the creaking is in the crank area:

1. Check to make sure that the chainring bolts are tight, and tighten them if they are not (Fig. 8.5).

2. If that does not solve the problem, make certain that the crankarm bolts are tight (Fig. 8.2). If they are not, the resulting movement between the crankarm and the bottom bracket spindle is a likely source of noise. If your crank is of a different brand than your bottom bracket, check with the manufacturers or your local shop to make sure that they are recommended for use together. Incompatible cranks and spindles will never properly join and are a potential problem area.

3. Rust and alternating wet and dry cycles can breakdown the glue bond on a Shimano cartridge bottom bracket (Fig. 8.10) that holds the cup(s) onto the cartridge. If the cartridge can move within the cup, it will creak. Fix it by removing the bottom

TROUBLE-
SHOOTING
CRANK AND
BOTTOM-
BRACKET
NOISE

bracket (Section VIII-10), slathering grease inside the cup(s) and around the outside of the cartridge where the parts meet. Grease the cup threads too, because if the cup moves against the bottom bracket shell it can also make noise. Tighten it back in (Fig. 8.15).

4. The bottom bracket itself can creak due to improper adjustment, lack of grease, cracked bearings, worn parts or loose cups. All of these things require adjustment or overhaul procedures, outlined in Sections VIII.C and VIII.D of this chapter.

5. Now for the bad news. If creaking persists, the problem could be rooted in your frame. Creaks can originate from cracks in and around the bottom bracket shell, so be sure to check for that. The threads in your bottom bracket shell could also be worn to the point that they allow the cups to move slightly. Neither of these is a good sign, unless, of course, you were hoping for an excuse to buy a new frame.

VIII-14: CLUNKING NOISES

1. Crankarm play: Grab the crankarm and push on it side to side.

a. If there is play, tighten the crank arm bolt (Fig. 8.2; torque spec is in Appendix E).

b. If there is still crankarm play and you have a cup-and-cone bottom bracket (Fig. 8.11) or a cartridge-bearing bottom bracket with a lockring on either side (Fig. 8.12), adjust the bottom bracket spindle end play (Section VIII-8, see steps 11–15).

c. If bottom bracket adjustment does not eliminate crankarm play or you have a nonadjustable cartridge bottom bracket (Fig. 8.10), the bottom bracket is loose in the frame threads, and you

should tighten it up. With a cup-and-cone bottom bracket, you can go back to Section VIII-8, and start over, making sure that the fixed cup is very tight. A cheater bar (extension tube) may need to be used on the fixed-cup wrench to tighten it to high enough torque. Adjustable-cup lockrings need to be equally tight (Fig. 8.18), once the spindle endplay is adjusted properly.

d. The lockrings and fixed-cup flanges must be flush with the bottom bracket shell all of the way around; if they are not, the bottom bracket must be removed, and the bottom bracket shell must be faced (cut parallel) by a shop equipped with a facing cutter.

e. If the crankarm play persists, or the bottom bracket fixed cup or lockring will not tighten up completely or keep coming loose, then the bottom bracket cups must either be stripped or undersized, or the frame's bottom bracket shell threads are stripped or oversized. Either way, it's an expensive fix, especially the frame replacement option! Get a second opinion if you reach this point. If you can find a Mavic-style bottom bracket (Fig. 8.14), you can still use the frame.

2. Pedal endplay: Grab each pedal and wobble it to check for play. See "Overhauling Pedals," Section IX.B in Chapter 9, if they are loose.

VIII-15: HARD-TO-TURN CRANKS

If the cranks are hard to turn, you really ought to overhaul your bottom bracket (see Section VIII.D above) — unless you want to continue intensifying your workout or boosting the egos of your cycling companions. The bottom bracket may be shot and need to be replaced.

TROUBLE-
SHOOTING

VIII-16: INNER CHAINRING DRAGS ON CHAINSTAY

Your bottom bracket spindle is too short, the square hole in your crankarm is deformed so that the crank slides on too far, or you have switched to a larger inner chainring. A misaligned frame, with either bent chainstays or a twisted bottom bracket shell, can cause chainring rub as well. With an adjustable cartridge-bearing bottom bracket with a lockring on either end (Fig. 8.12), it is possible that the entire bottom bracket is offset to the left. To move it to the right, screw the left cup in further, back the right cup out some, adjust out the end play, and tighten the lockrings back down (Fig. 8.18).

If the bottom bracket spindle is too short, you need a new one of the correct length.

If the square hole in the crank is badly deformed, you need a new crankarm. Otherwise it will continue to loosen up and cause problems.

If the chainring is too large, get a smaller one.

A badly misaligned frame needs to be replaced.

Note: See Section V-44 at the end of Chapter 5 (Fig. 5.41) on chain line to establish proper crank-to-frame spacing. The chainring might not be rubbing the frame, but the crank is still too far inboard if the derailleur cannot move inward far enough to shift to the granny gear. The mechanism on a Shimano "top-swing" front derailleur in particular can hit the seat tube and stop before the chain drops onto the inner ring. The problem is compounded with an oversized seat tube. And if your bottom bracket is too long, you can have the opposite problem — your front derailleur will not reach the large chainring.

pedals

For everything, turn, turn, turn . . .
— THE BYRDS

To best serve its purpose, a bicycle pedal needs only to be firmly attached to the crankarm and provide a stable platform for the shoe. A simple enough task, but you'd be amazed at the different approaches that have been taken to achieve this goal. Of the two basic types of mountain bike pedals, the standard cage-type pedal with a toeclip and strap (Fig. 9.2) is the simplest and cheapest. The type found on most mid- to high-end mountain bikes, the "clip-in" pedal (Fig. 9.1), has a spring-loaded shoe-retention system, much like a ski binding. Clip-in pedals are also called "clipless" pedals because they have no toeclip.

Cage-type pedals are fairly common on lower-end bikes. They are relatively nonintimidating for the novice rider, and the frame (or "cage") that surrounds the pedal provides a large, stable platform (Fig. 9.2). Without a toeclip, the top and bottom of the pedal are the same, and you can use just about any type of shoe. If you mount a toeclip without a strap, it can keep your foot from sliding forward and still allow easy release in almost any direction. When you add a toe strap and use a mountain bike shoe with aggressive tread, the combination works well to keep your foot on the pedal while riding even the roughest of singletrack. When tightened, the strap allows you to pull up on the upward part of the pedal stroke — giving you more power and a more fluid pedal stroke. Of course, as you add clips and straps, the pedal becomes harder to enter and to exit, especially with boots or shoes with aggressive tread designs.

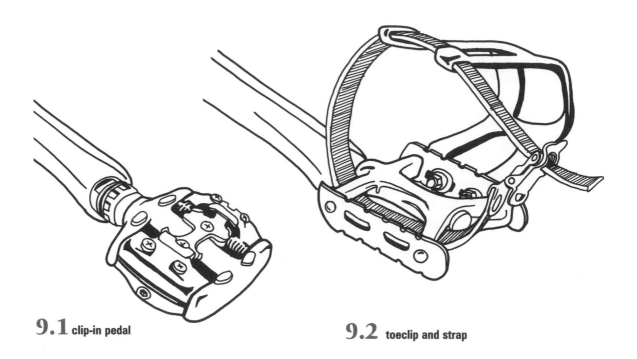

9.1 clip-in pedal

9.2 toeclip and strap

Clip-in models offer all of the advantages of a good clip-and-strap combination, yet allow easier entry and exit from the pedal. These pedals are more expensive and require special shoes and accurate mounting of the cleats. Your choice of shoes is limited to stiff-sole models that accept cleats for your particular pedal. Once you have them dialed in, you will find that clip-in pedals waste less energy through flex and slippage and allow you to transfer more power directly to the pedals. This greater efficiency explains their universal acceptance among cross-country mountain bike racers. Referring to the shoe sole, most clip-in mountain pedals are "SPD" compatible, where SPD stands for Shimano Pedaling Dynamics. Shimano produced the first successful clip-in mountain pedal in the mid-1980s and set the shoe standards. "SPD-compatibility" indicates that the cleat mounts with two side-by-side 5-by-0.8mm-thread screws, spaced 14mm apart, screwing into a movable threaded cleat-mounting plate on a shoe with two longitudi-

nal grooves in the sole (Fig. 9.6). It does not necessarily mean that one company's cleat will work with the pedal of another company.

Note: Some pedal cleats do work with other brands of pedals. Appendix F is a cleat compatibility chart that shows how well many common cleats do or do not work with particular pedals. Be careful. Cleats and pedals do not mix and match and you might find yourself unable to disengage at a most inopportune moment.

This chapter explains how to remove and replace pedals, how to mount the cleats and adjust the release tension with clip-in pedals, how to troubleshoot pedal problems and how to overhaul and replace spindles on almost all mountain bike pedals. Incidentally, I use the terms "axle" and "spindle" interchangeably.

IX-1: PEDAL REMOVAL AND INSTALLATION

Note the right pedal axle is right-hand threaded, and the left is left-hand (reverse) threaded. Both unscrew from the crank in the pedaling direction.

A. Removal

1. Slide the 15mm pedal wrench onto the wrench flats of the pedal axle (Fig. 9.3). Or, if the pedal axle is designed to accept it, you can use a 6mm Allen wrench from the backside of the crank arm (Fig. 9.4). This is particularly handy on the trail, since you probably won't be carrying a 15mm wrench anyway. But if you are at home and the pedal is on really tight, it will probably be easier to use the standard pedal wrench. Some pedals, like the Time ATAC with plastic body (Fig. 9.14) and Time TMT, have no wrench flats and can only be removed with a 6mm Allen wrench (Fig. 9.4).

2. Unscrew the pedal in the appropriate direction. The right, or drive-side, pedal unscrews counterclockwise when viewed from that side. The left-side pedal is reverse threaded, so it unscrews in a clockwise direction when viewed from the left side of the bike. Once loosened, either pedal can be unscrewed quickly by turning the crank forward with the wrench engaged on the pedal spindle.

9.3 removing or installing pedal with 15mm wrench

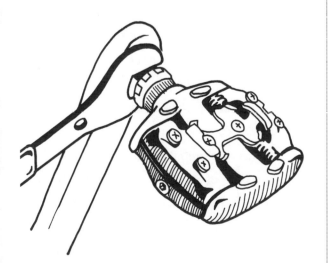

9.4 removing or installing pedal with a 6mm Allen wrench

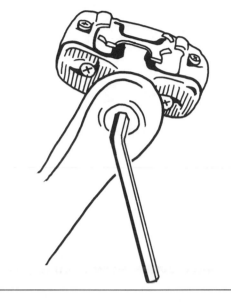

B. Installation

1. Use a rag to wipe the threads clean on the pedal axle and inside the crankarm.

2. Grease the pedal threads.

3. Start screwing the pedal in with your fingers, clockwise for the right pedal, counterclockwise for the left.

4. Tighten the pedal with the 15mm pedal wrench (Fig. 9.3) or a 6mm Allen wrench (Fig. 9.4). This can be done quickly by turning the cranks backward with the wrench engaged on the pedal spindle.

IX.A SETTING UP CLIP-IN PEDALS

Setting up clip-in pedals involves installation and adjustment of the cleats on the shoes, and adjusting the pedal-release tension.

IX-2: INSTALLING AND ADJUSTING PEDAL CLEATS ON THE SHOES

The cleat is important because its position determines the fore-aft, lateral (side-to-side) and

9.5 removing rubber cover concealing the cleat holes

9.6 cleat setup on a SPD-compatible shoe

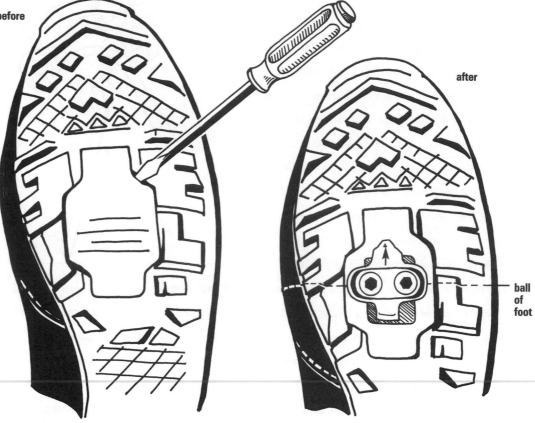

before

after

ball of foot

SETTING UP
CLIP-IN
PEDALS

rotational position of your foot. If your pedals aren't properly oriented, it could eventually cause hip, knee or ankle problems.

1. If your shoe has a precut piece of rubber covering the cleat-mounting area, remove it. Cut around the cover's outline with a knife, pry an edge up with a screwdriver (Fig. 9.5), and yank it off with some pliers. Warming it up with a hair dryer beforehand softens the glue.

2. Put the shoe on, and mark the position of the ball of your foot (the big bump behind your big toe) on the outside of the shoe. This will help you position the cleat fore and aft. Take the shoe off, and continue drawing the line straight across the bottom of the shoe (Fig. 9.6).

3. If there are threaded holes in your shoe sole to accept the cleat screws, skip to step 4. If you do not have threaded shoe holes, you must install the backing plate and threaded cleat plate that came with your pedals. Remove the shoe's sock liner, put the rectangular backing plate inside the shoe over the two slots, and put the threaded plate on top of it with the threaded protuberances sticking out through the slots, rather than up at your foot.

4. Lube the cleat screw threads, and screw the cleat that came with your pedals to your shoe; this usually requires a 4mm Allen wrench. Make sure you orient the cleat in the appropriate direction. Some cleats have an arrow indicating forward (Fig. 9.6); if yours do not, the instructions accompanying

your pedals probably specify which direction the cleat should point. Also note if the right and left cleats are different (see "Note" under next step).

5. Position the cleat in the middle of its lateral- and rotational-adjustment range, and line up the mounting screws over or, preferably, 1cm behind the mark you made in step 2 (Fig. 9.6).

Note: Cleats for Time ATAC pedals (Figs. 9.14 and 9.22) have no lateral or rotational adjustment; just set the screws at your mark and tighten the cleat down, making sure the arrow on the cleat points forward. Put the cleat with the imprinted stars onto the right shoe for more float range; put it on the left shoe for less float. You may now tighten the screws, skip the remaining steps and go riding! (Incidentally, the older model Time TMT pedal, of which few were sold, also had only fore aft cleat adjustment, but the only shoe you could use with it was Time's mountain shoe of the time. The ATAC pedals work with any SPD-compatible shoe.)

6. Snug the screws down enough that the cleat won't move when clipped in or out of the pedals, but don't tighten them down fully yet. Follow the same steps with your other shoe.

7. To set the lateral position, put the shoes on, sit on the bike, and clip into the pedals. Ride around a bit. Notice the position of your feet. Pedaling is more efficient the closer the feet are to the plane of the bike, but you don't want them in so far that they bump your cranks. Take the shoes off and adjust the cleats laterally, if necessary, to move the feet side to side. Get back on the bike and clip in again. (Again, Time cleats have no lateral adjustability.)

8. To set the rotational position, ride around some more. Notice if your feet feel twisted and uncomfortable. You may feel pressure on either side of your heel from the shoe. If necessary,

remove your shoes and rotate the cleat slightly. Some pedals offer free-float, allowing the foot to rotate freely for a few degrees before releasing. Precise rotational cleat adjustment is less important if the pedal is free-floating. Again, Time cleats have no rotational adjustability.

Note: On Speedplay Frogs (Fig. 9.16), angle the cleat slightly toward the outside of the shoe, and tighten the mounting screws just enough that the cleat can still turn. Clip into the pedal and rotate the heel inward until it just touches the crankarm. Tighten the cleat in this position. Frogs have no inward release; this sets the inward stop.

9. Once your cleat position feels right, trace the cleats with a pen so that you can tell if the cleat stays put. While holding the cleat in place, tighten the bolts down firmly. Hold the Allen wrench close to the bend so that you do not exert too much leverage and strip the bolts.

10. If the cleat holes are open to the inside of the shoe, place a waterproof sticker over the opening inside, and replace the sock liner.

11. When riding, bring the 4mm Allen wrench along, since you may want to fine-tune this adjustment over the course of a few rides.

CLEAT AND CLIPPING-IN PROBLEMS

If your cleat will not engage the pedal, or not without excessive downward force, you may have to trim some of the rubber lugs on the bottom of the shoe. If the tread is too tall, it won't allow the cleat and pedal to engage without pushing down so hard that you squish the offending knobs. Even if you can clip in, the friction will be so high that the free-float will not work. Look where the pedal contacts the shoe knobs, and trim them in that area with a sharp knife.

If the screws in your cleat plate are stripped, you will need to change them. Some cleat plates have two sets of threaded holes, in which case you can move the cleat to the other set of holes. If yours does not, or if the other sets of threads are also unusable, you can install a new threaded cleat plate. Many cleats come with spare backing plates and threaded plates. You interchange plates from inside the shoe — open the shoe wide, remove the shoe's sock liner and the cover concealing the screw slots, and pull out the old backing plate and threaded plate. Use new screws in the new threads or you could repeat the problem.

IX-3: ADJUSTING RELEASE TENSION ON CLIP-IN PEDALS

If you find the factory release-adjustment setting to be too loose or too restrictive, you can adjust the release tension on most clip-in pedal brands; exceptions are Time and Speedplay. The adjusting screws are usually located at the front and rear of the pedal (Fig. 9.7). The screws affect the tension of the nearest set of clips. The adjusters are usually operated with a small (usually 3mm) Allen wrench. Old OnZa H.O. (Fig. 9.8) and Look (Fig. 9.15) pedals are adjusted differently; see Section IX-4 below.

Before starting, clean your shoe cleats and the pedal clips. Lubricate the clip edges and cleat ends with dry lubricant (so you don't track it onto your carpet), and the pedal springs with wet chain lube (Fig. 9.23). Whenever you have trouble getting in or out, start with this step.

1. Locate the tension-adjustment screws. They are usually on either fore and aft end of the pedal; you can see the screw in Figs. 9.7 and 9.9–9.13.

2. To loosen the tension adjustment, turn the

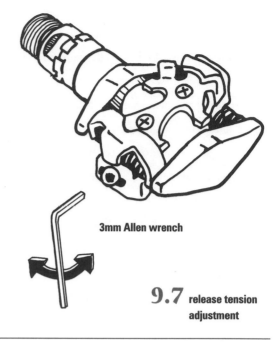

3mm Allen wrench

9.7 release tension adjustment

elastomer bumper

9.8 OnZa H.O. clip-in pedal, pre-1997

screw counterclockwise, and to tighten it, turn it clockwise (Fig. 9.7). It's the classic "lefty loosey, righty tighty" approach. There usually are click stops in the rotation of the screw. Tighten or loosen one click at a time (one-quarter to one-half turn), and go riding to test the adjustment. Many types include an indicator that moves with the screw to show relative adjustment. Make certain that you do not back the screw out so far that it comes out of the spring plate.

Note: *With Ritchey Scott, Girvin, Topo, Wellgo and other dual-rear-clip/dual-rear-spring pedals, you will*

ADJUSTING
RELEASE
TENSION ON
CLIP-IN
PEDALS

9.9 removing axle from Shimano clip-in pedal

9.10 removing axle from Scott pedal

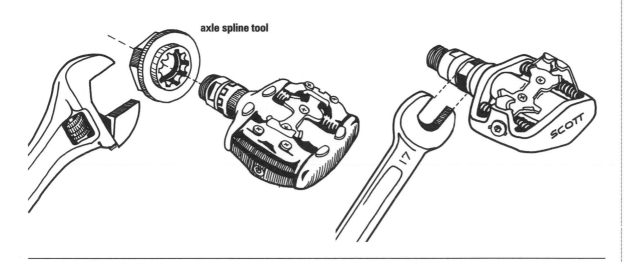

axle spline tool

decrease the amount of free-float in the pedal as you increase the release tension.

IX-4: ADJUSTING TENSION OF OTHER TYPES OF PEDALS

A. Time pedals (Fig. 9.14) have no tension adjustment; they offer high retention and lots of float, yet they require low entry and release force and, therefore, require no adjustment.

B. Old double-sided Look mountain pedals have a single 5mm bolt that adjusts both sides. It has a large window like a ski binding with a pointer to show the relative adjustment. The even older, one-sided Look models resembling Look road pedals have a small slotted screw in the center to adjust the tension. More recently, Look SL-3 pedals (Fig. 9.15) have a 3mm adjustment screw with spring tension indicator on either side that is reached through a hole in the top of the rear clip.

C. Old OnZa H.O. clip-in pedals (Fig. 9.8) rely on elastomer bumpers to provide release tension. You adjust them by changing the elastomer. Bumpers of varying hardness are included with the pedals. OnZa's black bumpers are the hardest, and the clear ones are the softest. There are several grades in between. The harder the bumper, the greater the release tension. To replace bumpers, unscrew the two Allen bolts holding each bumper on (Fig. 9.21). Pull the old bumper out and put in the new one. While you are at it, make sure that the Phillips screws that hold in the cleat guides are tight, since they have a tendency to loosen up and fall out. In fact, it wouldn't hurt to put a small dab of Loctite on the threads while you're checking them.

D. Speedplay Frogs (Fig. 9.16) have no tension adjustment; ease of release can be adjusted by rotating the cleat on the shoe sole to change the release angle.

IX.B: OVERHAULING PEDALS

Just like a hub or bottom bracket, pedal bearings and bushings need to be cleaned and regreased regularly. Most pedals have a lip seal around the axle where it enters the pedal. Pedals without one get dirty inside very quickly.

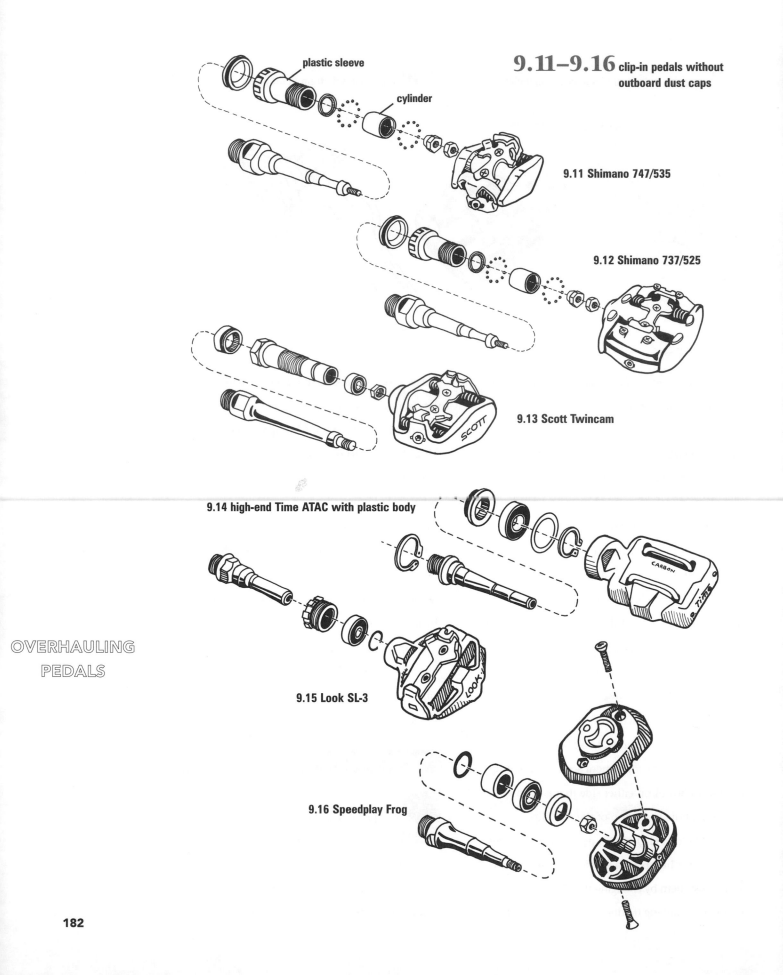

9.11–9.16 clip-in pedals without outboard dust caps

plastic sleeve

cylinder

9.11 Shimano 747/535

9.12 Shimano 737/525

9.13 Scott Twincam

9.14 high-end Time ATAC with plastic body

OVERHAULING
PEDALS

9.15 Look SL-3

9.16 Speedplay Frog

First remove the pedal from the bike (Figs. 9.3 and 9.4) and inspect it to figure out which section of directions to follow for overhauling.

There is a wide variation in mountain bike pedal designs. This book is not big enough to go into great detail about the inner workings of every single model. Speaking in general terms, pedal guts fall into two broad categories: ones that have cartridge bearings and/or bushings (Figs. 9.13–9.16 and 9.21), and those that have loose ball bearings (Figs. 9.11, 9.12 and 9.18).

Many pedals are closed on the outboard end and have a nut surrounding the axle on the inboard end (Figs. 9.9–9.13). The axle assembly installs into the pedal as a unit and is accessed by this inboard nut. The axle assemblies on older pedal designs — and some newer models — are accessed from the outboard end by removing a dust cap (Figs. 9.18, 9.21 and 9.22).

Before you start, figure out how the pedal is put together so you will know how to take it apart; the following paragraphs and the illustrations on subsequent pages should help. In a few cases, what the pedal guts are like may not be clear until you have completed step 1 in the overhaul process.

Shimano pedals usually have two sets of loose bearings and a bushing that comes out as a complete axle assembly (Figs. 9.11 and 9.12). You will see the tiny ball bearings at the small end of the axle (Fig. 9.17).

Most Taiwan-made clip-in pedals use an inboard bushing and an outboard cartridge bearing (Figs. 9.13 and 9.21); Codas also have an additional needle bearing between the two. Brands include Wellgo, VP, Ritchey, Scott, Coda, Girvin, Topo, Nashbar, OnZa, Exus and Norco. Some of these are

9.17 tightening Shimano locknut

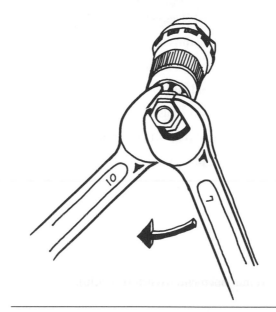

accessed from the crank side; others are accessed via an outboard dust cap. Speedplay pedals also have cartridge bearings and bushings; they differ in that they are opened like a clamshell (Fig. 9.16).

All Look, plastic-body Time ATAC, and Time TMT mountain pedals have an inboard cartridge bearing and an outboard needle bearing (Figs. 9.14 and 9.15). The axle assembly is accessed from the crank side.

Some pedals — even clip-in models (older Tioga comes to mind) — have no bearings at all. Instead, they just use bushings inside a plastic axle sleeve.

IX-5: OVERHAULING PEDALS CLOSED
ON THE OUTBOARD SIDE

 This includes Shimano, Time ATAC with plastic bodies, Time TMT, recent Ritchey, Look, Coda, Scott, Tioga, Exus and some VP and Wellgo models.

1. With the tool designed for your pedal (Figs. 1.2–1.4), remove the axle assembly. On most varieties, this is accomplished by unscrewing the nut

surrounding the axle where it enters the inboard side of the pedal (Figs. 9.9 and 9.10). See note below regarding thread direction. High-end Time ATACs with plastic bodies, recent butterfly-shaped Ritcheys, and old Time TMTs use a different approach. These pedals all rely on a snapring on the inboard end (Fig. 9.14) that must be removed with snapring pliers (Fig. 1.4).

Shimano, Look and Exus take a plastic splined tool, but the Look tool is not compatible with the other two. Use a large adjustable wrench to turn the tool (Fig. 9.9). Most other pedals take a 17mm or 18mm open-end wrench (Fig. 9.10).

Note: The threads inside the pedal body are reversed from the crankarm threads on the axle; the internal threads on the drive-side pedal are left-hand threaded, and vice versa. That means the right axle assembly unscrews clockwise and the left axle assembly unscrews counterclockwise. It's confusing, but like bottom bracket threads, pedal bodies are threaded so that pedaling forward works to unscrew the assembly.

The nut is often plastic and can crack if you turn it the wrong way, so be careful. Hold the pedal body with your hand or a vise while you unscrew the assembly. The fine threads take many turns to unscrew.

Time, Ritchey and Look pedals: All Look, recent Ritchey and old or current high-end Time mountain pedals have a large inboard cartridge bearing and an outboard needle bearing cartridge. These bearings tend to stay very clean and seldom require overhaul.

Axles in Time plastic-body ATACs, recent Ritchey and old Time TMTs are removed via a snapring on the crank side (Fig. 9.14). Popping the snapring out requires inward-squeezing snapring pliers. Now skip to step 3 with any of these.

There are three versions of Look clip-in moun-

tain pedals. The oldest models, marketed under the Look and Campagnolo names, clip in only on one side and resemble Look road pedals in design and function. Later Look models resemble most double-sided mountain clip-in pedals and take a large steel cleat. Axle assemblies in the single-sided model are accessed with an 18mm open-end wrench, while double-sided Looks (Fig. 9.15) require a special splined tool purchased separately.

Speedplay Frogs have a cartridge bearing and a needle bearing, which can be regreased without opening the pedal. Remove the Phillips screw from the outboard end of the pedal body and squirt grease in with a fine-tip bicycle grease gun (Fig. 1.3) until it squirts out the axle end. If you decide to open a Frog (reminds you of junior-high biology, doesn't it?), the pedal comes apart like a clamshell by unscrewing the single bolt on each side with a 2.5mm Allen wrench (Fig. 9.16). Before you put it back together, put a thin bead of automotive gasket sealer all of the way around the edge of one pedal half to seal water out.

2. Once you have removed the pedal body, take a look at the axle/bearing/bushing assembly. You will notice either one or two nuts on the thin end of the axle. These nuts serve to hold the bearings and/or bushings in place. Remove the nuts.

If the axle has just a single nut on the end (Figs. 9.13 and 9.16), simply hold the axle's large end with the 15mm pedal wrench and unscrew the little nut with a 9mm wrench (or whatever fits it). The nut may be very tight, since it has no locknut.

If the axle has two nuts on the end, they are tightened against each other. To remove them, hold the inner nut with a wrench while you unscrew the outer nut with another (Fig. 9.17).

Shimano and older Tioga pedals use two nuts in this fashion; on Shimanos, the inner nut acts as a bearing cone — be careful not to lose the tiny ball bearings as you unscrew the cone!

3. Clean all of the parts.

If it is a loose-bearing pedal, use a rag to clean the ball bearings, the cone, the inner ring that the bearings ride on at the end of the plastic sleeve (it looks like a washer), the bearing surfaces on either end of the little steel cylinder, the axle and the inside of the plastic axle sleeve (Figs. 9.11 and 9.12). To get the bearings really clean, wash them in the sink in soap and water with the sink drain plugged; the motion is the same as washing your hands, and it results in both the bearings and your hands being clean for a sterile reassembly. Blot dry.

If, on a pedal with a cartridge bearing (Figs. 9.13–9.16), the bearing is dirty or worn out, clean it if you can, otherwise replace it. These bearings often have steel bearing covers that cannot be pried off without damaging them, nor can the covers be replaced. If yours has plastic bearing covers, pry them off with a razor blade (Fig. 6.26), clean the bearing with solvent, let it dry, and repack it with grease.

Needle bearings (Time, Look, recent Ritchey and Coda) can be cleaned with a solvent and a thin bottle brush slipped inside the pedal-body bore.

On a bushing-only pedal, like older Tioga, just wipe down the axle and the inside of the bushings.

4. Lightly grease everything and reassemble the parts as they were, a simple process with bushings, cartridge bearings, and needle bearings — not so simple with loose bearings!

With a loose-bearing pedal, it is exacting work to place the bearings on their races and screw the cone on while they stay in place. On a Shimano (Figs.

9.11 and 9.12), grease the bushing inside the plastic axle sleeve, and slide the axle into the sleeve. Slide the steel ring, on which the inner set of bearings rides, down onto the axle and against the end of the sleeve. Make sure that the concave bearing surface faces out, away from the sleeve. Coat the ring with grease, and stick half of the bearings onto the outer surface of the ring. Slip the steel cylinder onto the axle so that one end rides on the bearings. Make sure that all of the bearings are seated properly and none are stuck inside of the sleeve.

To prevent the bearings from piling up on each other and ending up inside the sleeve instead of on the races, grease the cone and start it on the axle a few threads. Place the remaining half of the bearings on the flanks of the cone. Being careful not to dislodge the bearings, screw the cone in until the bearings come close to the end of the cylinder but do not touch it. While holding the plastic sleeve, push the axle inward until the bearings seat against the end of the cylinder. Make sure that the first set of bearings is still in place. Screw the cone in without turning the axle or cylinder. Tighten it with your fingers only, and loosely screw on the locknut.

5. Adjust the axle assembly. Time, recent Ritchey and Look skip this step.

Pedals with a small cartridge bearing and a single nut on the end of the axle, like Exus, Coda, VP, Wellgo, Topo, Girvin, Speedplay and Scott, simply require that you tighten the nut against the cartridge bearing while holding the other end of the axle with the 15mm pedal wrench. This secures the inner ring of the cartridge bearing against the shoulder on the axle, and proper adjustment is assured.

On pedals with two nuts on the end of the axle, hold the cone or inner nut with a wrench and

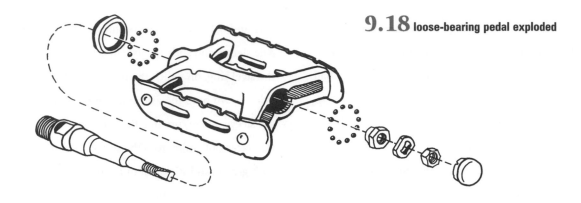

9.18 loose-bearing pedal exploded

tighten the outer locknut down against it (Fig. 9.17). Check the adjustment for freedom of rotation, and be sure there is no play. Readjust as necessary by tightening or loosening the cone or inner nut and retightening the locknut.

6. Replace the axle assembly in the pedal body.

Smear grease on the inside of the pedal hole; this will ease insertion and act as a barrier to dirt and water. Screw the sleeve back in place with the same wrench you used to remove it (Figs. 9.9 and 9.10). Remember: Pay attention to proper thread direction (see note in step 1). Tighten carefully; it is easy to overtighten and crack the plastic nut.

Time plastic-body ATACs, recent Ritchey and old Time TMTs: After replacing the axle assembly, pop the snapring back into its groove just inside the inboard lip of the pedal body.

7. Put the pedals back on your bike, and go ride.

IX-6: OVERHAULING LOOSE-BEARING PEDALS WITH A DUST CAP ON THE OUTBOARD END

Note: Many non-clip-in pedals are not worth the effort to overhaul, and not all economical pedals are accessible to overhaul. Assess the value of your pedals and your time before continuing.

1. Remove the dust cap with the appropriate tool. This could be a pair of pliers, a screwdriver, a coin, an Allen wrench or a splined tool especially for your pedals (Figs. 9.18 and 9.20–9.22); it's pretty easy to figure out which one is needed to remove the cap. If you see a cartridge bearing inside rather than loose balls, skip to Section IX-7.

2. Hold the wrench flats on the inboard end of the axle with a pedal wrench, and unscrew the locknut with the appropriate size socket wrench (as in Fig. 9.20).

3. Holding the pedal over a rag to catch the bearings, unscrew the cone. Keep the bearings from

9.19 dropping in bearings

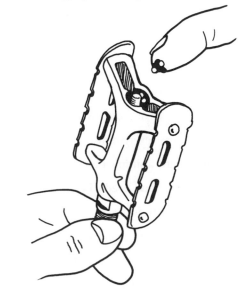

OVERHAULING LOOSE- BEARING PEDALS

9.20 removing locknut on OnZa H.O. pedal

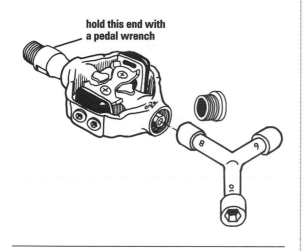

hold this end with
a pedal wrench

the two ends separate in case they differ in size or in number. Count them so you can put the right numbers back in when you reassemble the pedal. The guts should look like Fig. 9.18.

4. With a rag, clean the bearings, cones and bearing races. Clean the inside of the pedal body by pushing the rag through with a screwdriver. If there is a dust cover on the inboard end of the pedal body, you can clean that in place or after popping it out with a screwdriver.

5. If you want to get the bearings really clean, wash them in a plugged sink with soap and water. The motion is the same as washing your hands, and it results in both the bearings and your hands being clean for a sterile reassembly. Blot dry.

6. If you removed it, press the inboard dust cover back into the pedal body. Smear a thin layer of grease in the inboard bearing cup and replace the bearings. Once all of the bearings are in place, there will be a gap equal to about half the size of one bearing.

7. Drop the axle in and turn the pedal over so that the outboard end is up. Smear grease in that end, and replace the bearings (Fig. 9.19).

8. Screw the cone in until it almost contacts the bearings, then push the axle straight in to bring the cone and bearings together; this prevents the bearings from piling up and getting spit out as the cone turns down against them. Without turning the axle (which would knock the inboard bearings about), screw the cone in until it is finger-tight.

9. Slide on the washer and screw on the locknut. While holding the cone with a cone wrench, tighten

9.21 OnZa H.O. clip-in pedal exploded

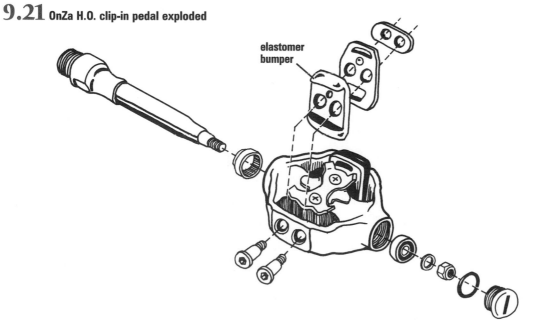

elastomer
bumper

9.22 Time ATAC Alium or Aliup HP exploded

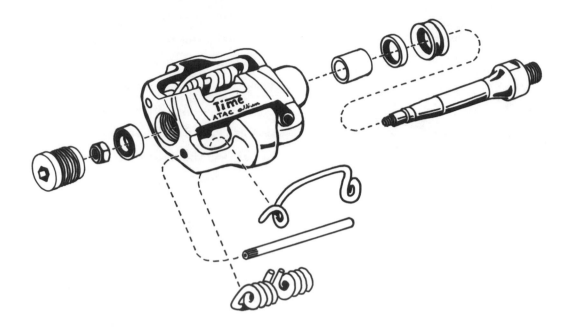

the locknut (similar to Fig. 9.17, but you will be holding the cone with a 13mm or so cone wrench, not a 10mm standard open-end wrench).

10. Check that the pedal spins smoothly without play. Readjust as necessary by tightening or loosening the cone and retightening the locknut.

11. Replace the dust cap.

12. Put the pedals back on and go riding!

OVERHAULING
CARTRIDGE
BEARING
PEDALS

IX-7: OVERHAULING CARTRIDGE BEARING PEDALS WITH OUTBOARD DUSTCAP

Time ATAC Alium and Aliup HP (Fig. 9.22), older Ritchey, OnZa H.O. (Figs. 9.8 and 9.20–9.21), some Wellgo, some VP, Nashbar and Norco, among others, have an axle end nut accessed from the outboard end by removing the dustcap. Inside is a brass bushing on the crank side and a sealed cartridge bearing on the outboard end.

1. Take off the dust cap; some take a 5mm or 6mm Allen wrench; others take a coin or a screwdriver.

2. Hold the crank end of the axle with a 15mm pedal wrench, and unscrew the nut on the outboard end with a socket wrench (usually 8mm, 9mm or 10mm [see Fig. 9.20]). The guts should look similar to Figs. 9.21 and 9.22.

3. Push the axle out the inboard end, freeing the outboard cartridge bearing.

4. Clean and regrease the axle and the inside of the pedal body hole. Replace the cartridge bearing if necessary. On Ritcheys and Time Aliums and Aliup HPs, the brass bushings inside the pedal body are also replaceable, but you need a special (unavailable) tool.

5. Push the axle back into the pedal body, slip the cartridge bearing onto the outboard end of the axle, and thread on the end nut.

6. While holding the crank end of the axle with a 15mm pedal wrench, tighten the little nut down against the cartridge bearing.

Note: *Ritcheys will still have side play at this point; the dust cap is an integral part of the assembly. Once it is tightened down, the play goes away.*

7. Replace the dust cap.

8. Put the pedals back on your bike (Figs. 9.3 and 9.4), and you're done. Go ride.

IX-8: LIGHTEN YOUR BIKE WITH AN AFTERMARKET TITANIUM SPINDLE

Some manufacturers offer aftermarket titanium axles for high-end pedals. Some offer only a titanium axle that is installed into the same sleeve, bushings and bearings as the one it replaces, while others sell a complete assembly, including the sleeve, bushings, and bearings.

If you are going to install a lightweight aftermarket axle or axle assembly into your pedals, make sure that you purchase one intended for your pedal brand and model. If all you are doing is replacing the axle, go ahead and follow the overhaul procedures outlined earlier in this chapter (Section IX-5 and IX-7). If you bought the entire assembly, just take out your old assembly. Again (I obviously feel the need to say this often), pay attention to the direction of the threads (see note in Section IX-5, step 1). Using the procedures in Section IX-5 or IX-7, install the new assembly.

Reinstall your pedals (Fig. 9.3 or 9.4). You'll be amazed how much lighter your bike feels ... or is that your wallet?

TROUBLESHOOTING PEDAL PROBLEMS

IX-9: CREAKING NOISE WHILE PEDALING

a. The shoe cleats are loose, or they are worn and need to be replaced (see Section IX-2).

b. Pedal bearings need cleaning and lubrication (see Sections IX.B and IX-5–IX-7).

c. The noise is originating from somewhere other than the pedals (see Chapter 8, troubleshooting section).

IX-10: RELEASE OR ENTRY WITH CLIP-IN PEDALS IS TOO EASY OR TOO HARD

a. Release tension needs to be adjusted (see Section IX-3).

b. Pedal-release mechanism needs to be cleaned and lubricated. Clean off mud and dirt, and drip chain lubricant on the springs (Fig. 9.23) and dry lubricant on the cleat contacts on the clips.

c. The cleats themselves need to be cleaned and lubricated. Clean off dirt and mud and put a dry chain lubricant or a dry grease like pure Teflon on the contact ends of the cleats.

d. The cleats are worn out. Replace them (Section IX 2).

9.23 lubing release mechanism

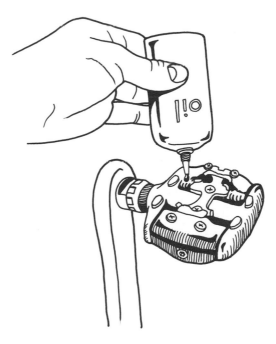

e. The knobs on the shoe sole that contact the pedal might be so tall that they prevent the cleat from engaging. Locate where the pedal edges contact the sole, and trim some of the rubber with a knife.

f. The clips on the pedal are bent down. Straighten them if you can, or replace them. If you can't repair or replace the clips, you may have to replace the entire pedal.

g. If it is hard to clip into your pedals, check the metal cleat guide plate at the center of the pedal. It is held on with two Phillips screws, and they may be loose or have fallen out.

h. Time ATAC spring clips can get bent and not hold the cleat as well. But they are replaceable by driving out the pin with a hammer and a punch (see Fig. 9.22).

IX-11: YOU EXPERIENCE KNEE AND JOINT PAIN WHILE PEDALING

a. Cleat misalignment often causes pain on the sides of the knees (see Section IX-2).

b. You need more rotational float. Consider a pedal that offers more float; those offering the most are the Time ATAC and Speedplay Frog.

c. If your foot wants to roll inward (pronate), but your shoe and pedal force your foot to roll outward, then there is likely to be an increase in the tension on the iliotibial (I-T) band, the tendon connecting the hip and calf. This will eventually cause pain on the outside of the knee. You need to see a specialist, because you will probably need custom foot-beds (insoles) to correct the problem.

d. Fatigue and improper seat height can also contribute to joint pain. Pain in the front of the knee right behind the kneecap can indicate that your saddle is too low. Pain in the back of the leg behind the knee suggests that your saddle is too high. (See Appendix C for seat-height guidelines.)

CAUTION

If any of these problems result in chronic pain, consult a specialist. If you experience foot pain, a specialist can make custom foot beds to fit inside your shoes. Custom foot beds can also correct leg misalignments emanating from the foot.

TROUBLE-
SHOOTING

saddles and seatposts

tools

4mm, 5mm, 6mm Allen wrenches

open-end wrenches of various sizes

adjustable wrench

grease

Even if you're on the right track, you'll get run over if you just sit there.

— WILL ROGERS

fter a few hours on the bike, I can pretty much guarantee that you will be most aware of one component on your bike: the saddle. It is the part of your bike with which you are most ... uh ... intimately connected. Nothing can ruin a good ride faster than a poorly positioned or badly designed saddle.

The seatpost connects it to the frame. Some have shock absorbing systems that cushion the ride. Some bikes, like the Softride, employ a flexible beam attached to the front of the frame instead of a seatpost.

X-1: SADDLES

Most bike saddles are simply made up of a flexible plastic shell, some padding, a cover and a pair of rails (Fig. 10.1). There are countless variations on (and a few notable exceptions to) this theme. Some have extra thick or high-tech gel cushions. Some have depressions, holes or splits in the shell to reduce pressure in sensitive areas. Some have rails made of titanium, hollow cromoly or even aluminum or carbon fiber. Others have synthetic covers, covers made from Kevlar or covers made from the finest full-grain leather money can buy. You can expect to spend anywhere from $20 to $200 for a decent saddle, and price may not be the best indicator of what makes a saddle really good — namely comfort.

You have a lot of choices when you decide to pick a saddle. My best advice is to ignore price, weight, fashion and looks, and choose a saddle that is comfortable. I could go on for pages about

10.1 modern lightweight saddle

10.2 Brooks leather saddle

hi-zoot gel padding, scientifically designed shells that flex in just the right places at just the right moment, and all sorts of factors that engineers consider when designing a saddle. None of it would count for squat if, after reading it, you ran out and bought a saddle that turned out to be a giant pain in the rear. Saddles are different because *people* are different. Try as many as you can before buying one.

The marketing war raging over saddles designed to prevent male impotency (Fig. 10.3) can blind a consumer's ability to select appropriately. If you buy a saddle out of fear, and it is uncomfortable, you have done yourself a disservice. Don't take it on faith or scientific studies that your saddle is protecting you. If it hurts or you get numb on it, it isn't working for you. What works for one person won't necessarily work for another.

Determine which saddle shape and design is the most comfortable for your body and then — and only then — start looking at things like titanium

rails, fancy covers and all of the other things that improve a saddle. I know a lot of people who need 300g or 400g saddles with tons of thick padding to feel comfortable on even a short ride. I know others who can ride for hours on a skinny little 200g Selle Italia Flite. It's a matter of preference. Any decent bike shop worth its weight in titanium should let you try a saddle for a while before locking you into a sale.

Brooks and Idéale saddles have no plastic shell, foam padding or cover. They are simply constructed from a single piece of thick leather attached to a steel frame with large brass rivets (Fig. 10.2). This was the main type of saddle up until the 1980s. Brooks still makes them and even offers them with titanium rails these days. This sort of saddle requires a long break-in period and frequent applications of a leather-softening compound that comes with the saddle or from a shoe store. Like a lot of old bike parts, you either love 'em or you hate

10.3 saddle designed to not contact the perineum

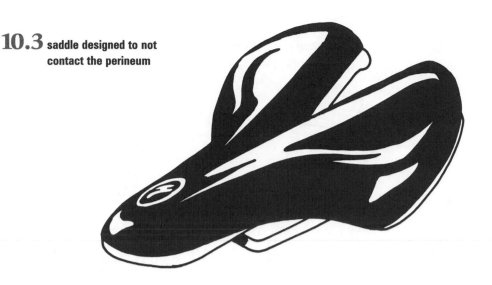

saddles and seatposts

'em. If you're not familiar with them by now, go out and buy a modern saddle (Figs. 10.1 and 10.3).

A saddle with a plastic shell and foam padding requires little maintenance, except to keep it clean; check periodically that the rails are not bent or cracked (a good sign that you need to replace your saddle).

X-2: SADDLE POSITION

Even if you have found the perfect saddle, it can still feel like some medieval torture device if it isn't properly positioned. Saddle placement is the most important part of finding a comfortable riding position. Not only does saddle position affect how you feel on the bike, but also with the saddle in the right place you suddenly become a much better rider. There are three basic elements to saddle position: tilt, fore-and-aft and saddle height (Fig. 10.4).

See Appendix C, Section C-3, for a detailed explanation of setting saddle and handlebar position. Following are some short guidelines.

Proper saddle height (Fig. 10.4) is key to transferring good power to the pedals. The ideal road-bike saddle height places your leg in a 90–95 per-

10.4 saddle adjustments

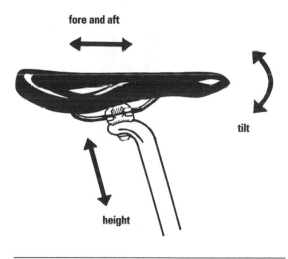

fore and aft

tilt

height

cent extension when you're riding; however, you may find that this position to be too high for riding singletrack. Make sure your seatpost is inserted past the limit line, however. Again, consult Appendix C.

To improve your balance and center of gravity when descending, you can bring the saddle height down — how far depends on you and the kind of riding you do. Pro downhillers prefer very low saddle heights when compared to pro cross-country riders.

The most common cause of numb crotch and butt fatigue is an improperly tilted saddle (Fig. 10.4).

SADDLE
POSITION

10.5 single-bolt seatpost   **10.6** single-bolt seatpost with small adjusting bolt   **10.7** two-bolt seatpost

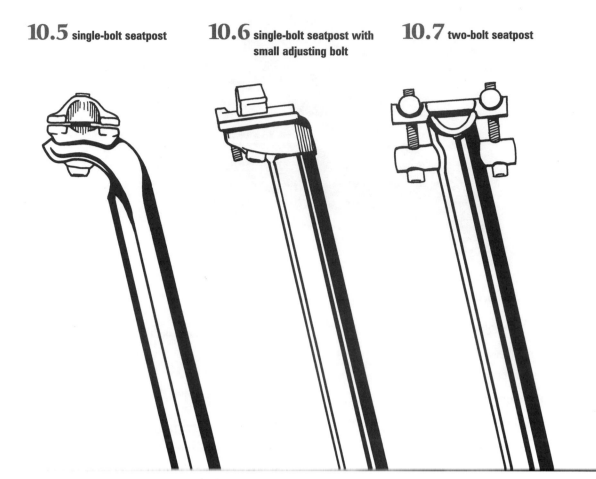

The general rule of thumb is that you should keep the saddle level when you first install it. After a while, some people find that they prefer a slight upward or downward tilt to their saddles. Other than perhaps for downhillers, I strongly recommend against making that tilt much more than a quarter-inch. Too much upward tilt and you place too much of your body weight on the nose of the saddle. Too much downward tilt will cause you to scoot down the saddle as you ride. That puts unnecessary pressure on your back, shoulders and neck.

Fore-aft position (Fig. 10.4) determines where your butt sits on the saddle, the position of your knees relative to the pedals and how much of your weight is transferred to your hands. Regardless of manufacturer, all saddles are designed to have your butt centered over the widest part. If this is not

where you sit, reposition the saddle. You want to position the saddle so that you have a comfortable amount of bend in your arms, without feeling too cramped or stretched out. If you find that your neck and shoulders feel tighter than usual and your hands are going numb, try redistributing your weight by moving the saddle back. Fore-and-aft saddle position also affects how your legs are positioned relative to the pedals. Ideally, your fore-aft position should be such that your knee pushes straight down on the forward pedal when your crankarms are in a perfectly horizontal position. If your saddle will not go back as far as you wish, and you have a short women's saddle, try replacing it with a standard-length men's model.

Butt pain is intimately connected to handlebar position, as are other aches and pains. The shorter the upper-body reach and higher the handlebars, the more weight will go on the butt. The longer the reach and lower the bars, the more the pelvis rotates forward and moves the saddle pressure point from the sit bones to the soft tissue of the perineum and genital area. As a general rule, a novice rider will want a shorter reach and higher bars and perhaps a correspondingly wider saddle than will an experienced rider. Once again, consult Appendix C.

X-3: SEATPOST MAINTENANCE

A standard seatpost requires little maintenance other than removing it from the frame every few months. When you do that, wipe it down, regrease it and the inside of the frame's seat tube, and then reinstall it. This keeps it clean and moving freely for the purposes of adjustability; it also should prevent the seatpost from getting stuck in the frame (a very nasty and potentially serious problem). I have outlined the procedures for installing a new seatpost and for removing a stuck seatpost in Section X-11.

Suspension seatposts require periodic tune-ups — see Section X-9.

Regularly check any seatpost for cracks or bends so that you can replace it before it breaks with you on it.

X-4: INSTALLING A SADDLE

Most seatposts have either one (Fig. 10.5) or two bolts (Figs. 10.6 and 10.7) for clamping the saddle. Good single-bolt systems have a vertical bolt (Fig. 10.5) while cheap posts have a horizontal crosswise bolt.

Remember those heavy posts on your first bike as a kid? Those steel seatposts had the single horizontal bolt that pulled together a number of

knurled washers with ears to hold the saddle rails. These weak seatpost clamps cannot hold up to adult use anymore; eschew them for posts with one or two vertical bolts holding aluminum clamshell clamp pieces together.

The two-bolt posts can rely on one of two systems. In one, the two bolts work together, pulling the saddle rails into the clamp (Fig. 10.7). On others, like the American Classic post, a smaller second bolt works to offset the force of the main bolt (Fig. 10.6). No matter what type you have, it is reasonably easy to figure out how to remove, install and adjust the saddle.

X-5: SADDLE INSTALLATION ON SEATPOST WITH A SINGLE VERTICAL CLAMP BOLT

Systems with a single vertical bolt (Fig. 10.5) usually have a two-piece clamp that fastens onto the saddle rails. On most single-bolt models, moving the clamp and saddle along a serrated curved platform controls saddle tilt. Before you tighten the clamp bolt, make sure there is not a second, much smaller bolt (or "set screw") that adjusts seat tilt. If it does, skip to the next section (X-6).

1. Loosen the bolt until there are only a couple of threads still holding onto the upper clamp.

2. Turn the top half of the clamp 90 degrees and slide in the saddle rails. Do it from the back where the space between the rails is wider. You might need to remove the top of the clamp completely from the bolt if it is too large. If you do disassemble the clamp, pay attention to the orientation of the parts so you can put it back together the same way.

3. Set the seat rails into the grooves in the lower part of the clamp, and set the top clamp piece on

10.8 saddle installation on single-bolt seatpost

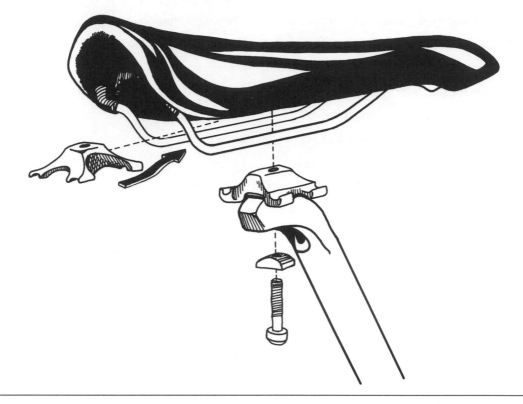

top of the rails (Fig. 10.8). Slide the saddle to the desired fore-aft position.

4. Tighten the bolt and check the seat tilt. Readjust if necessary.

X-6: SADDLE INSTALLATION ON SEATPOST WITH LARGE CLAMP BOLT AND SMALL SETSCREW

This type of post is illustrated in Fig. 10.6.

1. Loosen the large bolt until the top part of the clamp can either be removed or moved out of the way so that you can slide the saddle rails into place.

2. Set the saddle rails between the top and bottom sets of grooves in the seat clamp. Slide the saddle to the desired fore-aft position. Tighten the large bolt.

3. To change the saddle tilt, loosen the large clamp bolt, adjust the saddle angle as needed

by turning the setscrew, and retighten the clamp bolt. Repeat until the desired adjustment is reached.

Note: *On these types of seatposts, the setscrew may be either vertical or horizontal. On those with a vertical setscrew (Fig. 10.6), the screw is usually adjacent to the clamp bolt. A horizontal setscrew is usually placed at the top front of the seatpost, pushing back on the clamp. With such a setscrew, push down on the back of the saddle with the clamp bolt loose to make sure the clamp and setscrew are in contact.*

X-7: INSTALLING SADDLE ON SEATPOST WITH TWO EQUAL-SIZED CLAMP BOLTS

This type of post is illustrated in Fig. 10.7.

1. Loosen one or both of the bolts and open the clamp enough that the saddle rails slide into their grooves between the two sides of the clamp. On

10.9 saddle installation on two-bolt seatpost

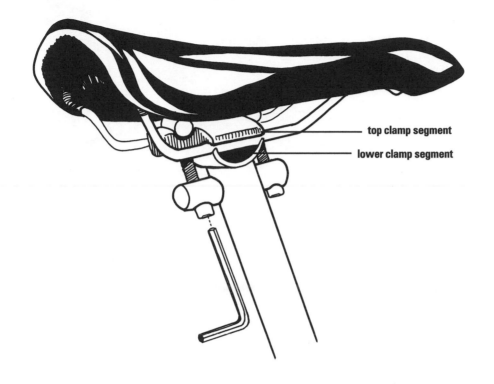

top clamp segment

lower clamp segment

some posts of this type, each piece that sits on top of and under the rails is shaped like a cylinder sliced longitudinally down the middle. Slide the top or bottom piece out, set the saddle rails in their grooves in the piece left in, and slide the piece you removed back in from the side.

2. Slide the saddle to the desired fore-aft position. Tighten down one or both of the clamp bolts completely.

3. Loosen one clamp bolt and tighten the other to change the tilt of the saddle (Fig. 10.9). Repeat as necessary. Complete by tightening both bolts.

X-8: SEATPOST INSTALLATION INTO THE FRAME

1. Check for irregularities, burrs and other problems inside the seat tube, visually and with your finger; if there are some, you may need to sand or otherwise clean up inside the seat tube. It may be necessary for a bike shop to ream the seat tube if a seat post of the correct size will not fit.

2. Grease the seatpost and the inside of the seat tube. Grease the seat lug binder bolt. If you are using a sleeve or shim to adapt an undersized seatpost to fit your frame, grease it inside and out, and insert it.

3. Insert the seatpost (Fig. 10.10), and tighten the seat binder bolt. Some binder bolts are tightened with a wrench (usually a 5mm Allen), and some have a quick-release lever (Fig. 10.11). To tighten a quick release, flip the lever open so that it is directly in line with the body of the bolt — in other words, about halfway open. Finger-tighten the nut on the other end, and then close the lever. It should be fairly snug, about tight enough to leave an impression in the heel of your hand for a

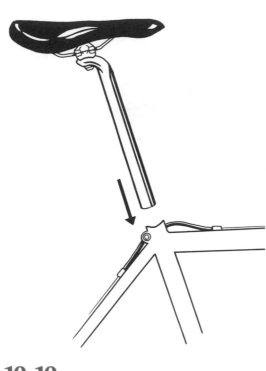

10.10 seatpost installation into the frame

10.11 closing quick-release seatpost binder

few seconds. Open the lever, reposition the end nut, and close the lever again as necessary to get the right closing force.

4. After the saddle is attached, adjust the seat height to your desired position. It is a good idea to mark this height on the post with an indelible marker or a piece of tape. This way, if you remove it, you can just slide it right back into the proper place.

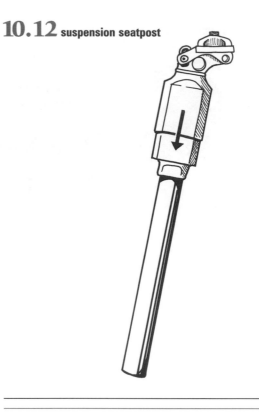

10.12 suspension seatpost

X-9: SUSPENSION SEATPOSTS

Shock-absorbing seatposts come equipped with some sort of spring — either a steel coil, an elastic polymer ("elastomer") or an air cushion. The telescoping elastomer spring type (Fig. 10.12) is probably the most common, and air shocks are the rarest. Some seatposts have linkages that swing the saddle on an arc, rather than up and down.

To adjust the "boing" in most suspension seatposts, you either change the amount of preload on the elastomer spring, or you replace the elastomer(s). With telescoping seatposts (Fig. 10.12) and even with some parallelogram-linkage posts, you must first pull the seatpost out of the frame. If you look up inside the post from the bottom, you will usually see a large slotted screw threaded into the walls of the post. If you tighten down clockwise on this screw, you will increase the preload on the spring and hence stiffen the seatpost. If you loosen this screw (counterclockwise),

10.13 saddle on Softride beam

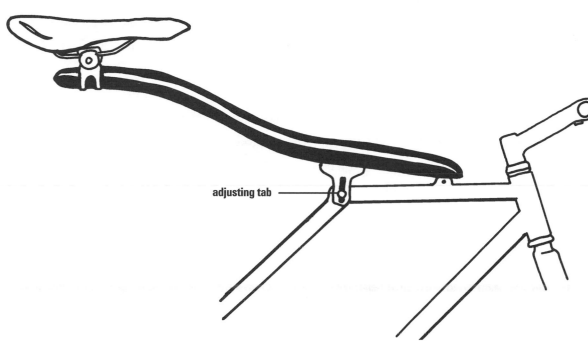

adjusting tab

you reduce the preload and soften the ride.

To change springs, you remove the spring completely, make the switch (remember to grease the elastomers!), and replace the screw. You will find that as you change preload or elastomer combinations, the height of your saddle changes, so expect to slide the seatpost up and down in the frame to adjust for that.

Some parallelogram-linkage posts can be adjusted by turning a preload screw behind the saddle clamp and/or pushing the elastomer out from the side and replacing it (or interchanging small elastomer plugs into a larger elastomer).

There are other suspension-seatpost designs out there as well, and it is difficult to provide instructions that apply to all of them. Fortunately, most shock-absorbing seatposts are tuned as above, and the others usually come with extensive instructions.

I recommend following the same regular maintenance schedule you would use for a standard

seatpost (Section X-3), in addition to maintenance of the suspension components.

X-10: INSTALLING A SOFTRIDE SUSPENSION BEAM ONTO FRAME

The frame must be built to accept the beam, or you must purchase a retrofit kit from Softride to install it on a standard frame.

1. Attach the beam to the front frame-mounting bracket with a steel pin. The underside of the beam's nose has a small steel eyelet that fits between two tabs on the bracket, which is located on the top of the frame's top tube (Fig. 10.13). With a soft hammer, tap the included pin through the bracket, through the eye on the bottom of the beam, and out through the hole in the other side of the bracket.

2. Attach the beam to the rear frame-mounting bracket, located a few inches behind the front eyelet. The rear mount on the beam consists of two

curved tabs separated by the width of the frame's mounting bracket that extend down. Long, curved slots in each tab (Fig. 10.13) are used to adjust the saddle height. Pass the bolt through one of the rectangular washers (with its knurled side pointing inward) and into the slot of one tab. Then pass it through the round end cap of the cylindrical frame mount, the frame mount itself and out through the second end cap, the other oval tab hole and the other rectangular washer. Screw on the nut after lining up the offset end cap holes so they fit into the mounting bracket with the bolt in place.

3. Swing the beam up to the desired height, with the fixing bolt loose. For starters, set it about an inch higher than what your normal seat height would be, to account for the beam's flex. If you reach the end of the adjustment in the bracket tab slots and the seat is still not as high as you need it to be, rotate the rear frame-mount end caps. The caps' offset holes offer two height positions for this very reason.

4. Tighten the fixing bolt. Readjust saddle height as needed.

X-11: REMOVING A STUCK SEATPOST

REMOVING A STUCK SEATPOST

LEVEL 3 This is a Level 3 job because of the risk involved. This may be a job best done by a shop, because if you make a mistake you run the risk of destroying your frame. If you're not 100 percent confident in your abilities, go to someone who is — or at least to someone who will be responsible if they screw it up.

1. Remove the seat binder bolt. Sounds easy enough.

2. Squirt penetrating oil around the seatpost and let it sit overnight. To get the most penetration, remove the bottom bracket (Chapter 8), turn the bike upside down, squirt the penetrating oil in from the bottom of the seat tube, and let it sit overnight.

3. The next day, stand over the bike and twist the saddle.

4. If step 3 does not free the seatpost, you will need to move into the difficult and risky part of this procedure.

You will now sacrifice the seatpost. Remove the saddle and all of the clamps from the top of the seatpost. With the bike upside down, clamp the top of the seatpost into a large bench vise that is bolted to a very secure workbench.

Congratulations, you have just ruined your seatpost. Don't ever ride it again.

Grab the frame at both ends, and begin to carefully apply a twisting pressure. Be aware that you can easily apply enough force to bend or crack your frame, so be careful. If the seatpost finally releases, it often makes such a large "pop" that you will think that you have broken many things!

5. If step 4 does not work, you need to go to a machine shop and get the post reamed out of the seat tube.

If you *still* insist on getting it out yourself, you should really sit down and think about it for a while. Will the guy at the machine shop really charge you so much money that is now worth the risk of completely trashing your frame?

Have you thought about it for a while? And still you insist on doing this yourself? Okay, but don't say I didn't warn you.

Take a hacksaw and cut your seatpost off a little more than an inch above the seat lug on your frame. (Now you obviously have completely destroyed your seatpost, so I don't have to warn about riding it again.) Remove the blade from the saw and wrap a piece of tape around one end. Hold on to the taped end and slip the other end into the center of the post. Carefully (no, make that very carefully) make two outward cuts about 60 degrees apart. Your goal is to remove a pie-shaped wedge from the hunk of seatpost stuck in your frame. Be careful — this is where many people cut too far and go right through the seatpost into the frame. Of course, you wouldn't do that, now would you? Once you've made the cut, pry or pull this piece out with a large screwdriver or a pair of pliers. Be careful here, too. A lot of overenthusiastic home mechanics have damaged their frames by prying too hard here. But you wouldn't do that, would you?

Once the wedge is out, work the remaining piece out by curling in the edges with the pliers to free more and more of it from the seatpost walls. It should eventually work its way out.

Now, once your seatpost is out of the frame, remember to go back and reread Section X-3 outlining the regular maintenance procedures required for a seatpost. In other words, take it out and apply grease every once in a while. You don't want to have to do this again, do you?

X-12: TROUBLESHOOTING PROBLEMS IN THE SEAT AND SEATPOST

1. **Loose saddle.** Check the bolts. They are probably loose. Tighten the bolts and set the desired saddle tilt, after setting fore-aft saddle position (Section X-2). Check for any damage to the clamping mechanism, and replace the post if necessary. If you need help, look up the instructions that apply to your seatpost.

2. **Stuck seatpost.** Having a stuck seatpost can be a serious problem. Follow the instructions in Section

X-11 carefully or you might damage your frame.

3. **Saddle squeaks with each pedal stroke.** The problem comes from the smooth leather or plastic moving against metal parts or from grit in the rail attachments.

On saddles that extend low on the sides, contact with the seatpost clamp or rails is likely the culprit. Greasing the contact area will eliminate the noise. Also, roughing up the leather at the contact point with metal will also quiet it down, since smooth leather sliding on metal can squeak.

Try also squirting chain lube into the three points where the rails are inserted into the plastic shell of the saddle, in case some grit working at the rails is making the noise.

4. **Creaking noises from the seatpost.** A seatpost can creak from moving back and forth against the sides of the seat tube while you ride. A dry seatpost can creak, so first try greasing it.

Some frames have an internal collar to adapt the seat tube to a certain seatpost diameter. Remember that the internal diameter of the seat tube is larger below the collar. I have seen bikes that creaked because the bottom of the seatpost rubbed against the sides of the seat tube below the extension of the collar. You can solve that problem by shortening the seatpost a bit with a hacksaw. If you do saw off the seatpost, make sure that you still have at least 3 inches of seatpost inserted in the frame for security.

Similarly, movement between the frame, sizing shims and the post can cause creaking. Greasing all of these parts well should eliminate it.

If the creaking originates from the seatpost head where the saddle is clamped, you should check the clamp bolts. Lubricate the bolt threads and you will be able to tighten them a bit more.

Shock-absorbing seatposts can squeak as they move up and down. Try greasing the sides of the inner shaft. Grease the elastomers inside, too.

5. **Seatpost slips down.** Tighten the frame binder bolt. If the seat-binder lug is pinched closed, and you still can't get it tight enough, you may be using a seatpost with an incorrect diameter, or the seat tube on your bike is oversized or has been stretched. Double-check the seat-tube diameter with a pair of calipers. Your local shop may have one.

Try putting a larger seatpost in the frame, and replace yours if you find one that fits better. If the next size up is too big, you may need to "shim" your existing post. Cut a 1-by-3-inch piece of aluminum from a pop can. Pull the seatpost out, grease it and the pop-can shim, and insert both back into your frame. Bend the top lip of the shim over to prevent it from disappearing inside the frame. You may need to experiment with various shim dimensions until you find a piece that will go in with the seatpost and will also prevent slippage. Go ahead, they're cheap.

TROUBLE-
SHOOTING

handlebars, stems and headsets

*The great thing in this world is not so much where you stand,
as in what direction you are moving.*

— *OLIVER WENDELL HOLMES JR. (1809–1894)*

On a bike, you maintain or change your direction largely by applying force to your handlebars. If everything works properly, variations in that pressure will result in your front wheel changing direction. Pretty basic, right? Right. But there is a somewhat complicated series of parts between the handlebars and the wheel that makes that simple process possible. The parts of the steering system are illustrated in Fig. 11.1. In this chapter, we'll cover most of that system by going over handlebars, stems and headsets. This chapter is designed to start at the outside of the handlebars and move toward the middle.

XI.A BAR ENDS

XI-1: INSTALLATION OF BAR ENDS

1. Slide the shifters, brake levers and grips inward to make room at the end of the bar for the bar end. See "Grip Removal," Section XI-3, for instructions on moving the grip, and Chapters 5 and 7 about shifters and brake levers.

2. Loosen the bolt on the bar-end clamp; it usually accepts a 5mm Allen wrench. Slide the bar end onto the bar (Fig. 11.2).

3. Tighten the clamp bolt enough that it just holds the bar ends in place. Rotate the bar ends to the position you like (see Section 5 of Appendix C for recommendations).

4. Tighten the clamp bolt. Make sure it is snug.

11.1 steering assembly (shown without brakes for clarity)

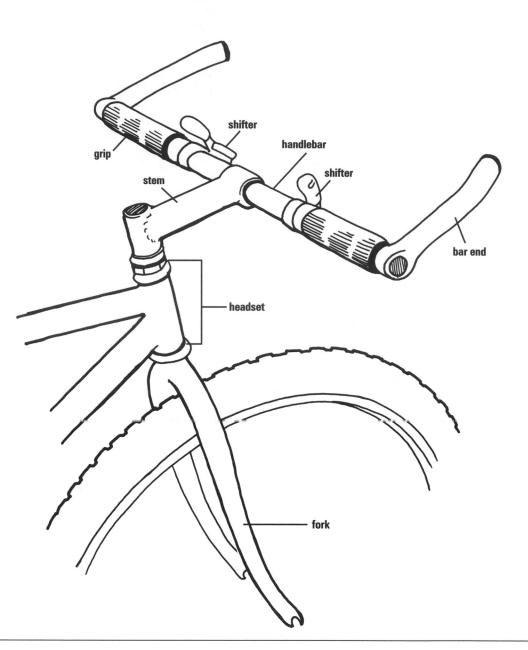

grip

shifter

handlebar

shifter

stem

bar end

headset

fork

BAR ENDS

Recommended torque is in Appendix E.

Note: *The ends of some superlight handlebars can be damaged by bar ends. These bars come equipped with small cylindrical aluminum inserts that support the bar under the bar end. Similarly, some composite bars have an aluminum reinforcement at the end to support them under the bar end. These bars cannot be shortened, as the bar ends will not have the support they need.*

Bar ends are meant to provide a powerful hand position while climbing, as well as an alternative stretched-out position while riding on smooth roads. They are not meant to be positioned vertically to provide a higher hand position. If you want your hands higher, get a taller, more vertical stem and perhaps bars that have a double bend to elevate the ends. This way you still have easy access to the brake levers.

11.2 grip and bar-end assembly exploded

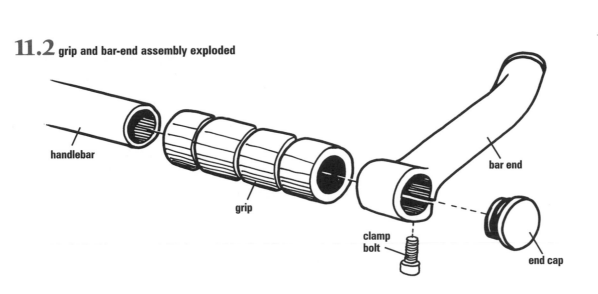

handlebar

grip

clamp
bolt

bar end

end cap

XI-12: REMOVE BAR ENDS

1. Loosen the bolt on the bar-end clamp; it usually accepts a 5mm Allen wrench.

2. Pull the bar end off (Fig. 11.2).

XI.B GRIPS

XI-3: GRIP REMOVAL

If the grip is shot, just cut it off with a knife. Otherwise:

1. Remove the bar ends and bar-end plugs (Fig. 11.2, Section XI-2).

2. Roll back an edge of the grip on itself.

3. Squirt water or, better yet, rubbing alcohol on the bar and the exposed grip underside (Fig. 11.3). Flip the rolled-up edge back down, and repeat steps 2 and 3 on the other end of the grip.

4. Starting at the ends, twist the grip back and forth as you pull outward on it (Fig. 11.4). The wet sections will slip easily, and the dry middle section will get moving as the ends twist.

PRO TIP

A syringe can be used to inject rubbing alcohol under the grip. The needle can be slipped under the grip from the end, and it can even be pushed through

11.3 using water to remove grip

11.4 grip removal

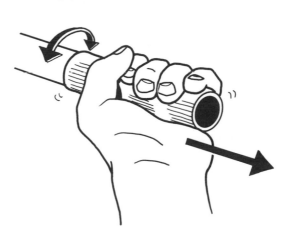

11.5 trimming grip to accommodate bar end

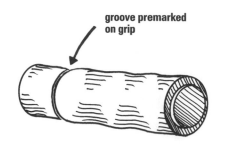

groove premarked
on grip

the grip. With alcohol underneath, the grip will slide off in seconds.

XI-4: GRIP INSTALLATION

1. Squirt rubbing alcohol or water inside the grip. Rubbing alcohol lubricates well and dries quickly (immediately, with a blast of compressed air!); water dries slowly, so the grip slips for a few days; hair spray and spray adhesives can be used to totally prevent grip slippage, but they are bad to breathe and set up permanently, thwarting subsequent removal and repositioning.

2. Twist the grip onto the bar.

Note: Some grips have a closed end. If you are going to use bar ends, you will need to cut off the closed end; you may also want to shorten the grip for your hand size or to adapt to a twist shifter. Some of these grips have a marked groove where they are meant to be cut with a pair of scissors (Fig. 11.5). Otherwise, you can cut them off anywhere you wish with scissors, tin snips or a knife. If you have a thin, lightweight handlebar you can easily cut off the end of the grip by hitting the end of the grip with a mallet or hammer after it is installed on the bar. The bar will cut a nice hole in the grip end like a cookie cutter!

Grips used alongside Grip Shift and other twist shifters are shorter than standard grips, as part of the

hand is sitting on the twist grip. Grips specifically designed for Grip Shift shifters are readily available in bike shops. If you can't find them, just cut yours down to the proper length.

XI.C HANDLEBARS

XI-5: HANDLEBAR REMOVAL

1. Remove the bar ends and grips (Fig. 11.2), at least from one side. It is easier to remove grips when the bar is clamped into the stem than when it is sitting on a workbench; therefore, if you are moving the parts to another bar, remove them while the bar is still on the bike. For instructions for removing bar ends and grips, see Sections XI-2 and XI-3.

2. Remove the brake levers and shifters. (Turn to Chapter 7 for information on brake levers and Chapter 5 for shifters.)

3. Loosen the bolt on the stem clamp surrounding the bar. This usually takes a 5mm Allen wrench.

4. Pull the bar out.

XI-6: HANDLEBAR INSTALLATION

1. Remove the stem-clamp bolt, grease its threads, and replace it. Grease the inside of the stem clamp, and grease the clamping area in the center of the bar.

2. Twist the bar to the position you find most comfortable. With a standard, single-bend bar, I prefer rotating the bar to the point that the ends point up and back, but it is all a matter of preference.

3. Tighten the bolt or bolts that clamp the bar to the stem to the recommended torque — see the torque table in Appendix E. This is particularly important with expensive, lightweight stems and bars. You can pinch and thereby weaken a lightweight handlebar by overtightening, and the high-strength tubing will crack right by the stem. Light

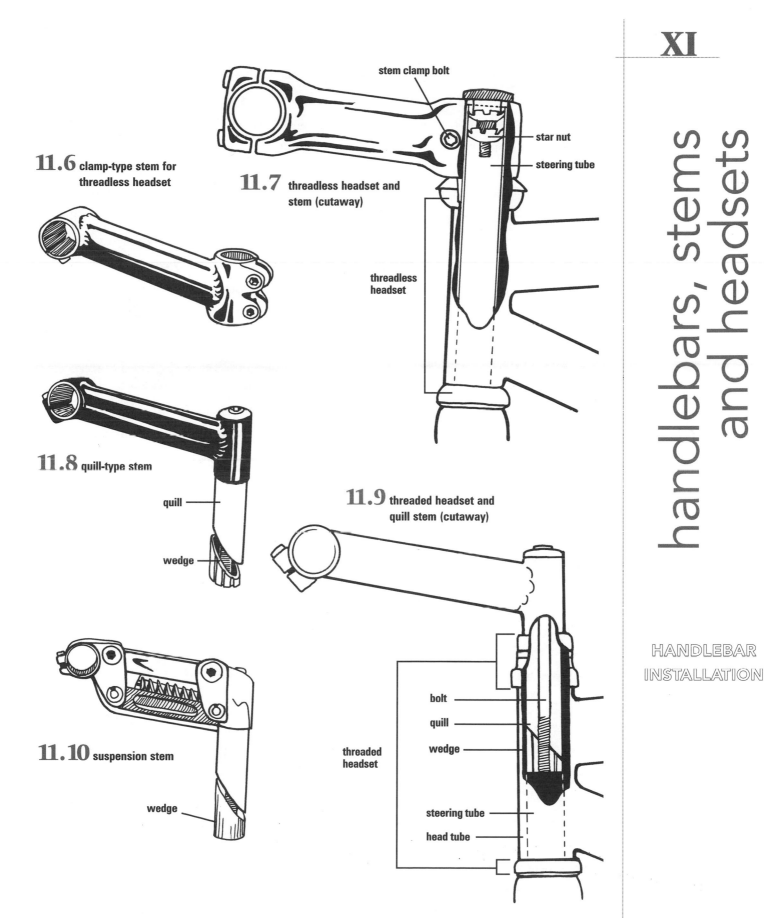

11.6 clamp-type stem for threadless headset

11.7 threadless headset and stem (cutaway)

stem clamp bolt

star nut

steering tube

threadless headset

11.8 quill-type stem

quill

wedge

11.9 threaded headset and quill stem (cutaway)

11.10 suspension stem

wedge

threaded headset

bolt

quill

wedge

steering tube

head tube

handlebars, stems and headsets

HANDLEBAR INSTALLATION

stems come with ever-smaller bolts with ever-finer threads, and overtightening can strip the threads inside the aluminum (or magnesium, etc.) stem. If you don't have a torque wrench and you have a lightweight stem with small bolts (e.g., M5 or M6 bolts, which take 4mm and 5mm hex keys, respectively), use a short hex key so that you can't get much leverage.

Also, make sure that there is the same amount of space between the stem and either edge of the front plate on a front-opening stem. Any stem whose clamp gap(s) gets pinched close to touching when tightened around the bar needs to be replaced, along with the handlebar.

XI-7: HANDLEBAR MAINTENANCE AND REPLACEMENT SCHEDULE

A bike cannot be controlled without handlebars, so you never want one to break on you. Do not look at your bars as a permanent accessory on your bike. All aluminum bars will eventually fail. If titanium, steel or carbon fiber bars are repeatedly stressed above a certain level, they will eventually fail as well. What that level is depends on the particular bar. The trick is not to be riding them when they fail.

Keep your bars clean. Regularly inspect the bars for cracks, crash-induced bends, corrosion and stressed areas. If you find any sign of wear or cracking, replace the bars. Never straighten a bent handlebar — replace it! If you crash hard on your bike, consider replacing your bars even if they look fine. If you have had a crash and see no problems with the bars, remove the bar ends and check whether the bar is bent at the edges of the bar end. A carbon-fiber bar can be broken internally and the damage may not be visible from the outside. If

your bars have taken an extremely hard hit, it's a good idea to replace them rather than gamble on their integrity. This is especially true with lightweight bars; the high hardness of the materials used may prevent visible bending, but they may be so weakened that they will shear off soon.

The Italian stem and bar manufacturer 3T recommends replacing stems and bars every four years. As with a stem, if you rarely ride the bike, this is overkill. If you ride hard and ride often, every four years may not be frequent enough. Do what is appropriate for you, and be aware of the risks.

XI.D STEMS

The stem connects to the steering tube of the fork and clamps around the handlebar. Stems come in one of two basic types: for (1) threadless (Fig. 11.7) or (2) threaded (Fig. 11.9) steering tubes. Some stems have shock-absorbing mechanisms with pivots and springs to provide suspension (Fig. 11.10).

Stems for threadless steering tubes (Fig. 11.6) have a clamping collar in place of the quill. Since

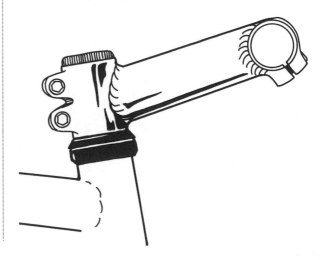

11.11 threadless headset cup held in place by stem

HANDLEBAR
MAINTENANCE
AND
REPLACEMENT
SCHEDULE
—
STEMS

the steering tube has no threads, the top headset cup slides on and off. In this case, the stem plays a dual role. It clamps around the steering tube to connect the handlebars to the fork, and it also keeps the headset in proper adjustment by preventing the top headset cup from sliding up the steering tube (Figs. 11.7 and 11.11).

Stems for threaded steering tubes (Fig. 11.8) have been the most common historically. They have a vertical "quill," which extends down into the steering tube of the fork and binds to the inside of the steering tube by means of a wedge-shaped plug pulled up by a long bolt that runs through the quill (Fig. 11.9).

Suspension stems used to be quite popular and were made for both threadless and threaded steering tubes. Some, like Softride (Fig. 11.10), use a parallelogram system with four pivots to prevent the handlebar from twisting as it moves up and down. Others, like Girvin, have a single pivot around which the bar swings in an arc. Both incorporate some sort of a spring for suspension, usually a steel coil or an elastic polymer ("elastomer"). Some suspension stems also come with a hydraulic damper to control the speed of movement.

XI-8: REMOVE CLAMP-TYPE STEM FROM THREADLESS STEERING TUBE

1. Loosen the horizontal bolts clamping the stem around the steering tube. Again, this should take about two or three turns.

2. With a 5mm Allen wrench, unscrew and remove the adjusting bolt in the top cap covering the top of the stem clamp and steering tube (Fig. 11.12). The fork can now fall out, so hold the fork as you unscrew the bolt.

3. With the bike standing on the floor, or while

11.12 loosening and tightening bolt on threadless-style headset

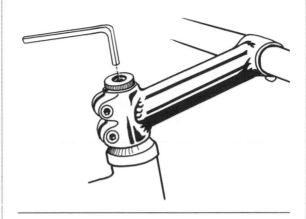

holding the fork to keep it from falling out, pull the cap and the stem off of the steering tube. Leave the bike standing until you replace the stem, or slide the fork out of the frame, keeping track of all headset parts.

4. If the stem will not budge, see Section XI-14A.

XI-9: INSTALL AND ADJUST HEIGHT OF STEM ON THREADLESS STEERING TUBE

Installing and adjusting the height of a stem on a threadless fork is much more complicated than installing and adjusting the height of a standard stem in a threaded fork. Here, the stem is an integral part of the headset (Fig. 11.7), so any change to the stem position alters the headset adjustment. That's why this procedure carries a Level 2 designation.

1. Stand the bike up on its wheels, so the fork does not fall out. Grease the top end of the steering tube. Loosen the stem clamp bolts, and grease their threads. Slide the stem onto the steering tube.

2. Set the stem height to the desired level. If you want to place the stem in a position higher than

11.13 measuring distance between stem clamp and top of steering tube

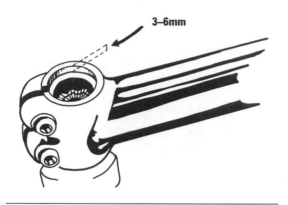

3–6mm

directly on top of the headset, you must put some spacers between the bottom of the stem clamp and the top piece of the headset. No matter what, there must be contact — directly or through spacers (and including the top crown on a double-crown fork) — between the headset and the stem. Otherwise, the headset will be loose.

3. Check the steering tube length: To adjust the threadless headset, the top of the stem clamp (or spacers placed above it) should overlap the top of the steering tube by 3–6mm (1/8–1/4 inch) (Fig. 11.13). If it does, skip ahead to step 4.

a. **Steering tube too short:** If the top of the stem clamp overlaps the top of the steering tube by more than 6mm (1/4 inches), the steering tube is too short to set the stem height where you have it. If you have spacers below the stem, remove some until the top edge of the stem clamp overlaps the top of the steering tube by 3–6mm. If you cannot or do not want to lower the stem any further, you either need: a fork with a longer steering tube, a stem with a shorter clamp or a stem that is angled upward more to attain your desired handlebar height. Stems for threadless steering tubes with different angles or with clamps of differing lengths are available. It is a

lot cheaper and easier than replacing the fork.

On many old suspension forks, you could simply replace the steering tube/crown assembly with a longer one and bolt your existing fork legs into it. But nowadays, to get a longer steering tube, you must replace the fork.

b. **Steering tube too long:** If the top of the steering tube is less than 3mm (1/8 inches) below the top edge of the stem clamp (or if sticks up above the top of the stem clamp), you have a choice. If you want the option to raise the stem for a higher handlebar position, stack some headset spacers on top of the stem clamp until the spacers overlap the top edge of the steering tube by at least 3mm.

If, however, you are sure you will never want the stem any higher, then go ahead and cut off the excess tube. First, mark the steering tube along the top edge of the stem clamp and remove the fork from the bike. Make another mark on the steering tube 3mm below the first mark. Place the steering tube in a padded vise or bike stand clamp. Using the lower mark as a guide, cut the excess steering tube off with a hacksaw or tube cutter.

There is a star-shaped nut that is inserted inside the steering tube (Fig. 11.7). The bolt through the top cap screws into it to adjust the headset bearings. If the star nut is already inside of the steering tube, and it looks like the saw is going to hit it, you must move the star nut down — see step 4 for how to do it.

Make your cut straight. Mark it straight by wrapping a piece of tape around the steering tube and cutting along it. If you are not sure your cut will be straight, start it a little higher and file it down flat to the tape edge. If you really want to be safe, use a tool specifically designed to help you make a straight cut. Park Tool's "threadless saw guide" will do the trick. Remember that you can always shorten the steering tube a little more, but you cannot make it longer! So apply the old adage of "measure twice, cut once." Use a round file on the inside of the tube and a flat file on the outside to remove any metal burrs left by the hacksaw or cutter.

When you have completed cutting and deburring, put the fork back in, replacing all headset parts the way they were originally installed (Figs. 11.17 and 11.20–11.21). Return to step 1 above.

4. Check that the edges of the star-shaped nut are at least 12mm below the top edge of the steering tube. The nut must be far enough down that the bottom of the headset top cap does not hit it once the adjusting bolt is tightened. If the nut is not in deeply enough, you need to drive it deeper into the steering tube after removing the stem. This is best done with the star nut installation tool (Fig. 1.4). The tool threads into the nut, and you hit it with a hammer until it stops; the star nut will now be set 15mm deep in the steering tube. If you do not have this tool, go to a bike shop and have the nut set for you. If you insist on doing it yourself, follow the steps to push the star nut in deeper as outlined below. Just remember that it is easy to mangle the star nut if you do not tap it in straight.

Pushing the star nut in further without the proper tool:

a. Put the adjusting bolt through the top cap, and thread it six turns into the star nut.

b. If the star nut is not already inside the steering tube, set it over the end of the steering tube and tap the top of the bolt with a mallet. Use the top cap as guide to keep it going in straight.

c. Tap the bolt in until the star nut is 15mm below the top of the steering tube.

Note: The wall thickness of steering tubes differs depending on if they are made of steel or aluminum, what grade and heat-treating they have, and what the fork is designed for. Therefore, the stock headset star nut may not fit in, and it will just bend when you try to install it. Even pros sometimes ruin star nuts. Not a big problem, since replacements can be purchased separately. If yours goes in crooked, take a long punch or rod, set it on top of the star nut, and drive it all of the way out of the bottom of the steering tube. Dispose of the star nut, and get another.

If you have an aluminum steering tube, its internal diameter (I.D.) will be undersized. Standard I.D. for a 1-inch steel steering tube is 22.2mm (7/8 inch), 25.4mm (1 inch) for a 1-1/8-inch steel steering tube and 28.6mm (1-1/8 inches) for a 1-1/4-inch steel steering tube. If the stock star nut from the headset does not fit, get one that is the correct size. Fork manufacturers often supply one with each fork. In a pinch, you can make an oversized stock star nut fit by bending each pair of opposite leaves of the star nut toward each other with a pair of channel-lock pliers to reduce the nut's width. Now you can insert the nut; be aware that it may not grip as well as a properly sized one.

5. Install the headset top cap on the top of the stem clamp (or spacers you set above it). Grease the threads of the top-cap adjusting bolt, and thread it into the star nut inside the steering tube (Fig. 11.12).

6. Adjust the headset before tightening the stem bolts. The steps are outlined in Section XI-16.

XI-10: REMOVE STANDARD QUILL-TYPE STEM FROM THREADED FORK

1. Unscrew the stem-fixing bolt on the top of the stem. It should take three turns or so. Most stem bolts take a 6mm Allen wrench.

2. Tap the top of the bolt down with a mallet or hammer (Fig. 11.15) to disengage the wedge from the bottom of the quill. If the head of the bolt is recessed down in the stem so that a hammer cannot get at it, leave the Allen wrench in the bolt and tap the top of the Allen wrench until the wedge is free.

3. Pull the stem out of the steering tube. If the stem will not budge, see Section XI-14B in this chapter.

XI-11: INSTALL AND ADJUST HEIGHT OF QUILL STEM IN THREADED FORK

1. Grease the stem quill, the bolt threads, the outside of the wedge or conical plug (Fig. 11.8) and the inside of the steering tube.

2. Thread the bolt through the stem and into the wedge or plug until it pulls it into place, but not so far as to prevent the stem from inserting into the steering tube.

3. Slip the stem quill into the steering tube (Fig. 11.9) to the depth you want. Make sure the stem is inserted beyond its height-limit line. Tighten the bolt until the stem is snug but can still be turned.

4. Set the stem to the desired height, line it up with the front wheel, and tighten the bolt. It needs to be tight, but don't overdo it. You can overtighten the stem bolt to the point that you bulge out the steerer tube on your fork, so be careful. Recommended torque for this bolt is in Appendix E.

XI-12: STEM MAINTENANCE AND REPLACEMENT SCHEDULE

A bike cannot be controlled if the stem breaks, so make sure yours doesn't break. Because aluminum has no fatigue limit, all aluminum parts will eventually fail. Steel and titanium parts repeatedly stressed more than about one-half of their

STEMS

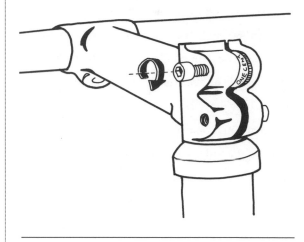

11.14 stick coin in crack to spread stem clamp

tensile strength will eventually fail as well. Stems and handlebars are not permanent accessories on your bike. Replace them before they fail on you.

Always clean your stem regularly. Whenever you clean it, be sure to look for corrosion, cracks, bends and stressed areas. If you find any, replace the stem immediately. If you crash hard on your bike, especially hard enough to bend the bars, replace your stem. It makes sense to err on the side of caution. Lightweight, expensive stems, in particular, need to be replaced after a violent impact, even if you see no visible signs of stress. The hard, thin material is not likely to bend, but it may be so weakened that it will break soon.

Italian stem maker 3T recommends replacing stems and bars every four years. As with a set of handlebars, if you rarely ride the bike, this is overkill. If you ride hard and ride often, every four years may not be frequent enough. Do what is appropriate for you, and be aware of the risks.

XI-13: SETTING STEM AND BAR POSITIONS

Complete treatment of this subject is in Appendix C, Section C-3. Here are some brief suggestions.

11.15 loosening stem wedge

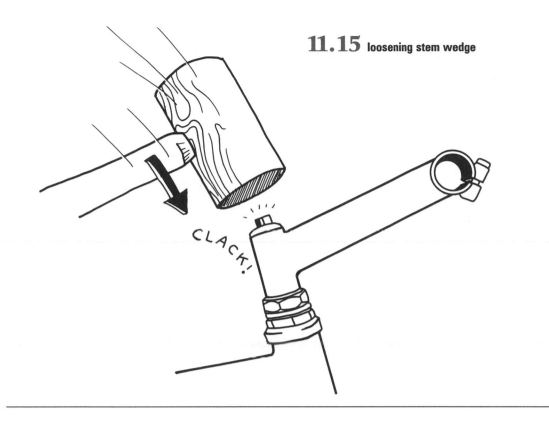

CLACK!

I recommend setting your handlebar twist so that the bends in the bars are pointed up and back. I also recommend setting your bar ends, if installed, so that they are horizontal or tipped up between 5 and 15 degrees from horizontal (Appendix C, Section 5).

Setting handlebar height and reach is very personal. Much depends on your physique, your flexibility, your frame, your riding style and a few other preferences. Again, this subject is covered in depth in Appendix C.

Since I do not know anything about you personally, I will leave you with a few simple guidelines:

• If you climb a lot, you will want your bars lower and further forward to keep weight on the front wheel on steep uphills.

• If you descend technical trails a lot, you will want your bars higher and with less forward reach.

• If you ride a lot on pavement, a low, stretched-out position is better aerodynamically. A low position means that the handlebar grips are about 7–12cm lower than your saddle. A stretched-out position would place your elbow at least 2 inches in front of your knee at the top of the pedal stroke.

XI-14: REMOVING STUCK STEM

A stem can get stuck onto or into the steering tube due to poor maintenance. Periodically regreasing the stem and steering tube will keep them sliding freely, and the grease will form a barrier to sweat and water getting in between the two. If your stem is really stuck, be careful; you can ruin your fork as well as your stem and headset trying to get it out. In fact, you're better off having a shop work on it, unless you *really* know what you are doing and are willing to accept the risk of destroying a lot of expensive parts.

A. Removing a stuck stem from a threadless fork

1. Remove the top cap (Fig. 11.12) and the bolts clamping the stem to the steering tube.

2. Spread the stem clamp by inserting a coin

into the slot between each bolt end and the opposing threadless half of the binder lug (Fig. 11.14). Tighten each bolt against each coin so that it spreads the clamp slot open wider. The stem should come right off of the steering tube now.

Note: *If your stem is the type that comes with a single bolt in the side of the stem shaft ahead of the steering tube (Fig. 11.7), loosen the bolt a few turns and tap it in with a hammer to free the wedge. It might still take some penetrating oil to free this type of stem from around the steering tube.*

3. If it still will not come free, you may have to use a vise, following instructions 6 and 7 in the next section (XI-14B) on freeing a quill-type stem. Failing that, your last resort is to saw through the steering tube at the base of the stem clamp and then replace the stem, the fork (or at least the steering tube) and the headset.

B. Removing a stuck stem from a threaded fork

1. Unscrew the stem bolt on top of the stem three turns or more. Smack the bolt (or the Allen wrench in the bolt) with a mallet or hammer (Fig. 11.15) to completely disengage the wedge.

2. Grasping the front wheel between your knees, make one last attempt to free the stem by twisting back and forth on the bars. Don't use all of your strength because you can ruin a fork and front wheel this way.

3. If your stem didn't budge, squirt penetrating oil around the stem where it enters the headset. Let the bike sit for several hours and add more penetrating oil every hour or so.

4. Turn the bike over, and squirt penetrating oil into the bottom of the fork steering tube so that it runs down around the stem quill. Let the bike sit

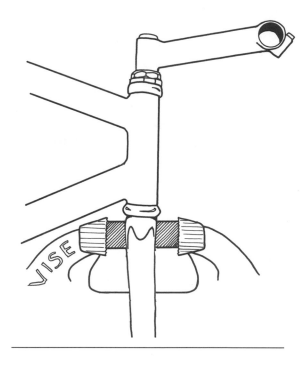

11.16 clamping fork crown in vise

for several hours and add more penetrating oil every hour or so.

5. Now that it's totally soaked in penetrating oil, try step 2 again. If the stem doesn't come free, you have to go to your workbench and use that heavy-duty vise. Is it solidly mounted? You'll need it to be.

6. Remove the front wheel (Chapter 2) and the front brake (Chapter 7). Put pieces of wood on both sides of the vise. Clamp the fork crown into the vise (Fig. 11.16). To fit it in the vise, you will at least have to remove the brakes. If you have an old suspension fork with crown-clamp bolts, remove the inner fork legs from the crown by loosening the crown bolts and yanking the legs out.

7. Grab both ends of the handlebar and twist back and forth. If this doesn't work, you may have to saw off the stem just above the headset and have the bottom of the stem reamed out of the steering tube by a machine shop. I told you that you should have gone to a bike shop.

REMOVING A
STUCK STEM

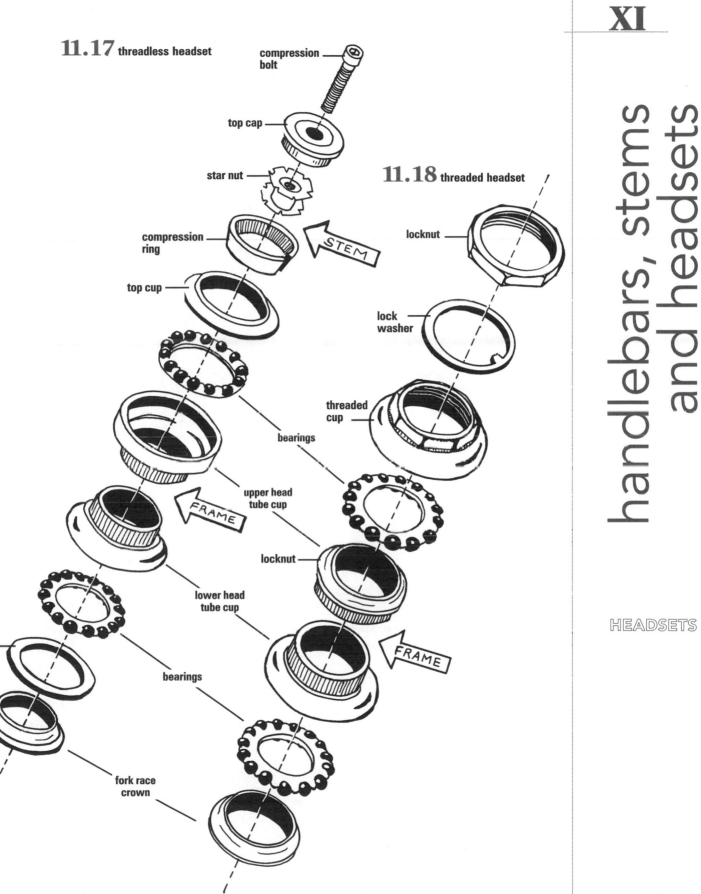

11.17 threadless headset

compression bolt

top cap

star nut

compression ring

top cup

bearings

upper head tube cup

lower head tube cup

seal

bearings

fork race crown

11.18 threaded headset

locknut

lock washer

threaded cup

bearings

locknut

STEM

FRAME

FRAME

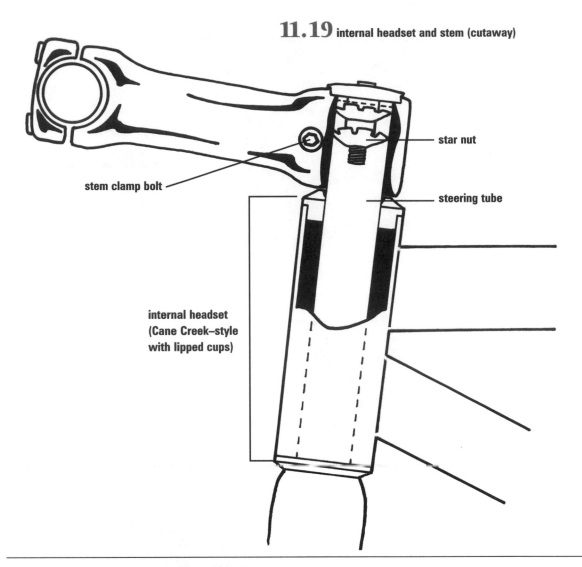

11.19 internal headset and stem (cutaway)

star nut

steering tube

stem clamp bolt

internal headset
(Cane Creek–style
with lipped cups)

XI.E HEADSETS

There are two basic types of headsets: threadless (Figs. 11.7, 11.17 and 11.19–11.21) and threaded (Figs. 11.9 and 11.18). They come in three sizes for mountain bikes: 1 inch, 1-1/8 inches and 1-1/4-inches, with 1-1/8-inches being by far the most common nowadays.

The Dia-Compe (now Cane Creek) AheadSet was the first threadless headset (Fig. 11.17), a lighter system than a threaded one, because it eliminates the stem quill, bolt and wedge. The connection between the handlebars and the stem is also more rigid than with an expanding stem wedge. Of

course, fork manufacturers prefer threadless headsets because they do not have to thread their forks and/or offer various lengths of fork steerers; steerer diameter is now the only variable.

On a threadless headset, the top cup and a conical compression ring slide onto the steering tube (Figs. 11.17 and 11.20–11.21). The stem clamps around the top of the steering tube and above the compression ring. A star-shaped nut with two layers of spring-steel teeth sticking out from it fits into the steering tube and grabs the inner walls (Fig. 11.7). A top cap sits atop the stem clamp and pushes it down by means of a long bolt threaded into the

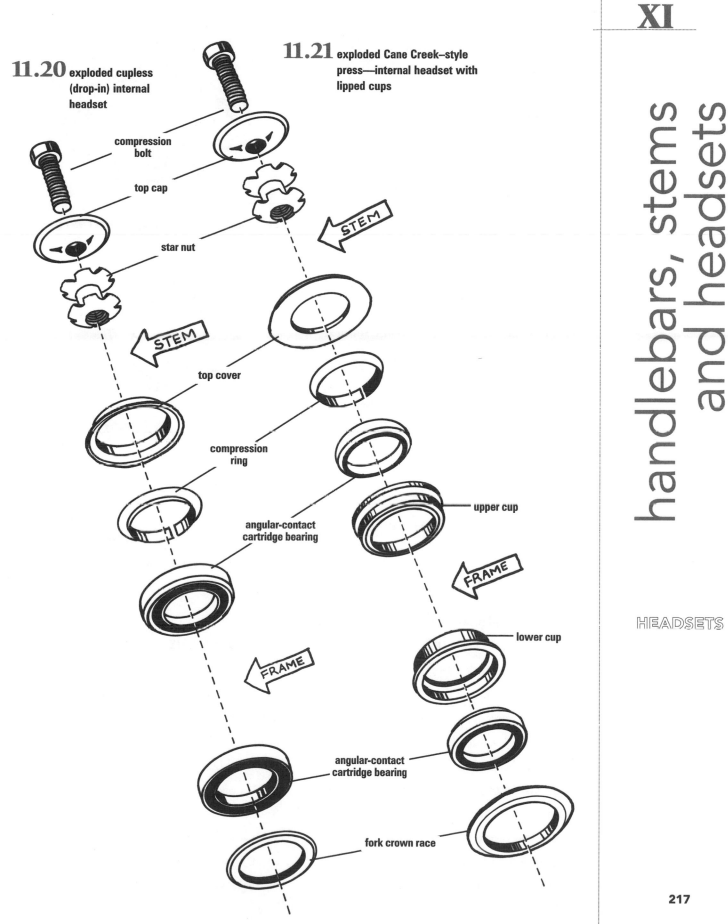

11.20 exploded cupless (drop-in) internal headset

11.21 exploded Cane Creek–style press—internal headset with lipped cups

compression bolt

top cap

star nut

STEM

STEM

top cover

compression ring

angular-contact cartridge bearing

upper cup

FRAME

FRAME

lower cup

angular-contact cartridge bearing

fork crown race

XI

handlebars, stems and headsets

HEADSETS

star nut to adjust the headset (Fig. 11.12). The stem clamped around the steering tube holds the headset in adjustment (Fig. 11.11).

The next generation of headsets are threadless internal ones, concealed inside the frame's steering tube (Fig. 11.19). Where standard threaded and threadless headsets have bearing cups that are pressed into the head tube (Figs. 11.17 and 11.18), internal headsets have bearings seated inside the head tube. The bearings either rest on a platform within the head tube itself (Fig. 11.20) or have cups with thin flanges that extend out to the edges of the head tube (Fig. 11.21). Otherwise, the headset is identical to and is adjusted the same as original threadless systems.

Prior to the 1990s, practically all headsets and steering tubes were threaded. The top bearing cup on a threaded headset has wrench flats, a toothed washer stacked on top of it and a locknut that covers the top of the steering tube. That locknut tightens against the washer and top cup (Fig. 11.18). A brake cable hanger (Fig. 7.4, Chapter 7) and extra spacers may be included under the locknut.

Most headsets, threaded or threadless, use loose ball bearings held in some type of steel or plastic retainer (or "cage") (Figs. 11.17 and 11.18) so that you are not chasing dozens of separate balls around when you work on the bike. A variation on this (Stronglight, some Ritchey) has needle bearings held in conical plastic retainers (Fig. 11.22) riding on conical steel bearing surfaces.

Cartridge-bearing headsets usually employ "angular contact" bearings (Fig. 11.23), since normal cartridge bearings cannot take the side forces encountered by a headset. Each bearing is a separate, sealed, internally greased unit.

CHECKING HEADSET ADJUSTMENT

11.22 needle bearings

11.23 cartridge-bearing headset lower parts

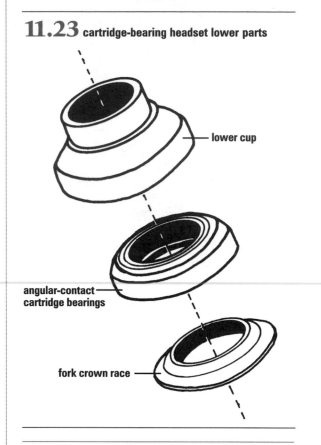

lower cup

angular-contact cartridge bearings

fork crown race

XI-15: CHECK HEADSET ADJUSTMENT

If your headset is too loose, it will rattle or clunk while you ride. You might even notice some "play" in the fork as you apply the front brake. If your headset is too tight, the fork will be difficult to turn, or at least gritty when you do.

1. Check for headset looseness by holding the front brake and rocking the bike forward and back. Try it with the front wheel pointed straight ahead and then with the wheel turned at 90 degrees to the bike. Feel for back-and-forth movement (or

play) at the lower head cup with your other hand. If there is play, you need to adjust your headset because it is too loose.

Note: *This task is more complicated with a suspension fork, and even with many brake types. There is always some side-to-side play in any suspension fork, as well as in many brakes; this makes it hard to isolate whether the play you feel is from the headset, the fork or the brakes. You have to feel each part as you rock the bike, and you may have to do some trial-and-error headset adjustment.*

If the headset is loose, skip to the appropriate adjustment section, XI-16 or XI-17.

2. Check for headset tightness by turning the handlebars back and forth. Feel for any binding or stiffness of movement. Also, check for the chunk-chunk chunk movement to fixed positions characterizing a pitted headset (if you feel this, you need a new headset; skip to Section XI-20). Lean the bike to one side and then the other; the front wheel should turn as the bike is leaned (be aware that cable housings can resist the turning of the front wheel). Lift the bike by the saddle so it is tipped down at an angle with both wheels off of the ground. Turn the handlebar one way and let go of it. See if it returns to center quickly and smoothly on its own. If the headset does not turn easily on any of the above steps, it is too tight, and you should skip to the appropriate adjustment section, XI-16 or XI-17.

3. If yours is a threaded headset, try to turn either the top nut or the threaded cup by hand. They should be so tight against each other that they can only be loosened with wrenches. If you can tighten or loosen either part by hand, you need to adjust your headset; go to Section XI-17.

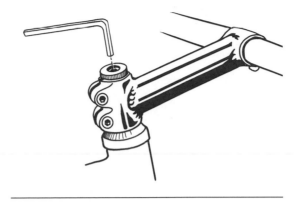

XI-16: ADJUSTING A THREADLESS HEADSET

Adjusting a threadless headset, whether it is the new internal type (Fig. 11.19) or the external type (Fig. 11.7), is much easier than adjusting the threaded style. It is a Level 1 procedure and usually only takes a 5mm Allen wrench.

1. Check the headset adjustment (Section XI-15 above). Determine whether the headset is too tight or too loose.

2. Loosen the bolt(s) that clamp the stem to the steering tube.

3. If the headset is too tight, loosen the 5mm Allen bolt on the top cap about one-sixteenth of a turn (Fig. 11.24). Recheck, and repeat as necessary.

If the headset is too loose, tighten the 5mm Allen bolt on the top cap about one-sixteenth of a turn (Fig. 11.24). Be careful not to overtighten it and pit the headset. If you're using a torque wrench, Dia-Compe recommends a tightening torque on this bolt of 22 in-lbs. Recheck the adjustment, and tighten or loosen further as necessary.

ADJUSTMENT PROBLEMS

a. If the cap does not move down and push the stem down, make sure the stem is not stuck to the steering tube. If it is, go to Section XI-14A earlier in this chapter.

b. Another hindrance occurs if the conical compression ring (Figs. 11.17 and 11.20–11.21) is stuck to the steering tube, preventing adjustment via the top cap bolt. With the stem off, gently tap the steering tube down with a mallet, and then push the fork back up to free the compression ring. Grease the ring and the steerer, and reassemble.

c. If neither the stem nor the compression ring are stuck, yet the cap still does not push the stem down, the steering tube may be so long that it is hitting the lip of the top cap and preventing the cap from pushing the stem down. The steering tube's top should be 3–6mm below the top edge of the stem (Fig. 11.13). If the steering tube is too long, add a spacer, or cut or file some off the top (see Section XI-9, step 3).

d. Another thing that can thwart adjustment is if the star nut is not installed deeply enough, so the cap bottoms out on the star nut. The highest point of the star nut should be 12–15mm below the top of the steering tube. Tap it deeper with a star-nut installation tool, or put the bolt through the top cap, thread it five turns into the star nut, and gently tap it in with a soft hammer, using the top cap to keep it going in straight (see Section XI-9, step 4).

e. With a double-crown fork, you must loosen the clamp bolts on the upper crown. There are three of them — one clamps the steering tube, and the other two each clamp one fork upper tube. If the headset is loose and these are still clamped, tightening the headset compression bolt cannot push the stem and top crown down more. After the headset is adjusted properly, retighten the bolts to the torque specified by the fork maker.

Once you have fixed the cause of the adjustment problem, return to step 1 above.

4. Tighten the stem clamp bolts to the recommended torque, which is given in Appendix E.

5. Recheck the headset adjustment. Repeat steps 2–4 if necessary. If it is adjusted properly, make sure the stem is aligned straight with the front wheel. Once the headset is adjusted properly, go find something else to do, because you are done.

XI-17: ADJUSTING A THREADED HEADSET

The secret to good adjustment is simultaneously controlling the steering tube, the adjustable cup and the locknut as you tighten the latter two together.

Note: *Perform the adjustment with the stem installed. Not only does it give you something to hold onto that keeps the fork from turning during the installation, but also there are slight differences in adjustment when the stem is in place as opposed to when it is not. Tightening the stem bolt can sometimes bulge the walls of the steering tube very slightly (Fig. 11.9), but just enough for it to shorten the steering tube slightly and throw your original headset adjustment off.*

1. Following the steps outlined in Section XI-15, determine whether the headset is too loose or too tight.

2. Put a pair of headset wrenches that fit your headset on the headset's top nut (which I will also call the "locknut") and top bearing cup (or "threaded cup" or "adjustable cup"). Headset nuts come in a wide variety of sizes, so make sure you have the proper size wrenches. Place the wrenches so that the top one is slightly offset to the left of the bottom wrench. That way you can squeeze them together to free the nut (Fig. 11.25).

Note: *People with small hands or a weak grip will need to grab each wrench out at the end to get enough leverage.*

ADJUSTING A
THREADLESS
HEADSET

—

ADJUSTING A
THREADED
HEADSET

11.25 loosening headset locknut

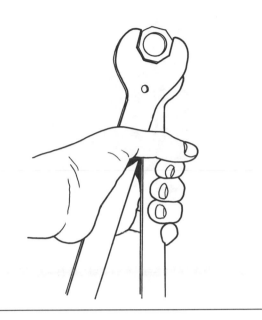

11.26 tightening headset locknut

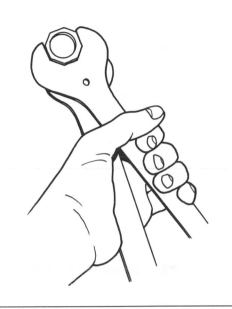

3. Hold the lower wrench in place and turn the top wrench counterclockwise about a quarter-turn to loosen the locknut. It may take considerable force to break it loose, since it needs to be installed very tightly to keep the headset from loosening up.

4. If the headset was too loose, turn the lower (or threaded) cup clockwise about one-sixteenth of a turn while holding the stem with your other hand. Be very careful when tightening the cup; overtightening it can ruin the headset by pressing the bearings into the bearing surfaces and make little indentations. The headset then stops at the indentations rather than turns smoothly, a condition known as a "pitted" headset.

If the headset was too tight, loosen the threaded cup counterclockwise one-sixteenth of a turn while holding the stem with your other hand. Loosen it until the bearings turn freely, but be sure not to loosen to the point that you allow any play to develop.

5. Holding the stem, tighten the locknut clock-

wise with a single wrench. Make sure that the threaded cup does not turn while you tighten the locknut. If it does turn, you either are missing the toothed lock washer separating the cup and locknut (Fig. 11.18), or the washer you have is missing its tooth. In this case, remove the locknut and replace the toothed washer. Put it on the steering tube so that the tooth engages the longitudinal groove in the steering tube. Tighten the locknut on again.

Note: You can adjust a headset without a toothed washer by working both wrenches simultaneously, but it is trickier and often comes loose while riding.

6. Check the headset adjustment again. Repeat steps 4 and 5 until properly adjusted.

7. Once properly adjusted, place one wrench on the locknut and the other on the threaded cup. Tighten the locknut (clockwise) firmly against the washer(s) and threaded cup to hold the headset adjustment in place (Fig. 11.26).

8. Check the headset adjustment again. If it is off, follow steps 2–7 again. If it is adjusted properly,

make sure the stem is aligned with the front wheel, and go ride your bike.

Note: *If you constantly get what you believe to be the proper adjustment, and then find it to be too loose after you tighten the locknut and threaded cup against each other, your steering tube may be too long, causing the locknut to bottom out. Remove the stem and examine the inside of the steering tube. If the top end of the steering tube butts up against the top lip of the locknut, the steering tube is too long. Remove the locknut and add another spacer.*

If you don't want to add another spacer, file off 1 or 2mm of the steering tube. Be sure to deburr it inside and out, and avoid leaving filings in the bearings or steering tube threads. Replace the locknut and return to step 5.

XI-18: OVERHAUL THREADLESS HEADSET

These instructions apply to both internal (Figs. 11.19–11.21) and external (Figs. 11.7 and 11.17) threadless headsets.

Like any other bike part with bearings, headsets need periodic overhauls. If you use your bike regularly, you should probably overhaul your loose-bearing headset once a year. Headsets with cartridge bearings (Fig. 11.23) need less frequent overhaul; some angular-contact bearings can be disassembled and cleaned and some cannot. With those that cannot, if a bearing fails, you either replace the bearing or, if it has press-in bearings (like Chris King and Dia-Compe's "S" series, Fig. 11.27), you replace the entire cup (Section XI-20).

Either place the bike upside down in the work stand or be ready to catch the fork when you remove the stem.

1. Disconnect or remove the front brake (Chapter

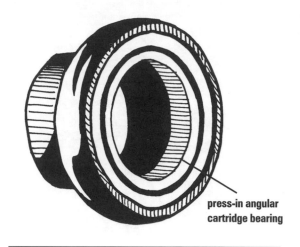

11.27 Chris King–style pressed-in sealed bearing

press-in angular
cartridge bearing

7), and unscrew the top cap bolt (Fig. 11.24) and the stem clamp bolts. Remove the top cap and the stem. If you have a double-crown fork, loosen the bolts on the top crown that clamp the steering tube and each fork inner tube, and pull the top crown off.

2. Remove the top headset cup by sliding the top cup, conical compression ring, and any other spacers above it, off of the steering tube (Figs. 11.17 and 11.20–11.21). It may take a tap with a mallet on the end of the steering tube, followed by pushing the fork back up, to free the compression ring.

3. Pull the fork out of the frame. The lower bearing and seal may come with it.

4. Remove any bearing seals. Remember the position and orientation of each.

5. Remove bearings remaining in the head tube or cups. Be careful not to lose any. Separate the top and bottom sets if they are of different sizes.

6. Clean or replace the bearings:

a. With standard ball bearing (Fig. 11.17) or needle-bearing (Fig. 11.22) headsets, put the bearings (leave the balls or needles in their retainers) in a jar or old water bottle along with some citrus-based solvent. Shake. If the bearings from the top

OVERHAULING
THREADLESS
HEADSET

and bottom are of different sizes, keep them in separate containers to avoid confusion. Blot the bearings dry with a clean rag.

b. Some cartridge bearings (Fig. 11.21) can be pulled apart and cleaned. Over a container to catch the balls, hold the bearing so the beveled outer surface that fits into the cup faces down, and push up on the bearing's inner ring. The bearing should come apart — the inner ring will pop up and out with the bearings stuck to its outer surface. It may take a little rocking of the inner ring as you push up. If the bearing does not come apart, first pry off the plastic seal covering the bearings with a knife or razor blade, as in Chapter 6, Fig. 6.26, and then try again. Wipe the bearings and bearing rings and seals with a clean rag.

If your bearings are the type that will not come apart, check to see if they turn smoothly. If they do not, buy new ones and skip to step 8.

7. Plug the sink, and wash the ball bearings in soap and water in your hands, just as if you were washing your palms by rubbing them together. Your hands will get clean for the assembly steps as well. Rinse bearings thoroughly and blot them dry. Air-dry completely.

With an angular-contact cartridge bearing that you disassembled, smear grease around the outside of the inner bearing ring, and stick the balls into the grease in the channel around the ring. With the outer ring sitting beveled side down on the table, push the inner ring with the balls attached down into it (the internal bevel on the inner ring should be facing up, opposite the bevel on the outer ring). Snap the bearing seals back into place.

8. Wipe all of the bearing surfaces with clean rags. Wipe the steering tube clean, and wipe the

inside of the head tube clean with a rag on the end of a screwdriver.

9. Inspect all bearing surfaces of loose-ball headsets for wear and pitting. If you see pits (separate indentations made by bearings in the bearing surfaces), you need to replace the headset — skip to Section XI-20.

10. Apply grease to all bearing surfaces. If you are using sealed-cartridge bearings, apply grease conservatively.

11. Turn the bike upside down in the bike stand. Place a set of bearings into (or onto) the top cup and a set into the cup on the lower end of the head tube. With a cupless internal headset (Fig. 11.20), set a bearing into the seat in the bottom of the head tube itself).

With loose-ball headsets, make sure you have the bearing retainer right side up so that only the bearings contact the bearing surfaces (note the different upper cup styles and bearing orientations in Figs. 11.17 and 11.18). If you have installed the retainer upside down, it will come in contact with one of the bearing surfaces, and the headset will not turn well. This is a bad thing, because assembling and riding it that way will turn the retainer into jagged chunks of broken metal. To be safe, double- and triple-check the retainer placement by turning each cup pair and bearing in your hand before proceeding. Most loose-ball headsets have the bearings set up identically top and bottom (Fig. 11.18) where the top piece of each pair is a cup, the bottom piece is a cone, and the bearing retainer rides the same way in both sets. Many headsets, however, place both cups (and hence the bearing retainers) facing outward from the head tube (Fig. 11.17).

Note: If you have loose ball bearings with no bear-

11.28 setting fork in head tube to seat bearings

ing retainer, stick the balls into the grease in the cups one at a time, making sure that you replace the same number you started with in each cup.

With angular-contact cartridge bearings, the beveled end faces into the cup (Fig. 11.23) or into the seat machined inside of the head tube (Fig. 11.20).

12. Reinstall any seals that you removed from the headset parts.

13. Slip the steering tube of the fork into the head tube so that the lower headset bearing seats properly (Fig. 11.28).

14. Slide the top cup, with the bearings in it (or on it), onto the steering tube. In the case of a cupless headset (Fig. 11.20), slide on the bearing alone.

Keep the bike upside down at this point; it not only keeps the fork in place, it also prevents grit from falling into the bearings as you put the cup on.

15. Grease the compression ring and slide it onto the (greased) steering tube followed by the top cover. Assure that the narrower end of the compression ring slides into the conical space in the top of the top cup (Figs. 11.17 and 11.21) or into the bearing of a cupless headset (Fig. 11.20). If you have a double-crown fork, slide the top crown onto the steerer and the fork upper tubes. Slide on any spacers you had under the stem. Slide the stem on, and tighten one stem clamp bolt to hold it in place.

16. Turn the bike over. Check that the stem clamp extends 3–6mm above the top of the steering tube (Fig. 11.13). If it does, install the top cap on the top of the stem clamp and steering tube, and screw the bolt into the star nut set inside the steering tube (Fig. 11.24).

If the steering tube is too long, remove the stem. Add a spacer or file the steering shorter until the stem clamp overlaps it by 3–6mm. If the steering tube is too short, remove spacers from below the stem, if there are any. If there are no spacers to remove, try a new stem with a shorter clamp.

17. Adjust the headset (Section XI-16). Go ride your bike.

XI-19: OVERHAUL THREADED HEADSET

Like any other bike part with bearings, headsets need periodic overhauls. If you use your bike regularly, you should probably overhaul your loose-bearing headset once a year. Headsets with cartridge bearings (Fig. 11.23) need less frequent overhaul; some angular-contact bearings can be disassembled and cleaned and some cannot. With those that cannot, if a bearing fails, you either replace the bearing or, if it has press-in bearings (like Chris King and Dia-Compe's "S" series, Fig. 11.27), you replace the entire cup (Section XI-20).

A bike stand is highly recommended when overhauling a headset.

1. Disconnect the front brake cable (Chapter 7), and remove the stem by loosening the stem bolt three turns, tapping the bolt down with a hammer to free the wedge (Fig. 11.15), and pulling the stem out.

2. Either turn your bike upside down or be prepared to catch your fork as you remove the upper portion of the headset. To remove the top headset cup, unscrew the locknut and threaded cup with headset wrenches. Place one on the locknut and one on the threaded cup. Loosen the locknut by turning it counterclockwise (Fig. 11.29). Unscrew the locknut and the cup from the steering tube. The headset washer or washers will slide off of the steering tube as you unscrew the threaded cup.

3. Pull the fork out of the frame.

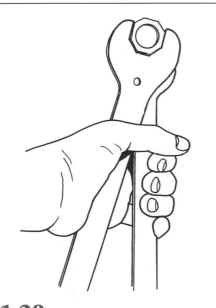

11.29 loosening headset locknut

4. Remove any seals that surround the edges of the cups. Make a point of remembering the position and orientation of each.

5. Remove the bearings from the cups. Be careful not to lose any. Separate the top and bottom sets if they are of different sizes.

6. Clean or replace the bearings.

a. With standard ball bearing (Fig. 11.17) or needle-bearing (Fig. 11.22) headsets, put the bearings in a jar or old water bottle along with some citrus-based solvent. Shake. If the bearings from the top and bottom are of different sizes, keep them in separate containers to avoid confusion. Blot the bearings dry with a clean rag.

b. Some cartridge bearings (Fig. 11.21) can be pulled apart and cleaned. Over a container to catch the balls, hold the bearing so the beveled outer surface that fits into the cup faces down, and push up on the bearing's inner ring. The bearing should come apart — the inner ring will pop up and out with the bearings stuck to its outer surface. It may take a little rocking of the inner ring as you push up. If the bearing does not come apart, first pry off the plastic seal covering the bearings with a knife or razor blade, as in Chapter 6, Fig. 6.26, and then try again. Wipe the bearings and bearing rings and seals with a clean rag.

If your bearings are the type that will not come apart, check to see if they turn smoothly. If they do not, buy new ones and skip to step 8.

7. Plug the sink, and wash the ball bearings in soap and water in your hands, just as if you were washing your palms by rubbing them together. This helps keep your hands clean for the assembly steps as well. Rinse bearings thoroughly and blot them dry. Let them air-dry completely.

OVERHAULING THREADED HEADSET

With an angular-contact cartridge bearing that you disassembled, smear grease around the outside of the inner bearing ring, and stick the balls into the grease in the channel around the ring. With the outer ring sitting beveled side down on the table, push the inner ring with the balls attached down into it (the internal bevel on the inner ring should be facing up, opposite the bevel on the outer ring). Snap the bearing seals back into place.

8. Wipe all of the bearing surfaces with clean rags. Wipe the steering tube clean, and wipe the inside of the head tube clean with a rag on the end of a screwdriver.

9. Inspect all bearing surfaces of loose-ball headsets for wear and pitting. If you see pits (separate indentations made by bearings in the bearing surfaces), you need to replace the headset. If that's the case, skip to Section XI-20.

10. Apply grease to all bearing surfaces. A thin film will do, especially with cartridge bearings.

11. Turn the bike upside down in the bike stand. Place a set of bearings in the top cup and a set in the cup on the lower end of the head tube. With loose-ball headsets, make sure you have the bearing retainer right side up so that only the bearings contact the bearing surfaces (note the different upper-cup styles and bearing orientations in Figs. 11.17 and 11.8). If you have installed the retainer upside down, it will come in contact with one of the bearing surfaces, and the headset will not turn well. This is a bad thing, because assembling and riding it that way will turn the retainer into jagged chunks of broken metal. To be safe, double- and triple-check the retainer placement by turning each cup pair in your hand with the bearing in between before proceeding. Most loose-ball headsets have

the bearings set up identically top and bottom (Fig. 11.18) where the top piece of each pair is a cup, the bottom piece is a cone, and the bearing retainer rides the same way in both sets. Many headsets, however, place both cups (and hence the bearing retainers) facing outward from the head tube (Fig. 11.17). Also, watch for asymmetry in ball size; some Ritchey headsets have smaller balls on top than on the bottom.

Note: *Stronglight and Ritchey needle-bearing headsets come with two pairs of separate conical steel rings. These are the bearing surfaces that sit on either side of the needle bearings (Fig. 11.22). On each set of conical rings, you will find that one is smaller than the other. Place the smaller one on the lower surface of each pair: the fork crown race and the cup on top of the head tube.*

If you have loose ball bearings with no bearing retainer, stick the balls into the grease in the cups one at a time, making sure that you replace the same number you started with in each cup.

With angular-contact cartridge bearings, the beveled end faces into the cup (Fig. 11.23).

12. Reinstall any seals that you removed from the headset parts.

13. Slide the steering tube of the fork into the head tube so that the lower headset bearing seats properly (Fig. 11.28).

14. Screw on the top cup, with the bearings in it, onto the steering tube. Keeping the bike upside down at this point not only keeps the fork in place, it also prevents grit from falling into the bearings as you thread the cup on.

15. Slide on the toothed washer (Fig. 11.18). Align the tooth in the groove going down the length of the steering tube threads. If you have one, install the brake cable hanger (Fig. 7.4) the same

OVERHAULING THREADED HEADSET

way. Screw on the locknut with your hand.

16. Turn the bike over. Grease the stem quill and insert it into the steering tube (Fig. 11.9). Make certain that it is in deeper than the imprinted limit line. Line the stem up with the front wheel, and tighten the stem bolt — see Appendix E for recommended torque.

17. Adjust the headset as outlined in Section XI-17.

XI-20: REMOVE HEADSET

1. Open the headset and remove the fork and bearings by following steps 1–5 of Section XI-18 or XI-19, depending on headset type.

2. If you have a cupless internal headset with bearings seated on steps machined into the head tube itself (Fig. 11.20), just pull the bearings out and skip to step 5.

With a headset with cups pressed into the head tube, slide the solid end of the headset-cup remover through one end of the head tube (Fig. 11.30). As you pull the headset-cup remover through the head tube, the splayed-out tangs on the opposite end of the tool pull through the cup and spread out.

3. Strike the solid end of the cup remover with a hammer, and drive the cup out (Fig. 11.31).

4. Remove the other cup by placing the cup remover into the opposite end of the head tube and repeating steps 2 and 3 on the opposite end of the end tube.

5. a. If you have a suspension fork (or a rigid fork with a clamp-together crown), you will usually find a notch on the front and back of the fork crown under the fork crown race. Clamp the steering tube in a vise or turn the fork upside down so that the top of the steering tube is sitting on the

11.30 inserting cup-removal tool

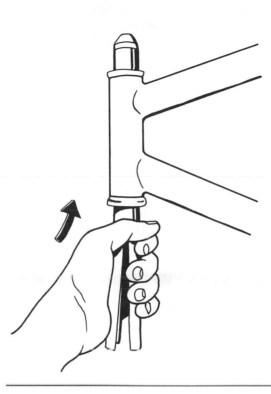

11.31 removing cup

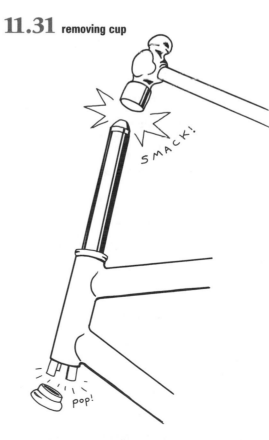

SMACK!

pop!

XI

handlebars, stems and headsets

OVERHAULING
THREADED
HEADSET

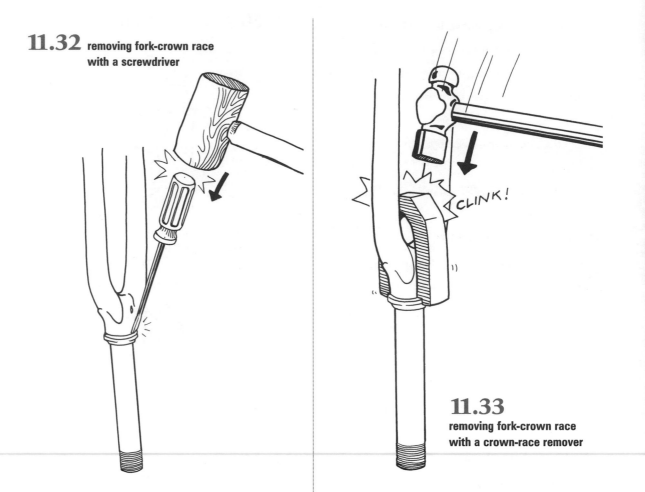

11.32 removing fork-crown race
with a screwdriver

11.33
removing fork-crown race
with a crown-race remover

workbench. Place the blade of a large screwdriver into the notch on one side of the crown so it butts against the bottom of the headset fork crown race. Tap the handle of the screwdriver with a hammer to drive the crown race up the steering tube a bit (Fig. 11.32). Move the screwdriver to the groove on the other side, and tap it again to move that side of the crown race up a bit. Continue in this way, alternately tapping either side of the crown race up the steering tube, bit by bit, until it gets past the enlarged section of the steering tube and slides off.

b. If you have a rigid fork, you can use a screwdriver to tap the crown race off as outlined above (Fig. 11.32). You can also do it more elegantly with a crown race remover or an appropriately sized bench

vise. Stand the fork upside down on the top of the steering tube. Place the U-shaped crown race remover so it straddles the underside of the fork crown and its ledges engage the front and back edges of the crown race. Smack the top of the crown race remover with a hammer to knock the race off (Fig. 11.33).

To do it with a bench vise, flip the brakes out of the way and slide the fork in, straddling the center shaft of the vise. Tighten the vise so its faces lightly contact the front and back of the fork crown with the lower side of the crown race sitting on top of them. Put a block of wood on the top of the steering tube to pad it. Strike the block with a hammer to drive the fork down and knock the crown race off of it (Fig. 11.34).

11.34 removing fork-crown race with a vise

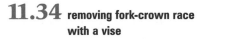

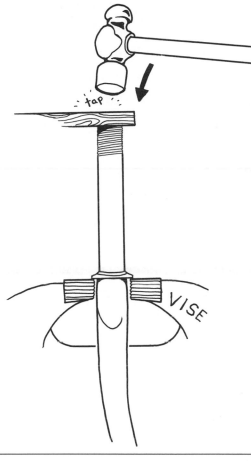

XI-21: INSTALL HEADSET

When you get a new headset, you can install it yourself if you have the necessary tools. Otherwise, get a shop to do it.

Frame and fork preparation

If this is a frame for a cupless internal headset, you shouldn't need to do anything except drop the bearings in, beveled end toward the head-tube seat, and follow steps 3, 6 and 7 in this section. If those seats are badly machined so the bearings are not parallel or the end of the tube is smashed, there is little you (or even most shops) can do — the frame probably needs to go back to the manufacturer.

With a headset with cups — be it an internal

(Fig. 11.21) or standard (Figs. 11.17 and 11.18) headset — on a new frame (or on one that has "eaten" headsets in the past), make sure that the head tube has been reamed and faced. If not, you will need a bike shop equipped with the proper tools to do it for you. Reaming makes the head tube ends round inside and of the correct diameter for the headset cups to press in. Facing makes both ends of the head tube parallel so the bearings can turn smoothly and uniformly. A head tube reaming-and-facing tool is shown in Fig. 1.5 in Chapter 1.

The base of the steering tube also needs to be turned down to the correct diameter for the crown race. The crown race seat on top of the fork crown must be faced in a way that places the crown race parallel to the head tube cups. This is generally only a concern with rigid forks; suspension forks are usually shipped with the tube properly machined to accept the fork crown race. But you do have to make sure that your crown race is the right size for your fork; there are various standard internal crown-race diameters for each steering-tube diameter.

The fork steerer (threaded or threadless) must also be cut to the proper length. Remember, you can always go back and cut more off. You can't go back and add any, so be careful! You can wait until the headset (and stem, in the case of a threadless headset) is installed. Or you can figure out the length first.

Once a threaded headset is installed, measure the excess length as in Fig. 11.36, remove the top nut, and cut that much off the top. Determining the steering-tube length for an already-installed threadless headset is detailed in Section XI-9.

You can find the stack height of a headset in the headset owner's manual, or a bike shop can look it

11.35 setting fork-crown race

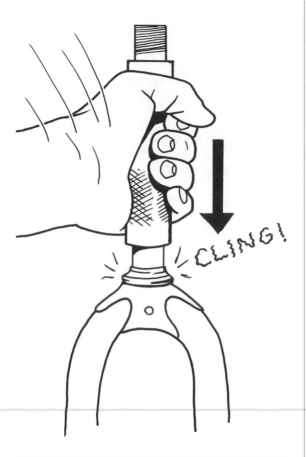

CLING!

INSTALLING
HEADSET

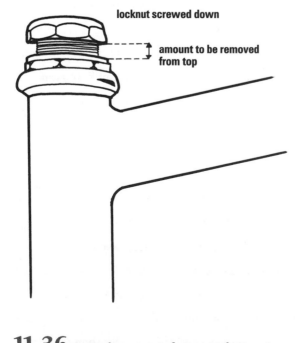

locknut screwed down

amount to be removed
from top

11.36 measuring amount of steerer tube to cut

up in their copy of *Barnett's Manual.* Armed with this information on your threaded headset, measure the length of the head tube and add the headset stack height to this length. If you are adding extra spacers or a brake cable hanger between the headset nuts, add their thickness in as well. This figure represents the length that the threaded steering tube must be from fork crown to top. If the steering tube is already more than 3–5mm shorter than this, you need to find another headset with a shorter stack height (or, if you have included spacers, remove a few). If the steering tube is longer than this sum, saw it down to length and then file off the burrs the hacksaw left on the inside and outside edges of the steering tube end.

You can pretty much follow the same steps if you are using a threadless headset. Add the headset stack-height to the length of the steering tube, spacers and stem clamp, and subtract 3mm from the total. This is the length the steering tube should be from fork crown to top. I recommend not cutting until the headset is assembled and the stem is installed so you can see if you want some spacers under the stem to raise your bars higher.

2. Put a thin layer of grease on the ends of the head-tube cups that will be pressed into the head tube, inside the fork-crown race, inside the ends of the head tube itself and on the base of the steering tube.

3. Slide the fork-crown race down on the fork steering tube until it hits the enlarged section at the bottom. Slide the crown-race slide punch up and down the steering tube, pounding the crown race down until it sits flat on top of its seat on the fork crown (Fig. 11.35). Some crown race punches are longer and closed on the top and are meant to be

11.37 pressing in headset cups with a headset press

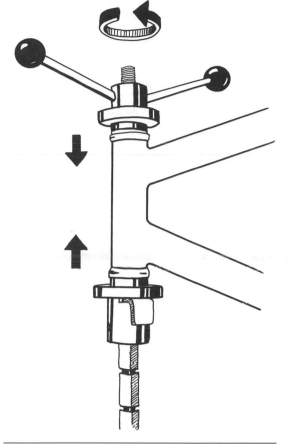

hit with a hammer rather than be slid up and down by hand.

Hold the fork up against the light to see if there are any gaps between the crown race and the crown.

Note: Extra-thin crown races can be easily bent or broken by the crown race punch. Chris King and Shimano both make support tools that sit over the race and distribute the impact from the punch.

4. Place the headset cups into the ends of the head tube. Slide the headset-press shaft through the head tube. Press the button on the detachable end of the tool and slide it onto the shaft until it bumps into one of the cups (Fig. 11.37). This same method, and often the same press, can be used for internal (Fig. 11.21) and external (Figs. 11.17 and

11.18) headsets with cups. You must make sure with internal cups that the press only makes contact with the outer cup flange and not the bearing seat. Find the nearest notch on the shaft and release the button. Some headset presses use a system of spacers and cones on both ends of the cups. Follow the instructions to set yours up properly. Whatever you do, be certain that the parts that make contact with the cups are not touching the precision surfaces the bearings roll in.

Note: Dia-Compe "S" and Chris King headsets have bearings that are pressed into the cups and cannot be removed (Fig. 11.27). If you use a headset press that pushes on the center of the cups, you will ruin the bearings. You need a press that pushes the outer portion of the cup and does not touch the bearings. Chris King makes tool inserts for this that fit most headset presses, and Park has a headset press with large flat ends that also works.

5. Hold the lower end of the cup press shaft with a wrench. That will keep the tool from turning as you press in the cups. Tighten the press by turning the handle on the top clockwise (Fig. 11.37). Keep tightening down on the tool until the cups are fully pressed into the ends of the head tube. Examine them carefully to make sure there are no gaps between the cups and the ends of the head tube.

Note: You can easily crush thin headset cups with a flat-surface headset press, so be careful and stop when the cups reach the head tube.

6. Liberally apply grease to all bearing surfaces. If you are using cartridge bearings (Fig. 11.23), a thin film will do.

7. Assemble and adjust the headset, following Sections XI-18 and XI-16 for a threadless headset, and Sections XI-19 and XI-17 for a threaded one.

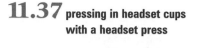

XI

handlebars, stems and headsets

INSTALLING HEADSET

XI-22: TROUBLESHOOTING STEM, BAR AND HEADSET PROBLEMS

1. **Bars slip**. Tighten the pinch bolt on the stem that holds the bars, but not beyond the maximum allowable torque (see Appendix E). With a front-opening stem, make sure that there is the same amount of space between the stem and the front plate on both edges of the front plate. With any stem, if the clamp closes on itself without holding the bar securely, be sure to check that the bar is not deformed and the stem clamp is not cracked or stretched; replace any questionable parts. You can slide a shim made out of a beer can between the stem and bar to hold it better if you have a heavy stem and bar, but don't try this with lightweight ones. Replacing parts is a safer option — there is always a reason why parts that are meant to fit together no longer do! With superlight stems and bars, you cannot just keep tightening the small clamp bolts like you can the larger bolts on heavy stems because you will strip threads and/or cause bar and stem failures.

2. **Bars make creaking noise while riding**. Loosen the stem clamp, grease the area of bar that is clamped in the stem, slide the bar back in place, and tighten the stem bolt. Also, sanding the hard anodized surface inside the stem clamp and on the clamping area of the bar can eliminate creaking.

3. **Bar end slips.** Tighten the bar-end clamp bolt. If you have to go beyond the specified torque, the bar or the bar end may be damaged and need to be replaced.

4. **Stem is not pointed straight ahead**. Loosen the bolt(s) securing the stem to the fork steering tube, align the stem with the front wheel, and tighten the stem bolt(s) again. (With a threaded headset, the bolt you are interested in is a single vertical bolt on top of the stem. Loosen it about two turns, and tap the top of the bolt with a hammer to disengage the wedge on the other end from the bottom of the stem (Fig. 11.15). With a threadless headset, there are one, two or three horizontal bolts pinching the stem around the steering tube that need to be loosened to turn the stem on the steerer. Do not loosen the bolt on the top of the stem cap (Fig. 11.12); you'll have to readjust your headset if you do.

5. **Fork and headset rattle or clunk when riding**. The headset is too loose. Adjust the headset (Section XI-16 or XI-17).

6. **Stem/bar/fork assembly does not turn smoothly but instead stops in certain fixed positions**. The headset is pitted and needs to be replaced. See Sections XI-20 and XI-21.

7. **Stem/bar/fork assembly does not turn freely**. The headset is too tight. The front wheel should swing easily from side to side when leaning the bike or lifting the front end. Adjust the headset (Section XI-16 or XI-17, depending on type).

8. **Stem is stuck on or in fork steering tube**. See Section XI-14.

wheel building

A child of five could understand this. Fetch me a child of five.
— GROUCHO MARX

tools

spoke wrench

truing stand

wheel dishing tool

13mm,14mm, 15mm
cone wrenches

17mm open end
wrench (or an
adjustable wrench)

spoke prep (follow
application instructions
on container)

optional

linseed oil

Congratulations. You have arrived at the task most often used to gauge the talents of a bike mechanic. Next to building a frame or fork, building a good set of wheels is the most critical and most creative of a bike mechanic's tasks. Despite the air of mystery surrounding the art of wheel building, the construction of a good set of bicycle wheels is really a pretty straightforward task.

Clearly, wheels are the central component of a bike. For any bike to perform well, its wheels must be well made and properly tensioned. Once you learn how, it is quite rewarding to turn a pile of small parts into a set of strong and light wheels upon which you can bash around with confidence.

You will be amazed at what they can withstand, and you will no longer go through life thinking that building wheels is something just the "experts" do. With practice, you can build wheels at your house that are just as good as any custom-made set and far superior to those built by machine.

This is not meant to be an exhaustive description of how to build all types of wheel spoking patterns, but you will learn here how to build the three spoking patterns that are used in virtually all mountain bike wheels. (If you are interested in a more comprehensive treatment of the subject of wheel building, I recommend reading *Barnett's Manual* by John Barnett, *The Art of Wheelbuilding* by Gerd Schraner or *The Bicycle Wheel* by Jobst Brandt.) You will learn in this chapter how to

12.1 the complete wheel

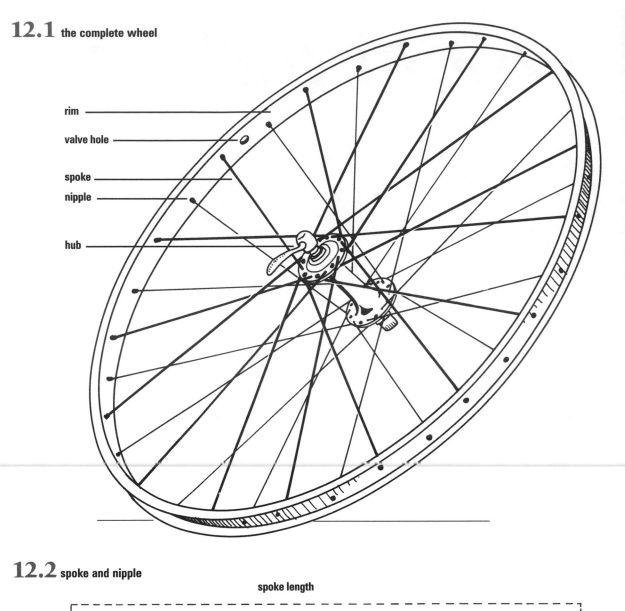

rim

valve hole

spoke

nipple

hub

12.2 spoke and nipple

spoke length

nipple

spoke

build wheels for either rim brakes or for disc brakes in the classic "three-cross" spoking pattern in which each spoke crosses over three other spokes (Fig. 12.1). Additionally, Section XII-7 details how to build radially spoked wheels, and Section XII-8 discusses heavier-duty wheels for big riders. Rear disc-brake wheels are in Section XII-9. So let's get started.

XII-1: PARTS

1. Get together the parts you need: a rim, a hub (make sure that the hub you are using has the same number of holes as the rim does), properly sized spokes and nipples to match. I suggest getting the spokes from your local bike shop. This way, a mechanic can help make sure you are getting the right spoke lengths (Fig. 12.2) and can

counsel you on what gauge (thickness) of spoke to buy, as well as what rim makes sense for your weight, budget and kind of riding you plan on doing. Remember: You must specify when purchasing spokes that you will be using a "three cross" spoking pattern (unless you are building a radial wheel — see Section XII-7). Make sure you also have a spoke wrench that is the right size for the nipples you are using.

Note: If you are just replacing a rim on an old wheel, do not use the old spokes. You won't save all that much money reusing the old spokes, and the rounded-out nipples and weakened spokes will soon make you wish you had gone ahead and spent the extra money on a new set.

Another note: If you are using thin 1.8mm (15-gauge) or thinner spokes, there may be some play between the hub holes and the spokes. This will work the spokes over time and bring on premature spoke breakage. DT sells spoke washers to go between each spoke head and the hub flange to take up this slack.

XII-2: LACING THE WHEEL

 For the sake of brevity and clarity, I do not mention using spoke prep compound with every instruction to thread a nipple onto a spoke. While spoke prep is not mandatory, I think that the wheel is improved if it is used. It encourages the nipples to thread on more smoothly, it takes up some of the slop between the spoke and nipple threads, and its thread-locking ability discourages the nipples from vibrating loose.

The spoke prep is applied to the spoke threads before putting each nipple on. You do not want too much, as it will be hard to adjust the nipples months and years down the road; you just want

12.3 "OCR" (off-center rear) rim laced correctly

the spoke prep in the dips of the threads. You can get the right amount if you dip the threads of a pair of spokes into the spoke prep and then take two more dry spokes, and roll the threads of all four spokes together with your fingers.

In the absence of spoke prep, at least dip the threads of each spoke in grease. Grease accomplishes everything spoke prep does, save for locking the threads.

1. Divide your spokes into four separate groups, two sets for each side of each hub flange.

12.4 first half of right-side spokes placed in hub

12.5 first spoke — right side up

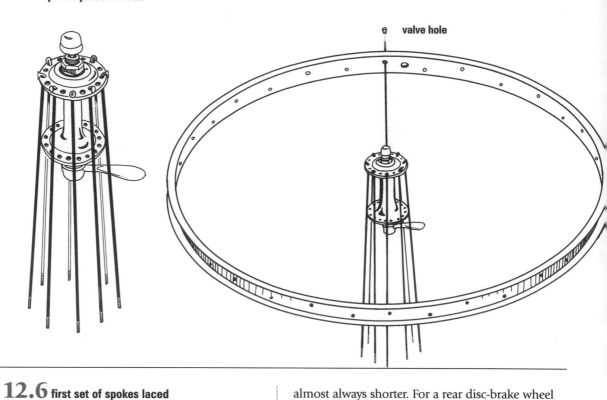

valve hole

12.6 first set of spokes laced

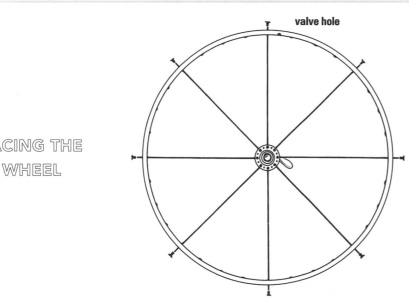

valve hole

Remember: If you are building a rear wheel (or a front disc-brake wheel — Fig. 12.26), you should be working with two different spoke lengths, since spokes on the drive side (or brake rotor side) are almost always shorter. For a rear disc-brake wheel or a radial wheel, skip to Section XII-9 or XII-7.

2. Hold the rim on your lap with the valve hole away from you. Notice that the holes alternate being offset upward or downward from the rim centerline. With an OCR rim (Fig. 12.3), have the spoke holes offset downward, toward your lap.

Note: If you are building a rear wheel with an off-center drilled rim (e.g., Ritchey OCR, Bontrager ASYM), make sure as you are lacing that you orient the rim so that the spoke holes are offset to the left (non-drive) side (see Fig. 12.3). If you are building a front disc-brake wheel with an off-center rim, make sure as you are lacing that you orient the rim so that the spoke holes are offset to the right (nonrotor) side. The rim is meant to reduce wheel dish by offsetting the nipples to reduce the otherwise very steep angle at which rear drive-side or front disc-side spokes normally hit the rim. The balanced left-to-right spoke tension should increase

12.8 lacing second set

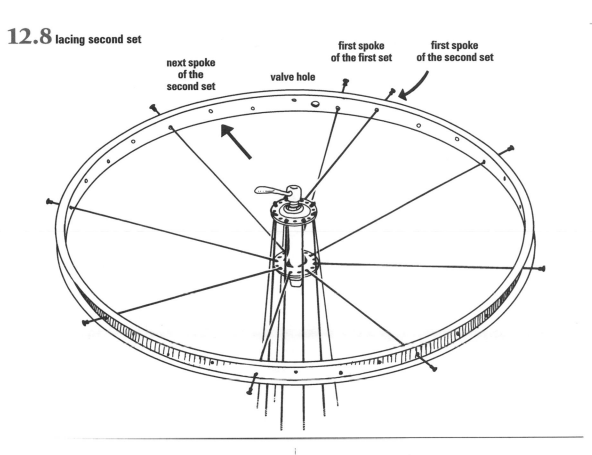

next spoke
of the
second set

valve hole

first spoke
of the first set

first spoke
of the second set

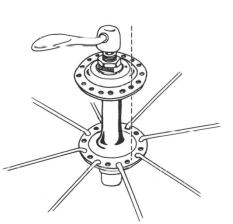

12.7 spoke-hole offset

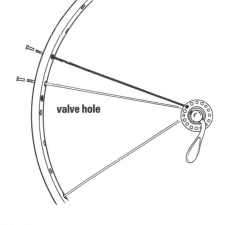

valve hole

12.9 diverging parallel spokes

the lifetime of the wheel, and the lower spoke angle moves the rear drive-side spokes away from the rear derailleur. Also, when using the chain on the dished titanium ninth (largest) cog of Ritchey's "2 x 9" drive-train, the derailleur does not snag the spokes since the rim offset moves them further inboard.

3. Hold the hub in the center of the rim, with

the right side of the hub pointing up. On a rear hub, the right side is the drive side. Standard front hubs are symmetrical; pick a side to be the right side. But if you are building a front disc-brake wheel (Fig. 12.26), I will ask you to call the left side the right side. In other words, follow the lacing instructions to the letter, except substitute the

12.10 second set of spokes laced

valve hole

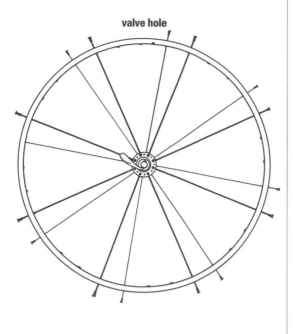

12.11 placing third set of spokes in hub

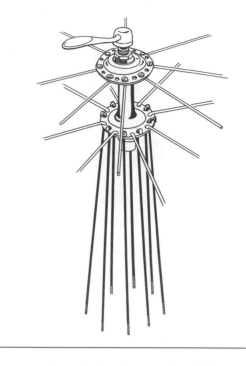

rotor side of the hub (which is actually the left side) whenever the instructions refer to the right side. That way, the spokes on both sides that oppose the braking force on the rotor will come out of the outside of the hub flanges. The wheel will hence be stronger, since these "pulling" spokes come into the rim from a wider angle. If you are building a rear disc-brake wheel, read Section XII-9 before continuing.

In the illustrations, the right side (or the rotor side of a disc-brake front hub — Fig. 12.26) is the one with the nut end of the quick release on it.

A. First set of spokes

4. Drop a spoke down into every other hole in the top (right side) hub flange so that the spoke heads are facing up (Fig. 12.4). Make sure if it's a rear wheel that you put the shorter spokes on the right (drive) side. Half of the holes you are looking at are normally countersunk deeper into the hub

flange to seat the spoke head, so use those holes.

5. Bring a spoke from the hub into the first rim hole counterclockwise from the valve hole and screw the nipple on three turns (Fig. 12.5). Notice that this hole is offset upward (on an OCR rim, this means that the hole is offset upward from the centerline of the spoke holes, not the centerline of the rim). If the first hole that is counterclockwise from the valve hole isn't offset upward, you have a misdrilled rim, and you must offset all instructions one hole.

6. Working counterclockwise, put the next spoke on the hub into the hole in the rim four holes away from the first spoke, and screw a nipple on three turns. There should be three open rim holes between these spokes, and the hole you put the second spoke into should also be offset upward.

7. Continue counterclockwise around the wheel in the same manner. You should now have used half of the rim holes that are offset upward, and there

12.13 lacing third set of spokes

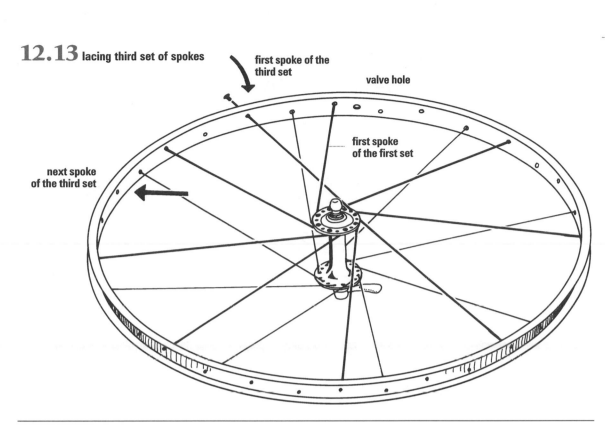

first spoke of the
third set

valve hole

first spoke
of the first set

next spoke
of the third set

---

should be three open holes between each spoke (Fig. 12.6).

8. Flip the wheel over.

B. Second set of spokes

9. Sight across the hub from one flange to the other flange. Notice that the holes in one flange do not line up with the holes in the other flange; each hole lines up in between two holes on the opposite flange (Fig. 12.7).

10. Drop a spoke down through the hole in the top flange that is immediately clockwise from the first spoke you installed (the spoke that is just clockwise from the valve hole). If this is a rear

---

12.12 rotating hub counterclockwise

12.14 third set laced

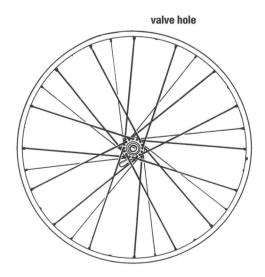

valve hole

12.15 lacing fourth set of spokes

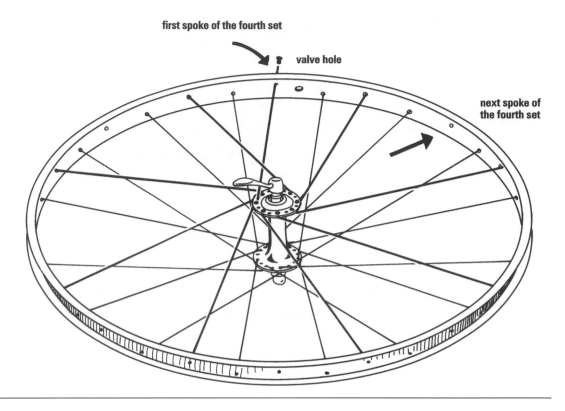

first spoke of the fourth set

valve hole

next spoke of the fourth set

wheel or a front disc-brake wheel, you are now using the longer spokes.

11. Put this new spoke into the second hole clockwise from the valve hole, next to the first spoke you installed (Figs. 12.8 and 12.9). This hole will be offset upward from the rim centerline.

12. Thread the nipple on three turns.

13. Double-check to make sure that the spoke you just installed starts at a hole in the hub's top (left side) flange, which is one-half-a-hole space clockwise from the hole in the lower flange where the first spoke you installed started. These two spokes should be diverging but still nearly parallel (Fig. 12.9).

14. Drop a spoke down through the hole in the top (left side) hub flange two holes away in either direction, and continue around until every other hole has a spoke hanging down through it (Fig. 12.8).

15. Working counterclockwise, take the next

spoke from the hub and put it in the rim hole that is three holes counterclockwise from the valve hole. This hole should be offset upward and four holes counterclockwise from the spoke you just installed. Thread the nipple on three turns.

16. Follow this pattern counterclockwise around the wheel (Fig. 12.10). You should have now used half of the rim holes that are offset upward, as well as half of the total rim holes. The second set of spokes should all be in upwardly offset holes, one hole clockwise from each spoke of the first set.

C. Third set of spokes

17. Drop spokes through the remaining holes on the right side of the hub, from the inside out (Fig. 12.11). Remember: If it's a rear wheel or front disc-brake wheel, these should be the shorter spokes.

18. Flip the wheel over, grabbing the spokes

you've just dropped through to keep them from falling out.

19. Fan the spokes out, so they cannot fall back down through the hub holes.

20. Grab the hub shell and rotate it counter-clockwise as far as you can (Fig. 12.12).

21. Pick any spoke on the top (right-hand) hub flange that is already laced to the rim. Now find the spoke five hub holes away in a clockwise direction.

22. Take this new spoke, cross it under the spoke you counted from (the one five holes away), and stick it into the rim hole two holes counterclockwise from that spoke (Fig. 12.13). Thread a nipple on three turns. Expect to bend the spokes some.

23. Continue around the wheel, doing the same thing (Fig. 12.14). You may find that some of the spokes don't quite reach far enough. If that's the case, push down on each one about an inch from the spoke elbow to help them reach.

24. Make sure that every spoke coming out of the upper side of the top flange (the spokes that come out toward you with their spoke heads hidden from view) crosses over two spokes and under a third. All three of these "crossing" spokes come from the underside of the same flange and have their spoke heads facing toward you. These crossing spokes begin one, three and five hub holes counterclockwise from the spoke that you just inserted into the rim (Fig. 12.14). This is called a "three cross" pattern because every spoke crosses three others on its way to the rim (over, over, under). Every upwardly offset hole should now be occupied on the rim.

D. Fourth (and final) set of spokes

25. Drop spokes down through the remaining hub holes in the bottom flange from the inside out (like Fig. 12.11, but with the other side of the hub up). On a rear or front disc-brake hub, these are again the longer spokes.

26. Flip the wheel over, grabbing the spokes to keep them from falling back down through the holes.

27. Fan the spokes out.

28. Pick any spoke on the top (left-hand) hub flange that is already laced to the rim. Now find the spoke five hub holes away in a counterclockwise direction.

29. Take that spoke, cross it over two spokes and under the spoke you counted from. Stick the spoke into the rim hole two holes clockwise from the spoke it crosses under (Fig. 12.15). Thread a nipple on three turns.

30. Continue around the wheel, doing the same thing until the wheel is laced like Fig. 12.1. You may find that some of the spokes don't quite reach far enough. If that's the case, push down on each

12.16 converging parallel spokes

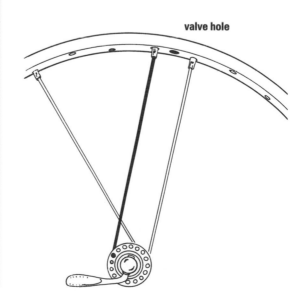

valve hole

XII

wheel building

LACING THE
WHEEL
—
FOURTH SET
OF SPOKES

12.17 pull rim to the right

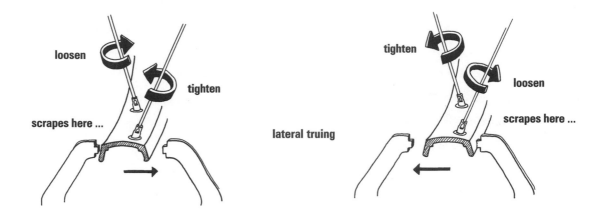

loosen

tighten

scrapes here ...

12.18 pull rim to the left

tighten

loosen

scrapes here ...

lateral truing

one about an inch from the spoke elbow to help them reach.

31. Make sure that every spoke coming out from the upper side of the top flange (the spokes that come out toward you with their spoke heads hidden from view) crosses over two spokes and under a third (Fig. 12.1). All three of these crossing spokes come from the underside of the same flange, and have their spoke heads facing toward you. The crossing spokes begin one, three and five hub holes clockwise from each spoke emerging from the top of upper (left) hub flange (Fig. 12.1).

Every hole should now be occupied on the rim. The valve hole should be between "converging parallel" spokes (Fig. 12.16) to make room for the pump head when inflating the tire.

If it is a rear wheel, note that the spokes coming out of the outside of the hub flange on both sides oppose the clockwise twist the chain applies on the cogs. Similarly, if it a front disc-brake wheel (Fig. 12.26), you will notice that the spokes coming out of the outside of both flanges oppose the twist the brake pads apply to the rotor. See Section XII-6 for more on this.

LACING THE
WHEEL
—
FOURTH SET
OF SPOKES

12.19 pull rim in

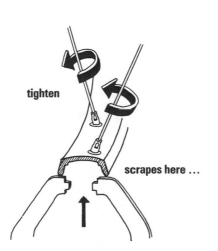

tighten

scrapes here ...

12.20 let rim out

radial truing

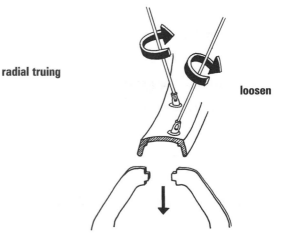

loosen

XII

wheel building

TENSIONING
THE WHEEL
—
TRUING
THE WHEEL

XII-3: TENSIONING THE WHEEL

1. Put the wheel in the truing stand.

2. Tighten each nipple with a spoke wrench until only three threads are visible beyond the bottom of the nipple (see Figs. 12.17–12.20 for rotation direction). From now on, every time you tighten or loosen a spoke nipple, turn it back the opposite direction an eighth-turn afterward. This unwinds the twist in the spoke that your tightening or loosening had just caused.

3. Press the spokes coming outward from the outer side of the hub flanges down with your thumb at the elbow to straighten out their line to the rim. Spokes coming out of the inner side of the flange do not need this.

4. Go around the wheel, tightening each nipple a half-turn. Do this uniformly, so that the wheel is not thrown out of true.

5. Check to see if the spokes are tight enough to give a tone when plucked. Squeeze pairs of spokes together and compare them with a good wheel with spokes of the same gauge; your wheel should have considerably less tension at this point.

6. Repeat steps 4 and 5 until the spokes all make a tone and are under less tension than an existing, good wheel.

XII-4: TRUING THE WHEEL

A. Lateral true

The side-to-side trueness is the most obvious wheel parameter when you spin it.

1. Make sure the hub axle has no endplay. If it does, adjust the hub (see "Hub adjustment," Section VI-14D in Chapter 6) to eliminate the endplay.

2. Optional: Put a drop of linseed oil around the top of each nipple on the tire side where it seats in the rim to lubricate the contact area between it and the inside of the rim hole.

3. Set the truing-stand feelers so that one of them scrapes the side of the rim at the worst lateral wobble (Figs. 12.17 and 12.18).

4. Ending a few spokes on either side of where the rim scrapes, tighten the spokes coming from the opposite side of the hub and loosen the spokes coming from the same side of the hub (Figs. 12.17 and 12.18). Start with a quarter-turn on nipples at the center of the scraping area and decrease the amount you turn each nipple as you move away in either direction. This pulls the rim away from the feeler. If it does the opposite, you are turning the nipples the wrong direction.

Remember: You normally turn something to the right to tighten and to the left to loosen, but tightening and loosening spoke nipples at the bottom of the wheel is the opposite of what you would normally do (Figs. 12.17–12.20). This is because the nipple head is underneath your spoke wrench. This does not apply if you rotate the wheel so you are looking down on the nipple from the top. Try opening a jar that is upside down and you will immediately understand the principle involved.

5. Work around the wheel in this way, bringing in the feelers as the wheel gets truer.

Note: On disc-brake rims, you may need to scrape decals off of the rim sides so they won't hang up on the truing-stand feelers and make it hard to tell where the real wobbles are.

B. Radial true

While not as obvious as side-to-side trueness, out-of-roundness is more important to the longevity of the wheel, since "uniformity of tension is the key to durability." — Portia Masterson of Self Propulsion Bike Shop in Golden, Colorado

6. Set the truing-stand feelers so that they now contact the circumference of the rim, rather than the sides (Figs. 12.19–12.20).

7. Bring the feelers in until they scrape against the highest spot on the rim (Fig. 12.19).

8. Tighten the spokes a quarter-turn where the rim scrapes. This will pull the rim inward. Decrease the amount of each turn (to an eighth-turn and less) as you move away from the center of the scraping area.

9. Work around the wheel this way, bringing the feelers in as the wheel becomes rounder. Loosen the spokes at a dip in the rim (Fig. 12.20).

If the spokes are too tight at this point, they will be hard to turn and will creak and groan as you turn them. When the spokes become hard to turn (i.e., the nipples feel on the verge of rounding off), loosen all of the spokes in the wheel a quarter-turn before continuing. Compare the tension with a good wheel with the same gauge spokes; the tension should still be lower in the wheel you are building.

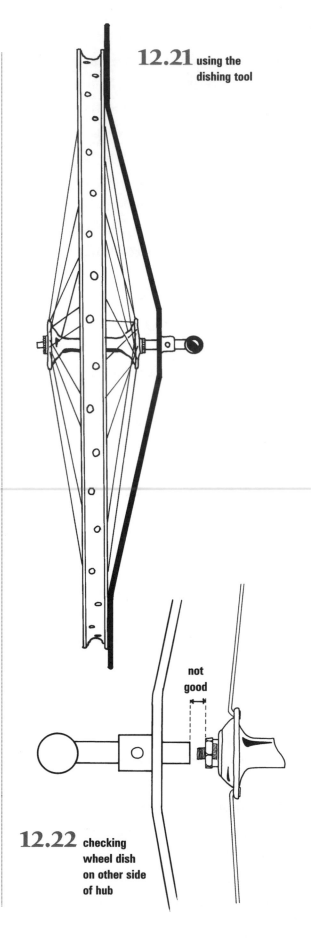

12.21 using the dishing tool

12.22 checking wheel dish on other side of hub

not good

XII-5: DISHING THE WHEEL

1. Place the dishing tool across the right side of the wheel, bisecting the center (Fig. 12.21).

2. Tighten or loosen the dishing gauge screw until the gauge contacts the outer face of the axle end nut (Fig. 12.21).

3. Flip the wheel over.

4. Place the dishing tool across the other side of the wheel.

5. Check the gap of the dishing gauge with this axle end-nut face (Fig. 12.22). Any gap between the dishing gauge and the axle end-nut face indicates

the amount the rim is offset from the centerline of the wheel. If there is no gap, but an overlap instead, reset the dishing gauge on this side (the previously overlapped side). Then flip it over and check the other side (i.e., repeat steps 3, 4 and 5 on the opposite side).

6. Put the wheel back in the truing stand.

7. Pull the rim toward the center (reducing the gap between the dishing tool and the axle end face) by tightening the spokes on the opposite side of the wheel from the axle end that had the gap between it and the dishing gauge. Tighten a half-turn each. If the spokes start getting really tight (they will creak a lot when tightening, the nipples will start rounding off, and the spokes will feel much tighter than the spokes in a comparable wheel), then, instead, loosen the spokes on the opposite side of the wheel a half-turn each.

8. Recheck the wheel with the dishing gauge by repeating steps 1–5.

9. If the wheel is still off dish (there is still a gap between the dishing gauge and the end nut when you flip it over), repeat steps 6–8 until the dish is correct (the gap is zero).

10. Prestress the spokes by squeezing each pair of spokes together with your hands (Fig. 12.23). They will make a "ping" noise as they unwind.

Leaning on the wheel is a quicker way to pre-stress the wheel, but this method has the potential to wreck the wheel if you are not careful. To proceed, set the axle end on the workbench and carefully press down on the rim with your hands at the 9 o'clock and 3 o'clock positions. This will affect an area of about three spokes on each side, so rotate the wheel three spokes, press down again, rotate three more spokes in the same direction, press

12.23 relieving tension

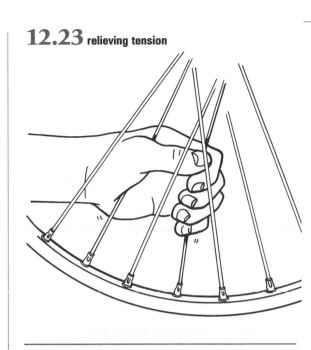

down again, and so on. After you finish one side, flip the wheel over and do the other side. Do not press down with all of your might; although a well-built wheel's lateral strength is impressive, it is still easy to destroy your work with too much pressure.

The amount of readjustment the spokes have to make will be reduced if you have been turning each nipple back an eighth-turn in the opposite direction after each rotational correction (as directed in Section XII-3, step 2). If none of your spokes are twisted, there will be no pinging and readjustment during prestressing.

If prestressing throws the wheel way out of true, the spokes are probably too tight. Loosen them all an eighth-turn. Some loss of wheel "trueness" is normal. If the loss is minor, you may overlook it.

11. Repeat "Truing the Wheel" (Section XII-4), followed by "Dishing the Wheel" (Section XII-5), prestressing the spokes frequently as you go. Keep improving the accuracy of the build this way.

12. Bring up the tension to that of a comparable wheel by making small tightening adjustments to

every nipple, adjusting dish and true after each time around, until the wheel is as you want it.

13. If the rim is oily, wipe it down with a citrus-based biodegradable solvent.

14. Congratulate yourself on building your wheel, and show it off to your friends.

XII-6: COMMENTS

Your wheel has some features that you won't find on machine-built wheels. Most significantly, on your rear wheel, the pulling spokes are to the outside. In plain speak, this means that you have a spoking pattern that best resists the twisting force on the hub produced by pedaling forces on the chain.

In the rear wheel you have just built, half of the spokes are called "pulling," or "dynamic," spokes, and the other half are called "static" spokes. The pulling spokes are the ones directed in such a way that a clockwise twist on the hub increases the tension in them. If you look at the wheel from the drive side, you will see what I am talking about.

You will also see that the static spokes do not oppose a clockwise twist on the hub. In fact, their tension decreases when you stomp on the pedals.

By placing all of the pulling spokes so that they come from the inside of the hub flanges out (i.e., the spoke heads are on the inward side of the flanges), we have attached the spokes doing the most work the farthest outward on the hub. This increases their angle to the rim, and hence their ability to oppose forces acting on the rim. Similarly, if you just built a front disc-brake wheel (Fig. 12.26), the pulling spokes opposing the braking force on the disc are to the outside of the hub flanges.

If you have chosen the appropriate parts for your weight and riding style, and have the proper

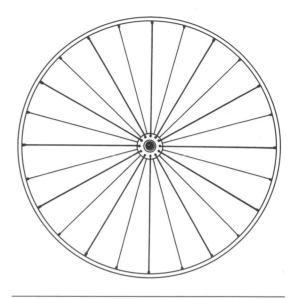

12.24 radially spoked front wheel

spoke tension, then you should have a strong wheel that will last you a long time. Congratulations!

XII-7: RADIALLY SPOKED WHEELS

With the advent of stronger rim materials and stiffer rim cross-sections, radially spoked wheels (Fig. 12.24) are currently very popular. They are very simple to lace up, and radial spoking offers a number of advantages, but a completely radial wheel can only be used on the front. On the rear, you must still use a crossing pattern on one side (usually the drive side) to oppose the twist on the hub caused by the chain (Fig. 12.25). Similarly, you cannot use a radially spoked wheel with disc brakes, as the spokes cannot oppose the torque the brake puts on the brake rotor.

A radially spoked wheel is vertically stiffer than a crossed one because radial spokes allow little opportunity for spokes to absorb energy in the spoking pattern. The radial wheel can be laterally stiffer, too, since all of the spokes can come to the outside of the hub flange and increase the pulling angle to the rim.

RADIALLY
SPOKED
WHEELS

12.25 radial/three-cross rear wheel

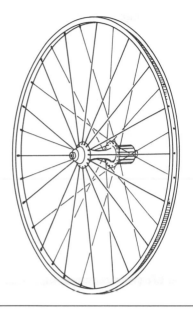

12.26 front disc-brake wheel

A radial wheel is lighter because the spokes are shorter. Further weight can be removed with fewer spokes, and radial spoking allows any even spoke count to be used (with nonradial patterns, the spoke count must be a multiple of four). And radial spoking allows the use of direct pull hubs and nail head spokes (straight spokes without elbows), eliminating a potential weak spot in each spoke.

Radially laced spokes line up behind each other and improve the aerodynamics of the wheel. Aero-shaped spokes can improve the aerodynamics further yet, but using aero-shaped spokes in a standard hub often requires you to slot the hub holes with a jeweler's file to get the spoke through. (If you slot the hub holes, make sure you only file downward from the hole. Slotting upward greatly weakens the hub and invites the spoke to rip the hub flange.) But aerodynamics is a very minor concern on a mountain bike (except perhaps a downhill bike, which can't use radial spokes anyway because of its disc brakes).

Speaking of torn hub flanges, the warranty of some hubs is voided when spoked radially.

Shimano has this stipulation. The stress is greater on hub holes with radial spoking because there is less material resisting the hub tearing out when the spoke is pulling straight outward than if it is pulling at an angle along the hub flange.

A. How to lace a radial front wheel (Fig. 12.24)

Simply drop all of the hubs from the inside of each flange outward and lace the spokes straight to the rim.

B. How to lace a rear wheel with a radial left side and a three-cross drive side (Fig. 12.25)

First lace the drive side following the instructions in Section XII-2A, steps 4–7, and Section XII-2C, steps 17–24. Now lace the left side spokes outward through the hub flange and straight to the rim.

The tensioning and truing steps are the same for radial and radial/three-cross wheels as for standard three-cross wheels, but radial spoke tension should be higher to help prevent the spokes from vibrating loose.

Note: These instructions place the radial spokes to the outside of the hub flange so that their angle to the rim (and hence their ability to oppose lateral forces on it) is highest.

XII-8: WHEELS FOR BIG RIDERS

Building wheels for heavy and tall riders requires greater lateral and vertical stiffness. The weight of the rider can more easily bend and laterally flex the rim, but it creates another problem as well. The heavier rider de-tensions the spokes at the bottom of the wheel more by making the rim more D-shaped at the bottom as it rolls. If the spokes are under less tension, or the nipple flanges periodically lose contact with the bases of the rim holes, the nipples can unscrew, and the wheel will fall apart. To achieve the necessary higher strength, you can add the following characteristics.

A. Spoke count and thickness

First, the spoke count needs to be high: Thirty-six or more spokes is highly preferable for riders over 190 pounds. The spokes need to be heavier, as thicker spokes have less stretch as well as less breakage. While 14/15-gauge (2.0mm/1.8mm) double-butted spokes will probably have no more breakage than straight 14-gauge (2.0mm) spokes (since most breakage occurs at the nipple or the elbow, where butted spokes are thick), butted spokes will stretch more, allowing spoke loosening.

B. Rim section and drilling

The deeper the rim, the higher its hoop strength (vertical stiffness and strength). Unfortunately for heavy riders, many deep V-section rims are also thinner to reduce weight and hence lose some strength. Very deep section rims work with low spoke counts because of this high hoop strength. The strongest wheel would be from a deep-section rim drilled for more spokes.

C. Spoking pattern

With 8-speed and 9-speed rear wheels, dish is high (one side is flatter than the other is), meaning that there is a great tension difference between spokes on the two sides. The loose spokes on the left can unscrew, especially under high pedaling forces, and the tight spokes on the right can break. As the chain twists the cogs clockwise, the spokes opposing the twist (the "pulling spokes") get tighter, while the "static spokes" are reduced in tension and can unscrew.

Using radial spokes on the left side (see Section XII-7 above) can counteract the problem of grossly uneven tension. With a radial left side, the chain twisting the hub forward always tightens all of the left side spokes, rather than loosening half of them as it would with a crossing pattern.

An off-center rim, such as a Ritchey OCR, can also help by reducing the wheel dish. The rim holes are offset to the left side (Fig. 12.3), so the drive-side spokes come to the rim at a lower angle and can work with lower tension. The left-side spokes come to the rim at a higher angle and can be under higher tension without forcing the use of dangerously high tensions on the drive side. Before lacing an off-center rim, make sure you read the note in step 2 of Section XII-2 above.

XII-9: LACING REAR DISC-BRAKE WHEELS

If you are building a rear disc-brake wheel (Fig. 12.28), you want the drive-side outer spokes oppos-

12.27 rear disc-brake wheel: first two sets of spokes completed, first spoke of third set installed

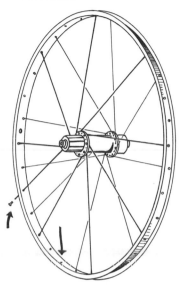

12.28 completed rear disc-brake wheel

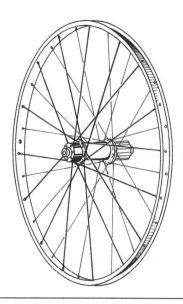

ing the chain force on the cogs, but you want the left-side outer spokes opposing the braking force on the rotor. This makes for a stronger wheel, by having the wider-angle spokes doing more of the work.

The drive side will be laced just the same as in the above Section XII-2 lacing instructions, but the nondrive side will be laced the opposite of the way the left side turns out in Section XII-2.

Lacing a rear three-cross disc-brake-wheel

A. First set of spokes

1. Follow steps 1–9 in Section XII-2.

B. Second set of spokes

2. Push a spoke up through the hole in the top flange that is immediately clockwise from the first spoke you installed (the spoke that is just clockwise from the valve hole).

3. Follow steps 11-13 in Section XII-2.

4. Drop one spoke down through each of the adjacent hub holes on either side of the newly laced spoke. Skip a hole, and continue around the hub

flange dropping a spoke down into every other hole.

5. Rotate the hub shell clockwise as far as you can.

6. Find the spoke five hub holes counterclockwise from the single spoke coming up out of the flange that you installed in steps 2 and 3.

7. Take this new spoke, cross it over the spoke you counted from (the one five holes away), and stick it into the rim hole two holes clockwise from that spoke. Thread a nipple on three turns.

8. Find the next spoke counterclockwise on the hub flange. Put it in the rim hole four holes counterclockwise from the spoke you just installed in step 7. Thread a nipple on three turns.

9. Continue counterclockwise around the top (brake-side) hub flange until all spokes whose heads stick out of the top flange are one rim hole counterclockwise from the first set of spokes installed in the rim.

C. Third set of spokes

10. Follow steps 17–27 in Section XII-2. After you complete step 22, the wheel should look like Fig.

12.27 (except the other fanned-out unlaced spokes coming out of the top flange are not shown).

D. Fourth (and final) set of spokes

11. Pick any spoke on the top (rotor-side) flange whose head is facing up and is already laced to the rim. Now find the spoke five clockwise hub holes away.

12. Follow steps 22-24 in Section XII-2.

13. Note that the drive-side outer spokes oppose the chain pull and the rotor-side outer spokes oppose the braking force on the rotor (Fig. 12.28). Your wheel is now laced. Give yourself a big pat on the back and then begin tensioning and truing your wheel, starting with Section XII-3.

LACING REAR
DISC-BRAKE
WHEELS

forks

If you come to a fork in the road, take it.

— *YOGI BERRA*

The fork serves a number of purposes. Most obviously, it connects the front wheel to the handlebars. Of course, the fork allows the bike to be steered, and supports the front brake. The fork also offsets the front hub some distance forward of the steering axis. This offset distance (called the "fork rake"), combined with the steering axis (the "head angle") and the wheel size, determine how your bike is going to handle and steer.

All forks, suspended (Fig. 13.2) or rigid (Fig. 13.1), provide at least a minimum amount of suspension by allowing the front wheel to move up and down. The simple facts, that the steering axis angles the fork forward from vertical and that the front hub is offset further forward still, make it possible for the fork to flex along its length and absorb vertical shocks. Suspension forks add a much greater range of vertical wheel travel.

All mountain bike forks are made up of a steering tube, a fork crown, fork legs (sometimes called "blades"), brake bosses (usually cantilever/V-brake posts, and/or disc brake mounts, but can also be roller-cam/U-brake posts) and fork ends (also called "dropouts" or "fork tips"). Figs. 13.1 and 13.2 illustrate these parts on a rigid fork and a suspension fork. Mountain bike forks are manufactured from steel, aluminum, magnesium, titanium, carbon fiber and countless combinations of these materials.

These days, most good mountain bikes come equipped with suspension forks (Fig. 13.2). Their most distinguishing feature is the spring inside. That spring can be made up of elastic polymer

tools

metric Allen wrenches

metric open-end wrenches

adjustable wrench

needle-nose pliers

safety glasses

soft hammer

long screwdriver

non-lithium grease

citrus degreaser

optional

torque wrench

ruler or calipers

a pair of dropout alignment tools

solid bench vise

snap-ring pliers

air pump for fork

metric socket wrenches

bike stand

medium thread lock compound (like Loctite 242)

anti-seize compound for titanium bolts

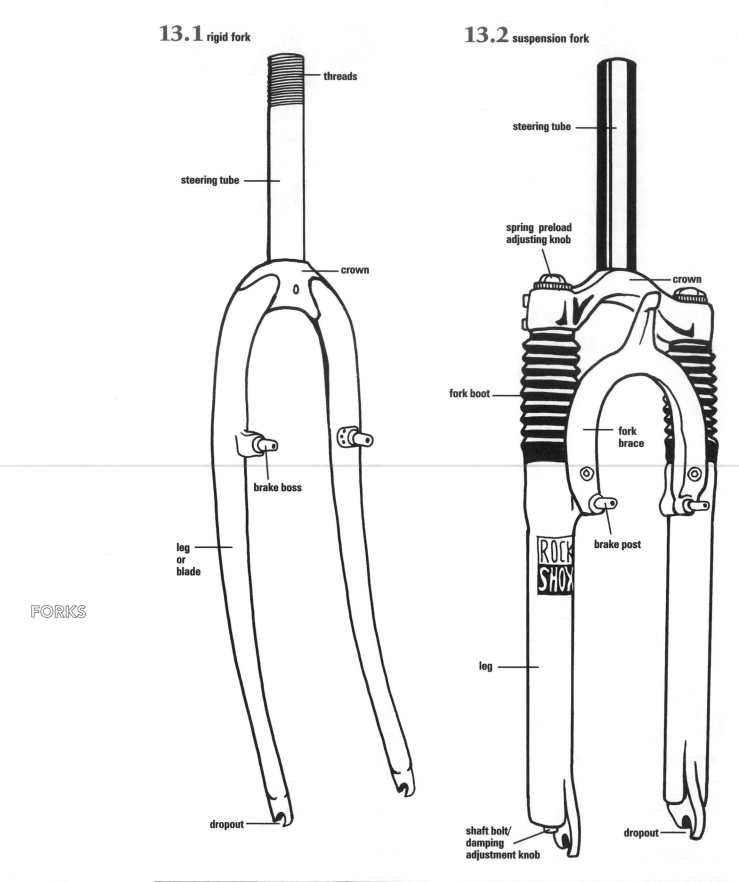

13.1 rigid fork

threads

steering tube

crown

brake boss

leg
or
blade

dropout

13.2 suspension fork

steering tube

spring preload
adjusting knob

crown

fork boot

fork
brace

brake post

leg

ROCK
SHOX

shaft bolt/
damping
adjustment knob

dropout

FORKS

bumpers (elastomers), compressed air, steel or titanium coils or a combination. A lot of suspension forks also include a damping system to control how fast the spring compresses and rebounds. It acts much like a shock absorber on a car or a door (you know — the thing that keeps your screen door from slamming).

Hydraulic damping systems are the most common, relying on the controlled movement of oil from one chamber to another. That flow is usually regulated by a system of holes that act to slow the rate of flow. Some dampers operate on a similar principle with compressed air instead of oil.

The most commonly used suspension fork design uses "telescoping" fork legs that consist of two sections: inner legs attached to the fork crown and steering tube and outer legs attached to the front hub that slide up and down over the inner legs (Fig. 13.3). Although this describes the vast majority of suspension forks, there are a number of variations that vie for a small piece of the fork market. Cannondale's "HeadShok" design incorporates rigid fork legs attached to a single shock unit inside the head tube, and its "Lefty" fork has only a single, telescoping, left leg. "Upside down" telescoping forks have thin lower legs sliding up and down inside fatter upper legs. There are also "linkage" suspension forks that use a system of pivots and movable arms attached to a spring.

XIII-1: FORK INSPECTION

For the most part, forks are pretty durable, but they do break sometimes. A fork failure can ruin your day, because the means of control of the bike is eliminated. Such loss of control usually involves the rapid transfer of your body directly onto the

13.3 how a suspension fork works

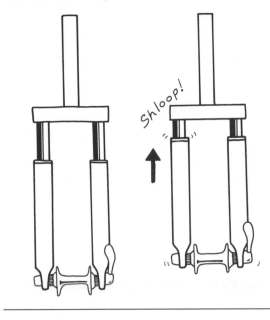

ground, resulting in a substantial amount of pain.

Ever since I first opened a frame shop, people have regularly brought me an amazing collection of forks that broke, sometimes with catastrophic consequences. Some had steering tubes broken either at the fork crown or in the threads. Others had fork crowns that broke or separated (releasing a fork leg or two), fork crown bolts that broke or fell out, fork legs that folded, cantilever posts that snapped, fork braces supporting the brake cable that broke off and front dropouts that broke off. Top caps can fly off of coil- or elastomer-sprung forks (and shoot up at your face!), and seals can blow on air-sprung forks, either one of which immediately bottoms out the fork. Pivots on linkage forks can break or fall apart. You can go a long way toward preventing problems like these by regularly inspecting your fork.

With that in mind, get into the habit of checking your fork regularly for any warning signs of impending failure — bends, cracks and stressed paint. If you have crashed your bike, give your fork a very thorough inspection. If you find any indication that your fork has been damaged, replace it. A new fork is cheaper than emergency room charges, brain surgery or an electric wheelchair.

When you inspect a fork, remove the front wheel, clean the mud off, and look under the crown and between the fork legs. Carefully examine all of the outside areas. Look for any spots where the paint or finish looks cracked or stretched. Look for bent parts, from little ripples in fork legs to skewed cantilever posts and bent dropouts (Fig. 13.4).

Put your wheel back in and watch to see if the fork legs twist when you tighten the hub into the dropouts. Check to make sure that a true wheel centers under the fork crown. If it doesn't, turn the wheel around and put it back in the fork. That way you can confirm whether the misalignment is in your fork or your wheel. If the wheel lines up off to one side when it is in one way and off the same amount to the other side when it is in the other way, the wheel is off, and the fork is straight. If the wheel is skewed off to the same side in the fork no matter which direction you place the wheel, the fork is misaligned.

I recommend overhauling your headset annually (Chapter 11, Sections XI-18 and XI-19), and when you do, carefully examine the steering tube for any signs of stress or damage. Check for bent, cracked or stretched areas, stripped threads (Fig. 13.4), bulging where the stem expands inside (threaded steerer) or crimping where the stem clamps around the top (threadless steerer).

With a threaded fork, hold the stem up next to the steering tube to make sure that, when your stem is inserted to the depth you have been using it, the bottom of the stem is always over an inch below the bottom of the steering tube threads. If you expand your stem in the threaded region, you are asking for trouble; the threads cut the steering tube wall thickness down by about 50 percent, and each thread offers a sharp breakage plane along which the tube can cleave.

On telescoping suspension forks: Check that any clamp bolts are tight (ideally, you would do this with a torque wrench to check that they are tightened to the torque recommended by the fork manufacturer). If you have titanium clamp bolts on your fork crown and you do lots of fast and rough downhill riding, consider replacing them annually; the heads of titanium fork crown bolts have been known to snap off. Nowadays, forks with crown bolts (Figs. 13.12 and 13.14) are rare, which is probably a good thing. Check for oil leaks, either from around the top of the outer leg or around the bolt at the bottom of the outer leg. Check for torn, cracked or missing seals around the top of the outer leg.

On linkage forks, there are a lot of bolts, pins and pivots that need to be checked regularly. Make sure that all bolts are tight and all pins have their circlips or other retaining devices in place so they do not fall out. Check for cracks and bends around the pivot points.

If you have any doubts about anything on your fork, take it to the expert at your bike shop. When it comes to forks, err on the side of caution—replace them before they need it.

XIII-2: FORK DAMAGE

If your inspection has uncovered some damage that does not automatically require fork replacement, here are some guidelines to go by and means of repair.

13.4 one messed-up fork

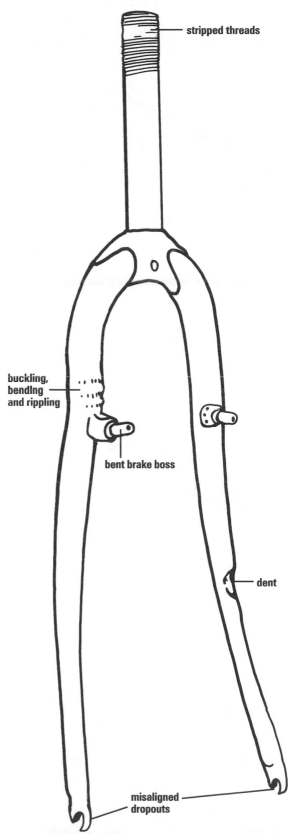

- stripped threads
- buckling, bending and rippling
- bent brake boss
- dent
- misaligned dropouts

forks

A. Dents

Not all fork dents threaten the integrity of the fork. On a rigid fork, a small dent usually poses little risk. A large dent (Fig. 13.4), of course, does. On a suspension fork, almost any dent can adversely affect the fork's operation, even if it does not pose a breakage threat. Most suspension fork parts are replaceable.

B. Fork misalignment

Within limits, a rigid steel fork can be realigned if it is slightly off center. (See Section XIII-5 in this chapter.) Rigid forks made out of any other material and suspension forks cannot be realigned. Don't try it!

C. Stripped steering tube threads

If the threads on the steering tube are damaged (Fig. 13.4) so that the headset slips when you try to tighten it, you need to replace it. The steering tube and fork crown assembly can be replaced on some older suspension forks. You don't usually have that option when it comes to rigid forks, so you have to replace the whole thing.

D. Obvious bend, ripple or crease in fork legs

Replace the fork if you feel or see ripples and bends in it (Fig. 13.4). The poor handling and potential breakage pose too great a threat to your safety to be worth saving a few bucks.

E. Bent or stripped cantilever bosses

On most suspension forks as well as some rigid forks, the cantilever studs can be unscrewed with an 8mm open-end wrench and replaced. It is a good idea to use a thread-locking compound like

FORK DAMAGE

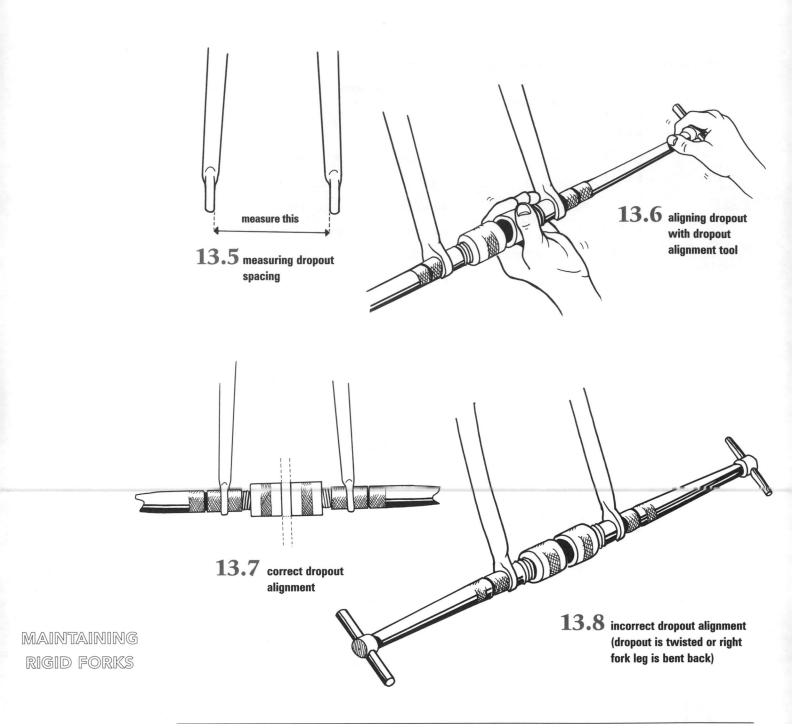

13.5 measuring dropout spacing

measure this

13.6 aligning dropout with dropout alignment tool

13.7 correct dropout alignment

13.8 incorrect dropout alignment (dropout is twisted or right fork leg is bent back)

Loctite 242 on the threads of the new mount.

With few exceptions, bent or stripped cantilever bosses on a rigid fork (Fig. 13.4) usually mean that you have to buy a new fork. If you have a frame builder in your area, he or she may be able to weld or braze a new one on a steel fork. You will also need to repaint the fork.

XIII-3: MAINTAINING RIGID FORKS

Beyond touching up the paint on steel forks and performing regular inspections, the only maintenance procedure to do with a rigid fork is to check the alignment if your bike is handling badly. You can perform minor realignment on a steel fork if you find that it is off center; note that it is risky enough to qualify as a Level 3 job. Do not try to realign titanium, carbon fiber, aluminum or suspension forks. (You've probably noticed that I am repeating myself here.)

XIII-4: CHECK FORK ALIGNMENT

LEVEL 2 You will need a ruler, a true front wheel and dropout alignment tools (Fig. 1.5). With any type of fork other than a rigid steel one, this procedure is diagnostic only, because you should not try to realign any other type of fork. (Again, you might have noticed that I am repeating myself.) Checking the alignment may help explain bike-handling problems.

If you find the alignment to be off more than a couple of millimeters in any direction with any fork other than a steel unsuspended one, you need a new fork. If your fork is new, misalignment should be a warranty item.

If your steel fork is more than 8mm off in any direction, you ought to get a new fork. If the dropouts of a steel fork are slightly bent, you can realign them. You can also take a moderately bent (between 2mm and 8mm off) steel fork to a frame builder or a bike shop for realignment. Make sure that whoever you take it to is properly equipped with a fork jig or alignment table and is well versed in the art of "cold setting" (a fancy term for bending) steel forks.

1. Remove the fork from the bike (Chapter 11, Sections XI-18 and XI-19).

2. With the front wheel out, measure the spacing between the faces of the dropouts (Fig. 13.5). Adult and high-quality children's bikes should have a spacing of 100mm between the inner surfaces of the dropouts. (Some low-end kids' bikes have narrower

spacing — about 90mm or so. If that's the type of bike you are working with, don't bother checking alignment; it isn't worth the trouble.) Remember that you are measuring the distance between the flat surfaces that meet the hub axle faces, not between wheel-retaining bumps. Dropout spacing up to 102mm and down to 99mm is acceptable. Beyond that in either direction means a trip to the bike shop for a new fork. If you have a steel fork, you can go to a bike shop or frame builder for realignment.

3. Clamp the steering tube of the fork in a bike stand or a padded vise. Install the dropout-alignment tools (Fig. 13.6). The tools are made to be used on either the fork or the rear triangle of the bike, so they have two axle diameters and spacers for use in the wider rear dropouts. Move all of the spacers to the outside of the fork ends so that only the cups of the tools are placed inside of the dropouts. Install the tool so that the shaft is seated up against the top of the dropout slot. Tighten the handles down.

4. Ideally, the ends of the cups on the dropout aligning tools should be parallel and lined up with each other (Fig. 13.7). The cups of Campagnolo dropout alignment tools are nonadjustable and are nominally 50mm in length; the ideal space between their ends is 0.1–0.5mm. The cups on Park dropout aligning tools (illustrated in Figs. 13.6–13.8) can be threaded in and out so that you can bring the faces up close to each other no matter what the dropout spacing. If they are lined up with each other, and the dropouts are spaced between 99mm and 102mm apart, continue on to step 5. If your steel rigid fork's dropouts are not lined up straight across with each other (Fig. 13.8) and the dropouts are within the 99–102mm spacing range, skip to Section XIII-5 to align them.

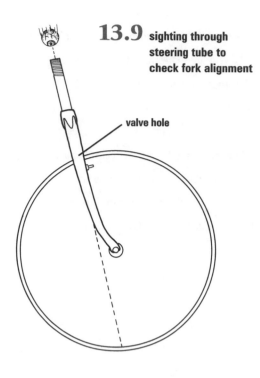

13.9 sighting through steering tube to check fork alignment

valve hole

13.10 correct alignment of valve hole in a straight fork

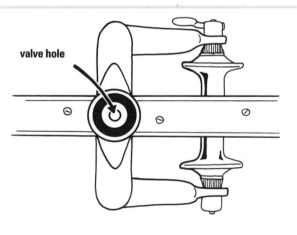

valve hole

CHECKING FORK ALIGNMENT

Note: It is crucial that the fork dropout faces are parallel before continuing with step 5, or the rest of the alignment procedures will be a waste of time. Clamping the hub into misaligned dropouts will force the fork legs to twist. If your dropouts are misaligned, any measurement of the side-to-side and fore-aft alignment of the fork legs will not be accurate.

5. Remove the tire from a front wheel. Make sure the wheel is true and properly dished (Chapter 12, Sections XII-4 and XII-5).

6. Install the wheel in the fork. Make sure the axle is seated against the top of the dropout slot on either side and that the quick-release skewer is tight. Lightly push the rim from side to side to be certain that there is no play in the front hub. If there is play, you first must adjust the hub (Chapter 6, Section VI-14D).

7. Look down the steering tube and through the valve hole to the bottom side of the rim (Fig. 13.9). The steering tube should be lined up with this line of sight through the wheel (Fig. 13.10). When you are sighting through the steering tube and the valve hole, you should see the same amount of space between either side of the rim and the sides of the steering tube while you see the seam side of the rim centered through the valve hole.

Turn the wheel around and install it again so that what was the right end of the hub is now the left, and vice versa. Sight through the steering tube and the wheel valve hole again. Placing the wheel in the fork both ways corrects for deformation in the axle or any wobble in the wheel. If the wheel is true, properly dished and the axle is in good shape, the wheel should line up exactly as it did before. If it does not line up, but the wheel is off by the same amount to one side as it is to the opposite side when the wheel is turned around, the wheel is off and the fork is fine side to side.

If this test indicates the fork is up to 2–3mm off to the side, that is close enough; continue on, please. If it is off by more than 3mm, get a new fork or have it aligned by a frame builder (if it is steel ... because, by now you know that you should

13.11 checking fork alignment with a ruler

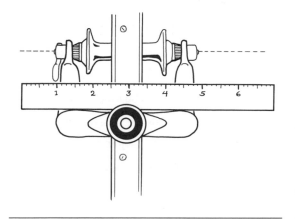

not try to realign suspension, titanium, carbon fiber or aluminum forks).

Note: If you are sighting through the wheel in this way, and you cannot see the bottom side of the rim through the valve hole because the hub is in the way, your fork has big problems. For the bike to handle properly, the front hub must have some forward offset from the steering axis (Fig. 13.9). This offset, or "rake," is usually around 4cm on a mountain bike. If you sight through the steering tube and see the front hub, the fork is bent backward so much that it has little or no offset! If this is the case, you need a new fork.

8. With the wheel in the fork, place a ruler on edge across the fork legs just below the fork crown (Fig. 13.11). Make sure the ruler is perpendicular to the steering tube.

9. Holding the ruler in place, lift the fork toward a light source so that you are sighting across the ruler and the front hub toward the light. The ruler's edge should line up parallel with the axle ends sticking out of either end of the hub (Fig. 13.11). This will tell you if one fork leg is bent back relative to the other one. If the axle lines up parallel to the ruler or very close to that, your fork alignment has checked out completely, and you can put it

back in the bike. If one fork leg is considerably behind the other, you need to get a new fork or have this one aligned.

XIII-5: ALIGN DROPOUTS ON RIGID STEEL FORK

LEVEL 3 You can only do this with a steel, nonsuspension fork!

Dropouts are easy to tweak out of alignment; simply pulling the bike off of a roof rack and failing to lift it high enough to clear the rack skewer will do it. Your forks may also have come with misaligned dropouts to start with.

If the dropout is bent more than 7 degrees or so, or if the paint is cracked at the dropout where it is bent, it is too dangerous to bend it back. Replace the fork.

1. Install dropout-alignment tools and check the alignment as described in steps 3 and 4 under "Check Fork Alignment," Section XIII-4.

2. If they are not lined up with each other, and the fork spacing is between 99 and 102mm, you can align the dropouts. If the fork spacing is wider than 102mm or less than 99mm, there is no point in aligning the dropout faces, because you must bend the fork legs as well to correct the spacing. Without an alignment table or fork jig, you cannot do this accurately. You should get a new fork or have a qualified mechanic or frame builder align your rigid steel fork.

If your fork spacing is between 99mm and 102mm apart, clamp the crown or unicrown of the fork very tightly between two wood blocks in a well-anchored vise.

3. Grab the end of the dropout-alignment tool handle with one hand and the cup of the tool with

the other. Bend each dropout until the open faces of the dropout-alignment tools are parallel, and the edges line straight up with each other (Fig. 13.7).

4. Remove the tools, and continue with Section XIII-4, step 5.

XIII-6: MAINTAINING SUSPENSION FORKS

Suspension forks (Fig. 13.2) are now the standard on mountain bikes. They offer a significant performance advantage and increase the versatility of the bike. Rapid improvements in the science of bicycle suspension have resulted in a proliferation of numerous types of forks. Of course, with this rush of technology, older models quickly become obsolete. Because of that, you should remember that the details outlined here are applicable to forks commonly used in 2002 and prior years. As of this writing, the market is dominated by telescoping forks with coil springs, elastomer springs, air springs or a combination inside. Many are also equipped with hydraulic damping systems. These forks share so many similarities that they lend themselves to common basic service steps.

You will be on your own if you have linkage-style forks or aftermarket upgrades retrofitted to forks; read your owner's manual carefully. Linkage-style forks rely on several pivot points, so there are plenty of places for things to go wrong. Be especially vigilant about inspecting these forks regularly.

The reality is that one of the most important things you can do in the way of suspension-fork maintenance is to check periodically with your bike shop to make sure your fork has not been recalled. If it has, make sure you get it to your shop or the manufacturer before riding it any more.

XIII-7: REMOVE FORK LEGS FROM FORK CROWN

This only applies to single-crown forks from prior to 1998 as well as to double-crown (a.k.a. "triple-clamp") forks — forks with a crown above and below the head tube. The inner legs in most later single-crown models are pressed into the crown and cannot be removed. If you have a slotted crown, pulling the inner legs out of the crown is a more convenient way to add or replace dust boots than pulling the outer legs off of the inner legs (Section XIII-14).

When pulling the inner legs out of the crown, you can leave the fork brace and brakes on and leave the fork in the bike when you do it. Removing the fork legs from the crown is not necessary to change coil springs or elastomers or to pump an air/oil fork.

1. Disconnect the brake cable by removing the cable end from the brake lever (Chapter 7, the reverse of Section VII-6, steps 8–10).

2. Loosen the crown bolts (shown in Figs. 13.12–13.14 and 13.21). If there are two bolts on each side of your fork crown, do not completely undo one bolt while leaving the other fully tightened. Doing that places a great deal of clamping force on the remaining tight bolt, and you can strip the head while you are trying to get it loose. Instead, unscrew one bolt about a quarter-turn and then do the same to the other. Then go back to the first bolt and loosen it by another quarter-turn. Repeat until the crown is loose enough to free the leg.

3. Pull both fork legs out of the crown(s) using a gentle rocking motion.

13.12 **1995 RockShox Judy fork exploded (the inner leg is shortened for clarity)**

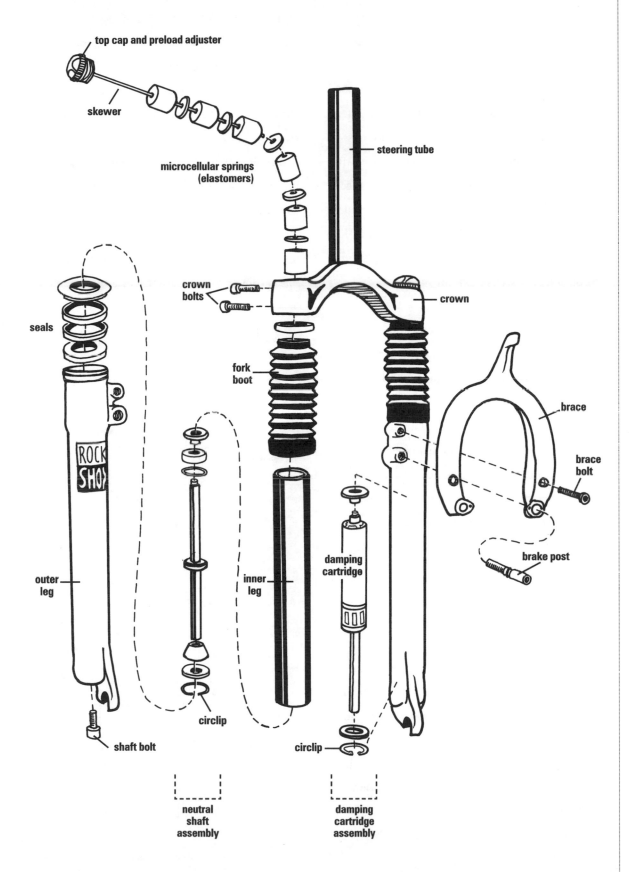

forks

SUSPENSION
FORK
EXPLODED

XIII-8: REMOVE AND INSTALL FORK BOOTS

Any telescoping forks will stay cleaner inside with fork boots on the inner legs (shown in Figs. 13.12 and 13.21) to keep dirt off of them and the seals at the top of the outer legs. But since the 2000 model year, this is less of a big deal, thanks to effective multiple sealing systems from manufacturers. Conversely, to check your fork's travel (Section XIII-10), you will need to remove the boots, if installed.

1. With a pre-1998 fork or a double-crown model, remove the fork legs from the crown (see Section XIII-7 above). Pressed-in legs require you to pull off the outer legs — see Section XIII-14, steps 1–4.

2. Pull the fork boots off.

3. To install boots, slide them on to the inner legs, with the large end down toward the outer legs. Make sure that you are using boots designed for your fork.

4. Pull the lip of each fork boot into the groove in the top of the outer leg. You may need to stretch the boot with a pair of needle-nose pliers to get it to slide over the outer leg behind the fork brace.

5. Replace the inner legs in the fork crown (see Section XIII-9 below) or in the lower legs (Section XIII-14, steps 5–9).

XIII-9: INSTALL INNER LEGS IN FORK CROWN

Again, this only applies to single-crown forks from prior to 1998 as well as to double-crown, or triple-clamp, forks (forks with a crown above and below the head tube).

1. Wipe the inner legs clean, and make sure the fork crown bolts are loose. Install the fork boots (Section XIII-8 above).

2. Insert the inner legs (a.k.a. "upper tubes")

REMOVING/
INSTALLING
FORK BOOTS
—
INSTALLING
INNER LEGS IN
FORK CROWN

into the fork crown. Some Manitou forks have a lip against which the inner leg is supposed to rest. Slide the inner leg up into the crown until it hits the lip. Otherwise, on single-crown forks, push the inner leg through the crown until the top of the leg sticks up no more than 2mm above the top of the crown (Fig. 13.14).

On triple-clamp forks, slide the inner legs up through both crowns. Make sure that the upper crown is the right shape and orientation to work with your head-tube length (Fig. 13.13). For instance, most RockShox triple-clamp forks specify that the lower crown must be located so that there

13.14 using zip tie to measure travel

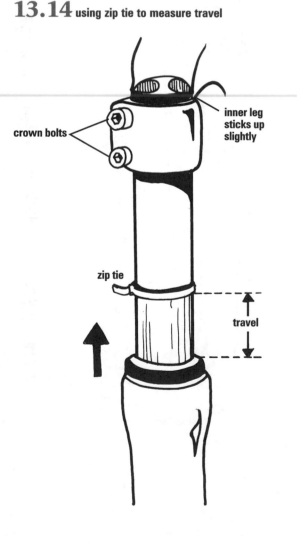

crown bolts

inner leg sticks up slightly

zip tie

travel

13.13 upper crown height and orientation for head tubes of different lengths with triple-clamp forks (example shown is for RockShox)

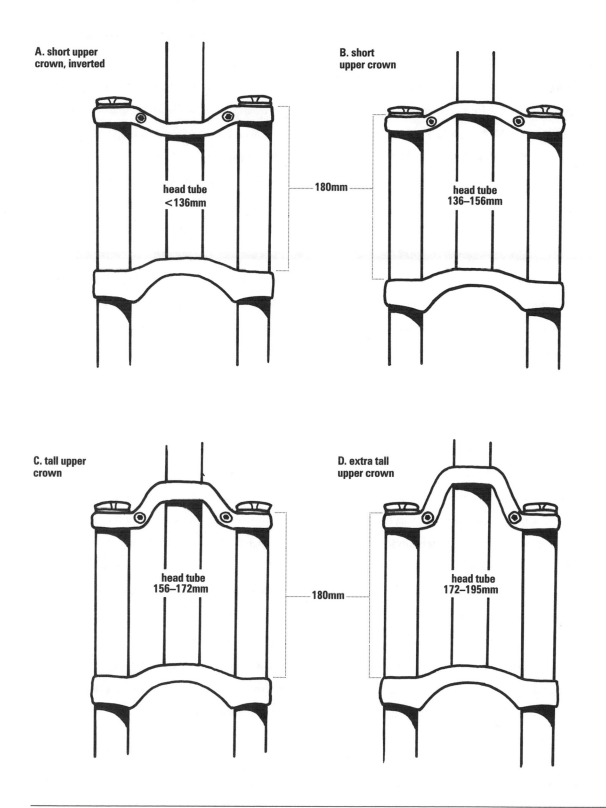

A. short upper crown, inverted

head tube
<136mm

180mm

B. short upper crown

head tube
136–156mm

C. tall upper crown

head tube
156–172mm

180mm

D. extra tall upper crown

head tube
172–195mm

UPPER CROWN
HEIGHT AND
ORIENTATION
FOR HEAD
TUBES OF
DIFFERENT
LENGTHS

are 180mm of exposed upper tubes above the lower crown. Upper crowns come in different heights (i.e., short, tall, extra tall) for different frame sizes, and they can be installed right-side up or inverted so that they clamp the upper tubes just below the top while ensuring that the specified length of upper tube extends above the lower crown (Fig. 13.13).

IMPORTANT CAUTION ON DOUBLE-CROWN FORKS

If more than the manufacturer's specified length of upper tubes is above the lower crown, then the lower crown will be too close to the tire and could hit it on large impacts, which can stop you and the bike dead and leave you that way. Furthermore, some triple-clamp forks have shims to be inserted into the lower crown's clamping slots or reinforcements around the upper tubes under the lower crown. To avoid fork failure, make sure you include whatever the manufacturer intended.

3. Tighten the crown bolts to the manufacturer's specified torque. If you have paired bolts on the crown (Fig. 13.14), alternately tighten each of the two bolts on each side.

On older single-crown forks, pre-1997 Manitous had a single M6 (tightened with a 5mm hex key) crown bolt on each side. 1997 Manitou forks use a small pair of M5 bolts (tightened with a 4mm hex key) on each side (Fig. 13.21), like RockShox (Figs. 13.12 and 13.14) or RST, and tightened to approximately the same torque. In 1999 and 2000, some RockShox forks utilized a small shim in their bolt-on single and double (Fig. 13.13) crowns, and these require considerably higher torque.

Fork crown bolts are critical bolts — make sure you tighten them to the required torque specified in Appendix E!

Using an anti-seize compound on titanium

bolts and a medium thread-lock compound on steel bolts is generally recommended.

XIII-10: MEASURING FORK TRAVEL

A. Measure sag

"Sag" is the amount of fork compression that occurs when the rider sits on the bike without moving. You'll need a friend to help you. Have your friend measure the distance from the top of the outer leg to the bottom of the fork crown when you are on the bike and when you are off of the bike. The difference between the two measurements is the sag. The sag can also be measured using the trusty zip-tie method (Fig. 13.14):

1. After removing the fork boot, if installed (Section XIII-8 for old forks, XIII-14 for the rest), tighten a plastic zip tie around one inner leg, and slide it down against the top of the outer leg.

2. Get on your bike.

3. Get off your bike. When you are off your bike, measure the distance from the top of the outer leg to the zip tie (Fig. 13.14).

Note: To measure the amount of travel you normally use while riding, go ride with the zip tie on. Hit bumps and check the travel after you stop.

B. Measure maximum possible travel

The fork's full travel can be measured by eliminating the spring from the fork. It is generally close enough to just go by the manufacturer's advertised travel, if no modifications have been made to the fork.

1. Holding the wheel down and pulling up on the crown, measure the distance from the crown to the top of the outer leg.

2. Remove the springs from both fork legs.

13.15 **removing spring stack from Manitou SX**

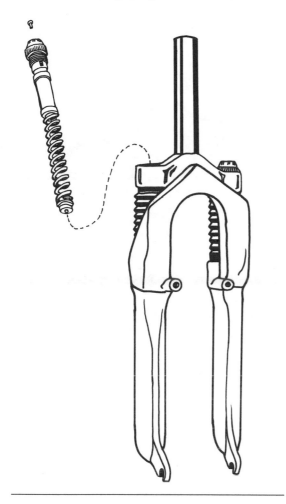

forks

With a coil spring and/or elastomer fork, remove the top cap (Fig. 13.15), usually from both sides of the fork crown. Some forks have plastic knurled nuts (Figs. 13.12 and 13.15), while others need to be removed with a wrench (usually 22mm). On some forks, loosening the crown bolts makes it easier to unscrew the cap.

With an air-oil fork, release the air from both legs. On older RockShox Mag-series forks, remove either the Phillips screw (Fig. 13.17) or the plastic snap-on cap covering the air hole, turn the compression damping adjustment to the highest setting, moisten the needle of a ball-pumping adapter, and stick it down into the hole to release

the air. On RockShox SIDs, original models require a moistened ball needle, whereas subsequent models up to 2001 have an inset Schrader valve and require a special pump adapter that is screwed into the valve for inflation. Current air forks from RockShox, like those from almost all other manufacturers, have standard Schrader valves. On forks with Schrader valves, simply remove the valve cap and push down on the valve pin to let the air out. Also, some air forks have valves on both ends of one leg, the bottom one being a negative spring.

Note: You do not remove the air or the springs from both legs of any Manitou TPC (Twin Piston Cartridge) fork — almost all post-1998 Manitou models — or RockShox Psylo, Duke or post-2001 SID Race and SL. These forks have all of the springs in one leg, and the other leg contains only the damping system. So just let the air or the coils or elastomers out of the one leg containing them.

3. **Measure the distance** from the bottom of the crown to the top of the outer leg when the fork is fully extended and when it is fully compressed. The difference between these numbers is the total available travel you have. Note that negative springs and top-out and bottom-out cushions make this a bit less simple. Pull the fork up to full extension before removing the springs, and lean on it with your full weight after removing them.

When riding with zip-ties on the inner legs, check if you are using up the total travel when you hit big bumps. This helps you determine the proper spring, preload and damping to use. If the fork is adjusted properly for the course you are riding, it will bottom out (i.e., use the full travel) at least once on the course; otherwise, you are not using the fork's full potential.

MEASURING
FORK TRAVEL

CAUTIONARY NOTE

Measure the distance from the top of your tire to the bottom of the fork crown, and make sure that it is more than your total fork travel. If it is less, the crown can hit your tire on full compression and stop you dead (literally!). Use a smaller tire if necessary to ensure that the tire cannot hit the crown.

XIII-11: MINOR MAINTENANCE OF TELE-SCOPING SUSPENSION FORKS

On old fork models, if you do this procedure frequently and keep the inner legs covered with fork boots, you can greatly increase the life of the seals as well as the time between fork overhauls. A dry or dirty dust seal rubbing on a dry or dirty inner leg usually causes stickiness in suspension forks.

1. With the fork boots off or slid up, wipe off the outside of the seal on top of each outer leg and the length of the inner leg between the outer leg and crown.

2. Put a thin coat of Teflon-fortified lubricant on the outside of the seals and inner legs (the area under the zip-tie in Fig. 13.14).

3. Pull the fork boots back into position. You may need to stretch the bottom of each fork boot with needle-nose pliers to get it in the groove around the top of the outer leg and behind the fork brace.

XIII-12: TUNING COIL SPRING/ ELASTOMER FORKS

Telescoping elastomer and coil spring suspension forks (Figs. 13.12, 13.15 and 13.21) are quite simple in principle and are generally straightforward to adjust and maintain. After you understand the why and the how of adjusting your coil/elas-

13.16 adjusting spring preload

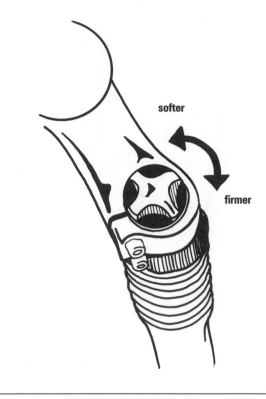

tomer spring fork from this section, you can use Section XIII-19 as a guide for dialing it in.

A. Setting spring preload

Spring preload, the amount of compression of the spring at rest, can be adjusted on most mid- to high-end coil spring/elastomer forks. On most mid- to high-end coil spring/elastomer forks, you can adjust the preload simply by turning the adjuster knobs on the top of the fork crown (Fig. 13.16) — even while riding, as you encounter terrain variations. With Manitou TPC or RockShox "Pure" damping systems, you only have one preload adjuster, as there are only springs in one leg (usually the left leg). (Note that the knob on the 2002 RockShox Psylo adjusts travel, not preload.)

Rotating the adjuster knobs clockwise gives a firmer ride by tightening down on (and thus short-

forks

ening) the spring stack. Rotating the adjuster knobs counterclockwise softens the ride. Make sure the top cap surrounding the knob does not unscrew from the fork crown; you may need to hold it tight with one hand (or a wrench) when you loosen the adjuster knob. Check the top cap occasionally to make sure it is not unscrewed or being forced out due to stripped threads. If its threads seem to be stripped, before you ride any more, get a new top cap right away; if the top cap pops off, the spring can shoot up into your face at high velocity.

Preloading the springs does not limit the full travel for large bumps; it determines the force required for a bump to initially compress the fork, and it uses up some of the spring's length and therefore makes it stiffen up faster as the fork moves. Varying the preload also changes the fork's sag, and it shortens the life of the springs, as they are being compressed even while your bike is hanging in the garage. It is better to change the spring stack (see XIII-12B below) to get the ride you want and minimize preload, using the preload adjustment only as a way to change the fork quickly during a particular ride.

B. Replacing elastomers and coil springs

To make major changes in the fork's spring rate, you must change the springs inside of the fork (Fig. 13.15). Manufacturers usually color-code the elastomers and coil springs for stiffness, though you can tell the difference between stiff and soft elastomer bumpers by squeezing them between your fingers. (Some manufacturers refer to the elastomers as "MCUs" for "Micro-Cellular Urethane," referring to small air voids trapped inside the urethane spring.) Extra springs usually come with the fork, or you can buy them from a dealer.

The fork needs stiffer springs (or more spring preload) if it sags excessively when you sit on it. Set your sag at about 20 percent of your fork's total travel, and closer to 10 percent for racing. The fork needs softer springs (or less compression damping — see the following section) if hard impacts with large bumps do not use the fork's full travel.

1. Unscrew the top caps (counterclockwise). On its old, pre-1998 forks, RockShox recommends that you first loosen the crown bolts to relieve inward pressure on the fork legs before unscrewing the caps. On some forks, the top caps can be unscrewed with your fingers, while others require a wrench (22mm is common) to unscrew the top cap. Again, on Manitou TPC or RockShox Pure damping systems, you only have springs in one leg.

2. Pull the springs out of the fork (Fig. 13.15). Oftentimes, they will come out attached to the top caps and snapped together to each other with plastic connectors. On many older (pre-1996 or so) forks, the top cap is connected to a rod (the "skewer" in Fig. 13.12) that runs through each of the elastomer bumpers. If the springs do not come out with the top caps, turn the bike upside down or compress the fork to get them out.

3. Clean any old grease off of the coil springs, elastomers, skewers, plastic connectors and whatever else you found in the fork.

4. Choose the coil springs and/or elastomers that you intend to use.

Again, when choosing the springs, don't be afraid to bottom the fork (as long as you do not use a tire bigger than recommended by the manufacturer so it can't hit the crown). If you do not bottom it once on the course, you are not getting the full potential out of the fork.

If any of the elastomers are misshapen or look squished or worn in any way, replace them. Some manufacturers provide a nominal and replacement length for coil springs and elastomers. Measure your springs and check them!

5. Apply a new coating of grease to the new parts and everything you just cleaned. Make sure you grease the outside of the coil springs to reduce the noise of the springs rubbing inside the legs.

In open-bath dampers, like in many Marzocchi and RockShox, hydraulic oil sloshes all around in the spring chamber, so there is no need to grease the springs. Make sure you don't let any dirt fall down into the leg.

6. Put the spring stack in the fork legs (Fig. 13.15), and screw the caps down. Be sure to retighten the crown bolts to the required torque, if you loosened them.

C. Fine-tuning damping

High-end elastomer- and coil-spring forks have a hydraulic damping cartridge or cylinder (Figs. 13.12 and 13.21) inside one or both lower legs. Some elastomer forks do not have these. (If there is no bolt at the bottom of the fork leg — as in Figs. 13.18 and 13.19 — it does not have a damper.) Of those with damping cartridges, not all are adjustable. You can be sure that almost any high-end fork (other than superlight race-only models) has adjustable damping — look for adjuster knobs on the top and bottom of the legs.

Compression damping

Compression damping controls the speed at which the spring compresses during the fork's downstroke. Speed of movement is controlled by oil (or compressed air, in the case of the Englund TotalAir system) moving through or around a piston that is being forced through the oil chamber. Varying the size of the hole or the thickness of the oil varies how easily the piston can move through the oil. Excessive compression damping will give you a harsh ride over repeated rocks, but it will feel good when you hit something big. Too little compression damping will lead to harsh bottoming out on big hits and will bob noticeably when climbing, but it will feel smooth over repeated rocks.

Some forks have a "lockout," which closes off the orifice in the compression-damping piston, thus preventing the fork from compressing rapidly. If you really slam into something with most lockout systems, you can still blow off the emergency shim stack covering the oil hole through the piston, and the fork will compress. The lockout knob is generally on top of the fork leg, but on a Cannondale single-sided Lefty fork with E.L.O. (electronic lockout), the lockout button is on the handlebar.

You can crank down your compression damping (or use the lockout, if you have it) to stiffen your fork for riding on smooth surfaces.

Rebound damping

Rebound damping controls the speed at which the fork returns to its original position after it has been compressed and released. As with compression damping, speed of movement is controlled by oil (or compressed air, in the case of Englund TotalAir) moving through or around a piston as it is being drawn back through the oil chamber. Varying the size of the hole or the thickness of the oil varies how easily the piston can move through the oil. The piston can be separate from the compression-damping piston (Manitou TPC or RockShox Pure damping), or the same piston can control both compression and rebound.

Rebound damping is too high when you get a harsh ride over repetitive bumps because the fork packs up (i.e., it keeps getting shorter with each bump, since it cannot return fully before the next impact). Too little rebound damping will let the fork snap back too fast (called "pogo-ing"). It is usually best to start with minimal rebound damping so the fork is very active and then reduce the damping to limit the pogo-ing effect.

Damping adjustments

On most Manitou TPC (Black, MARS, Xvert, SX) and some RockShox Psylo and post-2001 SID models, compression damping is adjusted by turning the knob on the top of the right-hand fork leg (except for early Manitou TPCs, which had the damping chamber in the left leg). This knob controls orifices in the upper piston. On Manitous with a lockout, the compression damping adjuster is eliminated in favor of the lockout lever. (You can still adjust compression damping, but you have to pull out the upper piston [Section XIII-16, Fig. 13.28] and turn a setscrew on the side of the shaft with a hex key.) On most forks with a damper only in one leg, a knob on the bottom of the same leg controls rebound damping by regulating orifices in the lower piston. On both the compression and rebound knobs, turning it clockwise increases damping and counterclockwise decreases it.

Some high-end RockShox forks (2000-model SID SL) have a damping adjuster on the bottom of the leg that you push in (its normal position) and turn to adjust rebound. If you pull the knob outward until it clicks and then turn it, you adjust compression damping.

On pre-TPC (pre-1998) Manitou Mach 5, SX,

SX-Ti or EFC, the rebound damping is adjustable by turning a knob at the bottom of the left leg. The Mach 5/SX/SX-Ti rebound damping adjuster knob is tall and made of black plastic (Fig. 13.18). Turning the knob clockwise increases rebound damping (and slows the return stroke), and counterclockwise decreases rebound damping. You can only change compression damping in these Manitou forks by varying the shim stack inside the damping unit.

On all pre-1997 adjustable RockShox Judy models, the compression damping is adjusted by inserting a 2mm hex key through the center of the hollow shaft bolt at the bottom of the left leg (the bolt is pictured in Fig. 13.19). Clockwise rotation increases compression damping. Later models, including Judy, SID and Psylo, have a removable knob attached to a 2.5 mm or 3mm hex key inserted through the bolt similar to Manitou (Fig. 13.18).

Early (1997–1998) Judy DH and DHO forks include an additional adjustable cartridge in the right leg to control rebound damping. It can also be adjusted with a 2mm hex key on a DH through the center of the hollow shaft bolt on the bottom of the right fork leg and on the DHO with a 3mm hex key or an optional knob. Clockwise rotation increases rebound damping (slows the return stroke). It is very important that you do not turn this adjuster any more than two full turns counterclockwise! RockShox Boxxer forks also have a compression damping adjuster at the bottom of the left leg and a rebound damping adjuster at the bottom of the right leg.

Marzocchi Bombers and subsequent models also have adjustable damping from the bottom of the leg.

13.17 inflating a RockShox Mag or early SID air-oil fork

If you have no damping adjustment knobs, you can also adjust damping by changing to different viscosity of hydraulic oil — see Sections XIII-15 and XIII-16 for how to do it. If the fork is moving too fast, go up 2.5 points in viscosity. To speed it up or adjust for wintertime cold, lighten the oil by 2.5 points.

XIII-13: TUNING AIR-SPRUNG FORKS

The lightest forks use compressed air as a spring. It would, after all, be hard to come up with a spring lighter than one made of air!

After you understand the why and the how of adjusting your air-sprung fork from this section, you can use Section XIII-19 as a guide for dialing it in.

A. Adjusting air pressure

Greater air pressure means a stiffer fork, and vice versa. It is a good idea to check your air pressure every couple of weeks, for all forks lose pressure over time.

Do not use a tire pump on the fork; the large stroke volume is poor for adjusting low volumes of air at high pressure. The gauge won't tell you how much air is left in the fork, and unless your fork takes a ball-inflation needle, you will lose most of the pressure when removing the pump head. You need a shock pump with a no-leak fitting, as the Schrader valves on air forks can lose air when removing the pump. Early RockShox SIDs, all Mag-series forks, and the air assist on post-2002 Judys use valves that require a ball-inflation needle (the kind you use for a soccer ball). SID forks from 1999 to 2000 require a special adapter that fits down in the recessed valve and prevents air from escaping as the adapter is removed. Newer shock pumps have a no-leak fitting built into the head that prevents leakage from any standard Schrader valve.

Pump to the desired pressure — something that varies widely with manufacturer. RockShox Mags run around 40psi, Hydra-Air Dukes and SIDs run around 55psi. Dual-Air Psylos, SIDs and Dukes, and Manitou MARS forks run around 120psi, and Englund air cartridges and White Bros. air forks run at around 80psi. Experiment with different pressures to find what you like best.

RockShox Mag 10, 20, 21, 21 SLTi: RockShox's pump looks like a large syringe with a dial gauge on it (Fig. 1.2). The air valve on each leg is located beneath either a Phillips screw or a plastic pry-off cap on top of the compression-damping adjusting knob (Fig. 13.17). Tighten down the compression-damping adjustment knob before inserting the pump needle to avoid pinching the rubber valve on the top of the adjuster rod inside, causing it to leak. Moisten the needle, and insert it into the valve hole (Fig. 13.17).

The fork needs higher air pressure if it sags excessively when you sit on it. Set your sag at about 20 percent of your fork's total travel — and closer to 10 percent for racing. The fork needs softer springs (or less compression damping — see Section XIII-12C) if hard impacts with large bumps do not use the fork's full travel. Remember that the main spring will be partially balanced by the negative spring, if you have one — see Section XIII-B. below.

B. Adjusting the negative spring

The negative spring in an air fork works against the main air spring to compress the fork. This makes the fork more compliant over small bumps and to behave more like a coil spring through its initial stage of travel (the fork will still have a progressive characteristic deeper in its travel). Early air forks did not have this, and the rider suffered on stutter bumps.

Air springs have a "progressive spring rate," meaning that as the spring is compressed, the force it takes to move the next increment of travel goes up exponentially, rather than linearly. A coil spring, on the other hand, has a "linear spring rate" through much of its stroke — it takes the same increase in force to move 1mm further in the travel, whether you are at the beginning or middle of the spring's compression. Also, the tight air seals in an air fork usually mean it has more "stiction" (coefficient of static friction — the force it takes to make it move initially) than a coil-spring fork. So it takes more force to get the air fork to move initially on a little bump, and the force it takes to keep moving further into the stroke on bigger bumps ramps up. A negative spring, by pulling the fork down, can help the fork react quickly to small bumps. A negative air spring will also start in its fully compressed

(hence fully ramped-up point), so as it moves through the stroke, its force ramps down rapidly while the main spring's force is ramping up rapidly, so the net spring rate of the fork is fairly linear.

Newer high-end RockShox Dual-Air forks (SID, Duke, Psylo Race) have an air negative-spring valve at the bottom of the left leg. It is simple with these forks to play with the balance between the pressure in your main air spring(s) and in the negative spring to find the ride you like. Some air forks (like RockShox Hydra-Air Dukes and SIDs and Manitou MARS and Black) have a coil negative spring, and many of these are not adjustable. Early (1998) SID forks have a coil negative spring on top of the cartridge shaft under the right-hand piston that is adjustable. There is a circlip constraining the top end of the spring, and you can clip it into any of six grooves to vary the compression of the negative spring. You have to take the fork apart and remove the cartridge to do it, though (Sections VIII-14 and VIII-15).

C. Adjusting damping

See Section XIII-12C on how and why to adjust damping on most air forks, as it is the same as on coil/elastomer forks.

Compression damping on old RockShox Mag-series forks can be adjusted by turning the knobs on top of the fork crown (Fig. 13.17); turning the knob clockwise increases the compression damping. Be aware that not all air forks have adjustable damping without disassembling and reconfiguring the damper.

D. Other adjustments

Changing air volume in an air-sprung fork is similar to varying preload in a coil/elastomer fork. Reducing air volume makes the fork stiffen up faster as it moves (i.e., the spring rate ramps up faster), and vice versa. For example, if you find an air pressure that works well, but you bottom the fork too often, you can decrease the air volume to stiffen the fork sooner with the same air pressure. On virtually any air fork, you can decrease the volume in an air cylinder by removing the valve and pouring some oil in. On the 1998 RockShox SID, you can change the air volume by changing the piston height; increase the volume by tightening the piston deeper into the fork and decrease it by unscrewing the piston. You get at the piston by releasing the air with a ball needle and unscrewing the top nut with an adjustable wrench. Screw the piston in or out with an 8mm hex key.

If you have the fork apart (Section XIII-14), you can change oil viscosity (Sections XIII-15 and XIII-16) or the size of compression- or rebound-damping bleed holes to change the speed of the fork (see Section XIII-12C) on compression or rebound. You can also change travel on some models (see Section XIII-17).

XIII-14: OVERHAULING FORKS WITH BOLTS AT THE BOTTOM OF THE OUTER LEGS

 Your fork needs overhauling if, as you gradually lean harder on your handlebars, it is hard to get started moving, and, when the fork finally does compress, it goes down chunk, chunk, chunk like a set of stairs.

On 1999 and later Manitou forks with the "Microlube" grease fitting on the back of the leg, you do not need to take the fork apart. Just inject the proper Manitou Microlube grease (it is thinner than most bicycle grease) with a fine-tipped grease

13.18 damping adjuster knob on Manitou SX fork

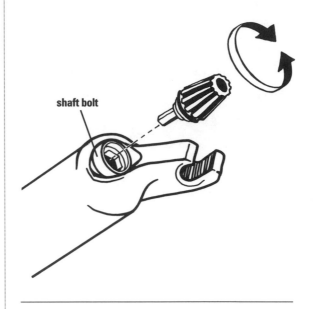

shaft bolt

gun into the grease fitting. A few squirts in each leg, and your fork will feel smooth again. However, you can still take it apart as described below if you want to.

These instructions apply to most mid- to high-end forks later than 1995 or so. The fork must have bolts on the bottoms of the outer legs to be disassembled in this way — see Figs. 13.18 and 13-19. (Forks without bottom bolts are usually either very old or low end. You can usually get these forks apart, too. You either need snapring pliers to remove the snapring at the top of each outer leg, or you need a long hex key to get at the head of the compression bolt way down inside after removing the springs. Keep track of everything and put it all back together the same way after cleaning and lubricating.)

1. Disconnect the front brake cable (Chapter 7) and remove the front wheel (Chapter 2, Section II-2). It is easier if you remove the fork from the bike as well (Chapter 11, Sections XI-18 and XI-19).

13.19 adjusting damping on early RockShox Judy fork

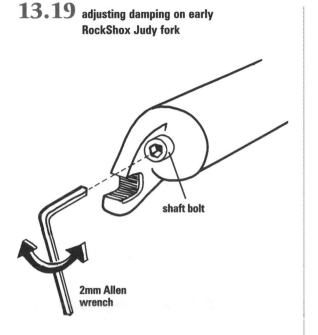

shaft bolt

2mm Allen wrench

13.20 freeing inner legs from lower bushings

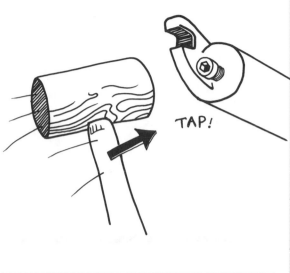

TAP!

forks

2. Unscrew the bolts on the bottoms of the fork legs (Figs. 13.18 and 13.19), leaving a few threads left engaged. If the bolts are not backing out, you are turning the shafts inside the fork along with them, and you may need to tighten down on the preload adjuster on a coil spring/elastomer fork (Fig. 13.16) or add air to an air fork (Fig. 13.17).

Note: The hex key size usually needed for these bolts varies from 4 to 8mm, and the bolt is sometimes hidden under a damping adjustment knob that you must first yank out (Fig. 13.18). Some forks (2000-year SID SL) have a damping adjuster knob you remove with a Phillips screwdriver and then use an open-end wrench on the bolt. Some air forks (SID Race and SL, Duke Race) have an air valve at the bottom of one leg for the negative air spring. After deflating this valve, you unscrew the bolt the valve emerges from with an open-end wrench.

WARNING

Do not unscrew the 5mm bolt in the center of a Manitou 8mm aluminum bolt. This is the damping

adjuster, and if you unscrew it a bunch of turns, you will break it. This will create an oil spill all over your work area, and you will have to buy a new damping unit. Use an 8mm hex key on the large bolt itself (Fig. 13.18) to unscrew it.

3. Before unscrewing the bolts completely (while they are still threaded in a few turns), tap the bolts with a mallet (Fig. 13.20) until the inner legs are free from the lower bushings. Remove the bolts. Do this over a bucket, in case your fork has an oil bath inside (or a blown cartridge that has leaked oil inside the leg). Pull the entire assembly that includes both lower legs and the fork brace off of the inner legs.

Note: On a fork with a removable fork brace (Fig. 13.12), there is no need to remove the brace. If you do remove it, be very careful not to overtighten the brace bolt or the brake post, as it is not hard to strip the threads in the aluminum or magnesium outer legs. Use Loctite on the threads.

4. With a clean, lint-free rag, clean the inner legs

OVERHAULING FORK LEGS

13.21 1997 Manitou SX partially exploded

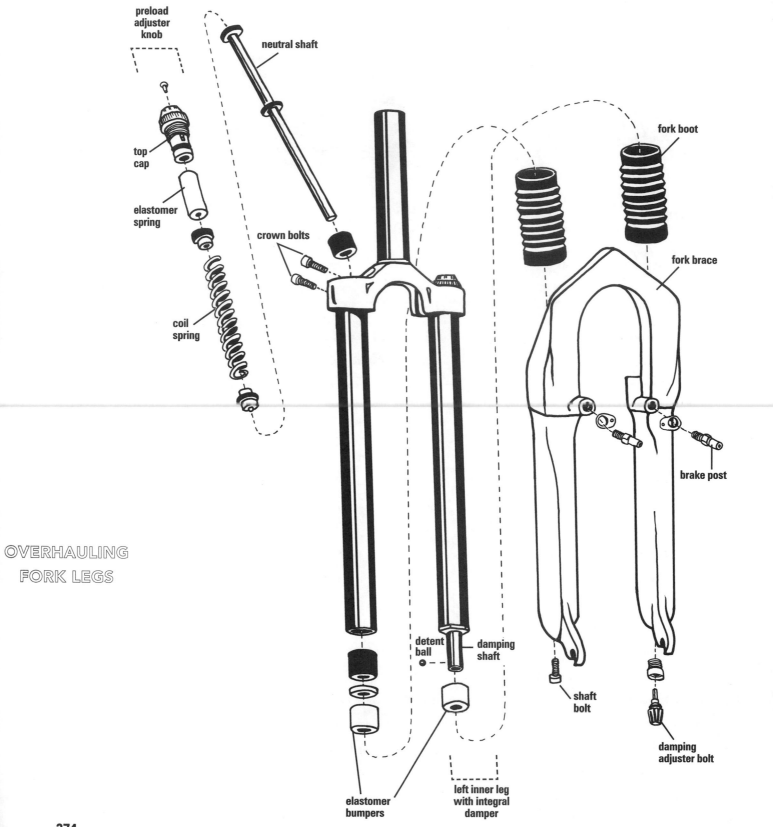

preload
adjuster
knob

neutral shaft

top
cap

elastomer
spring

crown bolts

coil
spring

fork boot

fork brace

brake post

OVERHAULING
FORK LEGS

detent
ball

damping
shaft

shaft
bolt

damping
adjuster bolt

elastomer
bumpers

left inner leg
with integral
damper

13.22 cleaning lower bushing   13.23 greasing lower bushing   13.24 greasing inner leg

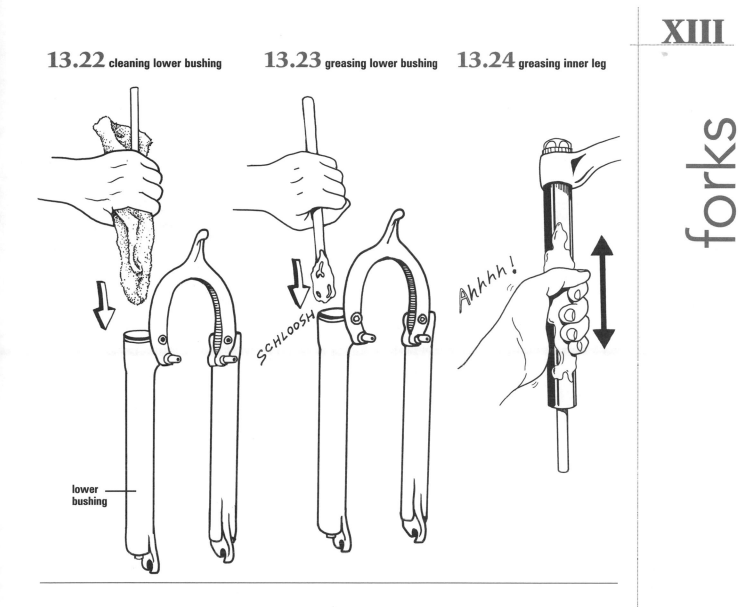

lower bushing

and the shafts sticking out of them. Check the damper shaft (Figs. 13.12 and 13.21) for surface abrasion or bending and for oil leaking from the damper. If you want to work on the damper, skip to the next sections (XIII-15 and XIII-16).

Note: *On many Manitous, there is an elastomer around the damper shaft that extends from the inner leg (Fig. 13.21). It is a good idea to clean and grease it, but, if you remove it, be ready to catch the steel ball that will fall out. This is the "detent" ball for the damper that puts the clicks in the damper adjustment!*

5. Clean the wiper seals and bushings inside of the outer legs. There are two bushings in each outer leg: one at the top and one halfway down. You need to reach the bottom one with the rag wrapped around a long rod (Fig. 13.22).

The top seals can be pried out and cleaned or replaced if need be. If there is a foam ring between two wiper seals, you may want to at least pull that out and clean it well with solvent so that it can do its job properly. Be sure to relube the foam ring with shock oil prior to reinstallation. If the bushings are shot (there would be slop of the inner leg wobbling inside the bushings), they can be replaced — it generally takes tools that only a well-equipped bike shop or service center would have.

6. Apply a thin layer of nonlithium grease (like "Judy Butter" or Englund "Slick Honey" lube) to the bushings and wipers in the outer legs. To grease the lower bushings, use a long rod (make sure it is clean), slather grease on the end of it, and reach down to the lower bushings with it (Fig. 13.23). It is counterproductive to grease between the upper and lower bushings, so don't do it. With your (clean) hand, smear a thin layer of the same grease on the inner legs (Fig. 13.24).

7. Slide the outer legs gently over the inner legs (after the fork boots, if you have them). Take care not to damage the upper dust seals or the lower bushings. Push the outer legs on completely. It may help if you spread the outer tube and fork brace assembly slightly while you rock it side to side to engage the bushings on the inner legs.

8. Replace the oil bath (Fig. 13.25), if your fork has a closed cartridge and a bath inside the outer legs. For example, in the bottom of a SID XC right leg, pour 100cc of 15-weight fork oil (or automatic transmission fluid); while in both legs of a SID SL and the left leg of a SID XC, pour 10cc of RedRum (RockShox thick red oil).

PRO TIP

OLD FORKS

If your fork does not have an oil bath or the Manitou Microlube system, you can keep it lubricated longer by putting an oil bath in. Squirt 15cc or so of automatic transmission fluid in through the bottom bolt holes before replacing the bolts (Fig. 13.25). It keeps lubricant sloshing around up to the upper bushings as you ride. Use a brass washer under your bottom bolt (Fig. 13.19) to reduce leakage. Don't do it on forks with internal shaft bolts you reach from the top, as you can crack the legs by tightening the bolts down onto trapped oil.

9. Put the shaft bolts (Figs. 13.18–13.19) back in the bottom of the outer legs, engaging the threads in the damper and neutral shaft. Push in the inner legs further, if the bolt threads do not engage.

10. Tighten the bolts. RockShox recommends 60 in-lbs of torque. Manitou recommends 110-130 in-lbs. See Appendix E for other torques.

11. Turn the fork upright.

12. Replace the oil bath in open-oil-bath systems. On SIDs and Dukes, pour 2ml of RedRum on top of the air piston, and replace the top caps. On Judys, drop the springs in both legs, and pour 120cc of 5-weight fork oil in with each spring.

13. Replace the springs (on coil/elastomer forks).

14. Replace the top caps. On air forks, inflate the main spring(s) and the negative spring (if included).

13.25 making an oil bath

OVERHAULING
FORK LEGS

13.26 removing cartridge-retaining circlip from RockShox inner leg

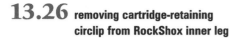

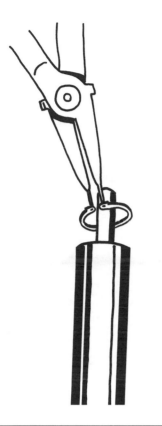

13.27 hand tighten old-style (pre-TPC) Manitou damper nut with O-ring slipped down around inner leg

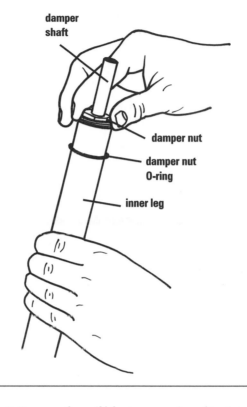

damper shaft

damper nut

damper nut O-ring

inner leg

XIII-15: DAMPER OIL CHANGE ON PRE-1998 MANITOUS AND REPLACING ROCKSHOX CARTRIDGE

This focuses primarily on Manitou pre-TPC dampers because they are easily worked on and built right into the inner leg; skip to Section XIII-16 for Manitou TPC and RockShox Pure damping systems.

RockShox HydraCoil and Marzocchi open-bath dampers get an oil change whether you want it or not when you pull the fork apart as above in Section XIII-14. For removing and replacing a closed RockShox cartridge, follow these instructions as well:

1. Start by taking the fork apart through step 4 in Section XIII-14 above.

2. Remove the coil/elastomer springs (Section XIII-12B) or deflate the air spring(s). If you don't, the shaft or cartridge on some forks will shoot out at you when you remove its retainer.

The temptation to push the damper shaft up and down will be great, but be very careful. The shaft is meant to be supported in the fork and move straight up and down, and if you put a side load on it, you can allow oil to leak out around the seal.

3. On most RockShox, if you want to remove and inspect (or replace) the cartridge and/or neutral shaft (Fig. 13.12), remove the circlip at the bottom of the inner leg with inward-squeezing snapring pliers (Fig. 13.26). When you replace the cartridge (or neutral shaft), orient the snapring so that its sharp edge faces away from the springs.

13.28 getting the Manitou TPC's top piston in and out

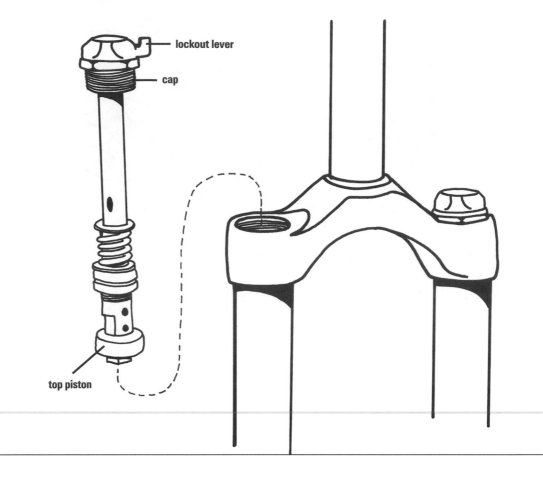

lockout lever

cap

top piston

Starting in the 1999 model year, some air-spring models require a special negative-spring/cartridge-removal tool that is essentially a hollow 15mm hex key. Be careful when you unscrew the cartridge retainer with this tool — it is left-hand threaded!

With an older, non-TPC Manitou (Fig. 13.21), unscrew the damper seal nut at the bottom of the leg (Fig. 13.27), with the fork upside down so oil won't pour out.

4. Pour out the old oil (we're back to talking specifically about Manitou now).

5. Add a little new oil of the weight you want. Automatic transmission fluid (ATF) is 15 weight and works fine for non-TPC Manitou forks if you don't have fork hydraulic oil. Slosh it around inside to rinse the damper clean, and pour it back out.

6. With an older, non-TPC Manitou damper, fill with new fork oil or ATF to the top of the inverted inner leg. Stroke the shaft a few times to get the air bubbles out and top off with oil again. Slide the nut back down onto the shaft and start it in the threads. Roll the rubber O-ring down off of the nut so it surrounds the fork inner leg (Fig. 13.27). Tighten the end nut down by hand. Air and excess oil are vented out through a hole under the nut's lip when the O-ring is not covering it. Replace the O-ring when its groove is about to go inside the tube, and tighten the nut with a wrench.

7. Continue with reassembly of the fork, Section XIII-14, step 5.

forks

XIII-16: CHANGING OIL IN MANITOU TPC OR ROCKSHOX PURE DAMPER

Manitou TPC (Twin Piston Cartridge) dampers rarely need oil changes due to the high oil volume keeping them cool and the absence of springs in the oil to grind aluminum into the oil. But they are easy to service when needed. RockShox "Pure" damping system, as found in high-end Psylo and post-2001 SID SL forks, is very similar to Manitou TPC, and almost the same instructions apply. You know if your Manitou is TPC or your high-end RockShox is Pure if it has springs (air, coil, or elastomer) in only one leg. (Many post-1999 low-end RockShox forks have a single-sided spring with single-piston cartridge in the other leg, but these are not Pure.)

1. The springs should be installed (or inflated) in the other leg so that the fork is at its full length. Keeping the fork right side up, unscrew the adjuster-knob cap on the top of the damper leg (usually on the right side, but early TPC dampers were in the left leg). (You may need to remove the lockout or adjustment lever first.) The upper (compression-damping) piston is attached to the cap — jiggle it as you pull the piston up and through the threads (Fig. 13.28).

2. Pour out the old oil.

3. Add a little new 5-weight fork oil (both TPC and Pure always use 5 weight). Slosh it around inside to rinse the damper clean, and pour it back out.

4. Keeping the fork straight up and down, pour in new 5-weight oil up to the level below the top of the crown specified in your fork owner's manual. You will need to fashion a dipstick out of a dowel rod or wire.

5. Slip the piston back in (Fig. 13.28) and tighten the cap back on. That's it for Manitou. Easy, huh?

6. For RockShox Pure, there is an extra bleeding step required to squeeze the air out, since the Pure damper, unlike the TPC, has no air in it. You stick a small plastic syringe (without a plunger in it) half full of 5-weight fork oil into the hole in the top cap. Remove the springs from or deflate the other leg. Stroke the fork up and down slowly to push air bubbles up into the syringe and pull oil down out of it. When no more air comes up, replace the springs or inflate the other leg to make the fork full length. Remove the syringe and screw the adjuster lever back on (remember to put the little detent ball — it makes the lever click — back onto its spring in the cap).

Piece o' cake, huh?

XIII-17: CHANGING FORK TRAVEL

 Changing travel on old forks requires a different damping cartridge, neutral shaft and spring stack (these parts are shown in Figs. 13.12 and 13.21). If you are persistent, you can probably find parts from at least an aftermarket supplier for many older high-end forks. You then take apart the fork as in Sections XIII-14 and XIII-15, put in the new pieces, reassemble it, and you are set. Just make sure that you check your total travel as in Section XIII-10B and that there is no way your fork crown can hit your tire when the fork is compressed fully. Although changing travel does not make the crown come down further, the temptation may be to use a bigger tire with the longer travel.

Manitou categorically recommended against changing travel for safety reasons until the 2002 Black fork, which has a travel-adjustment lever at the bottom of the left leg. You flip the lever to one of the two positions and push down once on the handlebar to engage the spring in its new position.

RockShox has made travel change easier and easier since the 2000 model year.

Changing travel on RockShox forks from 2000 and later

U-Turn

 On 2002 Psylo SL, XC and C forks, you just turn the orange "U-Turn" knob on top of the left leg to go from 80mm to 125mm of travel. The big coil spring itself screws down or up along large threads around the outside of a big plastic plunger to shorten or lengthen the fork. You can shorten it while riding, turning the U-Turn knob clockwise. You have to stop and take your weight off the spring to turn it counterclockwise and lengthen the fork.

Vari-Travel

 The next easiest travel change is in 2001 Psylo SL and Psylo XC forks. The "Vari-Travel" system simply requires removing the left top cap and removing the coil spring. Reach down inside with a long screwdriver and turn the screw on the top of the plunger. Each turn changes the travel by 1mm, and the length is infinitely variable from 80mm to 125mm (3 inches to 5 inches).

All Travel

 The SID SL and Psylo Race have one "All Travel" system, the SID XC has another, and Judys have yet another.

Judy. Judy Race, SL and XC forks have two plastic All Travel spacers installed inside each leg (Fig. 13.29). Each spacer is tubular with lips at one end to snap into a spring or insert into another spacer.

Note in Fig. 13.29 that if both spacers are on top of the plunger the shaft can stick out to full length, and the fork has 100mm of travel; placing both spacers under the plunger limits travel to 63mm, and one spacer above and one below gives you 80mm. Having spacers below the plunger limits travel by reducing the length of the shaft that can extend out of the bottom of the inner leg.

1. Pull the fork apart as in Section XIII-14 (steps 1–4) and remove the springs.

2. Using inward-closing snapring pliers, remove the snapring from the bottom of each inner leg (Fig. 13.26).

3. Carefully pry out the plastic ring, and pull out any washers and plastic rings you find in there.

4. Remove the shaft assembly.

5. If you want 63mm of travel, remove the spacers from the main spring, and slide them up onto the shaft, snapping the lips of the upper spacer into the bottom of the small spring that sits below the plunger (Fig. 13.29). For 100mm of travel (note that the 2001 Judy Race only goes up to 80mm), snap both spacers into the bottom of the main spring. For 80mm, snap one in the big spring and one in the small spring. Set both legs up the same.

6. Reinstall the plunger assembly and snapring (Fig. 13.26). On Judys, replace the springs and top caps (Fig. 13.29). Inflate SIDs.

7. Reassemble the fork as in Section XIII-14 (steps 5–14).

SID SL/Psylo Race. The SID SL and Psylo Race system is simpler.

1. Pull the fork apart as in Section XIII-14 (steps 1–4) and release the air from the valves.

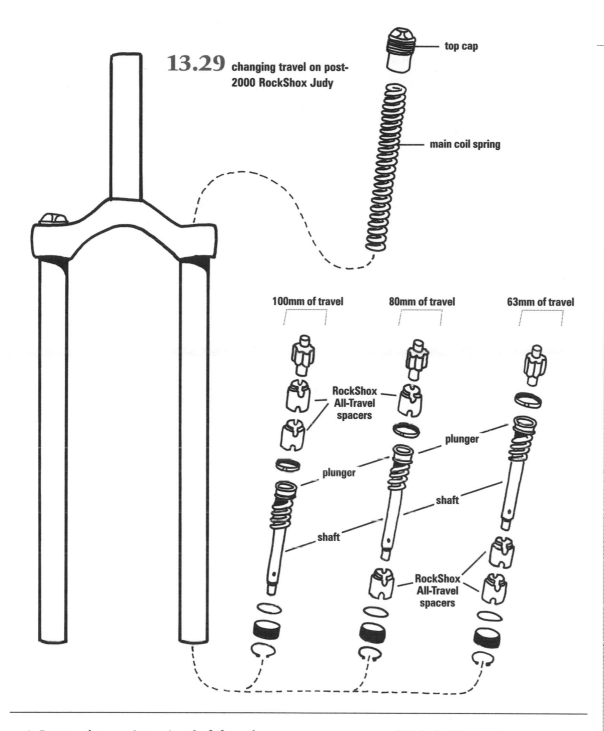

13.29 changing travel on post-2000 RockShox Judy

top cap

main coil spring

100mm of travel   80mm of travel   63mm of travel

RockShox All-Travel spacers

plunger

plunger

shaft

shaft

RockShox All-Travel spacers

2. Remove the negative-spring shaft from the left inner leg. On the Psylo Race, remove the standard circlip with snapring pliers (Fig. 13.26). On the SID, use the special SID cartridge removal tool, a hollow 15mm hex key that fits over the shaft and engages the threaded cap at the bottom of the inner leg. Put a 15mm socket or box wrench on the other end of the tool and unscrew it clockwise.

IMPORTANT

This SID cap is left-hand threaded!

3. The fork comes with a couple hard, cylindrical spacers split open on one side to snap onto the shaft between the piston and the glide ring below. Pop one in to reduce the travel by the length of the spacer.

4. Reinstall the plunger assembly and inflate the fork.

5. Reassemble the fork as in Section XIII-14 (steps 5–14).

SID XC

The SID XC system is the most interesting. Its packaging includes a single All Travel spacer identical to those on the Judy (Fig 13.29).

1. Pull the fork apart as in Section XIII-14 (steps 1–4) and release the air from the valves.

2. Remove both shafts from the inner legs with a small blade screwdriver to pry out the snap ring.

The cool feature of this fork is the reversibility of the negative-spring neutral shaft. If you want 80mm of travel, leave the All Travel spacer out of the fork, and set up the neutral shaft so that the end with a circumscribed line around it points down, and the piston is screwed into the opposite end. The scribed end is longer from the glide ring to the end, so having it down allows more shaft to extend out of the inner leg and — voilà! — more travel. The negative spring goes on the longer end, below the glide ring. Once you get it apart you'll see what I mean.

3. If you want a 63mm fork, you slide the All Travel spacer up onto the damper shaft (the shaft from the right leg), and snap it into the spring below the piston. Remove and save the thin spring guide that had been snapped into the spring.

4. The neutral shaft (from the left leg) must now be reversed. Unscrew the piston from the short end (without the circumscribed mark), and pull the negative spring off of the long end.

5. Screw the piston into the longer, scribed end, and put the negative spring onto the shorter, unscribed end. The negative spring has a tight-fitting plastic spring guide snapped into the piston end, so it does not slide easily. I find it simpler to snap the spring off of the guide and move them separately.

With the short end of the neutral shaft down and the All Travel spacer limiting the downward extension of the damper shaft, travel is shortened.

6. Reassemble the fork as in Section XIII-14 (steps 5–14).

XIII-18: OTHER SUSPENSION SYSTEMS AND UPGRADES

There are a number of variations on suspension forks. If you have something other than those described in this chapter, you should consult the owner's manual for service requirements and procedures.

There are also a number of retrofit units designed to improve the performance of the forks covered above. So you need not feel that you are stuck with a certain low level of performance from your fork. You can significantly upgrade a fork's performance without replacing it. Modern upgrades involve a lot more than just a few lightweight titanium fork bolts. Englund, for example, offers entire compressed-air (TotalAir) units to replace the elastomer spring and the hydraulic damper in a high-end coil- or elastomer-sprung, fluid-damped fork. It is air sprung, and the damping is controlled by airflow through small orifices rather than by oil.

Many of the evolutionary improvements on newer RockShox and Manitou models will retrofit into the older models if you can get the parts (for example, you can turn a Manitou Mach 5 into a Manitou SX-Ti).

XIII-19: SUSPENSION FORK ADJUSTMENT GUIDE

It is a good idea to have a short test course with a hill and some sharp turns in it. Make one change at a time and ride it again so you can isolate what each change does. Immediately after every ride, keep track of your observations in a notebook you keep by your bike, rather than waiting until you have time to work on your bike and have forgotten what you wanted to change. Much of the text below was taken (with permission) from a Manitou fork-tuning manual.

Before adjusting your fork, there are two important things to keep in mind:

1. A bottoming sensation (even if the fork is not bottoming) may actually be caused by the inability of the bike and rider to overcome an overly stiff spring or excessive damping.

2. A harsh sensation (even if the bike has soft springs) may actually be caused by a spring rate too soft for the bike and rider, causing the suspension to ride with much of the travel compressed (i.e., packed up).

Spring rate

Too soft: Bottoming of fork, high preload needed, front end too low on downhills.

Too hard: Fork rarely or never bottoms (e.g., fork does not use full travel).

Spring preload (coil/elastomer forks)

(Adjust the spring rate before you adjust the preload.)

Too little: Excessive static sag, front end too low entering turns, oversteering.

Too much: Not enough static sag, fork feels stiff/harsh, understeering, poor low-speed tight-turning ability.

Rebound damping

Too little: Fork extends too quickly and wheel springs up from ground after landing from jump,

difficulty in maintaining a straight path through rocks, front end attempts to climb the berm/groove while cornering, high ride height, understeering.

Too much: Harsh feeling, especially through successive rapid hits, bottoming after several successive large hits, failure to rebound after landing from jump, low ride height, oversteering, bottoming occurs even though compression damping and spring rate are correct.

Compression damping

Too little: Bottoming, fork dives while braking, oversteering, fork is unstable.

Too much: Harsh feeling, fork rarely or never bottoms, high ride height despite soft spring and/or little preload, understeering.

The following are some common ride symptoms and some fixes for them.

Fork too hard:

1. Decrease compression damping.

2. Decrease rebound damping.

3. Decrease spring rate.

4. Decrease oil viscosity.

5. Increase spring rate.*

Fork too soft:

1. Increase spring rate.

2. Increase compression damping.

3. Increase oil viscosity.

4. Replace worn-out oil in damper.

5. Put oil in (empty) cartridge.

*If you are running a spring rate that is too soft for your weight and ability, you can be misled into thinking that the spring rate is too stiff. This is because you are using up the fork travel before you begin to ride. Furthermore, the fork is working in a stiffer spring-rate range on smaller hits, giving the impression of the fork being *harsh and stiff. This is where the ride-height (sag) adjustment (Sections XIII-12B and XIII-13A) is important.*

Front end searching/nervous descending:

1. Increase rebound damping.

2. Increase spring preload.

3. Increase spring rate.

4. Decrease compression damping.

Front end "knifes"/oversteers:

1. Decrease rebound damping.

2. Increase spring preload.

3. Increase spring rate.

4. Increase compression damping.

Front end pushes or washes out in turns:

1. Increase rebound damping.

2. Decrease spring preload.

3. Decrease spring rate.

4. Decrease compression damping.

No response to small bumps:

1. Decrease compression damping.

2. Decrease spring preload.

3. Decrease spring rate.

4. Increase negative spring rate.

5. Decrease rebound damping.

6. Overhaul dirty fork.

SUSPENSION
FORK
ADJUSTMENT
GUIDE

frames

Come to kindly terms with your Ass for it bears you.
    —JOHN MUIR in How to Keep Your Volkswagen Alive

our Volkswagen is not a donkey ... and your mountain bike is not a Volkswagen. Still, you'd be well served to follow the sage advice given above and stay on good terms with your bike. In doing so, pay close attention to the frame, because it is the most important part of your bike. It is the one part of your bike that is nearly impossible to fix on the trail, and when it fails, the consequences can be serious. Therefore, get to know your bike. Come to kindly terms with it ... for it bears your ass ... or something like that.

XIV-1: FRAME DESIGN

The traditional "diamond," or "double-diamond," mountain bike frame design evolved from a combination of postwar cruiser bikes and road racing bikes. The rigid design of a road bike relies on a "front triangle" and a "rear triangle" (Fig. 14.1); never mind that the front triangle is not actually a triangle — or much of a diamond, for that matter. While the basic concept is similar, there are some notable differences between road and mountain bike geometries. Mountain bike frames feature a higher bottom bracket for more ground clearance; a longer and wider rear triangle for more tire clearance; a shorter seat tube for more standover clearance; brake bosses; and larger-diameter tubing. Another rigid-frame variation is the "elevated chainstay" design, in which the chainstays attach to the seat tube rather than to the bottom bracket shell. This design enjoyed great popularity for a few years. Its primary benefit is the elimination of "chain suck," the jamming of the chain between the chainring and the chainstay — and its primary drawback is added weight. When

14.1 rigid frame

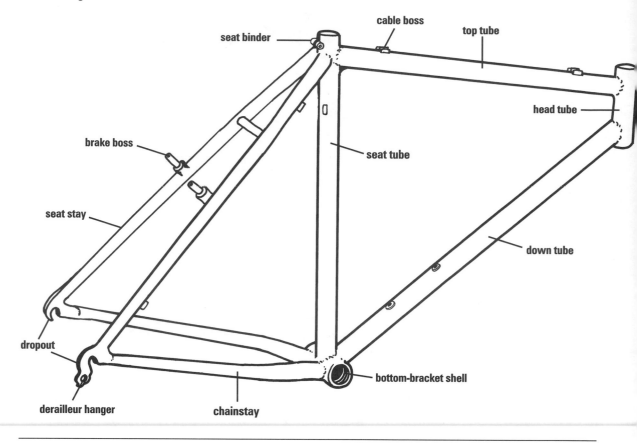

seat binder

cable boss

top tube

head tube

brake boss

seat tube

seat stay

down tube

dropout

bottom-bracket shell

derailleur hanger

chainstay

the chainstay-mounted U-brake and roller-cam brake (Figs. 7.45 and 7.46) went out of fashion, many chain suck problems evaporated, as did sales of elevated-chainstay rigid frames.

These and other modifications — sloping top tubes, large-diameter head tubes and the use of materials other than steel — are generally aimed at bringing a bike closer to the Holy Grail of bicycle design: low frame weight and price coupled with high frame strength and durability.

As a result of this pursuit, mountain bike frame design has changed radically in the short time since the inception of the sport. Take a look at a modern mountain bike and compare it to the Marin County Repack-style bikes of the late 1970s or the Crested Butte off-road "cruisers" that

popped onto the scene around the same time. The difference is amazing, even if you are just comparing modern design without suspension (Fig. i.2) to one of those early models made from or patterned after ca. 1940 Schwinn-style cruisers. Start looking at full-suspension models (Figs. i.3 and 14.2), and you have a whole new breed of animal. And full suspension has now become so common that you even find it on cheap department-store bikes.

XIV-2: SUSPENSION FRAME DESIGN

Rear suspension (also called "full suspension" because it is usually combined with a suspension fork) involves a design totally different than the traditional double diamond. Most suspension frames have a front triangle and a "rear swing arm" (Fig. 14.2).

14.2 rear-suspension frame

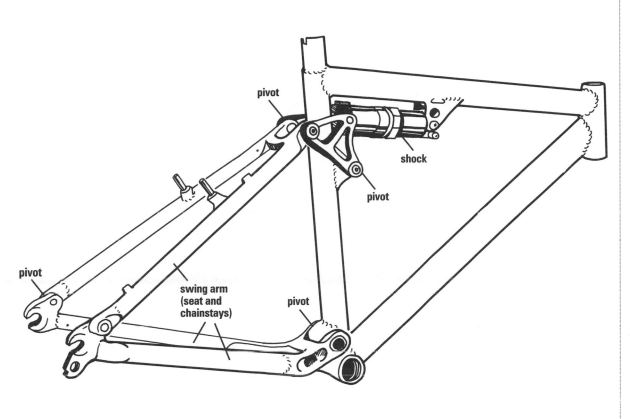

pivot

shock

pivot

pivot

pivot

swing arm
(seat and
chainstays)

There are almost as many rear suspension designs (and names for them) as there are suspension frame designers. Over the past few years, the changes have been fast and furious, and I'd wager that within another few years there will be a whole new crop of popular designs with a whole new crop of high-zoot names. While it would be pointless to go on at length about specifics of current designs, this chapter will divide suspension frames into broad categories and give general maintenance guidelines for them.

XIV-3: FRAME MATERIALS

The bicycle-frame-material revolution has been going on since the birth of the bicycle. Wood was the material of choice for the first bicycles, but that was soon replaced by steel, aluminum and even bamboo. Aluminum and steel are still the most commonly used materials used to build mountain bike frames, but the end of the cold war has seen titanium, carbon composites and metal matrix composites account for a significant share, too. Because the materials used in mountain bike frames come in a variety of grades with varying costs and physical properties, assume that I am talking about the highest grades used in bicycles. For example, the aluminum used in window frames is a lot different than the 6000- and 7000-series aluminum used in high-end bicycle frames.

Steel has the highest modulus of elasticity (a principal determiner of stiffness) as well as the highest density and tensile strength of any of the metals commonly used in frames. Aluminum has a much lower modulus, density or tensile strength than steel; and titanium has a modulus, density and tensile strength in-between the two. Metal tubing characteristics are maximized for bicycles by butting — placing thickness where it is needed and not where it adds useless weight, increasing diameter to add stiffness, and heat-treating and alloying to boost certain of the metal's physical properties. With intelligent use of materials, long-lasting frames of comparable stiffness-to-weight and/or strength-to-weight ratios can be built out of any of these metals.

Carbon fiber and similar composite frame materials consist of fibers embedded in a resin (plastic) matrix. These materials can be extremely light, strong and stiff. Bikes can be built by gluing carbon-fiber tubes into lugs (usually made of carbon fiber or aluminum), or they can be molded in a single piece ("monocoque" construction). The big advantage of composites is that they can be molded to be thicker where extra strength is needed. The tricky part is holding them together in a frame that does not come apart.

Metal-matrix composite frame materials contain hard materials included in the metal to increase its mechanical properties (usually its tensile strength). These added materials are not alloying materials (i.e., they are not melted together with the metal), as that would usually contaminate the metal. Rather, pieces of sandlike materials (aluminum oxide, silicon oxide, etc.) are worked into the metal without melting them. The trick with these materials is making them weldable without weakening the frame at the joints.

Frame builders have and will continue to experiment with all sorts of exotic materials and designs.

My recommendation regarding them is just not to be one of the first ones riding on a new material or suspension design. Let the engineers discover and correct the shortcomings before you jump on.

XIV-4: FRAME INSPECTION

You can avoid potentially dangerous or at least ride-shortening frame failures by inspecting your frame frequently. If you find damage, and you are not sure how dangerous the bike is to ride, take it to a bike shop for advice.

1. Clean your frame every few rides so that you can spot problems early.

2. Inspect all tubes for cracks, bends, buckles, dents and paint stretching or cracking, especially near the joints where stress is at its highest. If in doubt, take it to an expert for advice.

3. Inspect the rear dropouts and the welds around the brake bosses and cable hanger for cracks (see Fig. 14.1 for names and locations of frame parts). Check to be sure the dropouts, brake bosses and cable hangers are not bent. Some dropouts and brake bosses bolt on and are replaceable. (Some cable hangers are even glued in and replaceable). Otherwise, badly bent or broken dropouts, brake bosses, disc-brake mounts and cable hangers require having a new one welded or brazed on; a frame builder in your area may be able to do it.

4. Look for deeply rusted areas on steel frames. Remove the seatpost every few months and invert the bike to see if water pours out of the seat tube. Look and feel for deep rusted areas inside or for rust falling out. I recommend squirting a rust protective spray for designed for bicycle frames (Frame Saver) or WD-40 or oil inside your tubes periodically. Remember to grease both the seatpost and inside of

14.3 checking derailleur-hanger alignment

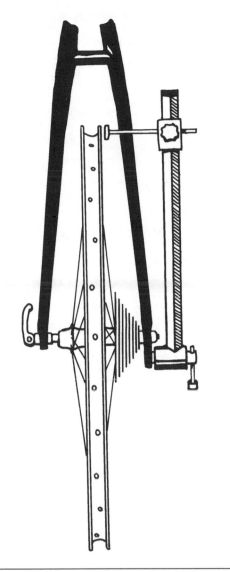

the seat tube when you reinsert the seatpost. After sanding off the rust, touch up any external areas where the paint has come off with touch-up paint or nail polish (hey, it's available in lots of cool colors).

5. On suspension frames, disconnect the shock. Move the swing arm up and down, and flex it laterally, feeling for play or binding in the pivots. Check the shock for leaking oil, cracks, a bent shaft or other damage.

6. Check that a true and properly dished wheel sits straight in the frame, centered between the

chainstays and seatstays and lined up in the same plane as the front triangle. Tightening the hub skewer should not result in bowing or twisting of the chainstays or seatstays.

XIV-5: CHECK AND STRAIGHTEN REAR DERAILLEUR HANGER

1. If you have a derailleur-hanger-alignment tool (Fig. 1.5), thread it into the derailleur hanger on the right dropout (Fig. 14.3).

2. Install a true rear wheel without a tire on it.

3. Swing the tool around, measuring the spacing between its arm and the rim all of the way around. The arm of the tool should be the same distance from the rim at all points. Some tools have a setscrew extending from the arm that you can adjust to check the spacing; others require you to measure it with a ruler or caliper.

4. If your tool has play in it, keep it pushed inward lightly as you perform all of the measurements, or you will get inconsistent data.

5. If the spacing between the tool arm and the rim is not consistent (within a millimeter or two all of the way around), carefully bend the hanger by pulling outward on the arm of the tool lightly where it is closest to the rim.

6. If the derailleur hanger is really bent, you may not be able to align it without breaking it (you may even have trouble threading the tool in because the threaded hole will be ovalized). If you have a replaceable bolt-on dropout, replace it.

7. If the threads or the hanger itself are really screwed up, and you do not have a replaceable dropout, see "Fixing Damaged Threads, Section XIV-8C below, for other derailleur hanger options.

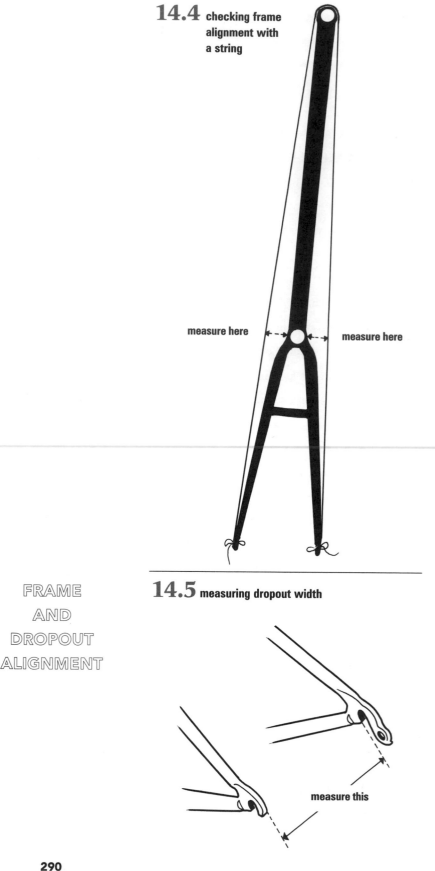

14.4 checking frame alignment with a string

14.5 measuring dropout width

XIV-6: CHECK FRAME ALIGNMENT AND ADJUST DROPOUT ALIGNMENT

 These are inexact methods for determining frame alignment. If your alignment is way off, these methods will tell you. If you find alignment problems, other than perhaps moderately bent dropouts or derailleur hanger, do not attempt to correct them. Adjusting frame alignment is a difficult and delicate task. If it can be done at all, only someone who is practiced at it should perform it with an accurate frame alignment fixture.

1. With the frame clamped in a bike stand, tie the end of a string to one rear dropout. Stretch it tightly around the head tube, and tie it symmetrically to the other dropout (Fig. 14.4).

2. Measure from the string to the seat tube on either side (Fig. 14.4). The measurement should be at least within a millimeter of being the same on both sides.

3. Put a true and properly dished rear wheel in the frame, and check that it lines up in the same plane as the front triangle. Make certain that the wheel is centered between the seatstays and chainstays (or swing arms). The hub should slide in easily without requiring you to pull outward or push inward on the dropouts. Tightening the hub quick release should not result in bowing or twisting of frame members.

4. Remove the wheel, and measure the spacing between the dropouts (Fig. 14.5). On most mountain bikes made since 1990, this spacing should be 135mm. Mountain bikes made between 1984 and 1990 or so should have a rear spacing of 130mm. Mountain bikes made prior to 1984 are likely to have a rear spacing of 125mm. Some high-end

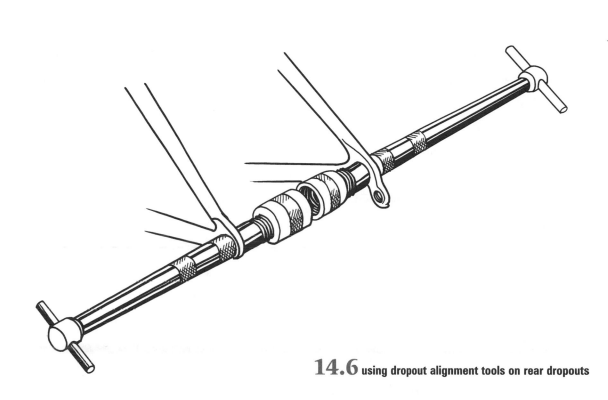

14.6 using dropout alignment tools on rear dropouts

cross-country mountain bikes (older Manitous, for instance) and downhill bikes have custom rear hubs with wider spacing (like 150mm) to decrease the wheel dish. Measure the width of the rear hub with a caliper to see what the rear-end spacing of the frame should be. No matter what the nominal measurement for your frame should be, if it is 1mm less or 1.5mm more than the nominal, it is acceptable. For instance, if you have a frame whose rear spacing should be 135mm, acceptable spacing is 134–136.5mm.

5. If you have dropout alignment tools, put them in the dropouts so their shafts are fully seated into the dropouts (Fig. 14.6). Arrange the tool spacers (and the cups, if they are adjustable) so that the faces of the cups are within a millimeter of each other. Tighten the handles on the tools. The tool cups should line up straight across with each other, with their faces parallel.

If the tools do not line up with each other, one or

both dropouts are bent. If you have replaceable bolt-on dropouts, go ahead and replace them. If you have a composite or bonded rear triangle of any kind, there is nothing you can do about it if your bike is not equipped with replaceable dropouts. If you have a steel rear triangle, you can align the dropouts by bending them carefully with the dropout alignment tools. Hold the cup of the tool with one hand and push or pull on the handle with the other. Aluminum or titanium rear dropouts can sometimes be aligned, but it is something you should have a shop do. Titanium is hard to bend because it keeps springing back, and you run a great risk of breaking aluminum by bending it.

6. Suspension frames have one other alignment feature not shared with rigid frames. To ensure proper swing-arm movement, every separate link in the swing-arm puzzle must be in perfect alignment with the next link so that there are no side forces applied to the pivots. If, for example, the rear

FRAME
AND
DROPOUT
ALIGNMENT

shock has to be forced into position between the two pivot points it connects, then there is unnecessary strain on the frame. These stresses will accelerate the rate of wear of the parts and compromise the linkage's ability to move smoothly.

XIV-7: CORRECTING FRAME DAMAGE

Other than alignment items covered above, the only frame problems you can correct are damaged threads, chipped paint and small dents. Broken braze-ons and bent, broken or deeply dented tubes require a frame builder to replace them, or a new frame is called for.

XIV-8: FIXING DAMAGED THREADS

 A mountain bike frame has threads in the bottom bracket shell, cantilever brake bosses, some disc-brake bosses, the water-bottle bosses and the rear derailleur hanger. Some bikes have a threaded seat binder, and some also have a small threaded hole in the bottom of the bottom bracket shell to which a plastic derailleur cable guide is bolted. Some frames also have a threaded front derailleur mount.

1. If any threads on the frame are stripped or cross-threaded, try chasing through the threads with the appropriate-sized thread tap. Then replace the bolt or other threaded part with a new one.

The following tap sizes are commonly found on mountain bikes:

Water bottle bosses and the hole for a plastic shift cable guide	M5 (5mm x 0.8)
Seat binders and brake bosses	M6 (6mm x 1)
Hayes disc brake post mounts	M6 (6mm x 1)
Derailleur hanger	M10 (10mm x 1)
Bottom-bracket shells	1.37 inches x 24

Note: Remember, the chain side bottom-bracket threads are left-hand threaded; the other side is right-hand threaded.

Whenever you retap any threads, first brush them clean and then use oil on the tap (use canola oil with titanium threads). Specific thread-cutting oil is not necessary on old threads since they are already cut.

2. Turn the tap forward (clockwise) a bit, then turn it back, then forward (two steps forward and one back), etc., to prevent the tap from binding and possibly breaking. Be aware that taps are made of very hard and brittle steel. If you put any side or twisting forces on small taps, they can easily break off. Be careful. If it breaks, you'll have a real mess, because the broken tap in the hole is harder than the frame, so it's impossible to drill the broken tap out. If you break off a tap in your frame, do not try to get it out yourself. Take it to a bike shop, a machine shop or a frame builder before you break off what little is left sticking out. Unless you put the tap in crooked, breaking one should not be a problem when retapping damaged frame threads, as these threads will be so worn; getting them to find any metal to bite into will probably be your biggest problem.

Important note: Tapping a bottom bracket shell takes a good amount of expertise. You really need expert supervision if you have never done it before and still want to do it yourself. In addition to making sure that you place the correct tap in the correct end of the shell, you must also be certain that the taps go in straight. Most bottom bracket taps have a shaft between the two taps to keep them parallel to each other (Fig. 1.5). They must both be started at the same time from both ends. If you mess it up, you can ruin your frame. So, if in doubt, ask an expert.

FRAME
DAMAGE
—
THREAD
DAMAGE

14.7 inserting dropout saver

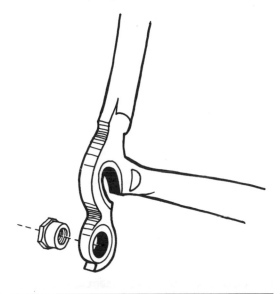

If tapping the threads and using a new bolt does not work, some specific remedies follow.

A. Brake bosses

Some brake posts are replaceable. Replaceable posts have wrench flats (usually 8mm) at the base, and they thread into a boss welded to the frame. If yours are not like this, you must take it to a frame builder to get a new boss welded on.

Threaded disc-brake mounts (i.e., Hayes-style post mounts) are usually part of the dropout. If the threads are stripped, then the entire dropout may need to be replaced.

B. Water-bottle bosses and threaded front derailleur braze-ons

Some bike shops have a tool that rivets bottle bosses into the frame. Check for this first, since you can avoid a new paint job that way, although such riveted bosses tend to loosen up over time. Otherwise, take it to a frame builder to get a new boss welded or brazed in.

C. Rear derailleur hanger threads

Some bikes have replaceable rear dropouts that bolt onto the frame. Another option is to use a "Dropout Saver" derailleur hanger backing nut (Fig. 14.7) made by Wheels Manufacturing and available at bike shops. A Dropout Saver is simply a sleeve threaded the same as your dropout *was*, with 16mm wrench flats on one end. You drill out the hole in your damaged derailleur hanger with a 15/32-inch drill bit, push the Dropout Saver in from the back side, and screw in your derailleur. Dropout Savers comes in two lengths, depending on the thickness of the dropout. Another option is to saw off the derailleur hanger with a hacksaw and use a separate derailleur hanger from a really cheap bike that fits flat against the outside of the dropout and is held in by the hub axle bolts or quick release. The final options are to have the dropout replaced by a frame builder ... or you could always get a new frame.

D. Seat binders

These can be drilled out and used with a quick release or a bolt and nut. Seat-binder threads rarely get stripped, however; it is usually the bolt that is the problem.

E. Bottom bracket shell threads

You can use a Mavic or Stronglight cartridge bottom bracket (Chapter 8, Section VIII-9C, Fig. 8.14), if you can still find one, as it does not depend on the threads in the shell to anchor it. You must have a shop bevel the ends of your bottom bracket shell with a special cutting tool, and they will have the tools to install the bottom bracket as well.

F. Bottom bracket cable-guide threads

A new hole in the bottom of the bottom bracket can be drilled and tapped, or the stripped hole can be tapped out with larger threads for a larger screw. Make sure the screw you use is short enough that it does not protrude into the inside of the bottom bracket shell.

XIV-9: REPAIR CHIPPED PAINT AND SMALL DENTS

Fixing paint chips is simply a matter of cleaning the area and touching it up. Sand any chipped paint or rust completely away before touching up the spot. Use touch-up paint for your bike, model paint or fingernail polish.

Small dents can be filled with automotive body putty, but there is little point to filling them if you are only doing a touch-up, since the area probably won't look that great anyway.

There are plenty of frame painters around the country who can fill dents, repaint frames and can even match original decals. Many of them advertise in bike magazines.

XIV-10: SUSPENSION FRAME MAINTENANCE

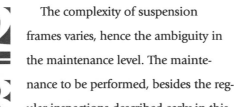

The complexity of suspension frames varies, hence the ambiguity in the maintenance level. The maintenance to be performed, besides the regular inspections described early in this chapter, is on the shock and the pivots.

A. Evaluate the condition of your suspension

You can tell if your suspension needs some lubrication while the bike is standing still. Stand next to the bike, pull the rear brake and push down lightly on the saddle. Gradually increase the pressure. Notice how much pressure it takes before the bike finally compresses. If the suspension does not compress as you push harder and harder, and then it finally goes down chunk, chunk, chunk, like a set of stairs, you've got a dry system. You need to clean and lubricate the pivots and the shock. There is no point to tuning the suspension until you have it moving smoothly.

If the swing arm begins compressing smoothly under a relatively gentle push, then you have a pretty clean, well-lubricated system.

B. Pivot maintenance

The pivots on any suspension frame require periodic attention. Pivots usually rely on cartridge bearings or bushings (usually steel on brass, but some are made of ceramic or plastic). They are held together by clamps with pinch bolts surrounding the pivot shaft or by through bolts or by pins secured with cotters or snaprings.

The shock also pivots on brass "eyelet" bushings on both ends of the shock body (Fig. 14.9).

Figure on cleaning and greasing pivot bushings after at least every 40 hours of riding. Inspect them for wear frequently. Check for wear by feeling for

14.8 removing bearing seal

REPAIRING
PAINT
AND DENTS
—
SUSPENSION
FRAME
MAINTENANCE

294

14.9 rear shock parts and adjustments

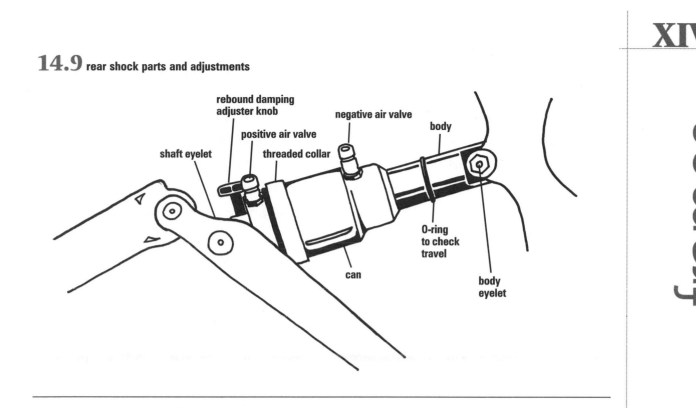

rebound damping
adjuster knob

negative air valve

body

positive air valve

shaft eyelet

threaded collar

O-ring
to check
travel

can

body
eyelet

lateral play and binding with the shock deflated or disconnected. Check the bushings for scoring and ovalization, and lubricate any squeaky ones. Replace worn bushings.

The above applies to pivot bearings as well, although they should wear longer than bushings as long as they are kept greased. Check them for lateral play and binding. They can be opened and repacked with grease like other cartridge bearings (Fig. 14.8). When they are worn out, they can be replaced, and they are often stock sizes that you can find at an automotive bearing store.

C. Shock maintenance

Keep the shock shaft, shaft seals and bottom-out bumper clean. Clean them after every ride, but do not use high-pressure water on them. Lightly lubricate the shaft or shock body (the part that slides in and out).

Keep the bushings in the "eyelets" (mounting holes on either end of the shock — Fig. 14.9) clean

and greased. Regrease the bushings once a month and/or after every 40 hours of riding.

Do a shock oil change at least once a year. The oil inside degrades over time, and damping is reduced. If you notice a damping loss, you need an oil change.

D. Tearing apart a shock

Many good mechanics are leery of hydraulic items like shocks, but hydraulics are often a simpler means of accomplishing something that would require much more complexity and more parts if done with a mechanical system. Like with a hydraulic disc brake, you may be amazed at how few parts there are inside. Just make sure you use your shock's manual and keep track of all of those parts!

Shim stacks on shock pistons, just like in fork dampers, can be changed to alter damping.

Replacement oil and springs can be obtained at many bike shops. So can knowledgeable shock service.

Special tools are recommended for many shock services, such as replacing air valves, glide rings, shaft bushings, shaft seals and pivot eyelet bushings. It may not make sense for you to own these tools, in which case a good relationship with a shock-literate shop is in order.

XIV-11: PIVOTLESS FRAME MAINTENANCE

 Suspension frames without moving pivots fall into two categories: beam bikes and bikes with a shock that depend on the flex of the chainstay, rather than on pivots.

The principal beam suspension used on mountain bikes is the Softride beam (Fig. 10.13), and Softride, Breeze, Otis Guy and Ritchey are some of the frame brands that have used it. Installation and replacement of the beam is covered in Chapter 10, Section X-10. Inspect the beam-mounting points on the frame periodically for fatigue indications (stretched, bulged or cracking metal or paint). There is not much else to say about Softride beams; they are fairly maintenance-free.

One of the simplest and lightest rear-suspension designs out there relies on a small shock behind the seat tube and flexing chainstays. The design was originally used in Moots frames and later adopted by Ritchey. Beyond checking the chainstays for indications of fatigue (stretched, bulged or cracking metal or paint), all you really need to do with these is to keep the shock lubricated and tuned to your weight and riding style.

XIV-12: REAR SUSPENSION TUNING

 There are three main variables to take into account when setting up the rear suspension system: sag, compres-

sion damping and rebound damping.

The four main types of shocks are air/oil (Fig. 14.9), air/air, coil spring (or "coil over") and elastomer (or "elastomer over"). In both air/oil and air/air shocks, compressed air acts as the spring. Air/oil shocks rely on the flow of oil through a small opening separating two chambers to slow the suspension movement. Air/air shocks operate on the same basic principle but rely on the movement of compressed air to damp the suspension. Coil-over and elastomer-over shocks use either a coil spring or an elastomer spring surrounding an oil chamber or gas/oil chamber. The oil provides the damping, and the pressurized gas provides an additional spring. Nitrogen is commonly used as the gas, as it is less likely to emulsify with the oil. This type of shock is not to be pumped by the consumer.

Air/oil and air/air shocks are tuned for the spring rate by varying the air pressure. You must have a shock pump with a no-leak head to pump these or to check the air pressure, as the air volume is so small and the air pressure is so high. Start with the pressure recommended by the bike manufacturer for your weight, and experiment from there. Because the location of the shock and pressure requirements vary from bike to bike, the recommendations will come from the bike manufacturer and not the shock manufacturer.

You can change the spring rate of most coil-over and elastomer-over shocks by turning a threaded collar around the shock body.

On rear shocks with hydraulic damping systems, damping is adjusted by varying the size of the orifices through which the oil (or compressed air) flows or by changing the viscosity of the oil. On many models, the damping orifices are adjusted with knobs (Fig. 14.9), but the technique varies from shock to shock, so be sure to read the owner's manual that came with yours.

Please review Chapter 13, Sections XIII-12 and XIII-13, on front suspension for an explanation of suspension spring rates, preload, compression damping, rebound damping and other considerations — it is the same for rear suspension. The same recommendations for setting up forks in Section XIII-19 apply to rear suspension, too.

The general recommendations below apply to cross-country full-suspension bikes as well as to downhill versions, although more specific downhill considerations are found in Section XIV-13.

A. Setting sag

Sag, or ride height, is the amount the bike compresses when you just sit on it. Ride height is not dependent on damping because there is no movement involved; it is only dependent on the spring rate and preload.

Sag is affected by changing your springs and/or your spring preload adjustment. A good rule of thumb is to set your springs so that sag uses up one quarter of the bike's travel.

On a coil-over shock, measure the shock shaft when you are off the bike. Have someone else measure it again when you are sitting on it. If less than 75 percent of the shaft length is still showing, increase the spring rate or preload. If more than 75 percent of the shaft length is showing, decrease the spring rate or preload. You can also measure the travel and sag either with an O-ring or zip tie around the shock body of air shocks or, with any shock, you can measure the height of the saddle above the ground at unloaded height, ride height

and full compression (with the shock disconnected or deflated).

Adjust the sag by adjusting the air pressure in an air/oil shock and by adjusting the spring preload, and/or by changing the spring on either a coil-over shock or an elastomer shock. The preload is usually set with both of these systems by turning a threaded collar surrounding the shock body that compresses the coil spring or the elastomers. If you have used more than six preload turns of the spring collar to reach 25 percent travel usage in ride height, you need a stiffer spring.

WARNING

Excessive preload on a soft spring can cause the spring to fail.

If the preload is zero and you get 25 percent sag, you've got the adjustment you are seeking. On steep downhill courses, more of your weight will be shifted to the front of the bike, so more sag in the rear is a good idea.

B. Compression damping

If adjustable, set the compression damping as light as possible without bottoming out the shock more than once or twice on your course. Some shocks have an adjustment knob.

C. Rebound damping

If adjustable, set the rebound damping as light as you can get without causing the bike to "pogo" (bouncing repeatedly after a bump). Do the "curb test," starting with the rebound knob fully counterclockwise. Ride off the curb and note how many times the shock bounces. You want only one bounce. Turn the rebound knob clockwise a quarter turn and ride off the curb again, repeating until you get only one bounce. Record the number of turns in of the knob it took.

If you can adjust your rebound on the fly, turn it up when you climb. It does not need to throw you up as much when you hit things, as you are going much slower, anyway. You will climb faster this way. Some shocks have a lockout lever that is great for this. Remember to reduce the rebound damping or open the lockout when you head back down.

D. Front and rear compatibility (balance)

You will want to have the front and rear suspension balanced so that everything works together like a beautiful symphony in motion. You can check the front-rear balance by standing next to the bike on level ground, lightly applying the front brake, and stepping straight down on the pedal closest to you while the crank arm is at bottom dead center. If the top tube doesn't tip forward or back as the suspension is compressed, the spring rates are well balanced. Next, sit on the bike in riding position. If one end drops noticeably more than the other, you need to increase the spring preload and/or spring rate on the end that dropped further (or soften the spring on the end that dropped less).

E. Shock mounts

Some shocks have adjustable attachment positions. Usually, these have a number of different mounting holes for one eye of the shock, but some frames (Cannondale Jekyll, for one) mount the body end of the shock via a threaded collar that can be turned to vary the position of the shock. Varying the shock position varies the head angle, bottom bracket height and ride height of the bike, and it

may also change the rear travel length as well.

Some frames also have adjustable head angles to accomplish similar things. A shallower head angle makes the bike more stable at high speed and gets the front wheel further out ahead for steep drops.

F. Riding it

Again, see Section XIII-19 and follow the guidelines about picking a test course and taking notes. You want to bottom out a couple of times on the front and rear on a course. If the suspension is never bottoming out, the spring is too stiff or the compression damping is too high.

Make setting changes in small increments. It is easy to overadjust. Make only one adjustment at a time.

Once you have balanced your front and rear end, any adjustment you make to the front you should also make to the rear, and vice versa.

Read your frame manual as well as your shock manual for adjustment methods and recommendations.

Suspension tuning is affected by: (1) rider weight, (2) rider ability, (3) riding speeds, (4) course conditions, (5) rider style and (6) rider's position on the bike. If any or all of these things change, so should the tuning.

Use the softest springs you can with little preload: You want to bottom out occasionally, but not frequently. If you are bottoming out too much, you need to change your compression damping or your spring rate. If the compression is slow, yet you are still bottoming out, your spring is too soft. You will feel beaten up on the intermediate hits, or, when bottoming out on a big hit, it will be harsh through the entire stroke. Stiffen the spring rate and lighten the compression damping. The ride height (again, you use up 25 percent of stroke when you sit on the bike) dictates some of your spring rate.

Preload makes the spring rate ramp up faster. If you can use a stiffer spring and back off on preload, you are a lot happier for it.

Set the compression damping to blow off quickly: Your plush spring won't bottom out harshly, anyway! The compression damping should be set high enough that on big hits you use up all of your travel, but the seat doesn't smack you in the butt when you hit bottom. Tighten up compression damping if you blow through the stroke and get bounced too hard.

Decrease the rebound damping to return quickly without pogo ing: You want a lively rebound, since a sluggish return will allow the suspension to pack up (as you go over stutter bumps, water bars or closely spaced rocks, the bike will ride lower and lower).

Again, if you have no damping adjuster, change your oil viscosity.

Tighten up the rebound damping if the bike springs back too fast: The rebound should not be so quick that you are getting bounced. Tighten it up for climbs, if you have a quick adjuster or lockout lever.

Damping is speed-sensitive. Don't worry about settings that feel good at low speeds being too light for high speeds; the shock will get stiffer as you hit things faster. At all speeds, you want the shock to pop back as quickly as possible without kicking back.

Damping is temperature sensitive. Oil is thick and sluggish in the cold, but when it gets hot, your shock gets really lively. You will need to adjust accordingly in summer, with stiffer springs and

firmer damping adjustments. You can lighten up your springs and damping adjustments even more in the cold of winter. Your overall speeds are slower, the grease and oil in the shock is thicker, and elastomer-over and coil-over springs will be stiffer. Lighter oil in the shock will help.

If you have no damping adjuster, you can vary the oil viscosity. Find out what oil weight you have from your manual, the shock manufacturer or a shop. Rely on manufacturer recommendations to help you decide on your new oil weight. Heavier oil slows the shock; lighter oil speeds it up. Changing the oil in your shock is a good idea, even if you like its performance. Replacing the oil is necessary periodically, because it breaks down with use, and there are little worn bits of your shock floating in it, sometimes even on a new shock. Using lighter oil in winter and heavier in summer is also a good policy.

XIV-13: DOWNHILL ADJUSTMENT RECOMMENDATIONS

Everything I said above in Section XIV-12 applies, with a few additions. Again, you are looking for a setup in which your front and rear shocks bottom out on the biggest bump on the course, but make sure it is at race speed.

On rougher courses, increasing the spring rate (or preload) will keep you from bottoming out so much. Compensate for small bumps by reducing rebound damping to keep the shock from packing in on successive hits. If the bike is bucking, increase damping a bit.

Note: Too much damping can sometimes cause bucking, not just too little. Heavily damped shocks will respond so slowly that they will pack in over repeated bumps, giving you a rigid bike and low ride height.

On smoother courses, try decreasing the spring rate (or preload) and increasing damping. Negotiating turns will usually be the major challenge, and the lower ride height (sag) provided by the softer springs will keep you closer to the ground. The greater sag will also increase the amount of negative fork travel (the amount the wheel can go down) available, which will help maintain tire traction in turns and when braking. Higher compression damping, while making the shock absorption slower, will still be fast enough to deal with isolated bumps and will eliminate the harshest bottoming out. Higher rebound damping will reduce the bouncing of the bike after the isolated bumps.

Where there is no general rough or smooth characterization of the course, set up your suspension to perform best on the sections in which you have the most trouble for the most elapsed time. In other words, don't set it up ideally for a tricky section you get through in a couple seconds; set it up for a challenging section on which you will spend half a minute.

DOWNHILL
ADJUSTMENT

cycling computers

tools

electrical tape

flat and Phillips
screwdrivers

*For a list of all the ways technology has failed to improve
the quality of life, please press three.*

— ALICE KAHN

cycling computer (Fig. 15.1) can
be a useful tool if it is set up cor-
rectly, and if you want the information. However, it can give you
incorrect information if not set
up properly, and it can also give you information
you might be better off not having.

XII-1: WHY HAVE A CYCLING COMPUTER?

Most likely, you ride your mountain bike
because you love it. Or at least that is why you
started. If having a computer on your handlebar
adds to your pleasure, then by all means use one.

You may love watching yourself eat up the miles
on a long ride. Or you may get a thrill from seeing
how fast you went on a gnarly downhill. Timing
yourself periodically on a favorite loop may bring
satisfaction as your times drop with improving fit-
ness. You may like watching your cadence or like to
work on keeping your pedaling rate in a certain
range. An altimeter feature may be fun to watch in
the mountains. An "electronic road book" feature
is cool for mapping trails.

You may have a specific workout schedule with
which a heart monitor or even a power meter can
assist you in realizing your goals more rapidly.
Effectiveness of interval training can be enhanced
with proper use of a power meter or at least a computer with a heart monitor. Duration, speed and
intensity of the intervals (and, at least as important, the intensity of the rest periods between intervals and the intensity of recovery rides between
interval days) can be monitored and even stored
for later playback.

15.1 Shimano Flight Deck mounted above the stem

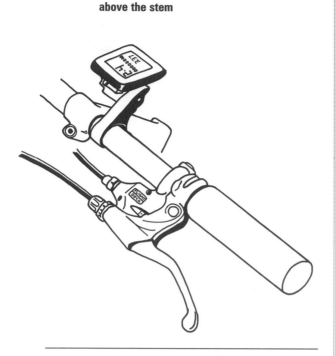

On the other hand, if you start using your computer to tell you whether you have ridden "far enough" or "hard enough" or "correctly" today, or this week, or this year, then you may want to reconsider using one. We all are probably compulsive enough in our work that we don't need to be compulsive in our play as well. My intention in writing this book is to add to your enjoyment of cycling, and I am not interested in you judging yourself harshly about what you have or have not done on your bike. It can be an insidious feature of a cycling computer — what starts as a fun way to monitor yourself can become a way in which you beat yourself up. And it can creep up on you. Bike riding devolves slowly from fun to drudgery without your noticing, until riding a certain way becomes another thing that you *have to* do. Yank the computer off your bike if you see this happen. Remember, even if you're a pro, you got into this for the *fun* of it!

XII-2: SETTING UP A CYCLING COMPUTER

Computers vary from brand to brand. Without having this book become an unmanageably large, dry tome, I can't go into the exact details of which buttons to push when for which computer. But I can give you some general guidelines that work for setting up any computer, and you can get the specifics about which buttons to push from the owner's manual or from a friendly guy at the bike shop.

A. Measure the circumference of the wheel and tire

1. Inflate the tire mounted on the wheel that will carry the magnet — generally this will be the front wheel. Wrap a piece of tape around the rim and tire in one spot on the wheel.

2. Put a piece of tape crosswise on a hard floor or driveway, and set the wheel on it so that the tape around the tire is lined up over it (Fig. 15.2).

3. Holding the ends of the axle, roll the wheel forward one revolution until the piece of tape is at the bottom again. If you ride your tires at low pressure (25–35 psi), you will get more accuracy if you inflate them only to say, 15 psi, and push down on the handlebar as you roll the bike forward.

4. Put another piece of tape on the floor lined up with the tape on the tire (Fig. 15.2).

5. With a tape measure, find the distance from the leading edge of one piece of tape on the floor to the other. This is the circumference of the inflated tire. Your computer needs this information to properly measure speed and distance, as it is counting revolutions of the wheel and must know distance covered with each revolution.

In the computer owner's manual, you will find either a way to enter the circumference, or you will find a table of code numbers corresponding to

15.2 rolling out the front wheel to measure its circumference

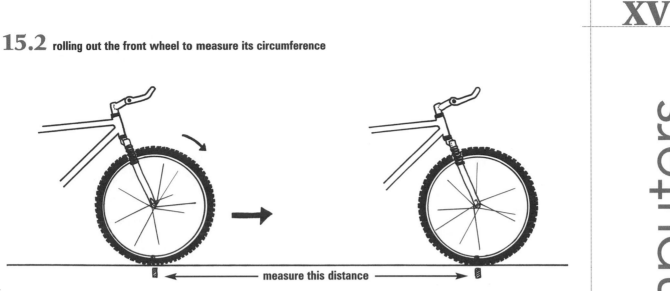

measure this distance

ranges of circumference and instructions on how to enter the proper code number. I know that everyone loses those instruction booklets, making it tough to reprogram when you change a battery or otherwise "zero out" your computer. File the instructions away. You will need them. But if you do lose them, go to the Internet. Many manufacturers post their instructions and those codes on their Web sites.

B. Install the computer and sensor

1. Snap the handlebar bracket mount around the handlebar next to the stem (Fig. 15.1). If it fits too loosely onto the bar, wrap the bar at that spot with one of the rubber pieces that come with the computer or with layers of electrical tape.

2. Tighten the screw to secure the mount, and snap the computer onto the mount.

3. If the computer has a wire to the sensor, wrap

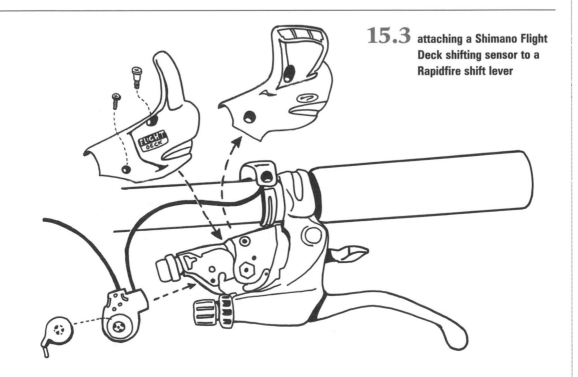

15.3 attaching a Shimano Flight Deck shifting sensor to a Rapidfire shift lever

the wire around the front brake cable to take up slack, and strap the sensor (Fig. 15.7) around the fork leg. With a wireless computer, you need only strap the sensor to the fork leg.

The sensor usually mounts to the inside of the fork leg about midway down, but the position may need to be changed later for optimal clearance with the wheel magnet. There is usually a built-in zip-tie on the sensor, or separate zip-ties are used to hold the sensor.

Secure the wire to the fork leg with tape or zip-ties.

Shimano cycling computers also have a wire and sensor that must be connected to each Rapidfire shift lever in order to sense when you shift (Fig. 15.3). If your shifter has a gear indicator, you will have to remove it to attach the computer sensor. You won't be putting the indicator back on; chuck it out or throw it in a drawer. To hook up the shifting sensor, you will be installing a plastic insert into the hole the gear indicator came out of — three of them come with the computer, and you will need to look in the manual to find out which one to use for your shifter. The same goes for figuring out which plastic screw-on cover will fit your lever to cover the shifting sensor.

4. Attach the wheel magnet (Figs. 15.4–15.6) to the spokes. Ideally, you want the magnet to sit fairly close to the hub, but clearance with the sensor will largely dictate the position.

Some magnets have a slot in the holder and hold the spoke into the slot with a collar and a screw tightened against the spoke (Fig. 15.4). Other magnets sit in a plastic housing that wraps around two spokes and is retained by a screw (Fig. 15.5). Some recent magnets come in a plastic housing that snaps onto the spoke (Fig. 15.6).

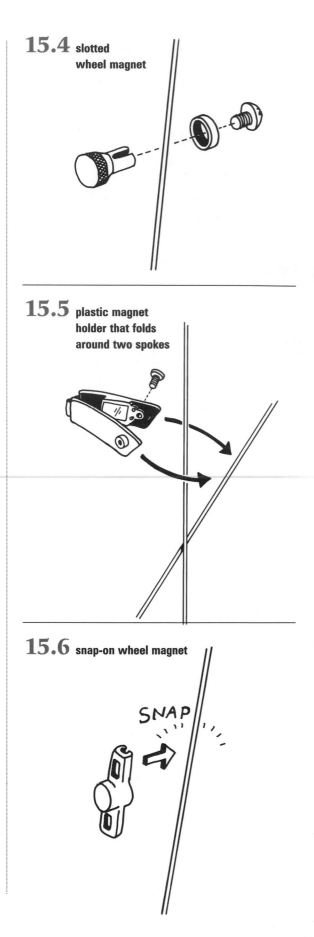

15.4 slotted wheel magnet

15.5 plastic magnet holder that folds around two spokes

15.6 snap-on wheel magnet

SNAP

To fit a magnet like in Fig. 15.4 on flat spokes, file the slot in the magnet holder wider, or use a plastic clip-on type like in Fig. 15.5 or 15.6.

Make sure the wheel magnet passes close to the sensor. If the computer does not indicate a speed when you spin the wheel, the positions of the sensor and/or the magnet need to be changed. Many sensors have a scribed line indicating where the magnet should pass (some sensors have lines at either end, giving you a couple of options). Make sure the magnet passes by the line and that it is close to the sensor (1–5mm away), but it doesn't touch (Fig. 15.7). You may need to slide the sensor and the magnet up or down the spoke and fork leg to get them the right distance apart.

5. If the computer has a separate cadence sensor and magnet, the magnet usually goes on the crank

15.7 position the magnet close to the sensor and align with one of the scribed lines

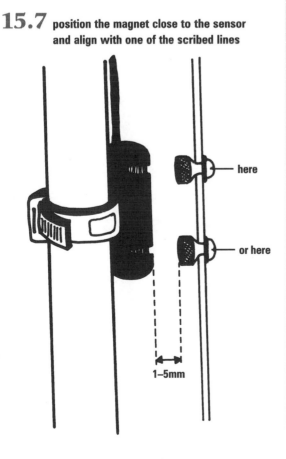

- here
- or here

1–5mm

15.8 replacing the computer battery

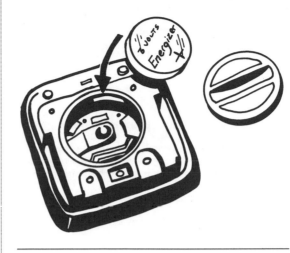

arm, and the sensor mounts to the chainstay. Shimano computers calculate cadence from wheel speed and gear size.

6. On a Shimano Flight Deck computer, you will also need to enter the number of teeth on each of your chainrings and each of your cogs so it can give accurate gear size and cadence information.

XII-3: POWER METERS AND HEART MONITORS

SRM power meters have strain gauges built into the spider arms on the right crank. Sensors near the bottom bracket pick up the torque on the crank wirelessly.

Heart monitors require no additional hookups on the bike, just a strap around your chest.

XII-4: DIAGNOSING COMPUTER PROBLEMS

A. No display

The battery probably needs to be replaced. Some computers have a battery not only in the computer (Fig. 15.8) but also in the sensor, so check both places. Some computers have two batteries in the computer itself. A bike shop (or a

XV

cycling computers

POWER
METERS AND
HEART
MONITORS
—
TROUBLE-
SHOOTING

camera store) should have a battery to match. You may have to reenter the wheel circumference and other data after changing the battery.

If the battery is not the problem, check for broken wires.

B. Computer is on, but speed does not register

The wheel magnet may be missing, or it may be too far from the sensor as it passes by. Adjust the positions of the sensor and the magnet so that the magnet passes close by the scribed line on the sensor but does not touch it.

C. Cadence reading does not display

Check that your computer does have a cadence feature. If so, check that the sensor and magnet on the crank and frame pass closely by each other (except with a Shimano Flight Deck, which calculates cadence from speed and gear size).

D. Computer reads wrong speed and distance

The wrong wheel size may have been entered. Follow the owner's manual for the button-pushing sequence to find the number programmed into the computer for wheel size. See Section XII-2A for instructions on measuring wheel circumference.

E. Can't find computer owner's manual

Here are a number of options:

1. Check the computer maker's Web site for an online owner's manual or ordering instructions for getting a new one.

2. Check with a bike shop for a new manual.

3. Get the contact information for the manufacturer or distributor from the bike shop, and contact the company directly.

4. Find a friend or shop employee who knows how to work your computer, and learn from them. Take notes.

TROUBLE-
SHOOTING

appendixes

troubleshooting index

T his index is intended to assist you in finding and fixing problems. If you already know wherein the problem lies, consult the Table of Contents for the chapter covering that part of the bike. If you are not sure which part of the bike is affected, this index can be of assistance. It is organized alphabetically, but because people's descriptions of the same problem vary, you may need to look through the entire list to find your symptom.

This index can assist you with a diagnosis and can recommend a course of action. Following each recommended action are listed chapter numbers to which you can refer for the repair procedure to fix the problem.

SYMPTOM	LIKELY CAUSES	ACTION	CHAPTER
bent wheel	misadjusted spokes	true wheel	6
	broken spoke	replace spoke	6
	bent rim	replace rim	12
bike pulls to one side	wheels not true	true wheels	6
	tight headset	adjust headset	11
	pitted headset	replace headset	11
	bent frame	replace or straighten	14
	bent fork	replace or straighten	13
	loose hub bearings	adjust hubs	6
	tire pressure really low	inflate tires	2, 6

SYMPTOM	LIKELY CAUSES	ACTION	CHAPTER
bike shimmies	frame cracked	replace frame	14
at high speed	frame bent	replace or straighten	14
	wheels are way out of true	true wheels	6
	loose hub bearings	adjust hubs	6
	headset too loose	tighten headset	11
	flexible frame/heavy rider	replace frame	14
	poor frame design	replace frame	14
bike vibrates	*see* "chattering and vibration when		
when braking	braking" under "Strange Noises"		
brake doesn't stop bike	misadjusted brake	adjust brake	7
	worn brake pads	replace pads	7
	wet rims	keep braking	7
	greasy rims	clean rims	7
	sticky brake cable	lube or replace cable	7
	steel rims in wet weather	use aluminum rims	12
	brake damaged	replace brake	7
	sticky or bent brake lever	lube or replace lever	7
	air in hydraulic brake	bleed brake	7
	worn disc brake pads	replace pads	7
	brake pads missing	install pads	7
brake rubs on rim	brake misaligned	adjust brake	7
see "bent wheel"			
chain falls off in front	misadjusted front derailleur	adjust front derailleur	5
	chain line off	adjust chain line	8
	chainring bent or loose	replace or tighten	8
chain jams in front	dirty chain	clean chain	4
between chainring	bent chainring teeth	replace chainring	8
and chainstay — called	chain too narrow	replace chain	4
"chain suck"	chain line off	adjust chain line	8
	stiff links in chain	free links, lube chain	4
	thick inner chainring teeth	use thinner chainring	8
chain jams in rear	misadjusted rear derailleur	adjust derailleur	5
	chain too wide	replace chain	4
	small cog not on spline	reseat cogs	6
	poor frame clearance	return to dealer	14
chain skips	tight chain link	loosen tight link	4
	worn out chain	replace chain	4
	misadjusted derailleur	adjust derailleur	5

troubleshooting index

SYMPTOM	LIKELY CAUSES	ACTION	CHAPTER
chain skips (cont.)	worn rear cogs	replace cogs and chain	6, 4
	dirty or rusted chain	clean or replace chain	4
	bent rear derailleur	replace derailleur	5
	bent derailleur hanger	straighten hanger	14
	loose derailleur jockey wheels	tighten jockey wheels	5
	bent chain link	replace chain	4
	sticky rear shift cable	replace shift cable	5
chain slaps chainstay	chain too long	shorten chain	4
	weak rear derailleur spring	replace spring or derailleur	5
	terrain very bumpy	ignore noise	n/a
derailleur hits spokes	misadjusted rear derailleur	adjust derailleur	5
	broken spoke	replace spoke	6
	bent rear derailleur	replace derailleur	5
	bent derailleur hanger	straighten or replace	14
knee pain	poor shoe cleat position	reposition cleat	9
	saddle too low or high	adjust saddle	10
	clip-in pedal has no float	get floating pedal	9
	foot rolled In or out	replace shoes or get orthotics	n/a
pain or fatigue when riding, particularly in the back, neck and arms	incorrect seat position	adjust seat position	10
	too much riding	build up miles gradually	n/a
	incorrect stem length	replace stem	11
	poor frame fit	replace frame	14
	incorrect handlebar height	adjust stem height or get stem with different angle	11
pedal(s) move laterally, clunk or twist while pedaling	loose crank arm	tighten crank bolt	8
	pedal loose in crank arm	tighten pedal to crank	9
	bent pedal axle	replace pedal or axle	9
	loose bottom bracket	adjust bottom bracket	8
	bent bottom bracket axle	replace bottom bracket or axle	8
	bent crank arm	replace crank arm	8
	loose pedal bearings	adjust pedal bearings	9
pedal entry difficult (with clip-in pedals)	mud in cleat or pedal	clean cleat and pedal	9
	spring tension set high	reduce spring tension	9
	shoe sole knobs too tall	trim knobs	9
	loose cleat	tighten cleat	9
	dry cleat and pedal	lubricate cleat and pedal clips	9
	cleat guide loose or gone	tighten or replace	9

SYMPTOM	LIKELY CAUSES	ACTION	CHAPTER
pedal release difficult (with clip-in pedals)	spring tension set high	reduce spring tension	9
	loose cleat on shoe	tighten cleat	9
	dry pedal spring pivots	oil spring pivots	9
	dirty pedals	clean and lube pedals	9
	bent pedal clips	replace pedals or clips	9
	dirty cleats	clean, lube cleats	9
	worn cleat	replace cleat	9
pedal release too easy (with clip-in pedals)	release tension set too low	increase release tension	9
	cleats worn out	replace cleats	9
rear shifting working poorly	misadjusted derailleur	adjust derailleur	5
	sticky or damaged cable	replace cable	5
	loose rear cogs	seat and tighten cogs	6
	worn rear cogs	replace cogs	6
	worn/damaged chain	replace chain	4
	see also "chain jams in rear" *and* "chain skips"		
resistance while coasting or pedaling	tire rubs frame or fork	adjust axle and/or true wheel	2, 6
	brake drags on rim	adjust brake	7
	tire pressure really low	inflate tire	2, 6
	hub bearings too tight	adjust hubs	6
	hub bearings dirty/worn	overhaul hubs	6
	mud packed around tires	clean bike	2
resistance while pedaling only	bottom bracket too tight	adjust bottom bracket	8
	bottom bracket dirty/worn	overhaul bottom bracket	8
	chain dry/dirty/rusted	clean/lube or replace	4
	pedal bearings too tight	adjust pedal bearings	9
	pedal bearings dirty/worn	overhaul pedals	9
	bent chain ring rubs frame	straighten or replace	8
	chainring rubs frame	adjust chain line	8
stiff steering	tight headset	adjust headset	11
suspension problems front or rear	fork needs tuning	tune fork	13
	fork needs overhaul	overhaul fork	13
	rear suspension misadjusted	tune rear shock	14
	rear shock dirty	overhaul rear shock	14
	suspension pivots worn/dirty	overhaul pivots	14
tire loses air or is flat	tire deflated	pump tire	6
	hole in tube	patch or replace tube	6
	bad valve	replace tube or valve	6
	hole in tubeless tire	patch or replace tire	6
	leaky seal around tubeless tire	seal, replace or Slime	6

STRANGE NOISES

Weird noises can be hard to locate; use this to assist in locating them.

SYMPTOM	LIKELY CAUSES	ACTION	CHAPTER
creaking noise	dry handlebar/stem joint	grease bar and inside stem clamp	11
	hard-anodizing of stem and bar	sand inside stem clamp	11
	dry stem/steerer joint	grease steerer and inside stem clamp	11
	cartridge BB moves inside cup	grease inside cup	8
	loose seatpost	tighten seatpost	10
	loose shoe cleats	tighten cleats	9
	loose crank arm	tighten crank arm bolt	8
	cracked frame	replace frame	14
	dry, rusty seatpost	grease seatpost	10
	see "squeaking noise"	*see* "squeaking noise"	
clicking noise	cracked shoe cleats	replace cleats	9
	cracked shoe sole	replace shoes	9
	loose bottom bracket	tighten BB	8
	loose crank arm	tighten crank arm	8
	loose pedal	tighten pedal	9
chattering and vibration when braking	bent or dented rim	replace rim	12
	loose headset	adjust headset	11
	brake pads toed out	adjust brake pads	7
	wheel way out of round	true wheel	6
	greasy sections of rim	clean rim	6
	loose brake pivot bolts	tighten brake bolts	7
	rim worn out and ready to collapse	replace rim ASAP!	12
	oily disc-brake rotor	clean rotor and pads	7
clunking from fork	headset loose	adjust headset	11
	suspension fork bushings worn	replace bushings	13
rubbing or scraping noise when pedaling	crossed chain	avoid extreme gears	5
	front derailleur rubbing	adjust front derailleur	5
	chainring rubs frame	longer bottom bracket	
		or move bottom bracket over	8
rubbing, squealing or scraping noise when coasting or pedaling	tire dragging on frame	straighten wheel	2, 6
	tire dragging on fork	straighten wheel	2, 6
	brake dragging on rim	adjust brake	7
	mud packed around tires	clean bike	2
	dry, dirty hub dust seals	clean dust seals	6
squeaking noise	dry hub or BB bearings	overhaul hubs or BB	6, 8
	dry pedal bushings	overhaul pedals	9

troubleshooting index

SYMPTOM	LIKELY CAUSES	ACTION	CHAPTER
squeaking noise (cont.)	squeaky saddle	grease leather-rail contact	10
		and oil rail attachments	10
	dry suspension pivots	overhaul suspension	13, 14
	rusted or dry chain	lube or replace chain	4
	dry suspension fork	overhaul fork	13
	dry suspension seatpost	overhaul seatpost	10
squealing noise when braking	brake pads toed out	adjust brake pads	7
	greasy rims	clean rims and pads	7
	loose brake arms	tighten brake arms	7
	flexible seatstays	use brake booster plate	7
	oily disc-brake rotor	clean rotor and pads	7

gear development

The gear table on the following page is based on a 26-inch (66cm) tire diameter. Your gear development numbers may be slightly different if the diameter of your rear tire, at inflation, with your weight on it, is not 26 inches. Unless your bike has 24-inch wheels or some other nonstandard size, these numbers will be very close.

If you want to have totally accurate gear development numbers for the tire you happen to have on at the time, at a certain inflation pressure, then you can measure the tire diameter very precisely with the procedure below. You can come up with your own gear chart by plugging your tire diameter into the following gear development formula, or by multiplying each number in this chart by the ratio of your tire diameter divided by 26 inches (the tire diameter we used).

To measure the diameter of your tire:

1. Sit on the bike with your tire pumped to your desired pressure.

2. Mark the spot on the rear rim that is at the bottom, and mark the floor adjacent to that spot.

3. Roll forward one wheel revolution, and mark the floor again where the mark on the rim is again at the bottom (Fig. 15.2).

4. Measure the distance between the marks on the floor; this is the tire circumference at pressure with your weight on it.

5. Divide this number by π (pi) — 3.14159 — to get the diameter.

Note: This roll-out procedure is also the method to measure the wheel size with which to calibrate your bike computer, except you do it on the front wheel with most computers.

CHAINRING GEAR TEETH

REAR HUB COGS	20	22	24	26	28	30	32	34	36	38	39	40	41
11	47	52	57	61	66	71	76	80	85	90	92	95	97
12	43	48	52	56	61	65	69	74	78	82	84	87	89
13	40	44	48	52	56	60	64	68	72	76	78	80	82
14	37	41	45	48	52	56	60	63	67	70	72	74	76
15	35	38	42	45	49	52	55	59	62	66	68	69	71
16	33	36	39	42	45	49	52	55	58	61	63	65	67
17	31	34	37	40	43	46	49	52	55	58	60	61	63
18	29	32	35	38	40	43	46	49	52	55	56	58	59
19	27	30	33	36	38	41	44	47	49	52	53	55	56
20	26	29	31	34	36	39	42	44	47	49	51	52	53
21	25	27	30	32	35	37	40	42	45	47	48	50	51
22	24	26	28	31	33	35	38	40	43	45	46	47	48
23	23	25	27	29	32	34	36	38	41	43	44	45	46
24	22	24	26	28	30	32	35	37	39	41	42	43	44
25	21	23	25	27	29	31	33	35	37	39	41	42	43
26	20	22	24	26	28	30	32	34	36	38	39	40	41
27	19	21	23	25	27	29	31	33	35	37	38	39	39
28	18	20	22	24	26	28	30	32	33	35	36	37	38
30	17	19	21	23	24	26	28	29	31	33	34	35	36
32	16	18	20	21	23	24	26	28	29	31	32	33	33
34	15	17	18	20	21	23	24	26	28	29	30	31	31
38	14	16	16	18	19	21	22	23	25	26	27	27	28
	20	22	24	26	28	30	32	34	36	38	39	40	41

CHAINRING GEAR TEETH

The formula is:

Gear development = (number of teeth on chainring) x (wheel diameter) ÷ (number of teeth on rear cog)

To find out how far you get with each pedal stroke in a given gear, multiply the gear development by 3.14159265 (π).

CHAINRING GEAR TEETH

42	43	44	45	46	47	48	49	50	51	52	53	
99	102	104	106	109	111	113	116	118	121	123	125	11
91	93	95	97	100	102	104	106	108	111	113	115	12
84	86	88	90	92	94	96	98	100	102	104	106	13
78	80	82	84	85	87	89	91	93	95	97	98	14
73	75	76	78	80	81	83	85	87	88	90	92	15
68	70	72	73	75	76	78	80	81	83	85	86	16
64	66	67	69	70	72	73	75	76	78	80	81	17
61	62	64	65	66	68	69	71	72	74	75	77	18
57	59	60	62	63	64	66	67	68	70	71	73	19
55	56	57	59	60	61	62	64	65	66	68	69	20
52	53	54	56	57	58	59	61	62	63	64	66	21
50	51	52	53	54	56	57	58	59	60	61	63	22
47	49	50	51	52	53	54	55	57	58	59	60	23
45	47	48	49	50	51	52	53	54	55	56	57	24
44	45	46	47	48	49	50	51	52	53	54	55	25
42	43	44	45	46	47	48	49	50	51	52	53	26
40	41	42	43	44	45	46	47	48	49	50	51	27
39	40	41	42	43	44	45	46	46	47	48	49	28
36	37	38	39	40	41	42	42	43	44	45	46	30
34	35	35	37	37	38	39	40	41	41	42	43	32
32	33	33	34	35	36	37	37	38	39	40	41	34
29	29	30	31	31	32	32	33	34	35	36	36	38
42	43	44	45	46	47	48	49	50	51	52	53	

CHAINRING GEAR TEETH

APPENDIX B

gear development

bike fit

MOUNTAIN BIKE FITTING

If you are getting a new bike, you might as well get one that fits you properly. Fit should be the primary consideration when selecting a bike; you can adapt to heavier bikes and bikes not painted your favorite color, but your body will soon protest on one that doesn't fit. The simple need to protect your more sensitive parts should keep you away from a bike without sufficient standover clearance (Fig. C.1), but there are a lot of other factors to consider as well. You need to make certain that your bike has enough reach to ensure that you don't bang your knees on the handlebar. You also need to check that your weight is properly distributed over the wheels so that you don't end up going over the handlebars on downhills or unweighting the front end on steep climbs. An

improperly sized bike is both inefficient and terribly uncomfortable. Therefore, take some time, and find out how you can pick the properly sized bike.

I've outlined two methods for finding your frame size. The first is a simple method of checking your fit on bikes at your local bike shop. The second is a bit more elaborate, as it involves taking body measurements. This more detailed approach will allow you to calculate the proper frame dimensions whether the bike is assembled or not.

C-1: SELECTING THE SIZE OF A BUILT-UP BIKE

1. Standover height

Stand over the bike's top tube and lift the bike straight up until the top tube hits your crotch. The wheels should be at least 2 inches off of the

C.1 bike height

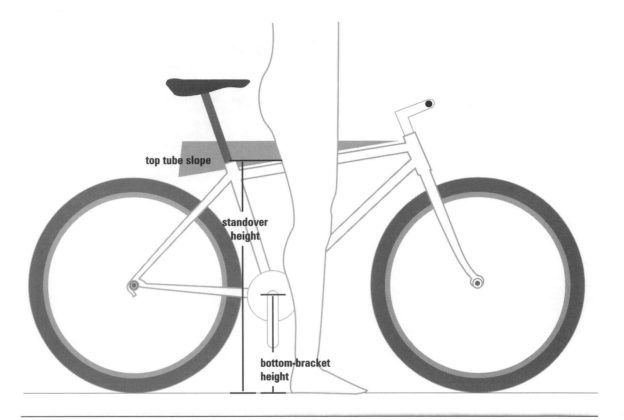

top tube slope

standover height

bottom-bracket height

ground to ensure that you can jump off of the bike safely without hitting your crotch. There is no maximum dimension here. Though it may seem like a lot, 5 or more inches of standover height is fine, as long as the top tube is long enough for you, and the handlebar height can be set properly for you.

Note: If you have 2 inches of standover clearance over one bike, do not assume that another bike with the same listed frame size will also offer you the same standover clearance. Manufacturers all seem to measure frame differently. They also slope their top tubes differently and use different bottom bracket heights (Figs. C.1 and C.2), all of which affect the final standover height.

All manufacturers measure the frame size up the seat tube from the center of the bottom bracket, but the top end of the measurement varies. Some measure to the center of the top tube ("center-to-

center" measurement), some measure to the top of the top tube ("center-to-top"), and others measure to the top of the seat tube (also called "center-to-top"), even though there is wide variation in the length of the seatpost collar above the top tube. Obviously, each of these methods will give you a different frame size for the same frame.

No matter how the frame size is measured, the standover height of a bike depends on the slope of the top tube (Fig. C.1). Top tubes that slant up to the front are common, so standover clearance is obviously a function of where you are standing. With an up-angled top tube, stand over it a few inches forward of the nose of the saddle, and then lift the bike up into your crotch to measure standover clearance.

A bike with a suspension fork will have a higher front end than a bike with a rigid fork would,

C.2 knee and toe clearance

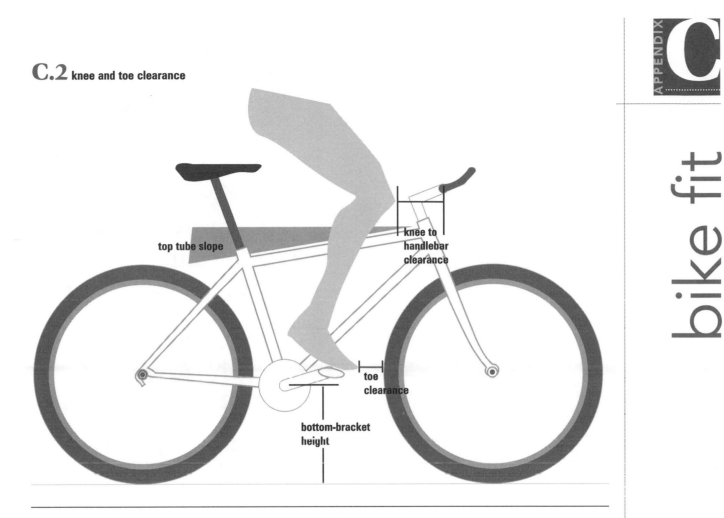

top tube slope

knee to handlebar clearance

toe clearance

bottom-bracket height

because the suspension fork has to allow for travel. This makes it difficult even to compare listed frame sizes from the same manufacturer to determine standover height.

Standover height is also a function of bottom bracket height above the ground. There is substantial variation here, especially with bikes with rear suspension whose bottom brackets are often very high so that ground clearance is still sufficient when the suspension is fully compressed.

Unless the manufacturer lists the standover height in their brochure and you know your inseam length, you need to actually stand over the bike.

Another note: *If you are short and cannot find a frame size small enough for you to get at least 2 inches of standover clearance, consider a bike with 24-inch wheels instead of 26-inch.*

2. Knee-to-handlebar clearance

Make sure your knee cannot hit the handlebar (Fig. C.2). Do this standing out of the saddle as well as seated and with the front wheel turned slightly. Be certain that your knees will not hit when you are in the most awkward pedaling position you might use.

3. Handlebar reach and drop

Ride the bike. See if the reach feels comfortable to you when holding the handlebar grips or the bar ends. Make sure you can grab the brake levers easily and that your knees do not hit your elbows as you pedal. Check to see that the stem can be raised or lowered enough to achieve a comfortable handlebar height for you.

Note: *Threadless headsets allow very limited*

4. Pedal overlap

"Pedal overlap" is a misnomer, since you are actually interested in whether the toe, not the pedal, can hit the front tire when turning sharply at low speeds. Sitting on the bike with the crankarms horizontal and the foot on the pedal, turn the handlebars and check that your toe does not hit the front tire (Fig. C.2). Toe overlap is to be avoided for any kind of slow-speed, technical riding, as pedaling up rocky terrain slowly can often result in the front wheel turning sharply back and forth as the feet pass by. Toe overlap is not an issue for most riding, because at higher speeds, turning the bike does not require turning the front wheel at enough of an angle to hit the foot.

C-2: CHOOSING FRAME SIZE FROM YOUR BODY MEASUREMENTS

You will need a second person to assist you.

By taking the three easy measurements shown in Fig. C.3, most people can get a very good frame fit. When designing a custom frame, I go through a more complex procedure than this, involving more measurements. For picking an off-the-shelf bike, this method works well. You can download a measurement form to fill in at www.zinncycles.com.

1. Measure your inseam

Spread your stocking feet about 2 inches apart, and measure up from the floor to a broomstick held level and lifted firmly up into your crotch. You can also use a large book and slide it up a wall to keep the top edge horizontal — as you pull it up as hard as you can — into your crotch. You can mark

C.3 body measurements

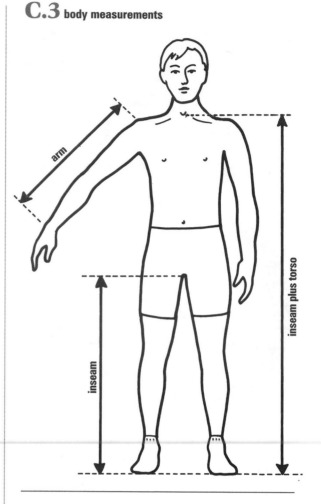

the top of the book on the wall and measure up from the floor to the mark. With the book method, it is harder to pull up enough to compress the soft tissue up against the bottom edge of the pelvis — so pull up hard.

2. Measure your inseam-plus-torso length

Hold a pencil horizontally in your sternal notch, the U-shaped bone depression just below your Adam's apple. Standing up straight in front of a wall, mark the wall with the horizontal pencil. Measure up from the floor to the mark.

3. Measure your arm length

Hold your arm out from your side at a 45-

bike fit

C.4 bike dimensions

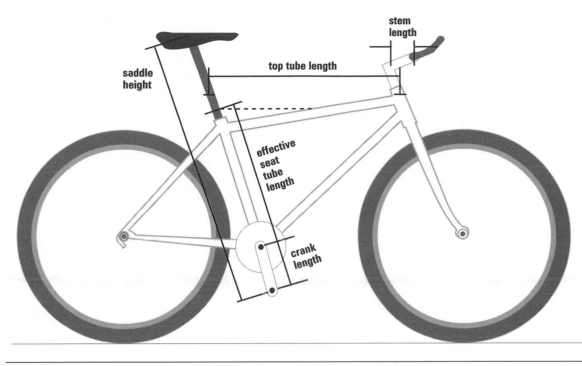

degree angle with your elbow straight as in Fig. C.3. Measure from the sharp bone point directly behind your shoulder joint to the wrist bone on your little finger side.

4. Find your frame size

Subtract 34cm to 42cm (13.5 inches to 16.5 inches) from your inseam length. This length is your frame size measured from the center of the bottom bracket to the top of a horizontal top tube. If the frame you are interested in has a sloping top tube (most mountain bikes do), you need a bike with an even shorter seat tube length. With a sloping top tube bike, project a horizontal line back to the seat tube (or seatpost) from the top of the top tube at the center of its length (Fig. C.4). Mark the seat tube or seatpost at this line. Measure from the center of the bottom bracket to this mark; this length should be 34–42cm less than

your inseam measurement. Also, if the bike has a bottom bracket higher than 29cm (11-1/2 inches), subtract the additional bottom bracket height from the seat tube length as well.

Generally, smaller riders will want to subtract close to 34cm from their inseam, while taller riders will subtract closer to 42cm. There is considerable range here. The top tube length (next step) is more important than a specific frame size, and, if you have short torso and arms, you can use a small frame to get the right top tube length, as long as you can raise your bars as high as you need them. Be aware that configurations of some full-suspension frames make measuring frame size challenging.

You really want to be sure that you have plenty of standover clearance, so do not subtract less than 34cm from your inseam for your seat-tube length; this should ensure at least 2 inches (5cm) of standover clearance. If you are short and cannot find a

C.5 saddle and stem position

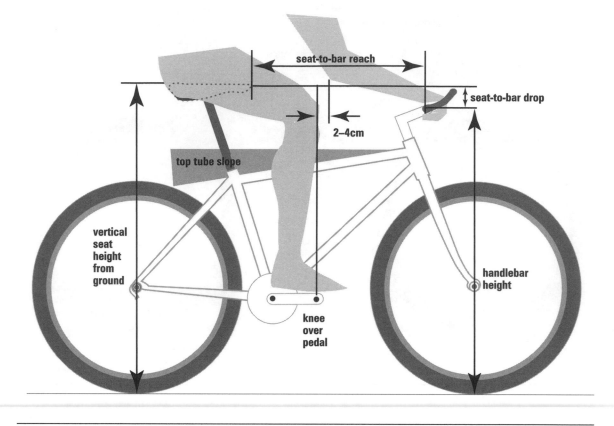

bike small enough for you to get at least 2 inches of standover clearance, consider one with 24-inch wheels instead of 26-inch wheels.

Note: *A step-through frame (i.e., "women's" frame, "mixte frame," or "girl's bike") having a steeply up-angled top tube meeting near the bottom bracket shell makes seat tube length for standover clearance nearly irrelevant. With a step-through bike, the only considerations will be horizontal and vertical reach to the bars.*

5. Find your top tube length

To find your torso length, subtract your inseam measurement (found in step 1) from your inseam-plus-torso measurement (found in step 2). Add this torso length to your arm length measurement (found in step 3). To find the top tube length,

multiply this arm-plus-torso measurement by a factor in the range between 0.47 and 0.5. If you are a casual rider, use 0.47; if you are a very aggressive rider, use 0.5, and, if you are in between, use a factor in between.

The top-tube length is measured horizontally from the center of the seat tube (or seatpost) to the center of the head tube (Fig. C.4). Obviously, the horizontal top-tube length is greater than the length found by measuring along the top tube on a sloping-top-tube bike, so don't just measure along your sloping top tube. Your body position is dictated by the horizontal distance forward of your hands from your butt — measuring along a sloping line does not give you useful information.

Note: *Full-suspension bikes often have a seatpost*

clamp that angles the seatpost back sharply along a line that would not intersect the bottom bracket. If you are tall and would have your seat high, your seat would end up far back of where it normally would on a bike of that size, and vice versa. You need to account for this shallow seatpost angle by estimating where the center of your virtual seat tube would be. Extrapolating a line from the center of your saddle to the center of the bottom bracket is one way. Measure from this imaginary line horizontally forward to the center of the head tube to find your top tube length.

6. Find your stem length

Multiply the arm-plus-torso length you found in step 5 by 0.10 up to 0.14 to find the stem length. Again, a casual rider will multiply by 0.10 or so, while an aggressive rider will multiply by closer to 0.14. This is a starting stem length. Finalize the stem length once you are sitting on the bike and see what feels best.

If you will have to accept a top tube length different from one that is ideal for you, you will need to make a corresponding adjustment of your stem length.

7. Determine crankarm length

Most mountain bikes come with 175mm cranks (measured hole-hole — see Fig. C.4), and it is rare to find another length on a bike or even available in a shop. But tall riders will often be better off with 180mm arms, and short riders with 170mm.

C-3: POSITIONING OF YOUR SADDLE AND HANDLEBARS

The frame fit is only part of the equation. Except for the standover clearance, a good frame fit is rela-tively meaningless if the seat setback, seat height, handlebar height, and handlebar reach are not set correctly for you.

1. Saddle height

When your foot is at the bottom of the stroke, lock your knee without rocking your hips. Do this sitting on your bike on a trainer with someone else observing. Your foot should be level, or the heel should be slightly higher than the ball of the foot. Another way to determine seat height is using your inseam measurement (Fig. C.3), found in step 1 under Section C-2, "Choosing Frame Size from Your Body Measurements" above. Multiply your inseam length by 1.09; this is the length from the center of the pedal spindle (when the pedal is down) to one of the points on the top of the saddle where your butt bones (ischial tuberosities) contact it (Fig. C.4). Adjust the seat height (Chapter 10) until you get it the proper height.

Note: These two methods yield similar results, although the measurement-multiplying method is dependent on shoe sole and pedal thicknesses. Both methods yield a biomechanically efficient pedaling position, but if you do a lot of technical riding and descending, you may wish to have a lower saddle for better bike-handling control.

2. Saddle setback

Sit on your bike on a stationary trainer with your crankarms horizontal and your foot at its normal angle at that point when pedaling. Have a friend drop a plumb line from the front of your knee below your kneecap. You can use a heavy ring, washer, etc. tied to a string for the plumb line. The plumb line should bisect the pedal axle or pass up to 2cm behind it (Fig. C.5); you will need to lean the knee out to get the string to hang clear. A saddle positioned fore-aft in this manner encourages smooth pedaling at high revolutions per minute, while 2 cm behind the pedal spindle encourages powerful seated climbing. You may also wish to experiment with a saddle position further forward; this can keep the front wheel on the ground on steep climbs.

Slide the saddle back and forth on the seatpost (Chapter 10) until you achieve the desired fore-aft saddle position. Set the saddle level or very close to it. Recheck the seat height in step 1 above, as fore-aft saddle movements affect seat-to-pedal distance, too.

3. Handlebar height

Measure the handlebar height relative to the saddle height by measuring the vertical distance of the saddle and bar up from the floor (Fig. C.5). How much higher the saddle is than your bar (or vice versa) depends on your flexibility, riding style, overall size and type of riding you prefer.

Aggressive and/or tall cross-country riders will prefer to have their saddle at least 10cm higher than their bar. Shorter riders will want proportionately less drop, as will less aggressive riders. Riders doing lots of downhills will want their bars higher; handlebars on downhill and dual slalom bikes are commonly higher than the saddle. Generally, people beginning mountain bike riding will like their bars high and can lower them as they become more comfortable with the bike, with going fast and with riding more technical terrain.

If in doubt, start with 4cm of drop and vary it from there. The higher the bar, the greater the tendency is for the front wheel to pull up off of the

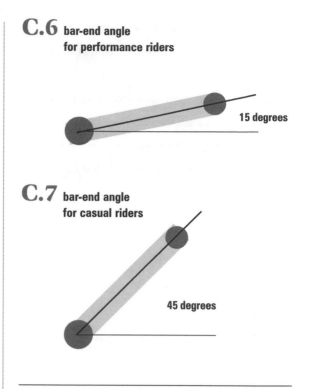

C.6 bar-end angle for performance riders

15 degrees

C.7 bar-end angle for casual riders

45 degrees

ground when climbing, and the more wind resistance you can expect. Change the bar height by raising or lowering the stem (Chapter 11), or by switching stems and/or bars.

Again, threadless headsets allow only limited stem-height adjustment without substitution of a differently angled stem.

4. Setting handlebar reach

The reach from the saddle to the handlebar is also very dependent on personal preference. More aggressive riders will want a more stretched-out position than will casual riders. This length is subjective, and I find that I need to look at the rider on the bike and get a feel for how they would be comfortable and efficient.

A useful starting place is to drop a plumb line from the back of your elbow with your arms bent in a comfortable riding position. This plane determined by your elbows and the plumb line should

bike fit

be 2–4cm horizontally ahead of each knee at the point in the pedal stroke when the crank arm is horizontal forward (Fig. C.5). The idea is to select a position you find comfortable and efficient; listen to what your body wants.

Vary the saddle-bar distance by changing stem length (Chapter 11), not by changing the seat fore-aft position, which is based on pedaling efficiency (step 2 above) and not on reach.

Note: There is no single formula for determining handlebar reach and height. I can tell you that using the all-too-common method of placing your elbow against the saddle and seeing if your fingertips reach the handlebar is close to useless. Similarly, the oft-suggested method of seeing if the handlebar obscures your vision of the front hub is not worth the brief time it takes to look, as it largely depends on elbow bend, the inclination of your neck, and front-end geometry. Another method involving dropping a plumb bob from the rider's nose is dependent on the handlebar height and elbow bend and thus does not lend itself to a proscribed relationship for all riders.

5. Bar end position

Performance riders should position the bar ends in the range between horizontal and pointed up 15 degrees (Fig. C.6). Bar-end angles in this range allow powerful pulling on the bar ends when climbing out of the saddle, since the bar ends are perpendicular to the forearms when standing. This bar-end angle also makes for a lower, more extended position when seated and grabbing the hooks of the bar ends. Find the bar-end position you find comfortable for pulling on when climbing standing or seated, and for pedaling seated on extended paved stretches.

Casual riders often prefer a higher angle (Fig. C.7) to pull with a straight wrist and closed fist while seated. Leave the bar end mounting bolts a bit loose, sit on the bike, and grab the bar ends comfortably. Tighten them down in that position.

Note: Do not use the bar ends to raise your hand position by pointing the bar ends vertically up. If you want a higher hand position, get a taller or more up-angled stem, and/or a higher-rise handlebar. Bar ends are not meant to be stood straight up and held on to for cruising along sitting up high; that is the mountain bike equivalent of flipping a road drop bar upside down to lift the hands. As with the road bar equivalent, you cannot reach the brakes when you need them.

glossary

adjustable cup: the nondrive-side cup in the bottom-bracket (Fig. 8.9). This cup is removed for maintenance of the bottom bracket spindle and bearings, and it adjusts the bearings. The term is sometimes applied to the top headset cup as well.

AheadSet: a style of headset that allows the use of a fork with a threadless steering tube (Fig. 11.7). The name is a trademark of Dia-Compe and Cane Creek.

Allen key (Allen wrench, hex key): a hexagonal wrench that fits inside a hexagonal hole in the head of a bolt.

all-terrain bike (ATB): another term for mountain bike.

anchor bolt (cable anchor, cable-fixing bolt): a bolt securing a cable to a component.

Answer Products: American bicycle- and motorcycle-component company and parent company of Manitou.

axle: the shaft about which a part turns, usually on bearings or bushings.

axle overlock dimension: the length of a hub axle from dropout to dropout, referring to the distance from locknut face to locknut face.

ball bearing: a set of balls, generally made out of steel, rolling in a track to allow a shaft to spin inside a cylindrical part. May also refer to one of the individual balls.

barrel adjuster: a threaded cable stop that allows for fine adjustment of cable tension. Barrel adjusters are commonly found on rear derailleurs, shifters and brake levers (Figs. 5.3, 5.25 and 7.1).

BB (*see* "bottom bracket" *or* "ball bearing").

bearing (*see* "ball bearing").

bearing cone: a conical part with a bearing race around its circumference. The cone presses the ball bearings against the bearing race inside the bearing cup.

bearing cup: a polished dish-shaped surface inside of which ball bearings roll. The bearings roll on the outside of a bearing cone that presses them into their track inside the bearing cup.

bearing race: the track or surface the bearings roll on. It can be inside a cup, on the outside of a cone or inside a cartridge bearing.

binder bolt: a bolt clamping a seatpost in a frame, a bar end to a handlebar, a handlebar inside a stem or a threadless steering tube inside a stem clamp.

bottom bracket (BB): the assembly that allows the crank to rotate. Generally the bottom bracket assembly includes bearings, an axle, a fixed cup, an adjustable cup and a lockring.

bottom bracket shell: the cylindrical housing at the bottom of a bicycle frame through which the bottom bracket axle passes.

brake boss (brake post or pivot; cantilever boss, post or pivot): a fork- or frame-mounted pivot for a brake arm (Figs. 13.1, 13.2 and 14.1).

brake pad (brake block): a block of rubber or similar material used to slow the bike by creating friction on the rim, hub-mounted disc or other braking surface.

brake post (*see* "brake boss").

brake shoe: the metal pad holder that holds the brake pad to the brake arm.

braze-on: a generic term for most metal frame attachments, even those welded or glued on.

brazing: a method commonly used to construct steel bicycle frames. Brazing involves the use of brass or silver solder to connect frame tubes and attach various "braze-on" items including brake bosses, cable guides and rack mounts to the frame. Although rarely done, it is also possible to braze aluminum and titanium.

bushing: a metal or plastic sleeve that acts as a simple bearing on pedals, suspension forks, suspension swing arms and jockey wheels.

butted tubing: a common type of frame tubing with varying wall thicknesses. Butted tubing is designed to accommodate high stress points at the ends of the tube by being thicker there.

cable (inner wire): wound or braided wire strands used to operate brakes and derailleurs.

cable anchor (*see* "anchor bolt").

cable end: a cap on the end of a cable to keep it from fraying (Fig. 5.18).

cable-fixing bolt (*see* "anchor bolt").

cable hanger: cable stop on a fork- or seatstay-arch used to stop the brake cable housing for a cantilever or U-brake.

cable housing: a metal-reinforced exterior sheath through which a cable passes.

cable housing stop (*see* "cable stop").

cable-fixing bolt: an anchor bolt that attaches cables to brakes or derailleurs.

cable stop: a fitting on the frame, fork or stem at which a cable housing segment terminates.

cage: two guiding plates through which the chain travels. Both the front and rear derailleurs have cages. The cage on the rear also holds the jockey pulleys. Also, a water-bottle holder.

Cane Creek: American bicycle component company and originator of the threadless headset. Originally known as Dia-Compe USA.

cantilever boss (*see* "brake boss").

cantilever brake: a cable-operated rim brake consisting of two opposing arms pivoting on frame- or fork-mounted posts. Pads mounted to each brake arm are pressed against the braking surface of the rim via cable tension from the lever (Figs. 7.23–7.25).

cantilever pivot (*see* "brake boss").

cantilever post (*see* "brake boss").

cartridge bearing: ball bearings encased in a cartridge consisting of steel inner and outer rings, ball retainers and, sometimes, bearing covers (Figs. 6.26 and 11.23).

cassette: the group of cogs that mounts on a freehub (Fig. 6.27). Also the group of chainrings that mounts on a spiderless crankarm (Fig. 8.8).

cassette hub (*see* "freehub").

chain: a series of metal links held together by pins and used to transmit energy from the crank to the rear wheel (Fig. 4.1).

chain line: the imaginary line connecting the center of the middle chainring with the middle of the cogset. This line should, in theory, be straight and parallel with the vertical plane passing through the center of the bicycle. This is measured as the distance from the center of the seat tube to the center of the middle chainring (Chapter 5, Section V-44, Fig. 5.42).

chain link: a single unit of bicycle chain consisting of four plates with a roller on each end and in the center (Fig. 4.6).

chainring: a multiple-tooth sprocket attached to the right crankarm.

chainring-nut spanner: a tool used to secure the chainring nuts while tightening the chainring bolts (Fig. 1.3).

chainstays: the tubes leading from the bottom bracket shell to the rear hub axle (Fig. 14.1).

chain suck: the dragging of the chain by the chainring past the release point at the bottom of the chainring. The chain can be dragged upward until it is jammed between the chainring and the chainstay.

chain whip (chain wrench): a flat piece of steel, usually attached to two lengths of chain (Fig. 1.3). This tool is used to remove the rear cogs on a freehub or freewheel.

chase, wild goose (*see* "goose chase").

circlip (snapring, Jesus clip): a C-shaped snapring that fits in a groove to hold parts together.

clip-in pedal (clipless pedal): a pedal that relies on spring-loaded clips to grip a cleat attached to the bottom of the rider's shoe, without the use of toeclips and straps.

clipless pedal (*see* "clip-in pedal").

cog: a sprocket located on the drive side of the rear hub (Fig. 6.27).

compression damping: diminishing the speed of compression of a spring on impact by hydraulic or mechanical means.

cone: a threaded conical nut that serves to hold a set of bearings in place and also provides a smooth surface upon which those bearings can roll. Can refer to the conical (or male) member of any cup and cone ball bearing system (*see also* "bearing cone").

crankarm: the lever attached at the bottom bracket spindle used to transmit a rider's energy to the chain.

crankarm-fixing bolt: the bolt attaching the crank to the bottom bracket spindle on a cotterless drive train (Fig. 8.1).

crankset: the assembly that includes a bottom

bracket, two crankarms, chainring set and accompanying nuts and bolts (Fig. 8.1).

cross three: a pattern used by wheel builders, that calls for each spoke to cross three others in its path from the hub to the rim.

cup: a cup-shaped bearing surface that surrounds the bearings in a bottom bracket, headset or hub (*see* "bearing cup").

damper: a mechanism in a suspension fork or shock that reduces the speed of the spring's oscillation.

damping: the reduction in speed of the oscillation of a spring, as in a suspension fork or shock.

derailleur: a gear-changing device that allows a rider to move the chain from one cog or chainring to another while the bicycle is in motion.

derailleur hanger: a metal extension of the right rear dropout through which the rear derailleur is mounted to the frame (Fig. 14.1).

diamond frame: the traditional bicycle frame shape.

dish: a difference in spoke tension on the two sides of the rear wheel so that the wheel is centered.

disc brake: a brake that stops the bike by squeezing brake pads against a circular disc attached to the wheel (Figs. 7.17–7.19).

double: a two-chainring drivetrain setup (as opposed to a three-chainring, or " triple," one).

down tube: the frame tube that connects the head tube and bottom bracket shell together (Fig.14.1).

drivetrain: the crankarms, chainrings, bottom bracket, front derailleur, chain, rear derailleur and freewheel (or cassette).

drop: the vertical distance between the center of the bottom bracket and a horizontal line passing through the wheel hub centers.

dropouts: the slots in the fork and rear triangle where the wheel axles attach (Figs. 13.1 and 14.1).

dust cap: a protective cap keeping dirt out of a part.

elastomer: a urethane spring used in suspension forks and swing arms.

ferrule: a cap for the end of cable housing (Fig. 5.18).

fixed cup: the nonadjustable cup of the bottom bracket located on the drive side of the bottom bracket (Fig. 8.9).

flange: the largest diameter of the hub where the spoke heads are anchored.

fork: the part that attaches the front wheel to the frame (Figs. 13.1 and 13.2).

fork crown: the cross piece connecting the fork legs to the steering tube (Figs. 13.1 and 13.2).

fork ends (*see* "dropouts").

fork rake (rake): the perpendicular offset distance of the front axle from an imaginary extension of the steering tube centerline (*see* "steering axis").

fork tips (fork ends) (*see* "dropouts").

frame: the central structure of a bicycle to which all of the parts are attached (Fig. 14.1 and 14.2).

freehub: a rear hub that has a built-in freewheel mechanism to which the rear cogs are attached (Fig. 6.27).

freewheel: the mechanism through which the rear cogs are attached to the rear wheel on a derailleur bicycle (Figs. 6.27 and 6.28). The freewheel is locked to the hub when turned in the forward direction, but it is free to spin backward independently of the hub's movement, thus allowing the rider to stop pedaling and coast as the bicycle is moving forward.

friction shifter: a traditional (nonindexed) shifter attached to the frame or handle bars. Cable tension is maintained by a combination of friction washers and bolts.

front triangle (main triangle): the head tube, top tube, down tube and seat tube of a bike frame (Fig. 14.1).

girl's bike (*see* "step-through frame").

goose chase, wild (*see* "wild goose chase").

Grip Shift: a trademarked shifter of the SRAM corporation that is integrated with the handlebar grip of a mountain bike (Fig. 5.25). The rider shifts gears by twisting the grip (*see also* "twist shifter").

headset: the cup, lockring and bearings that hold the fork to the frame and allow the fork to spin in the frame (Figs. 11.17 and 11.18).

head tube: the front tube of the frame through which the steering tube of the fork passes (Fig. 14.1). The head tube is attached to the top tube and down tube and contains the headset.

hex key (*see* "Allen key").

hub: the central part of a wheel to which the spokes are anchored and through which the wheel axle passes (Fig. 6.18).

hub brake: a disc, drum or coaster brake that stops the wheel with friction applied to a braking surface attached to the hub.

Hutchinson: French tire company.

hydraulic brake: a type of brake that uses oil pressure to move the brake pads against the braking surface.

index shifter: a shifter that clicks into fixed positions as it moves the derailleur from gear to gear.

inner wire (*see* "cable").

Jesus clip (*see* "circlip").

jockey wheel or jockey pulley: a circular cog-shaped-pulley attached to the rear derailleur used to guide, apply tension to and laterally move the chain from rear cog to rear cog (Fig. 5.39).

knobby tire: an all-terrain tire used on mountain bikes.

link: (1) a pivoting steel hook on a V-brake arm that the cable-guide " noodle" hooks into (Fig. 7.14); (2) (*see also* "chain link").

locknut: a nut that serves to hold the bearing adjustment in a headset, hub or pedal.

lockring: a large circular locknut. On a bottom bracket, the outer ring that tightens the adjustable cup against the face of the bottom bracket shell. On a rear shock, the threaded ring that tightens the coil spring on a coil-over shock or is used to secure the fore-aft position of the shock body on some air shocks.

lock washer: a notched or toothed washer that serves to hold surrounding nuts and washers in position.

Manitou: American suspension-fork and component company. Subsidiary of Answer Products. Maker of EFC, Mach, SX, X-Vert, and Black forks and TPC systems.

Marzocchi: Italian suspension-fork and component company.

master link: a detachable link that holds the chain together. The master link can be opened by hand without a chain tool (Figs. 4.12 and 4.13).

Mavic: French bicycle-component company. Subsidiary of Salomon, which is a subsidiary of Adidas.

Michelin: French tire company.

mixte frame (*see* "step-through frame").

mounting bolt: a bolt that mounts a part to a frame, fork or component (*see also* "pivot bolt").

needle bearing: steel cylindrical cartridge with rod-shaped rollers arranged coaxially around the inside walls.

noodle: curved cable-guide pipe on a V-brake arm that stops the cable housing and directs the cable to the cable anchor bolt on the opposite arm (Fig. 7.12).

nipple: a thin nut designed to receive the end of a spoke and seat in the holes of a rim.

outer wire (*see* "cable housing").

outer wire stop (*see* "cable stop").

pedal: platform the foot pushes on to propel the bicycle (Figs. 9.1 and 9.2).

pedal overlap: the overlapping of the toe with the front wheel while pedaling (Appendix C, Fig. C.2).

pin spanner: a V-shaped wrench with two tip-end pins. Often used for tightening the adjustable cup of the bottom bracket or other lockrings (Fig. 1.3).

pivot: a pin about which a part rotates through a bearing or bushing. Found on brakes, derailleurs and rear suspension systems.

pivot bolt: a bolt on which a brake or derailleur part pivots.

preload (*see* "spring preload").

Presta valve: thin, metal tire valve that uses a locking nut to stop air flow from the tire (Fig. 1.1).

quick release: (1) the tightening lever and shaft used to attach a wheel to the fork or rear dropouts without using axle nuts (Fig. 6.18); (2) a quick-opening lever and shaft pinching the seatpost inside the seat tube, in lieu of a wrench-operated bolt; (3) a quick cable release on a brake; (4) a fixing mechanism that can be quickly opened and closed, as on a brake cable or wheel axle; (5) any fixing bolt that can be quickly opened and closed by a lever.

quill: the vertical tube of a stem that inserts into the fork steering tube. It has an expander wedge and bolt inside to secure the stem to the steering tube (Fig. 11.8).

race: a circular track on which bearings roll freely (*see also* "bearing race").

Rapidfire shifter: an indexing shifter manufactured by Shimano for use on mountain bikes with two separate levers operating each shift cable (Figs. 5.22 and 5.23).

rear triangle: the rear portion of the bicycle frame, including the seat stays, the chainstays and the seat tube (Fig. 14.1).

rebound damping: the diminishing of speed of return of a spring by hydraulic or mechanical means.

rim: the outer hoop of a wheel to which the tire is attached (Fig. 12.1).

Ritchey: American bicycle and bicycle-component company.

RockShox: American suspension-fork and component company and maker of Mag, Judy, SID, Psylo and Duke lines.

roller-cam brakes: a brake system using pulleys and a cam to force the brake pads against the rim surface (Fig. 7.46).

saddle (seat): a platform made of leather and/or plastic upon which the rider sits (Fig. 10.1).

Schrader valve: a high-pressure air valve with a spring-loaded air-release pin inside (Fig. 1.1). Schrader valves are found on some bicycle tubes and air-sprung suspension forks as well as on adjustable rear shocks and automobile tires and tubes.

sealed bearing: a bearing enclosed in an attempt to keep contaminants out (Fig. 6.26) (*see* also "cartridge bearing").

seat cluster: the intersection of the seat tube, top tube and seat stays.

seat (*see* "saddle").

seatpost: the post to which the saddle is secured (Fig. 10.4).

seat tube: the frame tube to which the seatpost (and, usually, the cranks) are attached (Fig. 14.1).

Shimano: Japanese bicycle-component company and maker of XTR, XT, LX and STX component lines, as well as Rapidfire (shifters), SPD (pedals) and STI (shifting system).

sidepull cantilever brake (*see* "V-brake").

skewer: (1) a long rod; (2) a hub quick release (Fig. 6.18); and (3) a shaft passing through a stack of elastomer bumpers in a suspension fork (Fig. 13.12).

Slime: trademarked tire sealant consisting of chopped fibers in a liquid medium injected inside a tire or inner tube to flow to and fill small air leaks.

snapring (*see* "circlip").

spider: a star-shaped piece of metal that connects the right crank arm to the chainrings.

spokes: metal rods that connect the hub to the rim of a wheel (Figs. 12.1 and 12.2).

spring: an elastic contrivance that, when compressed, returns to its original shape by virtue of its elasticity. In bicycle suspension applications, the spring used is normally either an elastic polymer cylinder, a coil of steel or titanium wire or compressed air.

spring preload: the initial loading of a spring so part of its compression range is taken up prior to impact.

sprocket: a circular, multiple-toothed piece of metal that engages a chain (*see also* "cog" *and* "chain ring").

SRAM: American bicycle-component company and maker of Grip Shift, Half Pipes and ESP (derailleurs). Owner of Sachs, a German bicycle-component company.

standover clearance (standover height): the distance between the top tube of the bike and the rider's crotch when standing over the bicycle (Appendix C, Fig. C.1).

star nut (star-fangled nut): a pronged nut that is forced down into the steering tube and anchors the stem-cap bolt to adjust a threadless headset (Fig. 11.17).

steering axis: the imaginary line about which the fork rotates (Fig. 13.9).

steering tube: the vertical tube on a fork that is attached to the fork crown and fits inside the head tube.

step-through frame (women's frame, girl's bike, mixte frame): a bicycle frame with a steeply up-angled top tube connecting the bottom of the seat tube to the top of the head tube. The frame design is intended to provide ease of stepping over the frame and ample standover clearance.

straddle cable: short segment of cable connecting two brake arms together (Fig. 7.33).

straddle-cable holder (*see* "yoke").

swing arm: the movable rear end of a rear-suspension frame (Fig. 14.2).

threadless headset: (*see* "AheadSet").

three cross: (*see* "cross three").

thumb shifter: a thumb-operated shift lever attached on top of the handlebars (Fig. 5.21).

tire lever: a tool to pry a tire off of the rim (Figs. 6.4 and 6.5).

tire sealant (*see* "Slime").

toe overlap (toeclip overlap): (*see* "pedal overlap").

top tube: the frame tube that connects the seat tube to the head tube.

torque wrench: a socket wrench handle with a spring in it and an indicator to show how tight a bolt is (Fig. 1.4 or 2.12).

TORX wrench: a tool with a star-shaped end that fits in the star-shaped hole in the head of a TORX bolt (Fig. 1.4 or 1.7).

triple: a term used to describe the three-chainring combination attached to the right crankarm.

twist shifter: a cable-pulling derailleur control handle surrounding the handlebar adjacent the hand grip; it is twisted forward or back to cause the derailleur to shift (*see* also "Grip Shift").

U-brake: a mountain-bike brake consisting of two arms shaped like inverted L's affixed to posts on the frame or fork (Fig. 7.45).

UST: tubeless-tire system originated by Mavic, Michelin and Hutchinson in which the tire seals over a "hump" on the ledge inside a rim free of spoke holes on its outer circumference (Fig. 6.7).

V-brake (sidepull cantilever brake): a cable-operated cantilever rim brake consisting of two vertical brake arms pivoting on frame- or fork-mounted pivots pulled together by a horizontal cable. A brake pad is affixed to each arm, and there is a cable link and cable guide pipe on one arm and a cable anchor on the opposite arm (Figs. 7.12–7.14).

wheel base: the horizontal distance between the two wheel axles.

wild goose chase (*see* "chase").

women's frame (*see* "step-through frame").

yoke: the part attaching the brake cable to the straddle cable, on a cantilever or U-brake (Fig. 7.6).

torque table

One of the single biggest sources of mechanical problems (and breakage risk) is overtightening of fasteners, particularly on lightweight equipment. It is great to have the feel for what is tight enough, but many people do not have this. With some parts, particularly today's superlight stems and handlebars, it is incredibly important to tighten them to exact torque specification or you could have a stem or bar break while you are riding, which results in an immediate and terrifying loss of control of the bicycle. Even "old guard" mechanics, with their "feel" from years of practice, often overtighten the small, light bolts on lightweight stems.

It will be worth your while to review Section II-16 in Chapter 2 to help you develop a feel. Whether you do or don't have the touch, a torque wrench is a wonderful thing, if you know how tight things are supposed to be. Listed below are the standard tightening torque recommendations of Shimano, SRAM/Grip Shift, RockShox, Answer/Manitou, Marzocchi, RST, Cannondale, Avid, Hayes, Formula, Magura, Cane Creek, 3T, Cinelli, Deda, ITM, Salsa

and Dimension for their products, as well as some general recommendations from bsn.com. (Numbers listed as 3T also apply to Cinelli stems.)

Where there is only one number listed and not a range, that is the *maximum* torque allowable.

These torques apply to steel and titanium bolts; aluminum bolts are described as such in the table.

Conversion between units: The following table is in inch-pounds (in-lbs). Divide these in-lb settings by 12 to convert to foot-pounds (ft-lbs). Multiply in-lb settings by 0.113 to convert to Newton-meters (N-m).

BOLT SIZES

M5 bolts are 5mm in diameter and take a 3mm or 4mm hex key (except on derailleurs, where they often take a 5mm hex key or an 8mm box wrench).

M6 bolts are 6mm in diameter and generally take a 5mm hex key.

M7 bolts are 7mm in diameter and generally take a 6mm hex key.

M8 bolts are 8mm in diameter and generally take a 6mm hex key.

MANUFACTURERS' RECOMMENDED TIGHTENING TORQUES

BOTTOM BRACKETS AND CRANKS	INCH-POUNDS
crankarm fixing bolt	285–435
chainring fixing bolt (steel)	60–100
chainring fixing bolt (aluminum)	44
cartridge bottom bracket cups	435–610
standard bottom bracket fixed cup	609–695
standard bottom bracket lockring	609–695
pedal axle to crankarm	305–355

BRAKES	INCH-POUNDS

Cantilevers and V-brakes:

brake lever clamp bolt, M6	50–70
brake lever clamp — slotted screw	22–26
brake arm mounting bolt, M6	40–60
Avid split-clamp lever mounting bolts	28–36
brake cable fixing bolt, M5	50–70
V-brake pad fixing nut	50–70
cantilever brake pad fixing bolt	70–78
straddle cable yoke fixing nut	35–43
Shimano V-brake leverage adjuster bolt	9–13
Avid Arch Supreme arch-mounting bolt	35–40

Hayes disc brake:

rotor mounting bolts, M5	45–55
caliper mounting bolts, M6	100–120
single lever clamp bolt	15–20
split-clamp lever mounting bolts	20–30
hose nut	40 plus 1 turn
caliper bleeder	2 to seal
caliper bridge bolts	100–120
banjo bolt	50–60

Shimano disc brake:

rotor mounting bolts, M5	18–35
caliper mounting bolts, M6	55–70
lever clamp bolt	55–70
caliper bleed nipple	27–44
reservoir screws	2.5–4.5
pad axle bolt	20–35
banjo bolt	45–60

Avid disc brake:

rotor mounting bolts, M5	55
caliper mounting bolts, M6	80–90
mounting adapter bolts	80–90
cable-fixing bolt	40–60

BRAKES (CONT.)	INCH-POUNDS

Formula disc brake:

rotor mounting bolts, M5	42–47
caliper mounting bolts, M6	76–84
valve couplers	101–111

Magura hydraulic rim brake:

M6 center bolt	52
M5 housing clamp bolt	35
bleed screws	35
brake line sleeve nuts	35

Magura disc brake:

rotor mounting bolts, M5	35
master cylinder line fitting	35
caliper mounting bolts, M6	52

Coda disc brake:

rotor mounting bolts, M5	40–50
caliper mounting bolts, M6	69–78
lever clamp bolt	72–108
hose sleeve	69–78

Hope disc brake:

rotor mounting lockring	310

RockShox disc brake:

rotor mounting bolts, M5	50
caliper mounting bolts, M6	50
cable guide hardware	50

DiaTech disc brake:

mounting pins	62–80

DERAILLEURS AND SHIFTERS	INCH-POUNDS
front derailleur cable fixing bolt, M5	44–60
front derailleur clamp bolt, M5	44–60
rear derailleur cable fixing bolt, M5	44–60
rear derailleur mounting bolt	70–90
rear derailleur pulley center bolts, M5	27–34
Rapidfire shifter clamp bolt, M6	44
shifter clamp bolt for hex key, M6	53–69
shifter clamp bolt — slotted screw	22–26
shift lever parts fixing screw	22–24
Grip Shift lever mounting screw	17

HUBS, CASSETTES, QUICK RELEASES	INCH-POUNDS
hub quick-release lever closing	79–104
bolt-on steel skewer	65
bolt-on titanium skewer	85

torque table

MANUFACTURERS' RECOMMENDED TIGHTENING TORQUES

HUBS, CASSETTES, ETC. (CONT.)	INCH-POUNDS
nutted front hub	180
nutted rear hub	300
quick-release axle locknut	87–217
freehub cassette body-fixing bolt	305–434
cassette cog lock ring	260–435
Mavic cassette cog lock ring	354
Cannondale Lefty front axle bolt	133

PEDALS AND SHOES	INCH-POUNDS
pedal axle to crankarm	304–355
shoe cleat fixing bolt, M5	41–52
shoe spike, M5	34
toeclips to pedals, M5	25–45
Speedplay Frog spindle nut	35–40

SEATPOSTS AND SEAT BINDERS	INCH-POUNDS
seatpost saddle clamp bolt, M8	175–345
Thomson seatpost saddle clamp bolts, M6	60
Easton seatpost saddle clamp bolts	60–70
Campagnolo seatpost saddle clamp bolt, M8	194
cheap steel seatpost band-clamp bolt	175–345
two-piece seat binder bolt, M6	35–60
seat-tube clamp binder bolt, M6	105–140

STEMS AND BAR ENDS	INCH-POUNDS
single stem handlebar clamping bolt, M8	145–220
wedge expander bolt for quill stems, M8	140–175
ITM M8 bolts (single-bolt clamp or expander)	160
ITM M7 bolts	120
ITM M6 bolts (bar clamp, fork collar)	105
ITM M5 bolts (bar clamp, fork collar)	70
ITM aluminum M6 bolts in magnesium stem	53
3T M8 bolts (single steerer clamp; expander)	175
3T M8 bolts (single handlebar clamp)	220
3T M6 bolts (single steerer clamp)	130
3T M6 bolts (two-bolt front clamp plate)	130
3T Bono M6 bolts (two-bolt front clamp plate)	120
3T M5 bolts (front clamp, steerer clamp)	80
Deda M8 bolts (quill expander)	160
Deda M6 bolts (bar clamp, fork collar)	160
Deda M5 bolts (bar clamp, fork collar)	90
Deda M6 hidden steerer clamp bolt	130
Salsa SUL two-bolt face plate bar clamp, M6	120–130

STEMS AND BAR ENDS (CONT.)	INCH-POUNDS
Salsa one-bolt handlebar clamp, M6 bolt	140
Salsa one-bolt steerer tube clamp, M6 bolt	100–110
Dimension two-bolt face plate bar clamp, M6	80–90
Dimension two-bolt steerer tube clamp, M6	80–90
Dimension one-bolt handlebar clamp, M8 bolt	205–240
Bontrager M8 steerer tube clamp bolts	200
Easton MG60, EM90 fork collar bolts	50–60
Easton MG60, EM90 bar clamp bolts	70–80
Easton EA50, 70 bar clamp, fork collar bolts	60–70
bar end M6 bolt	120–140

SUSPENSION FORKS	INCH-POUNDS
RockShox Judy top cap	35
RockShox SID top cap	50
RockShox brake post	60
RockShox Judy cartridge shaft bolt	60
RockShox Judy neutral shaft bolt	60
RockShox SID shaft bolt, either leg	50
RockShox fork brace bolt	60
RockShox M6 fork crown clamp bolt	60
RockShox crown clamp bolt with shim	90
RockShox double-crown clamp bolt	90
Manitou EFC/Mach 5/SX cartridge bolt	10–30
Manitou neutral shaft bolt	10–30
Manitou brake post	90–110
Manitou EFC/Mach 5/SX cartridge cap	30–50
Manitou M8 (6mm key) crown clamp bolt	110–130
Manitou M6 (5mm key) crown clamp bolt	60
Manitou fork brace bolt	90–110
Marzocchi Bomber 26mm top plug	106
Marzocchi Bomber foot nut	106
RST Mozo brake arch bolt	70–80
RST Mozo fork crown clamp bolt	70–80

MISCELLANEOUS	INCH-POUNDS
AheadSet bearing preload, M6	22
fender to frame bolts, M5	50–60
water bottle cage bolts, M5	25–35

GENERAL MAXIMUM TIGHTENING TORQUE FOR UNTREATED SCREWS

SCREW SIZE	BOLT GRADE		
	ISO 8.8 (SAE 5) (in-lbs)	ISO 10.9 (SAE 8) (in-lbs)	ISO 12.9 (SAE n/a) (in-lbs)
M3	12	17	20
M4	27	39	46
M5	55	59	92
M6	93	133	159
M7	155	221	257
M8	230	319	381

(1 Nm = 8.851 in-lbs = 0.738 ft-lbs)

Note: Component manufacturers often use a large bolt for ease of the consumer, not because the product needs it. So tightening to the general spec of the bolt will be overtightening the part. It is far better to go by the torque recommendation for the part, not for the bolt. Steel bolts will take a lot more than aluminum bike parts will! Also, if the fit of the parts is bad (bikes are notorious for having undersized handlebars and seatposts, for instance), you may tighten to the specified torque and the part will still slip. If the fit is way off, the gap in a seat binder or stem binder can be closed down so much that the bolt will bend and fail prematurely.

pedal-cleat compatibility

Since the introduction of the SPD (Shimano Pedaling Dynamics) mountain bike pedal, there has been a flood of very successful competitors in a market once dominated by the Japanese component giant. Numerous manufacturers produce "SPD-compatible" pedals. But anyone who has tried more than one brand can attest to the fact that the phrase "compatibility" means different things to different people.

It is safe to assume that the cleats of any SPD-compatible system will mount on standard mountain bike shoes that have two lengthwise slots in the sole. What compatibility doesn't guarantee is whether those cleats will work in other pedals. Indeed, no manufacturer we found will even mention whether its cleats work in other pedals, and vice versa. I will, because pedal/cleat compatibility is an issue on the dirt. Riders want to try different equipment, so mountain bikes get traded around a lot.

Included, in addition to current models, are old standbys, many of which are no longer made,

namely Shimano 747, 737, 636 (and 525 — similar to 636; and A515 — similar to 737), OnZa HO and 1996 Scott pedals (which are representative of a slew of other concurrent Wellgo-made pedals under various brands). Note that OnZas produced since 1998 are completely different than the old HO and resemble 1997 Wellgo/Coda/Scott models in function. Note also that Wellgo cleats (with a WP number on them) come with many different brands of pedals. The same goes for VP, another Taiwanese pedal maker.

I first made this chart in 1997. When revising it in 2001, some of these pedals were no longer available, so I did not test the latest cleats on all of them, or vice versa — hence, the dash line in some boxes. Numbers like "96," "97" and "99" refer to the model year (1996, 1997 or 1999).

The listed pedals, along with private-label models virtually identical to some of these, represent the vast majority of the clip-in mountain bike pedals out there. All pedals were tested at midrange spring tension. Pedals are graded according to how easy they are to enter and release, how well they retain the foot when pulling up hard or bouncing over rough terrain, and how much they allow the foot to float rotationally.

Float is a must: It makes cleat setup much easier, can save your knees the agony of misadjusted cleats and prevents premature release when wending one's way through twisty single track or bouncing down a bumpy descent on the verge of losing control. High retention is also a must, as it can be very disconcerting, if not dangerous, to come out of the pedal when not expecting it. Ease of entry and intentional exit is also a must for convenient and safe use. As you can see, some pedals perform these functions better with another brand cleat than with their own.

Two pedals not on the chart are Speedplay and Bebop. Both are free-floating, and neither is compatible with any other cleats.

	PEDAL																	
	Shimano PD				Time ATAC	Ritchey Logic		Wellgo	Scott 2-Cam		Coda CO	Look	VP		Exus	Tioga	OnZa	
CLEAT	858	747	737	636	all	'96	'99	WPD-800	'97	'96	'97	SL3	103	104	E-M2	Clip-man	HO '93	HOX '98
SM-SH52	A	A	-	-	F	-	A	-	-	-	-	F	-	-	-	F	F	-
SM-SH51	A	A	A	A	F	D	A	C	C	B-	C	F	B	C	B+	F	F	C
SM-SH50	A	A	A	A	F	D	-	C	C	B-	C	F	B	C	B+	F	F	C
TIME ATAC	F	F	F	F	A+	F	F	F	F	F	F	F	F	F	F	F	F	F
Ritchey'99	A	A	-	-	F	-	A	-	-	-	-	F	-	-	-	F	F	-
Ritchey'96	-	B	B	B	F	A	-	C	A	A-	A	F	D	-	-	F	F	-
WP-98A	-	A	A	B	F	B-	-	C	C	B	C	F	B	C	B+	F	F	C
WP-97A	A	A	A	B	F	A	A	C	C	C	C	F	B	C	B+	F	F	C
LOOK SL3	F	F	F	F	F	F	F	F	F	F	F	A	F	F	F	F	F	F
OnZa HO	F	F	F	F	F	F	F	F	F	F	F	F	F	F	F	F	B+	F
VP E-C01	-	A	B	B	F	D+	-	C	C	C	C	F	B	C	B+	F	F	C
Tioga	F	F	F	F	F	F	F	F	F	F	F	F	F	F	F	B+	F	F

The grading scale is:
A+ = very easy entry and release, abundant float, and very high retention
A = good entry, good release, good retention, good float
A– = good entry, good release good retention, small float range
B+ = good entry, retention and float; hard or intermittent release (or break-in required)
B = good entry, retention and release; no float
B– = same as B with hard or intermittent release (or requiring break-in)
C = good entry, release and float; poor retention (foot can be pulled straight up and out)
C– = same as C, and pedal is fixed (no float)
D+ = can clip in, but foot can only be released by twisting inward
D = can clip but cannot release
F = cleat will not clip in

Note: *Combinations graded D+, D or F are not safe to ride with.*

illustration index

illustration index

bibliography

Barnett, John. *Barnett's Manual: Analysis and Procedures for Bicycle Mechanics.* 4th ed. Boulder, CO: VeloPress, 2000.

Brandt, Jobst. *The Bicycle Wheel.* Menlo Park, CA: Avocet, 1988.

Dushan, Allan. *Surviving the Trail,* Tumbleweed Films, 1993.

Langley, Jim. *Bicycling Magazine's Complete Guide to Bicycle Maintenance and Repair.* Emmaus, PA: Rodale Press, 1994.

Leslie, David. *The Mountain Bike Book.* London: Ward Lock, 1996.

Lindorf, W. *Mountain Bike Repair and Maintenance.* London: Ward Lock, 1995.

Muir, John, and Tosh Gregg. *How to Keep Your Volkswagen Alive: A Manual of Step by Step Procedures for the Compleat Idiot.* Santa Fe, NM: John Muir Publications, 1969.

Pirsig, Robert. *Zen and the Art of Motorcycle Maintenance.* New York, NY: William Morrow & Co., 1974.

Schraner, Gerd. *The Art of Wheelbuilding: A Bench Reference for Neophytes, Pros & Wheelaholics.* Denver, CO: Buonpane Publications, 1999.

Stevenson, John, and Brant Richards. *Mountain Bikes: Maintenance and Repair.* Mill Valley, CA: Bicycle Books, 1994.

Taylor, Garrett. *Bicycle Wheelbuilding 101: A Video Lesson in the Art of Wheelbuilding.* Westwood, MA: Rexadog, 1994.

Van der Plas, Robert. *The Bicycle Repair Book.* Mill Valley, CA: Bicycle Books, 1993.

Van der Plas, Robert. *Mountain Bike Maintenance.* San Francisco: Bicycle Books, 1994.

Zinn, Lennard. *Mountain Bike Performance Handbook.* Osceola, WI: MBI, 1998

Zinn, Lennard. *Zinn and the Art of Road Bike Maintenance.* Boulder, CO: VeloPress, 2000.

index

347

index

index

ABOUT THE AUTHOR

Lennard Zinn is a bike racer, frame builder and technical writer. He grew up cycling, skiing, running rivers and tinkering with mechanical devices in Los Alamos, New Mexico. After receiving a physics degree from Colorado College, he became a member of the U.S. Olympic Development (road) Cycling Team. He went on to work in Tom Ritchey's frame-building shop and has been producing custom road and mountain frames at Zinn Cycles since 1982.

Zinn has been writing for *VeloNews* since 1989 and is currently the senior technical writer for *VeloNews* and *Inside Triathlon* magazines. Other books by Zinn are: *Zinn and the Art of Road Bike Maintenance* (VeloPress, 2000), *Mountain Bike Performance Handbook* (MBI, 1998) and *Mountain Bike Owner's Manual* (VeloPress, 1998).

ABOUT THE ILLUSTRATOR

A former mechanic and bike racer, Todd Telander devotes most of his time now to artistic endeavors. In addition to drawing mountain-bike parts, he paints and draws wildlife for publishers, museums, design companies and individuals. Birds are his favorite subject, so he has included a little house sparrow.